Vance Packard and American Social Criticism

Daniel Horowitz

Vance Packard

& American Social Criticism

THE UNIVERSITY OF NORTH CAROLINA PRESS   CHAPEL HILL & LONDON

Library of Congress Cataloging-in-Publication Data

Horowitz, Daniel, 1938–

Vance Packard and American social criticism / Daniel Horowitz.

p.   cm.

Includes bibliographical references and index.

ISBN 0-8078-2141-1 (alk. paper)

1. Packard, Vance Oakley, 1914– . 2. Sociologists—United

States—Biography. 3. Historians—United States—Biography.

4. Journalists—United States—Biography.

5. United States—Social conditions—1945– . I. Title.

HM22.U6P274   1994

301′.092—dc20   93-35608

CIP

The paper in this book meets the guidelines
for permanence and durability of the Committee
on Production Guidelines for Book Longevity
of the Council on Library Resources.

98 97 96 95 94   5 4 3 2 1

With love and admiration to
Benjamin Horowitz and Sarah Esther Horowitz

Contents

Illustrations

Preface

           In the spring of 1985 I began to re-
search a chapter on Vance Packard for a book on the response of American
writers to affluence in the years after World War II. I interviewed Packard
in the spring of 1986 and in that summer went to Pennsylvania State
University to examine the material he had deposited there, covering the
period since 1957. A year later, when the chapter had grown to ninety
pages, I told him I might write a book on him alone, rather than just a
chapter on him in a work that included chapters on others as well. When I
arrived at his home in New Canaan for a second interview and entered his
living room, he pointed to more than forty boxes of material, mostly for the
period before 1957, and a tabletop copier. He informed me that he would
act as my research assistant, helping to reproduce anything I wanted. Not
long after that visit, I decided to write this book.

I did so for several reasons in addition to the availability of the material
in his living room and his willingness to cooperate. Ever since I began
teaching in the mid-1960s, I have taught widely read works by writers
trained as journalists, such as William H. Whyte, Jr., Betty Friedan, Alvin
Toffler, Anthony Lukas—and Packard. As I thought about doing this book,
I realized how long and how seriously I had considered the questions
raised by the careers of journalists: the complicated relationship between
reader and writer, the distance that separated authors who were professors from those who were not, the challenges that faced a free-lance
writer in America, and the impact of best-sellers on popular consciousness
and, in turn, on social movements.

In the years since 1986, Packard has cooperated with me eagerly and
fully. He sent me material he had discovered. He suggested people I could
talk to and then called in advance of my arrival, encouraging them to speak
freely. He answered my questions and responded to my requests for more
documentation and for verification of facts. Again and again, he displayed
the fundamental personal decency that his friends had mentioned to me.
His assistance has made my task both easier and more difficult. Easier,
because he placed in front of me none of those stumbling blocks that living
subjects often put in the way of inquiring scholars. More difficult, because
of the abundance of the material he uncovered and because of the sense of
gratitude that I felt toward him.

Despite his generosity, this is not an authorized or official biography. As
I understand those adjectives, for this to have been such a book, Packard

would have had to initiate the request that I write about his life, grant me exclusive access to material, and reserve to himself the right to read and comment on what I had written before it appeared in print. None of these conditions have obtained. In April 1988 we signed a simple agreement that gave me nonexclusive rights to draw on his papers. Except in the case of my use of one short document, Packard never asked to see what I was writing, nor did I offer him the opportunity to do so.

As I proceeded, I came to understand one of the reasons he respected my autonomy as an author. As a magazine writer from 1942 to 1956, Packard faced editors who carefully monitored what he wrote, often making sure that he changed the words that would appear under his name in order to suit the needs of his employer. When he emerged as a self-employed writer in 1957, he cherished his freedom to write as he pleased. Throughout his life he has remained a committed civil libertarian. I am sure there are other writers who, though they prize their own freedom of expression and fight to preserve it for others, would abandon these abstract principles when confronted by someone who is writing about them.

Though many of our conversations focused on his public life and our talk never became personal, he shared with me his thoughts, experiences, and memories. He still has a reporter's commitment to accuracy and an ample capacity to recall details and events. What developed over time was a somewhat formal and, I think, mutually respectful relationship. Sometimes as I returned home, I wondered what Packard thought of this historian who had entered his life and persisted in asking questions that were sometimes obvious and other times unexpected. He was, after all, a skilled interviewer himself, more sophisticated than his colloquial talk and unassuming manner suggested. In addition, in the past few years he has been writing a book in which he reflected on his life and work.

At moments he would jokingly talk about how he was trying to get me to show his life in a favorable light. For example, at the end of a letter in which he mentioned the considerable prescience with which he had written for forty years, he remarked, "The self-cheering goes on."[1] At other times he sent me signals that I interpreted as encouragement to offer a frank appraisal of his life. He once forwarded a marked-up copy of a review of Sally Bedell Smith's biography of William S. Paley. Packard underlined a number of passages, including some with quite negative statements about Paley's life. For example, he highlighted a passage where the reviewer noted that Paley emerged in the book as a "toweringly small man: insecure, petty, jealous, ungrateful, snobbish, . . . a philanderer" and also "a tyrannical father . . . a pathological liar; abusive, resentful, cruel, neurotic, hypochondriac, self-absorbed, tightfisted and greedy."[2] In the accompanying letter, Packard remarked, "Here is a good example of why well-researched biographies have a much better reputation as good reads than autobiographies, which, unless they are confessional, are usually suspected, with good reason, of being efforts at image protection and enhancement."[3]

Vance Packard and American Social Criticism differs markedly from what Packard might write of his own life. I well understood that my task was to present my interpretation of his life and work, not his. Though in correspondence and interviews he offered me his own views, I incorporated them into the text only when I believed they illuminated the past I was trying to recover. I suspect that he will want to correct some statements that I make, but I hope that most of those will concern issues of interpretation and few of them, questions of fact. Grateful as I am to him, in the end my commitment is to offer a book that both acknowledges and evaluates his contribution at the same time that it sets his life and writing in their historical contexts.

Acknowledgments

Without the assistance of Vance Packard, his friends, and family, this would have been a very different book, one in which I could have only begun to speculate on the connections between a life and a career. Packard has been unfailingly generous, straightforward, direct. He allowed me my independence, restrained his curiosity as to what I was up to, put no impediments in my way, responded to my inquiries quickly and fully, and respected the division of labor between biographer and subject. Virginia and Vance Packard welcomed me into their homes, bestowed upon me their legendary hospitality, and accommodated the idiosyncrasies of an inquiring historian. Andy Greenwood, the majordomo at the Packards' houses, displayed his culinary skills to a traveling scholar. I am also grateful to Cindy Packard Richmond, Vance Philip Packard, and Randall Packard, who in their distinctive ways offered their perspectives on their parents. The Packards' many friends talked candidly about a man they very much respected. The footnotes make clear my indebtedness to the many people whose conversations I drew upon; beyond the list of those cited lies an equally long one of those I did not—but who nonetheless provided background material as they gave of their time and opinions.

I began to study Vance Packard's life in 1985, as a fellow at the National Humanities Center, an estimable institution whose librarians, fellow scholars, and leaders (especially Charles Blitzer and Kent Mullikin) worked to create a world where ideas and friendships mattered. I continued with the project when I returned to Scripps College, where the staff of Honnold Library of the Claremont Colleges and the resources of the Nathaniel Wright Stephenson professorship eased the burdens of research and writing. I completed the study at Smith College. Here the interlibrary loan office of the William Allan Neilson Library brought distant resources within reach, and the always eager reference staff aided me in tracking down material. Silvana Solano worked her magic with photographs. Kay Worsley and Barbara Day kept the American Studies Program running smoothly, and the Committee on Faculty Compensation and Development materially aided my research. Most important, my colleagues continually gave encouragement with their help and their own exemplary commitment to scholarship.

I owe a special debt to those who made it possible for me to examine unpublished materials. In several cases, despite the best efforts of those who assisted me, nothing of any importance turned up. This was true for the New York Public Library's Crowell-Collier Collection, for the archives of the David McKay Company, for visual materials at major repositories of television shows, and for major collections in the history of advertising. Elsewhere, more success came my way. Dr. Bruce F. Kaufmann at Columbia's Graduate School of Journalism and Brenda Taylor of Little, Brown and Company facilitated my examination of key aspects of Packard's career. Above all, I am grateful to three people at Penn State who made my research trips so rewarding. Charles Mann presides over the Rare Books and Special Collections with a clear vision that enables scholars to draw effectively from its resources. Sandra Stelts made the Packard papers accessible and easy to use, helping me at every step of the way with her professionalism and good cheer. In addition, she and Ronald L. Filippelli were perfect hosts, making my stays much more pleasurable.

Dozens of scholars, too numerous to mention here, suggested leads, answered my inquiries, and responded to my ideas. Researchers helped at every step. Joel Dinerstein looked at material at the University of Texas at Austin. Mark Koerner reported on a television program that he viewed at the State Historical Society of Wisconsin. John M. Goots and Lisa Wajda located copies of the Associated Press material in local newspapers. Anna Graham and Nancy Palmer led me to issues of the *Boston Daily Record*. At Smith College, Suzanne M. Brendle, Frances E. Davey, Johannah L. Gray, Maura Sheehy, and Elaine Tan turned up hard-to-find material and checked for accuracy. Jennifer Mezey read an early version of the manuscript and offered trenchant observations. Pat Vidil's sophisticated analysis helped sharpen my argument, especially when it came to placing Packard's work in the context of collateral readings. Gina C. Rourke gave a penultimate draft a probing reading.

Before this book took its final form, several historians—Howard Brick, Daniel J. Czitrom, James Gilbert, David Oshinsky, Joan Shelley Rubin, David E. Shi, R. Jackson Wilson, Viviana A. R. Zelizer—prodded me to think hard about what it meant to combine biography with intellectual and cultural history. Cushing Strout brought to a reading of an early draft the same insistence on the rigorous exercise of intelligence that, when he taught me as an undergraduate, helped me realize the vital significance of a life dedicated to teaching and scholarship.

As I revised and revised, several people played key roles. Judith F. Chused, M.D., brought the skills of psychoanalyst and editor to bear on what I had written of Packard's childhood, pushing me to be more precise and nuanced. Nancy Grey Osterud's abundant knowledge of rural and family history greatly enriched my understanding of the situation Packard faced on his parents' farm. Robert H. Abzug applied his talents as a biographer and cultural historian to what I had to say about the contexts and nature of Packard's career. Thomas C. Leonard taught me about the world of popular magazines in the 1950s and helped me to articulate some of the major themes embedded in my narrative. Four sociologists—Gary T. Marx, Richard Fantasia, Peter I. Rose, and Raymond Mack—deepened my understanding of the relationship between Packard and professors. Janice Radway encouraged me to think through how best to analyze the letters Packard received.

Of inestimable importance was the support and criticism that I received from scholars who closely followed the development of this project. At two critical moments, Roland Marchand offered incisive critiques and then gave the University of North Carolina Press the green light. Again and again, Char Miller brought a unique set of skills to his reading of drafts: as historian and biographer he helped me clarify what I was saying; as someone who knew the Packard family in all of its settings, he suggested how to explore the relationships between the personal and the scholarly. Judith E. Smith's astute response to what I had written aided me in making the connections between Packard's life and major issues in the cultural and social history of the postwar period. Robert B. Westbrook's incisiveness prompted me to think through issues surrounding the role of the public intellectual, the history of social sciences, and the formation of a canon of social critics. More times than I can count, Lynn Dumenil welcomed my request for her to read yet another version; what I always received in return was the benefit of her precision as an editor, her intelligence as a historian, and her encouragement as a friend. On a daily basis, Helen Lefkowitz Horowitz took time from her own work on a biography of M. Carey Thomas to help me in innumerable and essential ways; at critical junctures, she read and reread everything I had written and offered a range of suggestions that unfailingly had the right combination of encouragement and criticism; at every step of the way, she was available to answer questions, provide advice, and give me the benefit of her careful judgments.

Others played significant roles in turning the research into a published book. Nikki Smith helped draft the legal agreement with Vance Packard. Jane Garrett was always available with the tact of a counselor and the wisdom of an editor. The staff of the University of North Carolina Press proved that their reputation for expeditiously and thoughtfully turning a preliminary draft into a published book was well deserved. From the beginning, Lewis Bateman expressed his confidence and interest in the project. From initial musings to finished manuscript, he guided me along with his humor and intelligence, but above all with his awareness of what it means to transform ideas into a book. Kathy Shaer skillfully guided me through the process of obtaining permissions. Jan McInroy was an exacting, precise, probing, and tactful copy editor. Pamela Upton ably served as project editor, orchestrating the steps from almost-final draft to published book.

Appropriately for a book about the intersection of family life and authorship, my own family supported my work. My parents, Miriam and William Horowitz, maintained their interest in the book and their confidence in their son the scholar. Judy and Len Katz provided models of sanity and good humor. For more than a third of a century, I have shared a life with Helen Lefkowitz Horowitz, one she has made immeasurably and immensely more wonderful than I could have imagined when we first met, between the publication of *Status Seekers* and *Waste Makers*. For more than two decades we have shared the pleasures and challenges of parenthood. I have dedicated the book to our children. When I began work on it, Sarah was a girl; now she is a young woman with a terrific sense of humor, a sharp intelligence, and a capacious interest in the past; throughout, she humored a father who must have seemed as eccentric as the one in Cindy Packard's novel. At the outset, Ben had just entered his teens; at the end, when the completion of the book and of his undergraduate education almost coincided, he remained a person with a focused intellect and an admirable spirit. Both Sarah and Ben are more than any father has the right to expect.

Vance Packard and
American Social Criticism

Introduction

When asked to describe the meaning of his life, Vance Packard responded that it was the story of lengthening intervals between writing assignments.[1] Beginning with daily commitments as a newspaper reporter, Packard moved to weekly ones when he worked for a news service. Next he provided articles for a monthly magazine. The success of *The Hidden Persuaders* (1957), *The Status Seekers* (1959), and *The Waste Makers* (1960) at last gave him the freedom to allow longer periods—two years, then four, and later six—between books. As he would be the first to admit, however, his career as a writer has achieved significance that goes beyond the length of time between publications.

Several experiences shaped Packard's outlook. His early years on a farm undergirded his vision of an America based on family, community, hard work, and individualism. Growing up in a Methodist household provided a moral basis for judging a postwar America that was dominated, he believed, by suburban sprawl, urban blight, conspicuous consumption, rampant commercialism, invasion of privacy, and fragmentation of the family. With a childhood illness, an iconoclastic uncle, and his family's move from farm to university town, he developed his skills as an observer, shaped his sense of himself as an outsider, and sustained himself in a complex relationship to the rewards that affluence brought him and the nation. In Professor Willard Waller (1899–1945), Packard found a mentor who not only shared his combination of engagement and ironic detachment but also structured the questions he asked and the methods he used to answer them. Coming of age politically during the 1930s, Packard developed a belief that America had not fulfilled its promise as a just society. Working for the mass media from 1937 until 1956 honed his skills as a journalist and put him in contact with the forces that were transforming America. Writing for a mass-circulation periodical for fourteen years sharpened his ability to compose prose, with extraordinary speed, that was easily accessible to a broad range of middle-class readers. Moreover, his work exposed him to the pressures and techniques of corporate publishing and advertising.

With the appearance of *Hidden Persuaders* in 1957, Packard's life took a dramatic turn. At that moment he found a successful writing formula, a new career, and a public interested in reading what he had to say. He followed his exposé of advertising with *Status Seekers* and *Waste Makers*. Within a period of four years, three different books that Packard wrote reached the number one position on the *New York Times* nonfiction best-seller list, an achievement that few, if any, other American authors have ever matched.[2]

If his later works were not as successful in the bookstores as the earlier ones, they were hardly inconsequential. Though *The Pyramid Climbers* (1962) broke little new ground, *The Naked Society* (1964) was among the first books, if not the very first, to warn Americans about the full range of new dangers to their privacy. *The Sexual Wilderness* (1968), Packard's most sustained attempt to produce a work that met scholarly standards, stood at a crucial turning point in the line of popular books on sexuality. *A Nation of Strangers* (1972), arguably his best book, examined American experiences with rootlessness. *The People Shapers* (1977) took on the task of exploring how scientists were setting out to transform human lives. *Our Endangered Children* (1983) entered the crowded field of treatments of family life and fully revealed how much Packard clung to family values without being tempted to give them the ideological cast offered by the fundamentalist right. In *The Ultra Rich* (1989), he returned full circle to his role as fascinated reporter and to themes he had explored in the late 1930s. Throughout his career, writing was important to Packard for a whole range of reasons, not the least of which were the satisfaction of his abundant curiosity and creativity as he pulled together the data for a book in order to draw a complete picture of the major changes reshaping America.

Combining prodigious research, a lively style, and a keen sense of the dramatic, for more than three decades Packard produced jeremiads warning against the threats posed to middle-class America. Throughout his career, he articulated the liberalism he had developed by the 1950s, one grounded in a dedication to individualism, family, and responsibility. There was remarkable continuity in his commitments. Randall Packard pointed to his father's "tremendous consistency in attitudes": a belief in family values, an appreciation of small communities, a distaste for the commercialization of American culture, a concern for the natural environment, and a commitment to social justice. He had sustained a faith, Vance Packard himself recalled in 1988, "in every person's right to personal dignity and a reasonable chance for personal fulfillment. These rights, I have believed, are enhanced when people work together to create an environment of an affectionate family, a shared community and a society committed to equalitarian goals." Displaying his self-irony, Packard added, "Maybe Moses or Jefferson or my Boy Scout Oath said the same."[3]

These core values underwrote a critique of American society that was both ambivalent and powerful. By the mid-1960s, however, Packard was no longer at the forefront of American social criticism, and he was muting his tone. Determined to be taken more seriously, reacting against the cultural radicalism of the 1960s, and increasingly removed from the society that had amply rewarded him, Packard focused less on exposing how corporations were manipulating Americans. Over the years, his love of the preposterous and the fascinating, a penchant shaped by his years as a writer of human interest features, undercut his critical edge.

Although this book has most of the trappings of a biography, in some senses it offers less than a full rendering of a life and in some senses it offers much more. Anyone who writes on Packard faces problems in presenting a complete story. He kept a diary for less than a year, and even then only sporadically. The correspondence that exists focuses mainly on his career as a writer. His adult relationships have considerable bearing on his private life but relatively little on his public one. Although this study begins to suggest some of what makes him tick, it is not a psychobiography. Rather, it explores the intersection of the personal, cultural, political, and social. Not everyone who had childhood experiences like his became a free-lance writer eager to provide well. No other author of the postwar period who struggled to gain freedom of expression shared all of Packard's early influences. Moreover, in the end, some things seem inexplicable; not everyone who suffered the early traumas that he did turned adversity into opportunity. Though this book reconstructs his public and private lives, its central focus lies elsewhere. In the end what remains important is Packard's life as a writer—the origins of his ideas and style, the cogency of his arguments, the nature of his influence, the contexts in which he worked, and the trajectory of his career. At the heart of this study are the relationships not only between his life and his words but also between his words and the trends in American life that they reflected and shaped.

Historians of American culture have mentioned Packard, when they have at all, principally in passing. Instead they have focused on such authors as John Kenneth Galbraith, C. Wright Mills, Daniel Bell, Lionel Trilling, Norman Podhoretz, David Riesman, Reinhold Niebuhr, and Dwight Macdonald—people whose writings were more original, whose audiences were more sophisticated, whose impact on political debates and intellectual life was often more palpable, and who held major positions as professors or editors. Because they provided the ideological standards by which we have come to judge an age, it is instructive to compare Packard with those writers who focused their lives on Manhattan or Cambridge rather than New Canaan, on little magazines or universities instead of best-selling books, and on anti-Stalinism instead of a combination of traditional values and liberal politics.

Packard's career thus raises the issue of why a list of important social critics includes some people and leaves out others. Students of American literature, having revealed the time-bound criteria used to decide which authors deserve attention, have not only expanded the literary canon but also reformulated the principles of selection. In the process, at times they have begged the question of whether *The Scarlet Letter* is of higher quality than the sentimental novels written by Nathaniel Hawthorne's female contemporaries. Literary scholars have contrasted those (like Packard) who were nostalgic, derivative, and popular with others whose works were complex, original, and less accessible.[4]

Loaded opposites, these contrasting terms make it difficult to give a writer like Packard his due. Those who popularize the work of others do not fare well at the hands of critics. If the purpose of highly original and sophisticated writing is to present a profound analysis of society to a learned audience, the cultural work of more popular analyses is to raise the consciousness of millions of people. One author's complexity awakens us to a book's power as much as does another's influence. There is certainly abundant evidence that *Hidden Persuaders* and *Status Seekers* more closely reflected what millions of Americans thought than, for example, Bell's probing and ground-breaking essays in *The End of Ideology* (1960). Yet, tempting as it might be to think of comparisons between Packard and others in terms of juxtaposition rather than hierarchy, there are reasons why people still read Mills's *Power Elite* (1956) or Riesman's *Lonely Crowd* (1950) and not Packard's *Status Seekers*, William H. Whyte, Jr.'s *Organization Man* (1956) and not Packard's *Pyramid Climbers*, Christopher Lasch's *Culture of Narcissism* (1979) and not Packard's *Nation of Strangers*.

A number of factors have prevented Packard from earning the appreciation given writers whose works are more profound and systematic: his rushed and omnivorous style, the contradictions between his life and his books, the derivative quality of his works, his lack of engagement with theoretical issues, the nostalgic and ambivalent cast of his vision, his career path, and the problems with his politics. Nonetheless, it is also important to realize that those who relegated Packard to the purgatory of middlebrow culture did so because they confidently believed, as Janice A. Radway has remarked in a somewhat different context, "that there is a single hierarchy of value within which all verbal products are ranged and that all such works aspire to the highest position."[5] This book approaches Packard's writing with a dual perspective that his most cosmopolitan critics usually lacked: that it is possible simultaneously to judge what he wrote and to acknowledge the impact he had on the audiences he addressed.

However, a study of Packard is also important because of the significant issues that his career raises. Without inherited wealth or, after 1956, institutional affiliation, Packard was among the handful of people of his generation who earned a substantial income over several decades by writing nonfiction. Unlike Betty Friedan, who also emerged from the world of magazine journalism and whose *Feminine Mystique* (1963) drew some of its inspiration from Packard's success, Packard did not sustain political involvement through a social movement. Unlike Ralph Nader, whose best-seller *Unsafe at Any Speed* (1965) catapulted its author into the public arena, Packard did not launch an organization that embodied the commitments his books expressed. In contrast with many writers whose careers were inextricably bound up in the life of a university, a publication, or a political organization, Packard was not enmeshed on a daily basis in a world where people, policy, and ideas intersected.

Packard thinks of himself as a self-directed nonconformist who, with the publication of *Hidden Persuaders* in 1957, gained freedom from the clutches of the organization man's world. In fact, of course, the situation is more complicated than that. His career illuminates the dilemmas and ironies of the free-lance social critic in America. By the late 1950s, he had liberated himself from the heavy hand of magazine editors; for the rest of his career, however, reviewers, book buyers, and publishers mediated between marketplace and freedom. At key moments, he found himself in a position where he had to live off the very system he was questioning and use the very methods he was critiquing. Packard could not help but absorb some of the values and methods he learned when he wrote for the mass media for almost twenty years.

Starting out as a reporter in the late 1930s, twenty years later he found himself cast (and he cast himself) as a social critic. That new identity was not without its problems; not the least of them was that reviewers would judge him by standards different from those applied to a writer of human interest stories. Others who worked in the world of magazines emerged as influential social critics: the muckrakers in the Progressive period; A. C. Spectorsky, John Keats, Friedan, and Whyte in the late 1950s and early 1960s; and, for a later period, Alvin Toffler, Charles Silberman, and the New Journalists. Those interested in the shifting patterns of recruitment of people into the ranks of public intellectuals have rarely paid attention to journalists. Rather, they have usually focused on people who used their positions in universities to reach a wider audience.[6] What Packard's career provides is an example of someone who emerged, however incompletely, from journalism and approached arenas usually occupied (and guarded) by public intellectuals.

If Packard straddled the worlds of journalism and social criticism, he stood in an even less easy relationship to academic life. Spending the second half of his youth in a university community and being inspired by one of his professors, he sought throughout his career to bring the findings of social and behavioral scientists to the public. He never wished to join the ranks of professors, but he nonetheless was eager for their respect. Though he cherished his hard-won freedom, his sensitivity to the response of academic reviewers caused shifts in his approach to what and how he wrote. The traffic between academics and nonacademics is, however, a two-way street. Though there is a little evidence that what Packard wrote influenced sociology, the response of sociologists to what he said illuminates the development of that discipline specifically and of the relationship of academics to nonacademics more generally. Packard's most famous best-sellers appeared at a time when sociologists had turned away from the task of reaching a broad audience. Later, when Packard sought to win the approval of academics by writing books that were more serious and careful, some professors had become more eager to reach a nonacademic audience. These changes brought Packard more respect from some academics at the same time that professors offered him more competition.

Packard's changing relationships to his audiences raise a number of important issues about his career, about American social criticism, and about best-selling books. An analysis of letters from readers, a source rarely examined in a systematic manner for nonfiction writers, demonstrates the often contradictory ways in which his audience drew on what he wrote. Why Packard did not continue to attract an audience as large as the one that gravitated toward him from the late 1950s to the mid-1960s requires a complicated answer. In some ways it is an unfair question, for rarely has a nonfiction writer commanded a substantial audience for more than a decade, let alone for thirty or forty years. Although he had a following throughout his life whose size many authors would covet, after the mid-1960s he never found a topic, a vision, a style, or a policy that significantly shaped public opinion.

At every turning point in his professional life, his career was shaped by the eclipse of one medium and the rise of another. In the 1930s, radio programming diminished the immediacy of his human interest stories. In the mid-1950s, television's increasing command of advertising revenue was among the factors that put him in the line to collect unemployment checks. In the quarter century beginning in the mid-1960s, the New Journalism, television documentaries, and oral histories made Packard's style less compelling and his books less commercially successful. Yet he earned a handsome income from writing books and lecturing from 1957 at least until well into the 1970s. Between the late 1960s and the 1980s, book buyers from abroad began to fill some of the vacuum created by decreasing purchases at home. By the 1980s—if not before—real estate, long an important part of his family's economy, helped compensate for declining royalties.

Packard's writings also illuminate a number of themes central to American thought in the postwar period. His grounding of social reform in traditional values encourages us to continue to rethink the history of social thought in this century.[7] The story of American ideas changes considerably when told from the perspective of Fairfield County rather than Manhattan. Like many writers of his generation, Packard came to political consciousness at a time when the achievements of the USSR attracted as much attention as did the flaws of the United States. Though he then admired the Soviet experiment with all the naiveté of a farm boy, he did so without flirting with Marxism. From the late 1930s until the early 1950s, Packard increasingly appreciated what America stood for. Because this did not happen after a struggle to come to terms with a radical past that he had not experienced in the first place, Stalinism and anti-Stalinism were never the twin poles between which he moved. But Packard's most influential works (like Riesman's *Lonely Crowd* and Whyte's *Organization Man*, the books with which his own were frequently compared) sustained a sense of America's unfulfilled promise.

Packard's fifteen minutes of fame stretched into many years as he played a critical role in the transition from the 1950s to the 1960s. His contribution to that shift expands our understanding of how one era helped create the next and emphasizes the importance of social criticism written by journalists to the awakening of America's conscience. More specifically, it underscores how the adversarial culture of the 1960s drew on the mass culture of the previous decade. Packard gained a large readership in the late 1950s and early 1960s not only because of his skill as a writer but also because the social criticism he was offering was right for the times, coming as it did between the conservatism of the McCarthy years and the more tumultuous politics of the late 1960s. What made Packard so important was what made him so widely read: along with writers as diverse as Paul Goodman, C. Wright Mills, and John Kenneth Galbraith, he was among the first social critics to benefit from and foster a renewal of social consciousness during the late 1950s.

As did so many writers of his generation—including Goodman, Richard Hofstadter, and Lionel Trilling—by the late 1960s Packard found himself outflanked on the left by the college students he had helped bring to political awareness. By then, he had developed a commitment to self-realization; at the same time he watched with considerable misgivings as members of a younger generation explored the implications of a quest for selfhood that both resembled and differed from his. This experience led him to begin to move back and forth between the poles of rights and responsibilities. Unlike neoconservatives, however, during the presidency of Ronald Reagan Packard once again emphasized such issues as society's obligation to children, the inequitable distribution of wealth, and the pursuit of a nonmaterialistic way of life. Yet his life after the mid-1960s makes it possible to explore the dilemmas of liberalism.

Packard's writings also reflect other critical turning points. His shift from rugged to humanistic individualism stemmed in part from the institutional situations in which he found himself. The change in emphasis from the self-made to the self-realized person also provided him with an outlook that was more personal than political. This embrace of a psychological emphasis takes on added importance because he often blunted the more adversarial thrust of his social criticism by celebrating the self-determined person and by transforming social problems into opportunities for practical advice and personal growth. As times changed more than he did, his response seemed traditional, especially on issues of family and feminism. Whatever vicissitudes he faced and however much America changed, Packard's ideology stayed largely the same. Articulating a vision of a nation threatened by powerful manipulative forces, he urged Americans to be self-determined people who led balanced lives in a world dominated by large bureaucratic organizations. As Joan S. Rubin has recently noted about middlebrow writers in the years between two world wars, Packard was able, simultaneously, to appeal to familiar values such as self-reliance and family integrity "in a world grown impersonal and specialized, while meeting newer demands for information, social performance, and personal growth."[8]

What made Packard's outlook distinctive among postwar social critics was his commitment to producer values that had their origin in a Methodist household in rural America. Working for populism or Prohibition, those who had articulated these values in the late nineteenth and early twentieth centuries were modestly middle class but upwardly mobile white Protestants. Among their ranks were farmers, artisans, independent entrepreneurs, and shopkeepers who had drawn a contrast between the parasitical work of capitalists and what they saw as their own truly productive labor. However attenuated, his articulation of the producer ethic evoked a better world, characterized by hard work, simple living, individual worth, community cohesion, moral values, and local democracy—but constantly threatened by the corrupting power of wealth and commerce.

Opposing avariciousness and luxury, advocates of a producer ethic stood for a virtuous life based on civic responsibility, honest callings, unalienated work, widespread property ownership, and personal independence. They remained skeptical about the benefits of material progress, which they believed threatened to undermine a moral economy. They sought to limit the power of the wealthy, large-scale corporations, middlemen, and creditors. Instead, they wished to promote the autonomy of small-scale economic units and the self-determination of a free people. They envisioned a nation whose health relied not on the corruption that, they believed, increasing wealth brought but on the commitment to a moral order based on the integration of work and leisure, family and community, the human and the natural. The more distant the political arena, the more alien and corruptible; responsibility to the public well-being was local and personalized. To secure a better life, those who articulated the producer ethic relied on community discipline and moral values, not on a large and faraway government.

Typically, the promotion of these values came from people like those among whom Packard had grown up in rural Pennsylvania and not from a mid-twentieth-century writer who divided his time between a wealthy Connecticut suburb and a summer house on Chappaquiddick Island, off Martha's Vineyard. Yet like other exponents of the producer ethic, Packard remained ambivalent about many of the central dramas of American life, such as the search for success, the conflict between individualism and mass culture, and the tension between hard work and the material rewards it produced.[9]

Growing Up Absurd

From Granville Summit to State College, 1914–1932

"My Uncle Bill once told me that I was born a mistake" was the way Vance Packard thought he might begin his memoirs. Given the seven years since the birth of his older brother and what we know of family planning in the early twentieth century, his Uncle Bill was probably right when he told his nephew that his birth was unplanned. Yet even if what his uncle said was not true, hearing him say it strengthened Packard's perception of himself as an anomaly. The sense that he was an outsider not only reverberated with critical childhood experiences but also influenced the career he later chose and the drive with which he pursued it. At times, he pictured his early years as an idyll that Norman Rockwell might have painted, but, as he recognized, the real situation that he and his family faced was more troublesome.

Throughout his life, Vance Packard remained uneasy in his relationship to worlds he entered. Awkward in his presentation of self and having what he later called an "under-integrated personality," he conquered what he saw through observation, not participation.[1] Driven to earn recognition, he nonetheless remained skeptical about the rewards that success would bring. Opposing the spread of commercialism, he achieved success in the marketplace through his writing and real estate investments. Promoting self-realization, he remained dedicated to a moral vision of community responsibility for social well-being. He saw himself as a rebellious nonconformist, yet this characterization missed how deeply his life was embedded in and helped transform American society.

Childhood in Granville Summit

Born on May 22, 1914, in Granville Summit, Bradford County, Pennsylvania, Packard spent his early years as what he later called a "backwater farm boy" on his parents' farm in the north central part of the state.[2] During his youth, the population of the area declined as local residents left to seek opportunities elsewhere. The villages of Granville Township provided the focal points of local activity, containing as they did the elementary school, the Grange hall, the Methodist church, a store, a milk station, and a railhead. Farming in the area, remarked the authors of a report published in the year of Packard's birth, "presents difficulties and problems," stemming mostly from poor soil and hilly land.[3] The area was isolated: Canton and Troy, the nearest small towns, were about seven miles away, and the Packards rarely traveled the thirty miles to Elmira, New York, the closest small city. Packard's paternal ancestors had probably come to Massachusetts from England in 1638; the family moved to Bradford County in the early 1800s. By the time Vance was born, his father's relatives owned much of the land in the township, with patterns of settlement and marriage combining to make community and kin inseparable. As Packard came of age, the more successful of his male relatives, remembered by him as "jovial achievers," were just beginning to gain a foothold in the middle class as farmers and small town businessmen.[4]

Born and raised in Granville Township and with only an eighth-grade education, Packard's father, Philip J. Packard (1879–1963), initially earned a living by transporting animals, logging timber, and shoveling coal. In 1902 he married Mabel L. Case (1881–1962), and they soon purchased their own farm, an older brother having inherited the family property. Before she agreed to wed, Mabel insisted that Phil give up drinking alcohol, chewing tobacco, and chasing women.[5] Moral reformation and the bonds of matrimony turned him from a rambunctious young man into a model husband and an amiable, well-respected citizen. As a father, Phil Packard was a disciplinarian, punishing his children physically with firmness but without rancor. Vance Packard later noted his own "proneness to inap-

*Packard family outside their farmhouse in Granville Summit, shortly after
Vance's birth, 1914. From left to right: LaRue, Vance, Mabel, Pauline, Philip.
(Used by permission of Vance Packard.)*

propriate behavior," something that emerged most clearly when he played
childhood pranks. In response came "thunder and lightning" from his
father. As his son recalled, "He'd holler and I'd jump."[6]

Mabel Case grew up in an orphanage, where she received a high school
education. At age seventeen, she began her career as a public school
teacher. Vance Packard saw little of his mother's family, few of whom lived
near Granville Summit. Those who did live close by were poor, barely
respectable, and "somber."[7] Within the home she was very much the
austere schoolmarm—"an aloof, tense person of rectitude," her son remembered, someone who probably saw her son "as a special challenge
posed by the Lord in His Wisdom." She played the piano at the local
Grange and the organ at the Methodist church, where she also taught
Bible classes. A genteel lady who faced unladylike conditions on the farm,
she constantly strove to uphold standards of decorum. "Dad wanted to be a
farmer," Vance Packard's sister later remarked, "Mom didn't want to be a
farmer's wife." As one of the better-educated people in the local community, Mabel Packard looked down on farming. Instead, she sought education for Vance and for his two siblings, Pauline and Charles LaRue, who
were respectively ten and seven years older than their brother. With "a

strong drive for Culture," she "dug deep," her son recalled, "into our skimpy funds to pay door-to-door salesmen for sets of encyclopedias and classics." She endowed Vance, her favorite child, with the sense that books were stepping-stones over which he could move to a world beyond the confines of his social and geographical lot.[8]

Like other women who had taught school before they settled down to the life of a farmer's wife, Mabel Packard felt trapped. She enjoyed few worldly pleasures, lived with a keen sense of isolation, and faced a continual round of chores. Her social aspirations exceeded her ability to achieve them, and she believed she was superior to most of the women she encountered. In a world where bloodlines were so central, she found herself caught in the web of her husband's extended family. She had to live within a family context, yet as an orphan and as a woman in the midst of her husband's world, embedding herself in a kinship network was problematic. Unlike her peers, she entered local social worlds principally through connections she inherited from her husband, not through ones she herself initially established.[9]

Phil Packard had more reason to be satisfied with his lot. An outgoing man who lived in a community filled with his relatives, he felt very much at home. The division of labor on the farm enabled him to accord Mabel the respect she deserved. He provided his family with a modicum of comfort, purchasing their first new car in 1922. Simple and small, their five-room home lacked central heat, an indoor bathroom, and electricity. As a youth, Vance Packard remained unaware of whatever problems the ups and downs of the economy posed for the family. There was always enough food on the table, much of it produced on the farm. Hard work on their 105 acres yielded income from the grain raised on the few fertile stretches of land, the lumber cut from the woods, the milk taken from the dozen or so cows that grazed on the hillsides, the eggs laid by the chickens, and the sale of animal skins.[10]

Beyond the household, life centered on extended family and local institutions. The Packard kids did the kinds of things farm children in the region had done for generations—invented games, trapped animals, gathered maple sap from the trees, and rode horses to the village school. On Saturdays, the Packards went to meetings and family gatherings at the Grange hall. On Sundays they traveled to the Methodist church, where both parents were active members and where the children attended Sunday school. Genuinely religious, Phil and Mabel studied the Bible and punctuated their days with prayer. Doing their best to lead Christian lives, they supported temperance and missionary work.[11] Occasionally, members of the household had contact with the world beyond the township. The train stopped not far from the farm to pick up milk and to take Pauline to high school and, later, to a teacher training college.

People like Vance Packard's parents shared a set of assumptions about how to live. Phil took care of the cows, the animal skins, the barn, and the land. Mabel tended the house, the garden, the chickens, and the children.[12] Despite considerable separation of work into masculine and feminine spheres, the household derived a sense of cohesion from cooperation rather than from equality. The divided responsibilities, quite common for farm families in which there was some aspiration to middle-class standing, ensured that physical effort would not exhaust the wife. Yet unlike their urban middle-class peers, rural women such as Mabel Packard constantly interacted with their husbands. Husband and wife shared a sense that her education and his identity as a yeoman made them superior to those who had neither a high school degree nor the independence of a farmer. Her role as a civilizing mother helped ensure that the children would turn out to be something other than farmers and that Mabel would secure the honor that both partners felt she deserved. The commitment to the female virtues of piety, purity, and domesticity made sure that husband and wife recognized what governed public behavior. In community affairs, the spheres in which they operated were both segregated and overlapping. Phil's world beyond the home revolved around the Farm Bureau and, later, the Dairymen's League; Mabel's, around the Sunday school, Ladies' Aid Society, and support of missionary work. Yet they participated together in the Methodist church, the Grange, and even in activities sponsored by local women's organizations, especially those that supported Prohibition.[13]

In works published as an adult, Vance Packard evoked the pleasures of life in Bradford County. In 1972, he wrote of meeting "people as families at Grange Hall suppers on Saturday nights. . . . at church festivities, at cattle auctions, at the milk station, at the icehouse pond, and at the contests on the steep road leading to Granville Summit on Sunday afternoons." Similarly, he celebrated the inclusiveness of the community where he spent his early years. Everyone, he remarked in 1960, "regardless of age or economic status, used to go to these socials: the blacksmith, the storekeeper, the farmers big and little, the farm hands and all their children." When he talked about the pleasure he derived from contributing to the family's well-being by tending skunk traps and cleaning the henhouse, he contrasted the simple, productive work on a farm early in the century with more modern and alienating conditions found in American cities, suburbs, and large corporations fifty years later.[14]

The experiences and memories of the world in which Packard spent his early years provided a set of values that shaped his career. Although as a writer he romanticized the conditions that obtained during his childhood, much of his later critique of mid-century society came from his own heartfelt assessment of the virtues of the life he left behind. In similar farm communities the lines between men and women were clear yet intersecting. With family, kin, and community integrated, there was little room for unbounded individualism. Because people relied on hard work more than on superficial symbols of social class, a rough egalitarianism held the community together. People bought and sold goods and services, but they did not systematically use market yardsticks to judge people's worth. Day in and day out, they understood the human and concrete dimensions of work. They depended on products they themselves made or purchased, items that they rarely imbued with qualities they did not inherently have. Husbands and wives, parents and children, farm owners and neighbors worked together as partners, without relying excessively on the exchange of money or experiencing sharp social divisions. Middlemen, speculators, immigrants, and African Americans, though present in the county in small numbers, were beyond the pale in the stories farm people commonly told about their own lives.[15]

Threats to the Pastoral

Tragedy, however, intervened in this idyll. Vance later remarked that Mabel Packard, deeply dissatisfied with being a farmer's wife, at times seemed on the verge of a nervous breakdown. Phil Packard, though more content with his own lot, did not adjust easily to some of the changes modern life brought. Once, having tried to stop his car by yelling "Whoa" instead of using the brakes, he sat in the automobile as it crashed through the garage. Vance Packard knew relatives on his mother's side who had difficulty with alcohol or mental illness. During World War I, an aunt, who had married a German American and lived in Elmira, was subjected to attacks on her family as "Huns." As a result, her husband lost his job. In the early 1920s, the Ku Klux Klan burned crosses on the hills in the township in order to intimidate Roman Catholics in Troy.[16]

Packard grew up acutely aware of the difference between insiders and outsiders. He did not know that Roman Catholics were Christians, and he did not meet one of them until he moved away from the county. His first encounter with an African American was within a context fraught with drama and racism. At the annual fair in Troy, the locals played a game called Hit the Nigger on the Head, in which they would win a prize if they could throw a baseball and hit a black man's face that stuck out from a hole in a white sheet. Mabel Packard dragged her son away from the scene, remarking that it was denigrating to black people. What Packard remembered as his "first big philosophic thought" also involved a contrast between the familiar in Granville Summit and the strange in the world beyond. Walking by himself one day when he was seven or eight, he remembered his parents' talk of India. "I could understand outposts such as Troy, Canton, Towanda," he recalled, "but India left me shaking my head."[17]

During Packard's youth, economic changes that originated beyond the boundaries of Bradford Country set off bitter fights among local residents.[18] New methods of transporting and storing milk had opened markets in cities up to three hundred miles away. Powerful monopolistic corporations gained control over milk distribution and threatened the independence and economic well-being of dairy farmers. Organizing themselves into a marketing cooperative called the Dairymen's League before World War I, most of the farmers in the region strongly opposed Sheffield Farms, a powerful, privately owned distributor. In these years, members of the league articulated a vision that contrasted greedy middlemen and monopolistic corporations with virtuous farmers whom they envisioned as real producers struggling so they could live a simple life and prevent corruption of the commonwealth. Though some dairymen remained skeptical of coordinated action because it smacked of trade unionism and they feared it might undermine their independence, many banded together to fight corporate monopolies and protect their own interests.

Disagreements divided communities. Neighbors hurled the epithet "scab," dumped milk on its way to market, fought at the creamery, and stopped speaking to one another altogether. Phil Packard, a longtime member of the Grange who had helped bring the Dairymen's League to the county, considered the struggle against the distributors, his son recollected, a "great moral battle." As a child, Vance Packard heard discussions about the conflict between the league and Sheffield Farms, a bigger topic of conversation, he recalled, than World War I. He remembered his father's returning home with injuries from a fight between the opposing forces. He listened to his Uncle Bill hollering "a lot about how farmers were being screwed on milk prices by middlemen." Young Packard paid attention as members of his family talked about "a commitment to prudence and hard work and a suspicion of riches."[19] The conflict over the Dairymen's League was undermining what remained of the community's dream of harmony. The increasingly competitive, capital-intensive, and centralized nature of dairy farming, along with the economic turbulence caused by World War I, challenged Phil Packard's position as an independent farmer who worked marginal land.

If these conditions influenced the family's economic position, more personal events contradicted the picture of an idyllic life on the farm and often made Vance feel at odds with the world. Packard's mother was unable to nurse him. "I have this obsession," he later remarked. "I think it has to do with my mother's milk. Whenever I see an empty glass, I have to fill it."[20] The family accepted a doctor's diagnosis that something in the cow's milk he drank caused eczema, a skin disease he suffered from for at least eighteen months beginning around his first birthday. "The irritation is intense," a medical specialist remarked in a contemporary textbook, "causing the child to suffer agony" and the skin to have "a most pitiable aspect." His parents administered a number of remedies, eventually tying their son's hands and feet when they could not keep an eye on him, so he would not further irritate his skin by scratching.[21] With blisters and scabs over almost his entire body, he doubtless appeared to his peers as freakish. The condition made him incapable of having some of the childhood experiences available to them and hampered the normal development of motor skills. Phil and Mabel Packard did not overprotect their son, something that would have undermined his sense of self-respect. As they took care of their child's condition, they may well have given him more attention and comfort than he would have received under normal circumstances.[22]

At a critical period in the development of his sense of self, Packard experienced the consequences not only of physical restraint but also of a sense of being distinctive. As a young man, he looked and carried himself differently from his classmates. As the novelist John Updike remarked about the effect of his own skin disorder, it promoted "the sense of another presence coöccupying your body and singling you out from the happy herds of healthy, normal mankind."[23] Limiting his ability to participate fully in the world, the eczema strengthened Packard's sense of detachment and his inclination to observe. Being physically restrained as a child was among the factors that made issues of independence and individualism central to him as an adult. Childhood experiences fostered an approach to researching and writing that was more absorptive than original. Conditions of his youth, reinforced by later situations, encouraged Packard to develop a sense of the importance of family. What he endured as a child made him hungry for success and eager to be an adequate provider. Although such circumstances might have daunted or severely limited others, he learned to channel his response effectively.

Packard's relationship with his Uncle Bill reinforced these childhood experiences. Packard later recalled that he "adored" his uncle, the "great hero of my formative years," who shaped his personality and his view of the world. Bill Packard, wounded in a World War I battle, came home skeptical about the wisdom of fighting as a way of settling national disagreements. The experience also transformed him, as it did many returning veterans, into someone unwilling to accept the pieties and certainties that made many middle-class Victorians optimistic and sentimental. His uncle, Packard remembered, was the "village radical" and "a hell-raiser" with "a marvelous sense of the preposterous" who enjoyed speaking freely as he set his nephew "straight about every son of a bitch in the county," fostering in him an "anti-establishment attitude." Uncle Bill was a Democrat in a largely Republican community; Vance's parents, like many people in the township, had switched to the Republican party around 1920 because they associated the Democrats with saloons and urban machines. Uncle Bill's radicalism, however, was more temperamental than political. Retrospectively, Packard credited his uncle with having started him on the road to being "a skeptic," an "individualist," and "a nonconformist." Uncle Bill, who, Packard remarked in 1935, "always had sort of a sneaking desire" to be a journalist, also influenced his nephew's career choice.[24]

Later in his life, Vance Packard noted things about himself that help explain both his attitudes and some of the reasons for his success as a writer. When he looked back, he wrote that he was "always an observer" who wanted to "escape involvement." As a child, he developed what he later called "a habit of amiable nosiness and a wariness of standard wisdom." These phrases expressed his sense of himself as someone who examined rather than participated. Similarly, when he remarked that drives for "status" and "scorn for Success" were life's "twin pulls," he recognized the mixed feelings he had toward the rewards brought by hard work.[25] Early experiences made him different from the farm children among whom he grew up—his powers of observation compensated for his difficulty in fitting into the standard mold. Seeing himself as an outsider and harboring an ambivalence toward the rewards ambition might bring shaped his work as a social critic. Although he relished being a nonconformist, doubtless there were times when he was envious of the experiences and skills that others enjoyed. These conflicting impulses intensified his ambition but ensured that he would satisfy it in both nonmaterialistic and materialistic ways.

The commitment of his parents to temperance, a reform movement that drew on the producer ethic and in which Methodists played an especially prominent role, had a lasting impact on Packard. His parents' evangelical faith connected the eradication of vice with the Social Gospel that at-

*Packard family in a more formal picture, several years before their move
from Bradford County, ca. 1919. From left to right: Philip, LaRue, Mabel,
Vance, Pauline. (Used by permission of Vance Packard.)*

tempted to Christianize the world so that social divisions would be healed. Those who fought for Prohibition believed that special interests were corrupting society, threatening family integrity, and undermining democracy. They opposed the evils that they associated with cities and commerce, often keeping the objects of their concern at a safe distance. As a religious historian noted, Methodists "were impressed not so much by the social evils from which the poor suffered as by the vices to which they succumbed."[26] Speaking for the respectable middling interest, people like Phil and Mabel Packard resented the ostentatiousness of the wealthy, the militancy of labor, the power of corporations, the corruption of politics, and the expressiveness of immigrants. To solve social problems, they relied not on the state but on the community's enforcement of a moral way of life that centered on the traditional values of hard work, responsibility, and self-discipline. Central to their vision was the nuclear family, which they believed shaped character and conscience.

The contrasting orientations of an ebullient father and a schoolmarm mother, his mother's feeling that she was better than her neighbors, his believing himself to be a "mistake," and his confining illness all left their marks on Packard. The Methodism of his youth instilled in him a strong ethical sensibility that would find secularized expression in the moral outrage that marked his social criticism. His mother's insistence on the importance of education and his parents' commitment to prudential values would influence how he carried out his calling. His father's desire for independence, as well as his position as a producer of tangible and useful goods, gave his son a basis for evaluating economic activity. Life on a farm instilled in him a respect for the natural environment. Moreover, Uncle Bill taught young Packard to strip away pretense so he could see people and situations directly. The farm and villages gave him a yardstick against which he could judge the changes he witnessed in America after World War II. If he was a naive farm boy, he was also learning to be a moral skeptic.

Youth in State College

The family's move from Granville Summit to State College around the time of Vance's tenth birthday in 1924 proved to be a major turning point in his life. The aspirations of Mabel Packard for her children and her unhappiness with the lonely life of a farmer's wife were the principal impulses behind the change from isolated farm to academic community. The difficulties Phil Packard faced as a small, independent farmer also played a part. Whatever reluctance he felt about the move, as a second son who himself had two sons and a daughter, Phil knew that the resources he commanded were not enough to sustain his household or launch his children. Though he was giving up considerable independence, he realized that changes in the production and distribution of milk were undermining what was left of his dream of being a yeoman farmer. The Packards sold their farm, and the county agent helped Phil obtain a job on the farms that Pennsylvania State College used for teaching and research.[27]

Phil and Mabel reacted to the move in dramatically different ways. For Vance's mother, the new situation was nearly ideal. She now resided in a small university town that had more than enough resources to help her overcome her sense of isolation. "Instead of tending chickens," her son recalled, she watched over the college students the family boarded in order to increase its income. She was able to see all three of her children graduate from college, the first members of the extended families to do so. Initially at least, the move was traumatic for her husband. For five months he suffered from a gastrointestinal illness that the family believed was brought on by his being uprooted from the world where he had spent most of his life. But it was not long before Phil Packard turned adversity into challenge. Starting as a farmhand, within a year he was a foreman and two years later became the supervisor of the university's farms. The family lived in a series of houses on the campus, eventually ending up in one that was close to the center of the university and had a splendid view of Mount Nittany.[28]

The move to State College was also traumatic for Vance. In 1936 he recalled that the "sudden" shift "worked violently on me." The change from rural community to university town made him keenly aware that he was "a farmer's son dropped in the midst of well-manicured sons and daughters of professors." He believed that the change developed in him a "definite inferiority complex" and "a seething ambition." As a youngster, he "tried to be 'best' at everything from marbles to going with the prettiest girl." His three years as a Boy Scout, from age twelve to fifteen, he remembered, gave him recognition and "a sense of belonging," helping him to make the shift "from being a farm boy to being a college townie." Earning the rank of Eagle Scout, he commented much later, made him a "shining success story" by giving him "self-confidence" and a way to compete with the children of professors. Yet Packard's sense of not belonging persisted, especially when his relationship to the academic world was involved: in 1938, on an application for a fellowship at Harvard, he claimed that his "father was a member of the faculty at Penn State."[29] The long-term consequences of the move were profound. Once and for all, the Packards left a world of familial and communal connectedness. What Phil Packard now had to face as a farmer his son would confront later as a writer, the question of what happened to identity in a bureaucratic world where you tried to do honorable work under conditions beyond your control. Few sons are able to reverse their father's loss, but Vance Packard did that by later switching from bureaucratic employee to independent producer.

State College was strikingly different from Bradford County—"contrasting worlds" Packard would later call the two places. It was a small town, not a sparsely populated rural area; the location of the state university, not a provincial backwater. A famous author, not farmers and relatives, came to visit. The new house was on a campus he could roam at will, not a farm on which his labor was critical. In the years between the move and his entrance into college, Packard found himself straddling divergent worlds. A religious home stood in contrast to the secular realm of school and peers. Once in State College, Packard's parents remained active in church affairs. During several summers, the family, true to its commitment to Christian good works, hosted children from poor neighborhoods in New York.[30] Sharing his quarters with boarders during the academic year, Vance was simultaneously a high school student and a roommate of collegians, some of whom encouraged his interest in ideas. Trips back to Granville Township during the summer reminded him of the differences between where he had come from and where he was. A townie who lived on campus, once again he was an outsider looking in on worlds he felt excluded from.

His adolescent rebellion took telling directions. Packard recalled his parents as "just hopelessly old-fashioned ex-farmers."[31] He gave his sister a "terrible time" when she was his schoolteacher. In public settings he was frequently mischievous and demonstrated little sense of how to behave properly, a condition his parents struggled unsuccessfully to remedy.[32] In late June of 1932, around the time he graduated from high school, he gave his first speech, at a meeting of young people involved in the work of the Women's Christian Temperance Union. He expressed the hope that "the line of temperance will continue to surge upward and a serious liquor problem will be a thing of the past." Soon after, when he had "been lured to the other side," some teetotalers saw him returning empty beer bottles to a local emporium.[33] By giving a speech in support of Prohibition, Vance Packard paid homage to his parents and aligned himself with the forces of self-denial. When he returned the beer bottles, he proved that he would not be denied the means of satisfying his thirst. This act announced his independence from his parents as he defined himself as a modern, secular person.

In high school, Packard was an outsider, a joiner whom his popular peers never fully accepted and a youth who sought to change that situation by excelling in sports and journalism. He was physically and sexually ungainly.[34] Nor did he fit into the established groups of high school students. A childhood friend remembered him as a "nonconformist," who was "all over the place" physically and mentally. There was an energy and awkwardness that made his behavior seem more erratic than that of other adolescents. At high school parties, he exhibited an unusual dancing style, something that hardly made him popular with girls.[35] He continued, as he recalled, with "efforts at comedy as a way to get attention." In his senior year, a classmate listed Packard's "favorite pastime" as "being radical."[36]

During Packard's high school years, sports and journalism were more important than good grades. Like most of his peers, he was not very studious. A slight young man, as an end on the football team he came up against opponents who loomed over him. Yet on the field he achieved distinction far beyond what his physical stature alone promised, something made clear several years after graduation when the local newspaper announced his selection as a member of his high school's "all-time all-star" team. His interest in journalism grew out of participation in athletics, expanded when he became sports editor for the school newspaper, and culminated with his serving as editor of the yearbook. With the increased achievements in journalism, he recalled several years later, his "ambitious fervor" and sense of inferiority lessened, helping to diminish his sensitivity to his rural origins. Still, his peers, he remembered, rarely considered him when "looking for a leader."[37]

Although there was little to indicate to Packard's contemporaries that he would gain the level of achievement he did, in retrospect what struck those who knew him was his exceptional determination.[38] What he lacked in physical stature and grace, he made up in competitiveness and tenacity. "When he wanted something," one of his high school classmates remarked years later, "no one could stop him; his forte was endurance. He never lost sight of his goal."[39] A childhood friend recalled that "no matter what he did, Vance wanted to be the best at it, he wanted to finish first."[40] The quotation under his picture in the high school yearbook, taken from Shakespeare's *Twelfth Night*, captured some of the qualities that characterized this country boy, qualities that would later stand him in good stead as a writer: "This fellow is wise enough to play the fool. And to do that well craves a kind of wit."[41]

Starting Out in the Thirties

Penn State, 1932–1936

Vance Packard's experiences as an undergraduate at Penn State shaped his politics and focused his ambition. These years also led him to reaffirm his stand as a nonconformist and pointed him toward a career that would combine journalism with the social and behavioral sciences. In his work on undergraduate publications, he commented on collegiate customs and sharpened his sense of himself as an ironic observer. Events on campus, across the nation, and around the world awakened his interest in politics. In the end he was a reluctant college rebel, a person whose stance, like that of his favorite uncle, was more iconoclastic than radical.[1] An "indifferent" student most of the time, he learned from Willard Waller, the professor who most influenced him, what it meant to develop an engaged yet ironic intelligence.[2] Waller reinforced the sense of himself that Packard had already developed. By the time he graduated in 1936, Packard had begun to learn what it meant to combine rebellion and observation as central elements in his stance toward the world.

From State College to Penn State

Though he continued to live at home, when he entered Penn State in the fall of 1932 Packard crossed the line between town and gown. Located in a hilly area in the middle of the state, the university dominated the region. State College was staunchly Republican, with its citizens voting against Franklin Roosevelt in 1932 and 1936. Perhaps the local newspaper spoke for many of the shopkeepers in town and professional employees at the university when a front-page editorial declared that the issue in the 1936 election was whether to accept the New Deal "or to attempt to return to our American system."[3] Expansion of the university protected the town and surrounding areas from the full impact of the Depression.[4] Across Pennsylvania factories shut down and banks foreclosed on mortgages. Yet Penn State flourished, bolstered by a campus building boom and an influx of students for whom college with an annual tuition of one hundred dollars seemed preferable to the uncertainties of the job market. Because of the relative prosperity of town and gown, Packard had little direct experience with the more dire consequences of the Depression. His family's real income was probably increasing at that time. To him and to many of his classmates, misery and suffering seemed far away and life in State College comparatively idyllic. On rare occasions, however, he caught "glimpses" of what life was like outside State College. Hitchhiking to see a friend before he matriculated, Packard went through Detroit and Toledo, an experience he recalled as providing "quite a jolt."[5]

Primarily an undergraduate institution, Penn State was a relatively homogeneous and insulated environment. Most of the undergraduates came from native-born and middle-class backgrounds. African Americans and children of immigrants, more likely to go to Temple or Pitt, attended in relatively small numbers. There was, Packard recalled, "not a single Black, Hispanic, or Asian" in his graduating class of almost nine hundred. Fraternities and sororities dominated collegiate life, with more than 40 percent of the undergraduates pledging.[6] Still, there were moments when national and international events gave many students a sense that they were living at a time that called on them to take stands on critical issues. The end of Prohibition, the collapse of the banking system, and a faculty-sponsored relief drive for needy local residents reminded undergraduates of the connection between national conditions and their own lives. During the mid-1930s ominous stories from across the Atlantic captured the attention of Packard and many of his contemporaries. Adolf Hitler assumed power in early 1933. The Italians invaded Ethiopia in October 1935, and Germany occupied the Rhineland five months later.

In response to events abroad, a nationwide peace movement emerged during Packard's years in college. Achieving an unusual degree of unity in the mid-1930s, Communists, Socialists, liberals, and pacifists joined in organizing campus protests. Antiwar activity crystallized around the Oxford Oath, a commitment not to support the American government in any future wars. Taking it involved asserting individual responsibility in opposition to nationalism and militarism. For many collegians, participation in the peace movement meant a rejection of a prevailing student culture based on fraternities, sororities, and athletics, as well as skepticism regarding the equation of a college degree with worldly success.[7]

At Penn State the peace movement developed late, grew dramatically, and then declined rapidly. There was no organized activity in April 1934, when thousands of students at more cosmopolitan institutions waged a strike against war. A year later, in the spring of Packard's junior year, antiwar sentiment at Penn State intensified when protest briefly energized many on the campus. "1,500 Students Join Nation-wide Strike Against Imperialistic War," announced the headline in the campus newspaper. About two hundred students at Penn State, including Packard, took the Oxford Oath. But Penn State was not especially fertile ground for activism and the protests soon diminished.[8]

Most Penn State students remained relatively conservative or apathetic. The Depression and events abroad still seemed far away, and they had absorbed the politics of their mostly middle-class parents. In a straw vote in 1932, students selected Herbert Hoover by a two-and-a-half-to-one margin over Roosevelt; four years later, FDR lost the student poll by a margin of two to one. Moreover, student rebels were rarely militant or confrontational. Living in rural Pennsylvania, only a few of them took part in the labor struggles that influenced their peers on more urban campuses. The more radical groups that played such important roles elsewhere did not develop fully among undergraduates at Penn State.[9] In Packard's graduating class, there were thirty to fifty students who considered themselves politically active on the left, numbers insufficient to permit the intense factionalism that affected their peers at places like City College and Columbia.[10]

As was true elsewhere, adversarial and left-leaning undergraduates gravitated toward campus publications. Late at night student journalists, Packard included, would gather at a local eatery and argue over national and international events.[11] One of them wrote in 1935 that the only way to end war was through "the establishment of a *classless* society," a prospect achievable only through acceptance of the leadership of the Communist party.[12] Though very few students actually joined the party, the editors of the student newspaper were decidedly left-wing. Editorials criticized the American Legion and called for mass protests against an imperialist war. Undergraduate journalists attacked capitalists for trying to suppress radical protest and for supporting a war that served business interests. William Randolph Hearst came in for criticism, with one editorial denouncing him as "the-liar-in-chief of America." Another writer, characterizing violence against labor leaders and protestors as fascism that was "out-Nazi-ing Hitler," attacked those who red-baited students and faculty.[13]

At the outset, Packard was poised between contrasting worlds—fraternity brothers and rebels; athletes and writers; town and gown; his parents' home where he lived and the world of undergraduates where he spent much of his time. "Caught between two fires" of sports and journalism, as he put it in 1936, initially he went out for three teams and four publications.[14] Even though he was a joiner, one contemporary recalled him as "an outsider all of the time." Living at home, one of his classmates remarked, meant he "missed out on the allnight pingpong games, arguments, humor, general camaraderie, and carryings-on" that took place near the offices of the undergraduate publications.[15] More so than most late adolescents, he was still ill at ease in social situations.[16] He remained conscious of his rural origins in a world where most students with whom he associated were from small towns, cities, or suburbs.[17] Skeptical and ironic, he was also aware of what he described in 1936 as his "Babbitish tendencies," conformity to middle-class aspirations.[18]

His brother's intercollegiate wrestling championship earned Vance membership in one of the most socially prestigious and academically average of the fraternities. Perhaps he accepted the invitation because it enabled him to realize his dream of achieving acceptance and prestige. Yet before long he revealed the other side of his ambivalence by poking fun at the pretense of fraternities and demystifying their customs, something he would do a quarter of a century later for American suburban life in *Status Seekers*.[19] In a fraternity but not of the Greek world, at the end of his Penn State career Packard delivered a "farewell speech to the brothers." He boastfully wrote the young woman he was courting that after flattering them he offered criticism "as politely and ruthlessly as I could." He asserted that the house "was becoming the headquarters for tramp athletes and would-be big shots," something they could begin to remedy by improving the condition of the house library and by purchasing "some at least faintly classical victrola records."[20]

The Making of a College Journalist

Journalism stood at the center of Packard's life in college, preoccupying him "almost totally," he remembered, "to the neglect of academic work."[21] He joined the staff of the magazine *Old Main Bell*, ending up as managing editor in his senior year. However, the *Penn State Collegian* was the focus of his ambition. A wrestling injury turned him from participating in that sport to writing about it for the student paper. Rising to assistant editor, he had "one of the great disappointments of my life" when he lost out on his bid to become editor. The holder of this position, he wrote soon afterwards in a way that may have reflected his envy of insiders, was "given bids or membership to all the important organizations of the College." Although the reasons for the choice of someone else were complicated, Packard felt wrongfully deprived of victory. He believed his peers had passed him over because he "was a 'town-boy.'" His sense of rejection reverberated with memories of his childhood illness, his move to State College, his awkwardness as an adolescent and his marginal position in high school and college. Coediting the *Summer Collegian* in 1935 was what he called his "consolation" but in his senior year he had nothing to do with the paper.[22]

Campus journalism provided Packard with his political education. He generally agreed with the student editorials that opposed militarism, superpatriotism, fascism, curbs on free speech, and the red-baiting by the Hearst newspapers and the American Legion.[23] The Comintern's encouragement of the antifascist Popular Front and the New Deal's Second Hundred Days, both of which occurred in 1935, meant that the critical year of Packard's political coming of age occurred at a time when he, like many others, could feel that associating with the Left was well within the American tradition. The Popular Front helped students like Packard avoid having to make tough choices by blurring the differences between Russian Communism and the American tradition of democratic reform, between revolutionary goals and middle-class life. FDR's fight for the National Labor Relations Act, a soak-the-rich income tax, and the Social Security Act enhanced Packard's faith in the ability of the American political system to respond constructively in a time of economic crisis.[24] For him, as for many other college students who came to political consciousness in the 1930s, the impact of critical events was long-lasting and yet the resulting commitments to adversarial politics were tenuous.[25]

If Packard stood apart from the student mainstream, he distanced himself even further from his parents' Republicanism. Later calling himself "just another New Deal liberal crazy about FDR," on domestic political issues he mixed iconoclasm with liberal and left-wing positions.[26] He felt drawn to the democratic socialism of Norman Thomas, to the industrial unionism of the CIO, to the public works programs advocated by Harold Ickes, and to the ideas about national planning put forward by Rexford G. Tugwell. In one article, he revealed himself as a New Dealer who feared the hysteria and extremism of a mass movement led by Huey Long.[27] He saw the American Communist party, he remembered, as "still pretty much a joke." Like many whose commitment to the Soviet Union was even stronger, Packard believed that Communism was an acceptable solution to the USSR's problems but not to America's. If "ideological communism" had any appeal to him, he recalled, it was not only because it represented an "idealistic way to put down relentless capitalists in major industries" but also because it offered "participation, action."[28] Progressive politics provided a way to overcome isolation, to find in a group other than a fraternity a sense of belonging and acceptance.[29] Politics offered a way he could educate himself and aided in his struggle to maintain his sense of himself as a nonconformist. Adversarial politics also appealed because they promised to transport him into a world beyond the parochialism of Bradford County and State College. If his past was religious, rural, nationalistic, and confining, his future was secular, cosmopolitan, internationalist, and eye-opening.[30]

News from abroad also captured Packard's attention. The Italian invasion of Ethiopia in October 1935 and the events culminating in the outbreak of the Spanish Civil War in July 1936, he recalled, made him "outraged" and "passionately anti-fascist."[31] Although Germany's expansion tested his reluctance to sanction American involvement abroad, while in college Packard nonetheless remained opposed to American intervention to halt the Japanese conquest of China because it might lead to a conflict supported by "our industrialists' enthusiasm" for new markets. Only the elimination of "decayed, outmoded Nationalism," he observed, would bring about real peace, stop "the glorification of babies and motherhood," and cut short the careers of dictators. To overcome the "stagnation" in China, he commented, "Communism would work just as well" as Christianity.[32]

Above all, the situation in the Soviet Union captivated him. Although Stalin was laying the foundation for the Great Purge during the year before Packard left State College, the activities prominently reported from the Soviet Union included relatively good harvests and the adoption of a constitution that promised a wide range of freedoms.[33] Such stories made it possible for Packard to write early in 1936 that Walter Duranty provided the "best analysis of Russia I've read to date."[34] In the bestselling *I Write as I Please*, a book Packard read not long after its publication late in 1935, this apologist for Stalinism and the Moscow correspondent for the *New York Times* argued that "any altruistic end, however remote, may justify any means however cruel" that the Soviet regime used under Stalin, "the greatest living statesman." Duranty hailed the way the USSR had enshrined economic planning and the value of "communal pride and interest in everything that the community rather than the individual accomplished." He also suggested that a business-run and government-backed system of social insurance would provide the United States with "a bridge from 'rugged individualism' to 'capitalist collectivism' without" the coercion experienced in the USSR.[35]

Like many others of his generation, the USSR appealed to Packard because it served in the mid-1930s as a bulwark against fascism and as an example of a society that had used, he believed, rational planning to solve economic problems. In retrospect, he recalled that he was "distinctly a sympathizer willing to overlook a lot of rough stuff" in the mid-1930s. For Packard, as for Duranty, the long-term end of bringing the Soviet Union into the modern world justified the brutal means used to do so.[36] Packard also may have seen in the Soviet experiment the possibility of a more perfect society where communal values triumphed over selfish individualism.

As appealing to Packard as Duranty's views were, at least as compelling was the sense of adventure he conveyed about the life of a foreign correspondent. Duranty emphasized the freedom he had to say what he liked even though editors and publishers might object. Duranty talked about what he was doing with phrases similar to those Packard would use when he described his own situation a quarter of a century later.[37] The very title of Duranty's book, *I Write as I Please*, might have served as a motto for what Packard strove to achieve during his career. Finding his great folk heroes in foreign correspondents, by the end of his time at Penn State Packard looked forward to a career as a writer on international affairs. These years were the heyday of American journalists in Europe, who reached wide audiences by telling about their adventures. Packard devoured the writings of Vincent Sheean, John Gunther, and William L. Shirer. Like Duranty and even like Lincoln Steffens during part of his career, these international correspondents seemed compelling to Packard because of their antifascist positions, lively writing, broad appeal, and knack for being in the right place at the right time.[38]

If Packard admired the Soviet example, he kept his distance from political involvement generally and American radicalism specifically. Caution and humor, rather than advocacy or a strong ideological position, remained his metier.[39] "Yes, I'm a member of that radical group," he wrote in the spring of 1936, referring to the American Student Union in a way that made him sound more daring than he actually was. "I don't think it is

Communist (as everyone else seems to)—just slightly pinkish," he told the woman he was courting. "Maybe it will neutralize my Babbitish tendencies."[40] His skepticism and his preference for observation over involvement kept him wary of his radical classmates.[41] He disagreed with one, he wrote in his last semester, who wanted "to remake the world after his own pattern." When the student editor of the *Old Main Bell* wrote that he would "be partial to any piece submitted which attempts to brighten the dismal prospect of world capitalism," Packard privately asserted "that literature should be good in itself per se." He continued, "While my politics might be slightly tinged with Socialism, I don't believe that everything written must be revolutionary to be of value."[42]

Packard thus expressed himself politically more through words than through political action or organizational involvement. In an act that resembled a prank more than a public protest, he and his closest friend, Jack Barnes, threw their rifles under the bushes, behavior that got them kicked out of ROTC. Vance was more forthright in his opposition to militarism in words than in public deeds. In a term paper he wrote in early 1936, he described how ROTC courses tried to "ameliorate the hatred for war" many students felt and to make them "more sheep-like in case they are ever drafted for service."[43] Yet many of those who knew Packard were unaware of where he stood politically.[44] Some of his best friends in high school and college considered him a "parlor pink," a person curious about radical causes but hesitant about making commitments.[45] At some level he may have sensed the embarrassment or even danger that his embrace of controversial positions might pose for his father's employment at a local public university. This concern about the connection between politics and the ability to provide would emerge in his own life during the ensuing decades.

To Packard, reading was more important than political action. His three-year job in the university library sparked his curiosity about books and the organization of knowledge. "Often there was little shelving to do," he recalled, "and I would prop up my feet and browse through books that particularly intrigued me." He discovered the pleasures of seeking mastery through reading and writing as he voraciously consumed unassigned material on a wide variety of subjects.[46] This helped him develop what he later called "the habit of looking for The Big Picture," an interest in seeing things in their totality. His passion for the written word did not, however, enhance his performance in the classroom: his academic record was only slightly higher than average.[47]

What Packard read on his own reveals the nature of his informal education. The muckrakers of the Progressive period, especially Steffens, cap-

tured his imagination.[48] He also focused on works that influenced his contemporaries on the Left: John Chamberlain's *Farewell to Reform*, George
Soule's *Coming American Revolution*, and Granville Hicks's *Great Tradi-
tion*. Noticeably absent from the lists he kept were the names of writers
who dominated so much of American intellectual life in the 1930s: Charles
Beard, Alfred Bingham, James Burnham, Lewis Corey, Malcolm Cowley,
Max Eastman, Waldo Frank, Lewis Mumford, and Edmund Wilson. Similarly, among periodicals, he reported reading the *Nation* and the *New
Republic* (as well as *Time*, *Fortune*, and *Reader's Digest*), but not *New
Masses*, *Common Sense*, or *Modern Quarterly*. His literary taste gravi-
tated to European and American classics more than to proletarian novel-
ists like James T. Farrell or to modernists such as James Joyce or Franz
Kafka.[49]

What Packard read, wrote, and did in college underscores how different
his experiences were from those of the intellectuals who dominated so
much of the ideological battleground in America from the 1930s on.[50] To
begin with, although Packard felt he was an outsider, he had no personal
connection with the forces that fostered a sense of marginality in others.
What influenced Alfred Kazin or Daniel Bell, who also started out in the
thirties, was the immigrant experience, urbanism, socialism, Judaism, and
poverty. Though Packard shared with people like Dwight Macdonald and
Edmund Wilson a white Anglo-Saxon Protestant heritage that underwrote a sense of being at home in America, he lacked their elite educations
and cosmopolitan outlooks.

Issues such as the failure of capitalism, the pervasiveness of class struggle, and the fundamental reconstruction of American society did not pre-
occupy Packard. Because he neither considered joining the Communist
party nor battled with those who did, the anticommunist views that he
later developed were neither vitriolic nor highly charged. Indeed, his pro-
Soviet attitude was apparently not connected to a critique of America that
grew out of disillusionment with the economy's performance during the
Depression. He never seriously believed that the USSR provided a viable
alternative to a failed American economic system or was the first step
toward the realization of a revolutionary dream.[51] As he viewed events
abroad, Packard was an admirer of many aspects of Stalinism; on domestic
issues, he stood between the New Deal and Norman Thomas's socialism. A
commitment to the American values of experimentation and rationality
may well have connected his outlook on events in the United States and
the USSR. In that context, FDR and Stalin were for Packard both pragmatic leaders, doing their best under adverse conditions. He found the
Soviet example appealing in varied ways. As an antifascist, he was pleased

that some nation would lead the battle against Nazi Germany. As a reader of foreign correspondents, he shared a sense of excitement about dramatic events across the ocean. As the son of a man who did not succeed as a yeoman farmer, perhaps he saw the dream of socialist agriculture as redeeming his father's difficulties and providing an alternative to his success as supervisor of farms at Penn State. Finally, as his parents' child, he allowed Communism to replace Christian missionary activity as the way of dealing with people in less-developed countries.[52]

Although he read *The Communist Manifesto* and occasionally used Marxist phrases, like most other college students who shared his politics Packard knew little if anything else of Marx. His heroes were foreign correspondents, not union members, African American sharecroppers, or revolutionary writers. He did not participate in heated political discussions like those that took place in the cafeteria at City College, the cafes of Greenwich Village, or the offices of the *New Republic*. Unlike the Trotskyite anti-Stalinists who rejected Popular Front antifascism and centered their lives on the *Partisan Review* in the late 1930s, Packard did not combine radical politics with literary modernism. Their belief that there was a connection between mass culture and the Popular Front's celebration of proletarians would have made little sense to him. When he attacked middlebrow commercialism, he did so because of its optimistic celebration of the hollow myth of success.[53]

Nothing keeps Packard's commitments in perspective better than the recognition that the lion's share of his college journalism focused not on public policy but on the culture of undergraduates. The unwritten codes by which students lived fascinated him; deciphering them was central to the process of his coming of age. His articles revealed his suspicions of the claims of authority over the individual and his interest in demystifying social customs. They also emphasized an outsider's penchant for rebelliousness that was more cultural than political, that spoke more of youthful skepticism than of ideological commitment. After fraternity rush had developed in entering students "an exaggerated opinion" of their "relative importance," he said at the beginning of his freshman year, the few remaining customs brought them "quickly back to earth," thus preventing them from becoming "the most conceited young asses on the face of this earth." A year later, he warned male students that they could not become a "College Man without being drastically remodeled." Perhaps reflecting the irony that his brother's achievements had gained him entry into a prestigious fraternity despite his awkwardness, Packard noted that if a prospective fraternity member exhibited "smoothness," he could "afford to be choosy."[54]

Vance Packard in his senior year at Penn State, 1935.
(Used by permission of Vance Packard.)

The "more painful and tremendously more significant" challenge, Packard wrote in a way that may have reflected his own experience, came in the students' "intellectual life." Initially, they would "tenaciously" hold on to the views they came to college with and would denounce the professor "as being one of Satan's henchmen." Gradually, as undergraduates listened to professors speak favorably about the ideas of Bertrand Russell, H. L. Mencken, or Charles Darwin, they became tormented by the tension between old and new ideas. Eventually, Packard predicted, "the entire structure of your previous views will totter for a moment and then crumble underneath you. Then you will doubt everything!" In the end, Packard concluded, the crisis was as much stylistic as intellectual. The student could consider himself a "College Man," he remarked, only when he "thoroughly sand-papered the rough-edges" of personality, "ironed out" his "home-town peculiarities," and developed his own "philosophy of life."[55]

Packard returned to these themes in the fall of his senior year. He poked fun at new students because they expected college to "scrub off that rustic complexion and convert them into campus dandies, to inoculate them with some sort of higher education, to enlighten them as to the secret of becoming a howling success in the world; and then, after four years, to eject them at the other end of the roller of this College Mill fairly reeking with culture and education." In contrast and perhaps offering his sense of his own development, Packard held up the ideal of the genuinely engaged student who would not be excessively concerned with grades and who avoided the "pitfalls of mass attitudes." Such an undergraduate, he wrote, would demonstrate the essential elements of a true education: emancipation from "herd-opinion"; the capacity for "self-criticism"; the development of "an attitude of true urbanity."[56]

Packard's writings on student culture also revealed his increasing distance from his parents. If father and son had their first political disagreements over the New Deal, the areas of conflict quickly expanded. In college, Packard came to see missionary activity, which his parents had long supported, "as a case where over-enthusiastic Christians (so-called) were meddling in other people's affairs."[57] His mother and father, he wrote in 1935, were unhappy when they discovered that he was reading about teenage sexual activity, about the way "a modest red-light district was an asset to any town," and about "the worldly tricks the preachers used to drum up trade." They believed, he wrote with his usual bravado to the woman he was courting, that it was "a disgrace that people should write such horrid things—let alone making us innocent sheep in college read it." To counter their impression that their son was "going to the devil all over again," Packard thought he might bring home *The Man Nobody Knows*,

The Fallacies of Organic Evolution, and *Why I Believe in God,* and "strew them promiscuously about my room for a couple of weeks." He concluded, "That always quiets them."[58]

Although Packard later acknowledged that during his college years he experienced no wrenching crisis of belief, he still had to deal with the tension between the old and the new—Methodism and skepticism; the Republican party and FDR; and the myth of success and the knowledge that the Depression had threatened the American Dream.[59] By dwelling on the relationship between the individual and the social environment, he could forge his own identity in the context of influence from classmates and professors. When he explored outmoded rituals, he was also expressing his feelings toward customs that both repelled and fascinated him. Warning newcomers about what they would face reminded him that, even though he had what he described as Babbitish tendencies, he was an outsider who looked skeptically and uneasily at the dominant undergraduate mores.

Whatever disappointments Packard experienced as an undergraduate, he recalled the summer of 1935 as a "glorious" time. It was then that he met and fell in love with Virginia Mathews, the woman he would marry three years later.[60] Born in 1912 in Nicholasville, Kentucky, she had moved to Susquehanna, Pennsylvania, as a child. There, her father ran a motion picture theater and worked as a commercial artist while her mother managed a restaurant. After two years at the University of Kentucky, she transferred to Penn State, where she majored in art education, graduating in 1935.[61] Virginia found Vance "frank" and "smooth."[62] Until they met, Packard later wrote, he had used "dozens of forms of guile, artifice, white lying and outright flimflamming" as he chased after young women whom his peers considered desirable, "the best-looking girl or the best dancer or the girl with the highest status within my range." Virginia was different from the others Packard pursued, and in the long run she strengthened the nonconformist, status-scorning side of the man she married. What struck Packard when he met her, he remembered, was that she was "unvaryingly frank, honest and proud about everything she did and was and wanted to be, and she expected me to be the same."[63]

The summer of 1935 was also important because at last Packard was editing the campus newspaper, albeit only the summer version. "Large Crowd Will Attend Tonight's Dance—We Hope," announced one headline of an article he wrote, with typical flippancy; he then proceeded to note that a small crowd would mean that he would not get free tickets to the next dance. When the business manager insisted that a column on window shopping focus on stores that advertised in the *Summer Collegian,* Packard's work on the paper exposed him to something he would encounter again in the 1950s, the connection between writers and business managers.[64] Although he and his coeditor paid some attention to weighty issues, they ended their stewardship with an editorial that was noticeably noncommittal, especially when compared with the serious and ideological cast of the student newspaper during the academic year.[65] Perhaps this contrast prompted a member of the university staff to congratulate Packard. The dean of men remarked that the coeditors had "put more life, color, joy and good taste in the *Collegian* (summer or winter) than it has shown for yeahs and yeahs."[66]

One of Packard's summer editorials deserves special mention for its prophetic value. Facetiously suggesting summer reading to students, Packard pointed to *American Magazine* as a "sunshine-dispersing gazette" that offered optimism and inspiration to "the great American Middle Class." Each issue, Packard commented, contained "stirring success" stories and was "just brim full of cheery, inspirational articles on how you, too can" be president, a lion tamer, or a tennis champion.[67] Little did Packard know that within two years he would be authoring similar features for a Hearst newspaper and within seven he would be working for the very magazine he now attacked, writing the kind of copy he had satirized as an undergraduate journalist.

Willard Waller as Mentor

What confirmed Packard's stance as a nonactivist rebel was the influence of sociology professor Willard W. Waller (1899–1945), who taught at Penn State from 1931 to 1937. One of Packard's contemporaries described Waller's influence on Packard as "profound"; another spoke of Packard as "the fruit of Waller."[68] The sociologist, Packard later asserted, "shaped my life more than any other teacher I ever had." Packard noted that he "became so immersed" in the books to which Waller's course led him that he could not "separate his input from the rest." During their years at Penn State, student and teacher published debunking articles on undergraduate culture. Waller, Packard remarked years later, was "a genial, acerbic skeptic who greatly whetted my own interest in human behavior" when he was a college student. They shared an iconoclasm, a commitment to a qualitative and accessible sociology, an interest in student culture and the family, and many elements of a stance toward politics. Some of Waller's impact on Packard may have stemmed from the ways in which the teacher's irreverence reverberated with the nonconformity Vance Packard had absorbed from his Uncle Bill. When Packard labeled Waller an "amiable skeptic," he was also describing both himself and his uncle.[69]

Waller was a product of the Chicago School of Sociology, a group of scholars who drew their inspiration from, among other sources, urban journalism and Progressive reform.[70] Behind their work lay assumptions of the Protestant tradition of muckraking—especially the idea that the public, grounded in a moral outlook, would correct a situation once they learned the facts.[71] The Chicago School stood in opposition to sociologists who, during the 1920s and 1930s, insisted that the field be objective in its stance and rigorous in its use of theory and quantitative methods. The Chicago School was famous for its emphasis on personal investigation and observation, case studies, anecdotal evidence, survey methods, and an interdisciplinary approach. One of its leading practitioners, Robert Park, came to sociology from journalism, as did other notable users of observation and anecdotal evidence, from Franklin Giddings to Christopher Jencks. What Waller wrote was thus dramatically different from the more "scientific" sociology that Talcott Parsons, George Lundberg, Samuel A. Stouffer, Paul Lazarsfeld, and Robert Merton were developing in the 1930s and 1940s and that would come to dominate the discipline by the 1950s.

Waller's approach was personal, demystifying, realistic, and often impressionistic. At Penn State he quickly earned a reputation as an ironic and energetic teacher, particularly popular with students who worked on undergraduate publications. He loved to shock students by attacking received wisdom and respected authorities. "Get the facts," someone recalled him telling his Penn State students, "know what is going on behind the scenes."[72] He presented a satirical and deterministic analysis of the relationships among people and between people and institutions. Rejecting the notion of a self-adjusting and harmonious society, he focused instead on conflict, tension, and divisiveness.[73] "One side of Waller," a historian has noted, in words not unlike those later used to describe Packard, "was the sociologist concerned about the scientific reputation of his work, but another side was the writer and former journalist who wanted to shock people."[74]

When Waller turned his attention to marriage and the family, subjects on which Packard would write in the postwar years, his observations were irreverent. Combining a flair for the dramatic, case studies filled with intimate details (some of them drawn from personal experience), and a highly readable style, he attacked the notions of romantic love and of the individual governed by free will. His classic 1937 article "The Rating and Dating Complex," which may have shaped what Packard said of his relationships with women in college, explored its subject as part of a "social scramble," in which students made elaborate judgments about the status of their dates. Waller was neither sanguine about proposals for radical reconstruction of the family nor sympathetic to the Victorian view of marriage as a couple living "together in perfect amity." Proclaiming sympathy for women's aspirations, he nonetheless evidenced unease about the way "women are doing men's jobs, and men are taking over the traditional tasks of women." Waller wanted to rework the division "of labor into that which truly belongs to man and that which rightfully may be assigned to women." With the roles recast, the "rivalry between the sexes may not so often arise, or if it does arise, may not disrupt families."[75]

A political maverick, Waller strengthened Packard's penchant for thinking of himself as a reluctant rebel, someone without a commitment to action. Waller was "a moralist rather than a political thinker" who "saw himself as a tough-minded realist," his biographers have written in words that also describe much of Packard's later approach.[76] When Penn State students pressed Waller for suggestions about how they should act in the political arena, he backed off from discussions of the implications of his analysis.[77] Insisting that he stood aside from politics, he explored the limitations rather than the possibilities of planning for social change. Waller argued that social problems emerged out of a conflict between the effort to improve conditions and the strength of basic mores and institutions such as private property, monogamy, individualism, Christianity, and nationalism. Until the reformer was willing to challenge these fundamental forces, he remarked, "he must continue to treat symptoms without removing their causes." Too often, Packard's teacher argued, the "liberal humanitarian" had deplored human misery that is a "necessary part of a social order which seems to him good."[78]

There was a gap between the power of Waller's analysis and his inattention to actual reforms.[79] This approach paralleled, if it did not actually influence, the stance toward politics that Packard took during much of his life, although the student replaced his teacher's pessimism with his own mixture of realism and optimism. Like his student, during the 1930s the mentor remained skeptical of radicalism. Waller described the "proselytizing radical" teacher who "must be willing, in order to preserve his own basic illusion, to endow students who follow him with more intelligence than they possess and to regard as exceedingly dull all students who have balance enough not to follow him."[80]

Though he knew about Waller before then, not until his last semester did Packard take a course from him.[81] In the paper he wrote for the class, Packard revealed why he had increasingly distanced himself from radical politics. Stung by his rejection as editor of the student paper, he was especially scornful of the clique that he believed controlled undergraduate publications, whom he described as "clever, good-natured, unscrupulous, and cynical." As he would more publicly in his books, he now sought to expose the corruption and pretense of hidden persuaders who, he felt, manipulated the lives of others. Though these peers pretended to be radicals, to Packard only one of them could "discuss proletarian revolt, social consciousness, and capitalistic oligarchy and leave the impression that he knows what he is talking about." The others, he concluded, derided "Fascism and Capitalism more as a hobby than from conviction." He argued that under the leadership of the person who had beaten him for the editor's position, the student newspaper vengefully demonstrated its "propensity for sensationalism" as it launched crusades. Consequently, the tactics the newspaper used "come closer to coinciding with those of Hearst than with those of any other figure in American journalism."[82]

Packard's paper demonstrated how rejection by the dominant newspaper clique taught him a number of important lessons. Tempted as he may have been by what he saw as the virtues of the USSR, he had a realistic view of how an editor's ideology could lead to censorship and control. Because the clique seemed fashionably left wing and made the newspaper more doctrinaire, Packard's antipathy to radical politics increased, encouraged by Waller's own skepticism about radicalism.[83] Packard's failure to become editor of the college newspaper sharpened his sense that he was an outsider even as it strengthened his determination to use his pen to gain recognition for himself and his point of view.

Interlude between College and Graduate School

Packard handed in this paper in mid-January 1936 and received his B.A. on the last day of the month.[84] Just before that, he asked Waller how to "avoid going bankrupt." In response, his mentor said "the only solution he knew (and the one he personally put into practice)" was "to continue taking in more than you give out," something "done best by constant reading."[85] In the ensuing months Packard embarked on a systematic program of reading. He also worked for the local newspaper, saving as much as he could for graduate school expenses.[86] His boss felt his work was plodding and unexceptional. Packard, he recalled, was "almost punchy" and "lived in a different world," the type of person who would forget to eat or might bump into a mailbox. He told the cub reporter to "forget about being a journalist" because he was not "cut out for it." By midsummer, the editor ended Packard's stint on the town paper.[87]

One incident in this interregnum between college and professional school revealed something of Packard's innocence. During the summer of 1936, his best friend sent him a letter addressed to "My dear radical-to-be" and signed "Comrade Barnes (No. 17642)." Columbia was "a hotbed of radicalism," Jack Barnes wrote, and Packard would not leave the journalism school "the same unsullied capitalist" that he was when he matriculated. If the revolution came to America, he predicted that Karl Marx's beard would "take the place of the Wrigley Fish on the sign in Times Square." All who joined the revolution, Packard learned, would have two weeks "in a mountain lair with their favorite concubine—except that we're going to use a more properly proletarian word and rearrange the marital code."[88]

Naive about the possible consequences of his action, Packard showed the letter to a local justice of the peace who much earlier had led a raid on the offices of the campus newspaper in order to find "subversive materials" that might uncover "Communist influence" on campus. Packard thought the judge might be "amused." Instead, he passed the information on to the FBI. Four years later, when there was concern about the German American Bund's "noisy anti-war activities," an FBI agent called on Packard and asked to see the letter that contained the details of the plot to take over New York City. Packard "tried to explain that it was a joke," but the agent persisted, and Packard handed over the letter.[89]

Pointing back to the harassment of his relatives during World War I and forward to the McCarthyism of the 1950s, the story was but one of several that illuminate how Packard's college years connected his childhood to his career. He was learning to combine his commitment to values of rural and small-town America with his newly awakened interest in politics and the social and behavioral sciences. From his mother came a love of books and a moral vision. From his father came a respect for people who worked hard, produced real wealth, and took advantage of opportunity. In his irreverence and insistence on seeing the world without pretense, Waller bore a striking resemblance to Uncle Bill. Moreover, Waller encouraged his student to make accessible to a nonacademic audience the fascinating phenomena that social and behavioral scientists uncovered. Events in Packard's childhood—in both Granville Summit and State College—developed in him those combinations of irony and open-eyed wonder, detachment and interest, desire to gain help from others and restlessness to be independent. Experiences in State College and at Penn State made him glance admiringly at the world of university professors. From early in his youth, he was an observer who wanted to take everything in and a nonconformist who both disliked and was fascinated by status. All of these qualities and experiences would shape him as a writer and social critic in the years to come.

White Collar

Columbia Graduate School of Journalism, *Boston Daily Record*,
and Associated Press, 1936–1942

When Vance Packard went from
State College to Manhattan in 1936, he set off on a course that would take
him far from rural and small-town Pennsylvania. In the fall he entered the
recently established Graduate School of Journalism at Columbia University, earning his master's degree the following June. He moved to Boston
for his first regular job and quickly produced a scoop, which in turn gained
him his own daily column. Nonetheless, work on the Boston newspaper did
not fully satisfy him, and, in any event, the newspaper terminated his job.
In 1938 he moved back to New York to begin a four-year stint with the
Associated Press Feature Service, writing human interest stories and
weekly reviews of the news. He married Virginia Mathews in 1938, and
their first child was born in 1942. At the end of the six years that stretched
from his departure from State College in 1936 to the beginning of his
employment with *American Magazine* in 1942, Packard's career had not

yet settled on the path that would lead directly to his emergence as a major American social critic.

Yet these years shaped his career. A series of events at home and abroad prompted him to rethink his attitudes toward the Soviet Union and the United States. Beginning with a dream of becoming an international correspondent, he ended up as an author of human interest stories. An ambitious country boy who was starting to make it in the city, he came to see himself as an independent nonconformist who faced work situations that threatened to compromise his autonomy and creativity. Individualism was attractive when compared with nazism and with occupational pressures for conformity. These experiences also increased his ambivalence toward traditional routes to success.

Graduate School of Journalism at Columbia University, 1936–1937

Although a number of experiences in high school and college caused him to admire what professors represented, Packard focused entirely on journalism, the area for which he had the most extensive experience and for which role models seemed most compelling. Like several of the campus journalists at Penn State, he focused his ambition on a career as a professional writer. Since Packard lacked the connections that might have brought him a job without further education and was attracted to the prestige of Columbia's newly established program, the next step seemed clear. His application to Columbia revealed a personally vulnerable but widely read and politically conscious college graduate who, with the help of further training and experience, would be well prepared to make his mark as a journalist. In writing about his vision of the place of newspapers in American society, Packard offered an answer that, although common in the 1930s, was not without risks. He boldly stated that it was "ridiculous" to think about trying to purge "the country of the Hearst Press without first remolding the mentality of the class that sustains it." Nonetheless, he identified the press as "the best available medium to carry out" the necessary "overhauling of society." Consequently, schools of journalism had to insist that the reporters they trained assume "a greater sense of social responsibility." Implicitly referring to himself, Packard commented that "the instrument for reform is available, awaiting only intelligent guidance." He felt he could help achieve these ambitious goals by becoming "either a foreign correspondent, a Washington correspondent, or a news columnist."[1]

Despite these expressions of confidence, a note of vulnerability ran through the application. He spoke of his childhood "inferiority complex" and his lack of a "healthy attitude toward" his studies in his early years at Penn State. Recalling his great disappointment at not becoming editor of the *Collegian*, he defensively tried to explain why his peers had not selected him. He also asserted that this rejection, coupled with a growing awareness of Columbia's lure, had prompted him to improve his academic record by taking his schoolwork more seriously. From his junior year on, he remarked, "all my plans were unconsciously based around my hope of going to Columbia."[2]

The application evidenced few signs of the jaunty style and ironic humor that marked the best of what he had written during his college years and little of the passion and wit that characterized the paper he had handed in to Willard Waller. Clearly, the admissions process was forbidding. Perhaps feeling very much the country boy petitioning those who guarded entry into a cosmopolitan, Ivy League university, he admitted that his knowledge of journalism was "vague and provincial" and that he looked forward to getting "my first taste of metropolitan life and metropolitan newspaper work." Graduate school, he concluded, having made no mention of the faculty that would teach him, would enable him "to more honestly evaluate my own potentialities as a journalist."[3]

Packard hardly impressed the admissions committee. His academic record had not markedly improved and what he wrote was not terribly persuasive. The letters of recommendation spoke more of his sense of humor, commitment to hard work, ambition, honesty, and friendliness than they did of achievement as a student or potential as a journalist. One member of the committee, noting that the applicant "may have the makings but I am not convinced," recommended that Packard's candidacy remain on hold along with others considered "border line." When Packard showed up for an interview in late June, the dean underlined the word "nervous" in his notes and characterized Packard as having "average mentality and promise." Nonetheless, in early July Columbia, not faced with an abundance of highly talented students who did not need financial aid, mailed Packard's letter of admission.[4]

Packard's accomplishments at Columbia belied the assessment of the admissions committee. Over the long term, he would prove to be an exceptionally productive and influential writer, an achievement the school recognized in 1958 when it gave him the Journalism Alumni Award and in 1963 when it honored him with its Outstanding Alumni Award. Even in the short term, however, Packard confounded expectations. He graduated fifth in his class and was an alternate for the Pulitzer Traveling Fellowship, which he would have used, had it been awarded to him, to travel around the world covering crises, just like the foreign correspondents he admired.[5] Perhaps Packard had failed to impress the admissions committee for the same reasons he seemed so unusual to some of his contemporaries. Once again his background and carriage threatened to make him an outsider. To some of his more urbane peers, he doubtlessly looked like a hayseed from a Pennsylvania farm. "Physically bumbling" and "able to think faster than he could act," Packard appeared to be less sophisticated than most of his classmates.[6] However, his ambitions were anything but provincial. Upon enrollment, he noted that his "chief interest" was "in national and world affairs—economics, politics."[7]

No Columbia professor affected Packard as much as Waller had done in college, but some were more important than others.[8] George Gallup, about to emerge as an influential pollster, taught him how to use the new survey techniques. Once a week, the Pulitzer prize–winning military historian Douglas Southall Freeman came up from Richmond, Virginia, where he was a newspaper editor, to offer a course on the news-of-the-week section. Walter B. Pitkin, who gave a class on feature stories, had recently authored the number one nonfiction best-seller *Life Begins at Forty* (1932). In a book that made academic research easily accessible to a middle-class audience and whose message would resonate in Packard's later writings, Pitkin encouraged people over forty to "learn to live more abundantly through adjusting work and play to the natural flow of energies." Calling on his readers to reject hard and routinized work, busy leisure, the gospel of success, and the struggle to keep up with the Joneses, Pitkin stressed seeking happiness through self-realization.[9] For his nonjournalism elective, Packard took an economics course from Michael T. Florinsky, an émigré who fled the Soviet Union not long after the Russian Revolution and whose teaching may have helped wean Packard from his sympathetic view of the USSR.[10]

The papers Packard wrote in graduate school reveal a young man coming to terms with complex moral and political issues, someone interested in exposing corruption, hypocrisy, and dishonesty.[11] A particularly revealing piece, on a strike in Pennsylvania garment factories, demonstrated his penchant for irony toward domestic radicals that his temperament and undergraduate experiences had fostered. This story also made him skeptical of the support that radicals gave to unions. "Nazi Berkshire Interests Control Hosiery Empire" ran the headline over an article in the *Socialist Call* that sparked Packard's interest in the story. If radicals saw a battle between good workers and evil capitalists, Packard viewed the situation as a morally ambiguous drama whose actors included industrialists fighting over patent rights; "Pennsylvania 'Dutch' workers from rural, conservative backgrounds"; union organizers who acted unscrupulously; and strikers who used razor blades to attack nonstriking laborers. Perhaps he spoke for himself when he noticed the "quandary" of "labor liberals" who, faced with workers who "complain that they only want to be left alone," found themselves in a difficult position when they took "their accustomed stand" for the union and against management.[12]

In another paper, written in late 1936, Packard sought to comprehend the changing landscape of national politics. Speculating on the future of the New Deal, he predicted a recovery, followed in 1939 and 1940 by another depression that would end the nation's "exceedingly fleeting experience" with prosperity. He believed that a world war could temporarily postpone the economic crisis, but that that crisis would be "even more severe" when it came later. Neglecting as it did fundamental structural problems, Packard's analysis was hardly radical. Yet he believed that the economic downturn might well lead to the ascendancy of the American Labor party under the leadership of John L. Lewis, someone he then admired. Packard's prediction of a victory of a third party on the Left led by Lewis, who reached the high point of his prominence in early 1937, revealed an impatience with traditional politics.[13]

Packard's analysis of the international situation reflected his departure from pacifism, the persistence of his antifascism, and his growing acceptance of President Franklin Roosevelt's foreign policy. Sympathetic with FDR's combination of neutrality and internationalism, he applauded the effort, "despite the cry of some liberals," to stop the flow of war materials to belligerents in the Spanish Civil War, especially Franco. While at Columbia, he published his first piece outside State College, an article in *Current History* that saw international treaties in the interwar period as "little more than diplomatic clichés" that no government honored. Packard continued to think, as he had since his political awakening in college, that the threat to world peace came from the fascists. His concern was not with a generic totalitarianism but with nazism. He wrote papers that detailed the Nazi threats to freedom of the press and individual liberties. He had every expectation that the fascist nations, needing "bugaboos to launch crusades at" and therefore pursuing anticommunism as a way to solve internal problems, would plunge the world into a war in which the Western democracies would join the Soviet Union.[14] Packard mentioned the USSR only in passing. Focusing so much on obtaining a professional education, he was not following the news about the Moscow trials. So he did not refer to the reign of terror carried out by Stalin's regime that was beginning to come to light, even though it would take thirty years before its full extent was revealed. He probably shared with others a belief that calling attention to problems in the Soviet Union would weaken the antifascist cause, especially at a time when Germany was on the march and when the USSR stood alone among the major nations in providing aid to Franco's opponents.

Cub Reporter at *Boston Daily Record,* 1937–1938

When Packard graduated from Columbia on 1 June 1937 and began his career as a professional journalist, he soon found himself in a predicament that would persist for at least two decades. Even as a graduate of Columbia's prestigious program, he was fortunate to obtain a regular job.[15] Yet to earn a living he had to practice a kind of journalism he had only recently derided. "I was so flattered I decided to take it despite my previous distaste for Hearstian journalism," he remarked a few years later about his job with the Hearst-owned *Boston Daily Record.* The paper, which frequently engaged in sensationalism and had a largely Irish American and working-class audience, was one that Packard at the time characterized as "a growing, lusty tabloid of about 340,000 circulation."[16]

Working for the newspaper chain whose politics and style he had recently denounced meant setting out on his career with considerable misgivings. He did not want to be a newspaper writer "for the rest of [his] life," if that meant being a "conventional" one. "I do not doubt but that if I write the kind of tripe Hearst wants," he told one of his professors a few weeks before graduation, "I will go places. But where?" He confessed that he had "little desire to be a success" if he ended up at the top but despised himself "for having achieved fame at the cost of double-crossing myself." He worried whether such a career would allow him to advance the world's knowledge, increase the happiness of others, or give his "own potentialities a fair outlet."[17]

Shortly after joining the paper, however, Packard got a break that separated him from his peers.[18] His chance came with a story in early July about a sailor who left his bride-to-be standing at the altar. Helping his paper fight circulation battles by working on attention-getting articles, Packard scooped his more seasoned colleagues when he found the young woman and convinced her mother to let him cover the couple's reunion. He went with the girl and the sailor to a secluded location from which he produced material for exclusive stories at the same time that he tried to negotiate a reconciliation. When the bride-to-be turned reluctant, the editor insisted that the young reporter play Cupid. "So I sat down on the bed beside her and explained that it was now time to get married. I told her," he recalled, " 'Look, this is going to ruin my whole story.' So we had the marriage."[19] The incident conflated two elements that would mark much of Packard's work—a commitment to marriage and a keen eye for material that would advance his career.

Ironically, his own triumph as a cub reporter now earned him an assignment that in the end proved to be confining. Packard's resourcefulness and writing ability led the editors to assign a daily column that appeared under his byline, the only one the paper allowed.[20] For four months beginning in early October of 1937, he wrote the column, called Success Struggles. Reflecting his parents' experience, his own recent personal history, what his editors believed would sell, and the dream of success that persisted in the mass media in the 1930s, his stories told of how hard work, character, and ingenuity enabled men and women to reach their goals. The heroes of the pieces were happiest when they did what they had always wanted to do—fulfill their lifelong hopes, rise from rags to riches, help others, fight for what they believed.[21]

The columns defined success not in terms of materialistic rewards but of obstacles overcome and visions realized. Even those born with silver spoons in their mouths avoided the role of the idle rich and achieved "spectacular and inspiring" success on their own terms. The rise of Henry Cabot Lodge, Jr., who had become a U.S. senator by age forty-two, Packard observed, was not "due to his family name" but to his hard work and his commitment to be a "relentless champion of the common man." In their climb to the top, the successful did not forget those above whom they had risen. Packard quoted the head of a large department store as saying, "Let us not use the word employee around here. We are all fellow-workers striving together for the same end." The wealthier among his subjects, he reported, lived unpretentiously and avoided notoriety. In short, Success Struggles portrayed an open society where exercise of long-cherished virtues enabled Americans during the Depression to realize their dreams, confounding skeptics who thought the rich and powerful were "born to wealth" and had their positions handed to them.[22]

In writing these features, Packard had to mix what he believed with what the genre and his job required. These pieces, with their celebration of entrepreneurship, struggle, and achievement, reflected the reluctance of many American newspapers to expose Depression-born conditions. Although he felt that having his own byline by age twenty-three made him seem "a phenomenal success," his dissatisfaction was apparent. He wanted to refuse the assignment but could find no way to do so "gracefully." Caught between conflicting desires for independence and achievement, he found himself stuck writing "'Business Office Musts,'" using a "formula" that was "rigid." The individuals usually had to be "poor to start, then overcome several thrilling obstacles, and thence become howling successes." Writing these pieces, he confided to a Columbia teacher, "somehow runs against my grain and seems to call for a good deal of hypocrisy."[23]

Packard soon proposed an alternative to his editors, a new column on Bostonians whose lives "hold a strong human-interest tug." Among the types of people Packard mentioned were women "who are not only uncommonly attractive but also uncommonly intelligent"; "Women Doing Men's Jobs—and vice-versa"; people with risky, "nasty," or "odd" jobs; individuals who were unselfishly heroic; and "pioneers" who were "trying to open up fields" in the same "bold and far-sighted" way that Western "frontiersmen" had once done. What resulted beginning in early February of 1938 was Exciting Lives, a series whose message differed markedly from that of Success Struggles. Rather than focusing mostly on the famous and the rich, the new series concentrated on Americans from ordinary backgrounds whose work was dangerous or unusual—window washer, air traffic controller, tattoo artist. Unlike the old columns, the new ones came closer to resembling the realistic case studies Waller had called for. Lacking the emphasis on conventional kinds of achievement and the celebration of America as an open society, Exciting Lives were success stories with a twist—the drama of people whose hard work led to real accomplishments based on satisfactions derived from an out-of-the-ordinary job well done.[24] The achievements of these people were not principally pecuniary; their heroism was dramatic but unrecognized.

Although these articles had a photographic quality, Exciting Lives matched neither the brilliant documentaries nor the radical politics of the more hard-hitting journalism of the 1930s. Packard focused on individuals with fascinating jobs, not dispossessed groups facing social adversity. His task was to intrigue the readers, not inspire them to right wrongs.[25] Although he minimized the importance of material rewards, Packard had neither cut loose from an emphasis on self-denial, character, and hard work nor begun to stress personality, leisure, and self-realization in the ways his teacher Walter Pitkin had done in his best-selling book.[26] For Packard, that shift would come when in the late 1950s his own life began after forty; for now, ambition and achievement remained qualities he emphasized in the lives of the people he wrote about. If he disliked the saga of rags to riches, he still extolled the virtues of individual effort directed toward a tangible goal.

The shift to Exciting Lives satisfied Packard only temporarily. To be sure, his position provided some satisfactions. He did have a white-collar job with a decent salary. Exposure to Massachusetts politics continued his education in the corruptibility of public service. He sharpened his skills as an interviewer, investigative reporter, and feature writer. He gained some control over his time and assignments and even had the opportunity to publish magazine articles. Moreover, he admired some of his fellow writers and he got "along beautifully" with the city editor, who, Packard said at the time, was "like a godfather" to him. His supervisors recognized his talents and rewarded him with a byline, as well as with two promotions and two pay raises in less than a year. His weekly earnings went from twenty-five to thirty dollars, a decent salary for a young bachelor during the 1930s.[27]

Nonetheless, Packard was eager to change his situation. He remained an outsider in a world in which his peers were Catholics and New Englanders.[28] He thought most of them turned out undistinguished copy, much of it "almost kindergarten stuff." He saw many of his fellow reporters as "broken-down drunkards" who were "not particularly intelligent." He worried that if he stayed on at the *Daily Record*, he would continue doing only "routine" articles. As a result, he feared he might lose his "critical viewpoint." Working for the Boston newspaper, he remarked at the time, had "revealed an aptitude for writing light feature material that disturbs me. I fear that feature writing will become so profitable that I will be reluctant to redirect myself toward writing national affairs when and if the opportunity comes."[29] His position resembled his father's situation, a result of what C. Wright Mills called a "bureaucratic usurpation of freedom." In the 1950s the Columbia sociologist, recalling the change among members of his own family from ranchers to salesmen, would write that "the twentieth-century white-collar man has never been independent as the farmer used to be."[30] Turning out human interest vignettes for a Hearst newspaper hardly measured up to the dream of being another Lincoln Steffens or Walter Duranty.

Publishing features for a mass audience intensified Packard's interest in the relationships among individualism, totalitarianism, and mass society. He read essays by Thomas Mann that provoked him to reflect on how his job was putting him in a position where he might have to compromise his craft and principles. By the spring of 1938 Mann had emerged as an important figure among antifascists who opposed pacifism. What Mann wrote nudged Packard toward interventionism and reinforced his antifascism; but it also underscored his awareness of the problematic nature of the mass culture he was creating. Mann argued that America had to embrace a democracy that was capacious yet realistic, virile, and disciplined.[31] Packard found especially compelling the work that Mann pub-

Shortly after beginning work in the summer of 1937 for the Boston
Daily Record, *Vance Packard relaxes on the beach at Nantasket,
Massachusetts, with Virginia Mathews. (Used by permission
of Vance Packard and Virginia M. Packard.)*

lished in August 1937. He focused on a section that emphasized how
totalitarianism debased culture and fostered "'mass drunkenness, which
relieves the individual of responsibility.'" Art, the German émigré wrote
in a passage that Vance quoted in a letter to Virginia, "'abhors the medi-
ocre as it abhors the cheap cliché, the trivial, the insipid and the base.'" In
contrast, Mann described a world where quality, distinction, and standards
reigned.[32] Packard's interest in Mann's work reveals the way in which the
cub reporter's political concerns and occupational location combined to
drive home the importance of individual autonomy and cultural standards.
His experiences underscored how fascist governments or profit-seeking
publications might exercise thought control as they pandered to a mass
audience.

Packard sought to counter the limitations of his job by living in an
apartment a few blocks from Harvard Yard and focusing his attention on
events at the university. In doing so, he once again found himself in a
position where he was an outsider. He applied to Harvard for a Nieman
Fellowship so he could develop expertise on national and international
affairs and continue his education in the social and behavioral sciences.[33]
However, winning the award would not solve the most pressing problem
he faced. Being in Boston meant separation from Virginia Mathews, something that caused him considerable pain and introduced a very consider-

able amount of strain into their relationship. The woman he would eventually marry was three hundred miles away, in Berwyn, Pennsylvania, working as a supervisor of art education in the public schools. Packard looked for jobs nearer her. He thought of launching a liberal paper in Lancaster, Pennsylvania. He sought the help of the Columbia dean in getting a position with the *Philadelphia Inquirer*. In line for one of the next vacancies there, he learned that the union had blocked the dismissal of writers whose departure would have opened up a position for him.[34]

His relationship with Virginia was in jeopardy from February to early May of 1938, when she was dating a successful dentist. "The clear break" between Vance and Virginia threw him "into the worst prolonged mental turmoil" of his life, something complicated by uncertainty over the continuation of his job with the Boston newspaper. Packard's attitude to wealth and success intensified the problems of separation, competition, and potential loss. In a letter he drafted to Virginia, he attacked the dentist's "large spending power for amusing, entertaining, diverting" her "in extravagant fashion." Vance felt she found in consumption something that gave her "a vicarious release to . . . [her] repressed urge to spend." Look carefully at the dentist, he remarked, "strip him of his spending power (car and dough) and look again."[35]

Reflecting the Depression-born fear of having to postpone marriage until means of support were available, Virginia questioned how she and Vance could get married and live on the salary of a reporter. Virginia may also have been echoing her mother's concern that Vance would not be a good provider, a sentiment that fueled his ambition to excel as a breadwinner. "I don't expect to be making $40 or even $50 a week for very long," he remarked, asserting that he could be a good provider, a commitment common to men who came of age in the Depression and one that influenced Packard for the rest of his life. "Probably that will soon look like small change because I've never doubted that I could get considerably more than my share of worldly goods if I wanted to go after them."[36] Yet although he was ambitious, he was also ambivalent about status and money. This incident brought to the surface his sense of the contrast between the solid middle class that behaved morally and the well-to-do who used money and power in immoral ways. The incident raised issues that he had first encountered in the events of his childhood. The connection between consumption and corruption drew on his parents' producer ideology and pointed forward to his writings on status seeking and material wastefulness twenty years later and on excessive wealth in the late 1980s.

As it turned out, Packard had to make a decision about his career sooner than he anticipated. On 6 May 1938, the *Daily Record* dropped him and almost twenty others. Costly battles for circulation, the loss of advertising revenue to radio, and the recession of 1937–38 placed daily newspapers under constant pressure. This was the first but not the last time that fundamental changes in the media threatened his livelihood. His editor recognized his strengths, noting his "natural talent for feature work" and his capacity to "distinguish intuitively those subjects that hold a strong appeal to readers from those that are simply trivial and gaudy."[37] Nevertheless, as the last hired he was also the first fired.

Associated Press Feature Service, 1938–1942

In late May 1938, shortly after his job with the Boston paper ended, Packard received an offer from the Associated Press Feature Service in New York. At the time, he realized that newspapers had to respond to the challenges they faced from magazines, radio, and movies by becoming more attractive and readable. In the spring of 1938 he told a prospective employer that by recognizing that readers, not advertisers, were their "gods," publishers could become less timid. He argued that this change would come only "when the present clash between capital and labor is settled," at which point publishers would begin to be "generous," "liberal," and "more sensible and courageous." Until then, those who controlled the papers, many of whom were "almost psychopathic cases" with "real phobias" about John L. Lewis and the National Labor Relations Board, would continue to think that workers were "after their blood."[38] As had been true two years previously when he was applying to Columbia, Packard was willing to tell someone who controlled his fate that the vested interests in publishing prevented journalism from being fair and progressive.

Packard moved to Manhattan and began working in mid-June with a starting salary of forty dollars per week, a figure that increased to fifty-five by 1940.[39] Initially he lived in Greenwich Village, where he saw people from Penn State, including a member of the Communist party who tried to recruit him. Once when Packard was out of town, friends used his apartment for a party meeting, boisterously singing the Internationale at three o'clock in the morning.[40] Not long after his move, Packard waxed rhapsodic about finding the unusual among ordinary people, a theme he had developed in Exciting Lives. Following a walk through a poor neighborhood in New York, he concluded that he "instinctively liked" most of those who dwelled there "more than I ever did the distinctly bourgeoisie . . . or the ultra ultra ultra people with dough." Like others who searched for Americans who were authentic, he found himself surprised that many of these common folk "seemed remarkably intelligent." He admired their ability to find pleasure in ordinary events such as playing stickball or swimming off a pier, activities that reflected "their simplicity, their more colorful personalities, their total lack of affectation."[41] Yet when not covering a story he shied away from making the effort to talk with people different from himself. When his parents, on a visit in the late 1930s, began talking with both a doorman and an African, Packard told them that in the city "one does not chat with people one does not know."[42]

The move from Boston involved welcome changes. Several months after he arrived in Manhattan, he and Virginia Mathews were married, on 25 November 1938. After living in Manhattan for a short period, they moved to an apartment in Queens.[43] His four years at the Associated Press offered him professional advantages that had not been available at the Boston newspaper. Its politics were not as conservative and its style not as sensational as those of the *Daily Record*. In addition, the AP had a higher status than the Hearst-owned tabloid. He now worked in the media capital of the nation, and the new position eventually offered him the chance to cover major national and international events. Packard had greater freedom to write on unusual subjects that he himself selected, although here, too, he eventually felt trapped by assigned formulas. The AP Feature Service depended on the decision of its hundreds of subscribing newspapers to print the material it offered. Consequently, in a 1940 memo to his staff, the editor of the service reminded his writers that "mighty few papers depend on us for run of the mill" material. Therefore, to be published extensively, stories had to have "a first class selling line, standout writing, eye-filling illustration, a sound fund of information or sheer novelty." The editor concluded that "one idea that can be ballyhooed is better than a dozen, plain, ordinary, quite commendable idea-ettes."[44]

At the outset, Packard concentrated on human interest features for the AP. Some of what he authored paralleled the Exciting Lives columns he had done in Boston. He also profiled those who had achieved national prominence, like the African American scientist George Washington Carver. Packard was able to get into print stories quite different from those he had published before. For example, a feature on the Amish, drafted when he was still in Boston, reflected his appreciation of pacifism and of people who lived simple lives and did not conform to mainstream standards. Moreover, Packard was at last able to connect two interests he had developed in college—journalism and the social sciences. He wrote pieces on such topics as scientific research on sleep and the industrial use of techniques for improving workers' morale.[45]

Although feature writing was originally his main task at the AP, Packard also sustained an interest in national and international events during momentous times. Framing his stint at the AP were the German conquest of Austria and Czechoslovakia at the beginning, and America's entry into World War II, near the end. Above all, it was the signing of the Nazi-Soviet nonaggression pact on 23 August 1939 that commanded Packard's interest. The agreement devastated many liberals and radicals who had seen the USSR as a bulwark against fascism, causing them to rethink their political commitments. It made war inevitable, ended the dream of a Popular Front, and undermined the special moral claim for the Soviet Union. The treaty galvanized Packard to write an article and submit it to the *New Republic*. Although never published, it illuminates the effect that the dramatic turn of events had on the twenty-five-year-old journalist. He was already somewhat realistic about Stalin's intentions, and so his reaction seemed relatively calm compared with that of the *New Republic*. In a tone more gloating or disappointed than shocked, Packard began his piece by attacking American Communists who explained the pact "as a 'great contribution' to world peace" or "a boon to democracy." Perhaps speaking for himself, he lamented the way the treaty betrayed "leftist ideals," disillusioned "Soviet sympathizers," and left "the Stop-Hitler crowd in a very bad hole."[46]

Packard's was not the reaction of an anti-Stalinist for whom the news of Soviet treachery only confirmed what he already knew. He had lost Russia as a bulwark against the spread of fascism, yet he showed little recognition that the treaty might have any consequences for American foreign policy. While the *New Republic* worried that the pact provided the excuse for attacks on "every worthy movement on the left," Packard used this piece to distance himself even further from Soviet sympathizers in the United States.[47] If the editors directed their outrage against Stalin, Packard, struggling to comprehend what had happened and not having learned any lessons from the Moscow trials, responded as a reader of Duranty's book might well have done. Although he did not engage in the tortuous rationalizations that many American Communists offered, he tried to understand the Soviet Union on its own terms. In important ways, Packard continued in a familiar vein. He saw Stalin as pragmatic, not treacherous. He remained sympathetic to the Soviet Union but distanced himself from dissenters, especially American Communists.

Not long after the Nazi-Soviet pact, Packard began working on the AP's one-page weekly summary of national and international events that appeared in about one hundred Sunday newspapers across the nation. For more than two years, beginning in early 1940, he edited this section.[48] Though he now had "total freedom" from editors and advertisers and could at last focus on major international events, he nonetheless found himself in a situation less attractive than that of the foreign correspondents he had admired in college. Covering foreign news during an important period, he was doing so as part of a bureaucratic job that relied on information gleaned from the Teletype, not from firsthand experiences as a roving international journalist. Regular in publication, as free of bias as possible, and controlled by rules that governed such a section, his writing once again had to follow a formula.[49]

What he wrote in the weekly news section and elsewhere revealed Packard's views of world and domestic events. His antifascism persisted, even as he shifted from neutrality to preparedness and then to internationalism.[50] He offered a generally favorable picture of the USSR as he rooted for it to stop the Germans.[51] He saw the Soviet Union not as a totalitarian or socialist nation but as a country acting in historic patterns shaped by its Russian past. He pictured Soviet leaders as heroic and nonideological and the USSR as a country populated by simple folk.[52] Like many others who had flirted with pacifism and radicalism in the mid-1930s, Packard by 1940 had come to rally around the American flag. He rejected extremism and criticized those groups he believed were impeding the fight against fascism. In one article in the middle of 1941, he wondered out loud "just how far an opposition can go during a national crisis without justifiably being charged with subversiveness." Relying on a red-baiting tactic he had earlier denounced, he found particularly "malodorous" the opposition of aid to democracies taken by "the red-speckled American Peace Mobilization." Doubtlessly describing himself, he noted that "many liberal interventionists feel a bit uncomfortable when they recall that as recently as 1935 they were taking the Oxford Oath, joining pacifistic groups and acclaiming Senator Nye for disclosing that munitions makers had prodded us into the World War." He admitted that there were "sincere pacifists" in the America First movement who offered "clean, hard-hitting criticism, even in wartime," something well within "the American tradition." Yet he felt that what left the isolationist organization "wide open to persecution" was its secrecy about the source of its funds, its anti-Semitism, and the welcome it extended "to viciously anti-democratic admirers."[53]

A key element in his response to those who threatened the war effort was his concern about the power of trade unions. Like many liberals of his generation, between the mid-1930s and the late 1940s Packard shifted from sympathy toward unions to skepticism. He admired the power of unions to deliver for their members, something he often wished would benefit middle-class employees as well. At the *Boston Daily Record*, he had noticed that the unionized printers had a washroom that "gleamed like Radio City," while the editorial staff had one that was a "mess."[54] His feelings toward unions had intensified when he wrote the story of the strike in Pennsylvania and when he did not get a job at the Philadelphia newspaper because of preference for a union member. Yet Packard approved of labor organizations that served ends he agreed with. While at the AP, he tried to start a union, in part because he saw organized workers getting more money than nonunionized journalists.[55] Although he never joined a union, this effort foreshadowed his postwar concern about what he saw as the enrichment of workers and the deteriorating condition of the white-collar middle class. In the late 1930s and early 1940s, what irked Packard was union interference in America's preparation for war. The culprit was John L. Lewis, the president of the United Mine Workers, whom Packard had once admired. When, beginning in the late 1930s, Lewis opposed FDR and American intervention into World War II, Packard began to criticize him. His antagonism intensified in March 1941 when job actions by coal miners, he felt, threatened to undermine the mobilization for the war.[56]

Packard's acceptance of American intervention, accompanied as it was by replacing the USSR with the United States as the bulwark against fascism, intensified his patriotism. Yet there is no evidence that the events of the late 1930s and early 1940s led him to a more wide-ranging celebration of America. During these years, many American liberals and radicals turned away from an appreciation of collectivism and a critique of America. Instead they defended liberal democracy, Western civilization, and American traditions. This move by others to the center and the right laid the groundwork for the Cold War celebration of the American Way. "Being for the United States," Norman Podhoretz would later write of anticommunist intellectuals, many of them Jews, "was a new experience" for people who used to think "of themselves as virtual foreigners in this country, as aliens."[57] In contrast, Packard made the transition to new positions in a manner that was gradual, free of trauma, and more private than public. Unlike many writers of his generation who would be influential in the 1950s and 1960s, he lacked an immigrant heritage, a declaration of loyalty to the USSR or the party, alienation from American institutions, and sustained participation in internecine ideological conflicts. However much he felt he was an outsider, Packard had never believed that he was a stranger to America. During the 1930s he had not been critical of American institutions, as had many of those who now came to a new sense of appreciation for the nation's strengths. The gradual development and more limited extent of his increasingly positive view of the United States enabled him to keep his distance from the Cold Warriors' claims of American exceptionalism and shape his social criticism in the late 1950s.[58]

The years at the *Daily Record* and the AP were important ones for Packard. He had learned to do formulaic writing so well that he garnered increased rewards and duties, but he also came to feel trapped. When work on the weekly news summary rotated to a colleague, Packard looked around for a new challenge. Because he considered the job at the AP a "dead end" at a "dull organization," he competed for positions at *Time* and the *New York Times*. A job with higher status, more pay, and greater freedom would begin to satisfy both his desire for independence and his commitment to provide for his family. In the summer of 1942, he bested two hundred applicants and began writing the Interesting People section for *American Magazine*, a mass-circulation monthly he had denounced in the pages of the *Summer Collegian* seven years earlier. With the birth of the Packards' first child, Vance Philip on 20 April 1942, and the move from Queens to a larger apartment in Westchester, the salary increase from sixty to ninety dollars a week was timely.[59]

The switch to *American Magazine* at the age of twenty-eight was a major turning point in Packard's career. Until this moment, he had divided his time between human interest profiles, features on the social and behavioral sciences, and coverage of national and international politics. Although at *American Magazine* he initially wrote on public affairs, the move set him on a path from which he would not deviate—away from political affairs and toward a focus on the social and behavioral sciences and human interest features. Ironically, at *American Magazine* he would find himself writing the kind of stories whose formulaic quality had bothered him since his junior year in college. Once again he would succeed at a job that compromised his creativity and autonomy at the same time that he remained ambivalent about the status brought to him by work he did not fully respect.

The Man in the Gray Flannel Suit

Darien, New Canaan, and *American Magazine*, 1942–1956

When he worked for *American Magazine*, from 1942 to 1956, Vance Packard shared many experiences with other white middle-class men of his generation. He bought his first house and then traded up to another, fathered several children, and worked for a large national corporation. In important ways, however, the Packard family's situation was different. They resided not in a new, cookie-cutter suburb but in an old and wealthy area between suburbia and country—too close to Manhattan to be rural but too distinctive to be ordinary. The household itself was unconventional for its time and place. Moreover, unlike most of his contemporaries, Packard was in a position to write about the mixed blessings of affluence in postwar America. As an author, he responded to his situation at *American Magazine* and, more generally, to the social and ideological forces shaping American life.

Life in Darien, New Canaan, and Chappaquiddick

Where the Packards lived during and after the war affected the choices available to Vance and the views he expressed. Around the time of the birth of their second child, Randall Mathews, on 30 May 1945, the Packards bought their first home, in the Connecticut suburb of Darien. With help from Vance's father and brother, they paid six thousand dollars for an abandoned and large fixer-upper that lacked heat and a kitchen.[1] In *Auntie Mame* (1955), Patrick Dennis described his fictional version of Darien as a place whose housewives and commuting husbands swore by the *Reader's Digest*. The novel's narrator remarked that he read its articles reluctantly, but "with snake bird fascination," on the "menace" in public schools, the pleasures of natural childbirth, and "how a community in Oregon put down a dope ring."[2] Darien also figured in *Gentleman's Agreement*, a 1947 novel by Laura Z. Hobson that came out as a movie in the same year. A reporter pretended to be a Jew so that he could experience anti-Semitism directly, uncovering it among respectable people, including his fiancée's family and local realtors bound by a gentleman's agreement that kept them from showing homes to Jews.

Auntie Mame and *Gentleman's Agreement* depicted situations familiar to Packard. The first opened with the scene of the narrator fixing up his house, something Packard would do over the years with continuing success.[3] Packard also wrote the kind of articles that fascinated *Auntie Mame*'s narrator. And, like Packard, the hero of *Gentleman's Agreement* yearned to cover national news but worked for a magazine editor who wanted him to write human interest stories. Though he did not change his identity to experience injustice, in *Status Seekers* Packard exposed anti-Semitism among the comfortable and powerful. Moreover, the connection between the movie and Packard was even more direct: one day when he drove up to the Darien railroad station, the film's director asked him to let the camera catch a view of his car, itself a Packard.[4]

In the spring of 1947, Vance reflected his sense of himself as an outsider when he noted in his diary that he tried "instinctively to avoid" most of the men with whom he commuted to New York, "and most of them try to avoid me." At work and in the suburbs, Packard was learning to hold his tongue. Reading what Henry Adams had written on the "benefit of silence" prompted him to remember a childhood friend who was able to win by using "calm silence" and by refusing "to argue his position." Packard felt relieved when he had the opportunity "to meet real individualists, even offensive ones." Life in Darien and work on *American Magazine* prompted him to think that maybe the "greatest threat to a happy future for Americans is the growing standardization brought on by mass production." He noted in his diary that "even ideas are mass disseminated and the typical American is simply a bundle of stereotypes." The nation, he wrote, had "become accustomed to ever increasing doses of excitement and stimulation" at a time when it was no longer able to meet these expectations because "television, movies, publishers eat through every fresh idea in a matter of weeks."[5]

Packard found solace in Joseph Wood Krutch's *Modern Temper* (1929). Struck by the way the atom bomb had fed disillusionment, Packard agreed with the book's argument that skepticism had overpowered faith in God, science, and nature. Paraphrasing Krutch, he wrote that "the farther man gets away from Nature—the greater each person becomes an intellectual concerned with self-realization." The book offered Packard a new justification for an appreciation of the USSR—as a simpler society that provided an elemental antidote to the spiritual malaise Krutch had seen overly comfortable Americans developing in the 1920s. In 1947 Packard, having witnessed his own and America's departure from the Depression in the eleven years since he left State College, was asking himself questions about the relationship between hard work, self-realization, material success, and spiritual satisfaction. "All societies," Krutch had written in a way that also applied to Packard, "which have passed the first vigor of their youth reveal their loss of faith in life itself" when they direct their "most eager attention" to "the activities which men are at liberty to pursue" once they have gained the necessities of life. Krutch's injunction to live life, without justifying it in some larger terms, appealed to Packard as he worried about how to deal with the tension brought on by helping to create a mass culture that he disliked.[6]

It did not take a reading of *Modern Temper* to persuade the Packards to move from Darien. They had become dissatisfied with life in a town whose "socially stuffy" inhabitants, they felt, succumbed to the pressures for conformity.[7] In 1948, at about the time of the birth of Cynthia Ann on 5 April, they sold the Darien house, which had increased in value through inflation, a housing shortage, and renovation, for $30,000. At a time when Vance's annual income from *American Magazine* was around $10,000, they purchased another house in neighboring New Canaan for $44,000.[8] So that Virginia could have access to a community of artists, they chose property in Silvermine, a section of town close to a well-established art community. New Canaan also provided Vance with the company of writers. In the decades following World War I, its reputation as a place where creative people settled had been enhanced by the presence of Maxwell E. Perkins, Van Wyck Brooks, Clifton Fadiman, Faith Baldwin, and Norman Cousins.

However, the creative people attracted to New Canaan tended to be more middlebrow and commercial than such writers as Arthur Miller and Lewis Mumford, who lived in the more rural areas to the north and west. The people who set the tone of New Canaan during the late 1940s and 1950s were the corporate officers, lawyers, and bankers who commuted to Manhattan while their wives ferried the children of the baby boom generation to school.[9] This was a world of business-oriented and internationalist Republicanism. In 1952, Packard called New Canaan "a New England village," and in 1972 he remembered it during the late 1940s as "a semi-rural town." Such descriptions could not hide the fact that it was about fifty miles from Manhattan and one of the nation's wealthiest communities.[10]

One version of life in places like New Canaan came from its sometime resident Sloan Wilson, whose best-selling novel *The Man in the Gray Flannel Suit* (1955) gave the 1950s one of its classic statements of life in the suburbs of Fairfield County and the office buildings of New York City. Looking back in his autobiography, Wilson was struck by the "ferocity with which everyone worked" in the postwar period as people felt they had to catch up. With little help taking care of the children, wives had their own round of obligations—fixing up houses, doing volunteer work, and learning do-it-yourself skills. They worked feverishly at preparing for parties and shared with their husbands "the thought of a mailbox without invitations as a calamity almost as bad as getting fired." Together spouses worried about money, for the relatively frequent pay raises barely outpaced the constantly spiraling expenditures. The consequent "financial tension which we brought upon ourselves," Wilson recalled, "sometimes became unbearable."[11]

For men, free time was also hard to come by. Commuting took up to two hours a day, added onto the standard eight-hour office job. Evenings were given to extracurricular writing projects and weekends to chores around the house. Dressed "either in gray flannel or in other drab hues," commuters into the city had about them, Wilson remarked, "the pervasive almost physical smell of fear" that came from the dread of being fired or of not being promoted with sufficient rapidity. Though most understood that unemployment, if it came at all, would probably be temporary, their ambitions were so high that they "knew perfectly well that the odds against achieving them were large." All of these pressures strained people's lives and resulted in alcoholism, adultery, neglect, divorce, and even suicide.[12]

Especially annoying to Wilson were writers who, working for magazines such as *Time*, complained about having to rewrite, about having to endure editors who were "sons of bitches," and about having to express in their articles what their supervisors wanted and not what they themselves believed. These were things, Wilson felt, that the writers should have realized were the conditions of their employment. "Never really reconciled . . . to being employees," these men could not fulfill their true ambitions—to be novelists, playwrights, or free-lance writers—because "like adolescents, they yearned for liberty without having the capacity for independence." Consequently, unable "to cut the cord that tied them to the mother company," magazine writers "had nothing but abuse for the parent who fed them." Even though such a writer might be a "flaming liberal" in private, publicly he had to conform.[13]

Though Wilson's picture did not always apply to Packard, it nonetheless shed light on the world that surrounded him and against which he was in many ways reacting. One thing that made his life different from those of many of his peers was that Packard did not serve in the military. At one time or another he considered a number of alternatives that would have enabled him to continue in journalism—including going to the USSR with the Office of War Information and traveling to China to work for the school of journalism that Chiang Kai-shek was establishing to help publicize the virtues of his regime. None of these options worked out, and during the spring of 1944, with his draft board closing in, Packard accepted an assignment as a combat correspondent for the Marine publication *Leatherneck*. Right after he resigned from *American Magazine* to take up this position, a change in the Selective Service rules exempted him from the draft. *American Magazine* rehired him.[14] Not having gone off to war, he was not in a desperate rush to catch up; indeed, he had a jump on his peers that gave him an edge in employment and in the housing market.

Vance and Virginia were not as affected by conventional social pressures as the people Wilson described. Their life among the artists and writers in Silvermine reflected and reinforced their relative freedom from these pressures. Still, to a considerable extent, Wilson captured the tension operative during that period that came from rising salaries bumping against escalating needs. Less involved in the rat race than many, Packard felt the pressures from editors that Wilson described, though necessity, desire, and luck eventually enabled him to cut his connection to bureaucratic employment. The tension that Packard experienced was not only between liberty and conformity but also between freedom and occupational restraint, a difficulty that would be resolved by his achievement of success as a free-lance writer. Yet Wilson aptly caught Packard's continuing impulse to criticize the source of his sustenance, though his outlook stemmed both from a reserved mother and a father who had conveyed to him an anger at the abuse of corporate power. A congenital optimist who never experienced the reversals that might have increased the risk of alcoholism or marital problems, Packard did not face the extreme conditions Wilson described, and that stability kept his streak of insecurity and anxiety in check. Less fearful of unemployment than of unfulfilled ambitions, Packard differed from the men Wilson wrote about. In the end, he was able to achieve his highest ambitions when, after 1957, he became both successful and free.

For the Packards, New Canaan was closer to their new heaven on earth than to the hell characterized by Wilson. On the top of a hill, out of sight of any other neighbor, and located on six and a half wooded acres across from a river, their second house had been built in 1915 by a partner in a major Wall Street investment banking firm as a wedding present for his daughter and her artist husband. Living there allowed Virginia, a painter herself, to be near the Silvermine Guild of Artists. The new location enabled Vance to straddle his ambivalence about status. He could live in a house and a community more prestigious than a Pennsylvania farm boy could ever have imagined, yet in a neighborhood of people who were both artistic and successful. Their friends were different from those in Darien: not organization men married to suburban housewives but men and women who were writers, professors, lawyers, theater producers; not only Christians and Republicans but also Jews, Democrats, and Independents. During most of the years from the end of World War II to the very late 1950s, Virginia worked full time as a supervisor of art education in the Darien schools, taking time off with the birth of each child and continuing to develop as an artist.[15]

In the 1950s, the Packards bought a summer home, one that became as important to them as their New Canaan residence. In 1940, Vance and Virginia had taken a "delayed honeymoon-vacation" on Martha's Vineyard, and in 1950 they began taking summer holidays on the adjacent Chappaquiddick Island. Their vacations there, Packard later wrote, were "probably our family's greatest experience in Togetherness," a time they went on walks during the day and spent the evenings reading aloud—from such books as *The Deerslayer* or a handwritten journal from a nineteenth-century ship captain that one of the children discovered in a closet. In 1953, for $8,500 the Packards purchased an abandoned, eleven-room turn-of-the-century home, five outbuildings, and fifty acres overlooking Katama Bay and beyond that the Atlantic Ocean, a property once owned by a New York real estate investor who had served as ambassador to Egypt. In the following summers, they fixed the house up, furnishing it for $213 with items acquired on the beach, at auctions, and in the local dump. Just as Packard had described New Canaan as a New England village, so he remarked that Chappaquiddick in 1940 was considered "wilderness," both phrases that revealed his sense of connection to a vanishing America.[16] In the 1940s and 1950s, Chappaquiddick, which still felt remote, was a community without pretension that attracted people who came for privacy, nature, and good value. Yet it was hardly wilderness. Their closest neighbors lived in a "grand old" and "rambling" 1906 house that best-selling author Clare Barnes, Jr., owned at the time and that a Rockefeller heir purchased and extensively renovated in the 1970s. Farther down the shore was a large summer house that Stanford White had designed in the mid-1890s for his aunt.[17]

New Canaan and Chappaquiddick provided ideal environments for raising a family, making friends, painting, and writing. Publishers in Manhattan were only a train ride away from New Canaan, and, like Martha's Vineyard, it was a place where artists, editors, and authors gathered. Before he was forty years old, this son of rural middle America had purchased two homes identified with the American upper class—something that over the long run would adversely affect the power of his pen to connect with a wider world, as these properties eventually sheltered him from the society he wrote about. Of at least equal importance, when income from writing diminished, the property gave him the intangible pride of having the wisdom of a good provider and the tangible pleasure of financial security. For the present, with mortgage payments and three children, the purchase of these houses committed the Packards to constant, often frenetic efforts to make ends meet by fixing up and then leasing their properties. These homes made clear how important land (literally, *real* estate) and privacy were to this farmer's son. With both properties, the setting, as much as the domicile itself, made it possible to create the sense of independence that Packard's parents had tried in vain to achieve.

The Packard Household

Life in the Packard household contrasted with the relatively conventional pictures of marriage and the family that Vance's articles in *American Magazine* offered. *Hell's Bells* (1983), a novel by Vance and Virginia's daughter Cindy, offered an embellished but generally accurate account of coming of age among the Packards. Dedicating the book to her parents, "who would like everyone to know this is a work of fiction," Cindy started out by having her protagonist talk of her "Wonder Bread years" in a "posh community" in Connecticut. Nonetheless, she noted, her youth "was anything but the safe, sane childhood one would infer from the locality." Her parents, who had both quit their regular jobs, were no longer "employed like normal folks." With the fictional father's inventing and the mother's mystery writing bringing in money on an irregular basis, the children found themselves in a house that had "the illusion of prosperity." Family members always faced a degree of uncertainty, wrote the novelist whose father lost his job when she was eight years old, because they lived "from patent pending to royalty statement."[18]

Then the fictional father accidentally produced an invention that provided a more stable income, Cindy wrote, having been twelve years old in 1960, the year her father published his third best-seller in a row. Now the fictional mother, under the cover of being a writer, could appear in public like "a typical suburban Mom" and involve herself "in an unending social whirl." Success enabled the father to become even more of an "'absent-minded professor,'" a phrase that "covered his multitude of sins quite nicely." Thus he was "incredibly stupid about matters which did not interest him," like how to operate a dishwasher or make a bed. Instead, when he was not writing or roaming "the house at all hours," he was dabbling in politics, playing golf or the stock market, remodeling the family's homes, and giving lectures "on the evils of a technological society."[19]

Watching *Ozzie and Harriet* on television provided the children in the novel with no guidance as to what life was really like. "I was aware my parents fought," Cindy Packard's protagonist noted, "but in that combative household, who didn't?" The parents taught their offspring "to think of life as A Great Challenge," expecting them to succeed and be creative but "not particularly" caring what they "excelled at." The children, raised by a "trial-and-error" approach, formed "a diverse menagerie." The oldest was "reared by draconian methods." When it became clear that this tactic did not work, the parents tried others with the next children. Feisty and antic interactions in the public realm plus "absolute privacy in one's own domain" dominated the household.[20]

His daughter's picture, however fictional, makes it clear that Vance Packard's experiences contrasted with those he had known as a son. If restraint as a child made him a fierce individualist, then the circumstances of his childhood and the impact of the Depression of the 1930s impelled him to value family in general and his role as provider specifically. Early on, considerable tension developed between the parents and their rambunctious first child, known as Vance P., who had a knack, his sister remembered, for "acting out of bounds" and whom the parents often did not know how to control.[21] Vance P. remembers his father as someone who observed more than he engaged, a father who was not physically affectionate and who spent little meaningful time with him.[22] With the two younger children, Randall and Cindy, themselves more well behaved, Vance Packard seemed more involved and effective as a father.[23] Still, to the children what was striking was that, although their father was around the house much of the time, he was nonetheless more present than available.[24] "Benign neglect" was how a friend characterized the parents' relationship to the children, noting that Vance and Virginia were always "deeply involved" in their own projects and that, in the end, their approach enabled the children to turn out so well and "develop their own very distinctive personalities."[25]

Virginia Packard stood in clear contrast to Vance's schoolmarm mother and to Packard himself. A skilled hostess and a teacher who brought in a steady income, Virginia was beautiful, energetic, intelligent, vivacious, and generous.[26] In public situations, hers was the dominant presence. "Strong-minded" and outgoing as a person, she exuded a sense of dash and competence that her husband lacked.[27] Unlike many husbands of his generation, Vance Packard remained very proud of his wife's career aspirations and achievements. Yet to Vance, Virginia's employment was necessary but not ideal. His own preference (and Virginia's as well) was to have his wife work at home as an artist, something that his success as a writer eventually made possible.

In the 1950s and early 1960s, Packard appeared to many of those who met him as an unassuming, fundamentally decent, but ambitious person. A colleague at *American Magazine* remembers him for his "energy, sheer energy," someone with "guts and determination" who would try to pass himself off as "just a farm boy from Pennsylvania."[28] Vance portrayed himself a country boy among the sophisticates, not someone who had the social skills or background to belong in the world of New Canaan and Ivy League graduates.[29] At first, a friend who knew him from Columbia days thought Vance's presentation of himself as a hayseed was just a persona; over time he came to realize this was authentic Packard.[30] One of his lifelong friends called him "genuinely offbeat, an American original."[31] "Naive and straitlaced" and with "highly moral attitudes on public behavior," Vance was also "cynical" about people. This combination made him continually both fascinated and shocked at what he witnessed in America.[32] Fumbling and even stammering, he had a "disarming quality" that encouraged people he interviewed to confide in him "without anticipating the result."[33] The phrase "absent-minded professor" was appropriate. When Virginia was giving birth to their first child, Vance was pacing the floor of the wrong hospital.[34] Writing about new gadgets for *American Magazine* and constantly fixing up houses with vigor and inventiveness, he was nonetheless not very interested in learning how to carry out ordinary tasks.

Driven but not egotistical, Vance Packard was unpretentious, often telling self-deprecating stories about himself.[35] He spoke in direct, colloquial language, and seemed less sophisticated than he was. He was "unassuming" and "reluctant to put himself forward."[36] Without pretense himself, he was an "enemy of pretense" in others.[37] Quite shy, he presented himself to the world as a genuinely modest person except when, on rare occasions, he was given to bursts of bravado.[38] Packard had boundless energy and curiosity, always trying to figure out what made people tick and things work. He struck one friend as "one of the nicest guys he ever met," someone who was "gentle, generous, and tolerant."[39] An "optimistic fool"—a label he later used to describe himself—Packard inwardly had more than a touch of insecurity.[40] About five feet nine inches and developing a middle-age girth, he did not cut an especially striking figure. A person who "thinks faster than he speaks," to one friend he often seemed "terribly uncoordinated" in his movements.[41] In fact, Packard was off in his own world, like the young man in State College, still daydreaming and even bumbling. Seen in the company of three active children and a striking wife, he was usually a tagalong, in public situations staying in the background and following rather than leading.[42] Surrounded by cartoonists and writers who were some of the funniest people in America and himself possessing a wry sense of humor and a keen eye for the preposterous, he never, Vance P. recalled, told a joke.[43]

The three children knew their parents were different, "different," Cindy recalled, "in way of being better."[44] The other mothers they knew chauffeured their broods and volunteered at local institutions; Virginia worked for money and was an artist. The fathers of their friends were corporate executives who commuted into New York. In contrast, Vance did not go into Manhattan to the magazine office on a regular basis. He dressed unfashionably, Vance P. said, and took the family on "unconventional vacations." In every respect but real estate, the family generally eschewed conspicuous consumption.[45] They relied on their 1938 Packard and did not buy a new automobile until 1950. The guests who came to the house were not advertising executives and corporate officials but writers and artists.[46] Among Vance's friends were the media historian John Tebbel, the author John Hersey, and two *New Yorker* cartoonists—Whitney Darrow, Jr., and Charles Saxon. By New Canaan standards, but especially by Chappaquiddick ones, the children did not feel they came from a wealthy family.[47] They sensed a combination of privilege and uncertainty.[48] Although they never lacked for things they wanted, until well into the 1950s they knew there was an issue of when and from where money would come.

Vance and Virginia encouraged their children to test the limits of conventional behavior. What characterized life among the Packards was creativity, not high culture; expressiveness, not self-control; nonconformity, not obedience to social norms. The tone the parents set was combative rather than placid. Vance and Virginia were always shouting, arguing, and disagreeing over myriad issues, especially money, but not in ways that made the offspring worry that the marriage was in jeopardy.[49] "They were always squabbling," a friend recalled, but never in a "mean or destructive" manner.[50]

Yet if the Packard household differed from those of the readers of *American Magazine*, it also resembled them in some important ways. Like many suburban dwellers, in social terms the Packards were relatively insulated. The only poor people, members of the working class, or African Americans the children met, they recalled, were those who helped in and around the house.[51] As someone brought up in the South, Virginia was more personally engaged with issues of race. Vance, with less direct experience, remained relatively uninformed when it came to African Americans.[52] Still, as Cindy recalled, her parents bent over backwards to make clear that all kids were equal, that their children were "just fortunate to be born white," and that there was nothing "so intrinsically special" about them that determined their skin color.[53]

The household was conventional in its relatively strict gender roles— with Vance in charge of things outside the house and Virginia of those inside. Vance believed he retained control of the major decisions, especially the financial ones. "Delegate, delegate, you have to be the one who delegates," he would later tell Cindy.[54] "At our house," he wrote in 1968, "the power struggle focuses upon who can push the most problems of handling finances onto the other's lap." A large range of decisions, he commented, could "be relegated to a weaker partner by the dominant mate."[55] Content in his own sphere and considerably removed from the world, his attitude was that Virginia should handle whatever problems arose.[56] Friends who understood the dynamics stated, however, that Virginia was "always the final authority on everything" in the household.[57] Like many spouses of writers, she arranged a busy social life and took care of the myriad details necessary to keep their worlds functioning and her husband writing. In the few days before the New Canaan house had to be readied for a summer renter, for example, she would handle all the critical arrangements and he would virtually disappear.[58] Virginia's importance to Vance's career was incalculable. As Packard's editor later commented, as an author's wife Virginia "gave two hundred percent effort to help him get ahead."[59]

Packard's politics were unconventional, at least in comparison with what he found at *American Magazine* and in much of New Canaan. In the fall of 1952, he and Virginia hosted a reception for U.S. senator William Benton, who was known, the town paper noted, as "the man who had the courage to stand up against McCarthyism."[60] Packard recalled that he "lost his heart" to Adlai Stevenson, though that commitment remained known principally within New Canaan.[61] In 1956, when Packard wrote a piece for the local paper that tried to define why he was a member of the Democratic party, he came up with an answer that emphasized temperament more than policy or social class.[62] In a way that revealed his social isolation and neglected the persistence of poverty and discrimination in America, he argued that there were not enough " 'little people' " to keep the Democrats in power in a world where "the 'little' brick layer drives a Cadillac."[63]

Rather, Packard argued that style and character divided the parties. Paralleling the shift of contemporary social scientists, such as Richard Hofstadter and Seymour Martin Lipset, to explanations of political differences that stressed symbolic and psychological factors more than economic ones, Packard said that "being a Democrat is a state of mind." Democrats, he observed, were less orderly and more forgiving, joyous, imaginative, and flexible. They were more likely to be "non-conformist," Packard remarked, doubtlessly conveying his sense of himself. If Republicans appealed to "social strivers," Democrats, he commented, again reflecting his self-perception, included among their numbers people whose incomes had increased but who were "horrified at the prospect of having to become 'respectable' and conform to 'middle-class morality.' "[64]

During these years, he also published two nonfiction books, writing a chapter a day for several weeks of his summer vacation.[65] He collaborated with Penn State professor Clifford R. Adams on *How to Pick a Mate: The Guide to a Happy Marriage* (1946), a book they wrote after readers responded enthusiastically to their 1944 article on the same subject. Part of the effort to restore family life to a domestic norm after the war, the book relied on Adams's theory of compatibility of partners and thus went against the grain of Willard Waller's sense of marriage as a battle between conflicting personalities. Packard and Adams expressed conventional views of gender roles but relatively enlightened ones of sexuality, and consequently, the book was banned in Peoria. Directed at returning veterans and their prospective brides, the book was a how-to primer, with tests that potential partners could take. It did not sell well, mainly because the title ensured that most women would not ask for it at a bookstore. The lion's share of Packard's income from the project came from a coauthored

Vance Packard poses for a picture on the dust jacket of Animal I.Q., *1950.*
(Used by permission of Vance Packard.)

column on courtship and marriage that appeared in *Woman's Home Companion* for six years beginning in 1946.[66]

The other nonfiction book that he produced during this period was *Animal I.Q.: The Human Side of Animals* (1950), on the intelligence of different species. Written with an irreverence about the claims of human beings to their distinctiveness, the book combined material from Packard's youth on a farm with his interest in the behavioral sciences and presented the discoveries of experts to a lay audience. Packard received an advance of fifteen hundred dollars, the Book-of-the-Month Club recommended it, and bookstores and reviewers—including Joseph Wood Krutch—responded favorably, resulting in moderately good sales. Yet Packard continued to think of himself as a magazine journalist, not a book author.[67]

The Celebratory Consensus in Cold War America

Packard's years at *American Magazine* coincided with a period of momentous changes in American life to which he, his audience, and his editors were responding. With the real gross national product growing, it was no wonder that economist John Kenneth Galbraith in 1958 labeled America "the affluent society." In the fifteen years after the end of World War II, the GNP grew by 250 percent, and per capita income increased by 35 percent. By the middle of the 1950s, America had become the first nation in history in which more workers wore white collars than blue ones. Moreover, many workers tasted a middle-class way of life as strong unions and gains in productivity strengthened their economic position. Millions of Americans, many of them the sons and daughters of immigrants, moved to suburbs where mass-produced houses, children of the baby boom, automobiles, televisions, and shopping centers marked their daily routines. It was the age of the "organization man" and "the man in the gray flannel suit," phrases that referred to those who worked in large bureaucracies and lived in new, often homogeneous suburbs.

Although the number of women who worked increased throughout the 1950s, many of those who shaped public opinion told women to value domesticity more than autonomy or liberation. Television, movies, and magazines emphasized the mutuality of parents who headed child-centered families. Obviously, the lives of American women were more complex and less compliant than the picture offered by the advertisements, stories, and advice columns of the *Saturday Evening Post* and *Look*. Yet the media had cultural power. In 1954 the editor of *McCall's* wrote the classic statement on "togetherness," which pictured husbands, wives, and children "creating this new and warmer way of life not as women *alone* or men *alone*, isolated from one another, but as a *family* sharing a common experience." In 1963 Betty Friedan described women who succumbed to the "feminine mystique" when they embraced homemaking, remained sexually passive, and subordinated themselves to men.[68] During the postwar period a version of "containment" connected domesticity and the Cold War.[69] As Vice President Richard Nixon told Soviet premier Nikita Khrushchev in the Moscow kitchen debate of 1959, the suburban house was the focal point of freedom and abundance.

To a considerable extent, national politics sustained the sense of contentment that affluence underwrote. Dwight D. Eisenhower, elected to the first of two terms as president in 1952, served as a symbol of peace, prosperity, and security. A bipartisan coalition accepted the consolidation of the New Deal social programs. Democrats and Republicans embraced the Cold War's doctrine of containment of Communism. Americans reasserted their historic anticommunism, and the Soviets tightened their grip on Central Europe. In 1946, Winston Churchill declared that "an iron curtain has descended across" Europe. A year later, the American president, announcing the Truman Doctrine, committed the nation for the first time in its history to the peacetime use of military aid to allies in order to stem the advances of a foe.

Of course, not everything was perfect in America.[70] McCarthyism generated a fearfulness that affected not just those directly attacked but also the millions who felt pressure to conform to society's definition of normalcy. For neither husbands, wives, nor children did the traditional home usually measure up to expectations. Nor did the American Century that Henry Luce had announced in 1941 continue to seem as certain as it once had, especially after the Communists took over China in 1949, the Soviets detonated their first atomic bomb the same year, and war broke out in Korea a year later. There were more social and ideological fissures in the 1950s than most celebrants of the era wished to acknowledge. A silent generation may have reigned on American campuses, but millions of young Americans identified with the apolitical rebelliousness portrayed in the 1955 movie *Rebel Without a Cause* and with the antic humor of *Mad Magazine*. In the mid-1950s a Beat Generation was emerging that questioned the nation's commitment to materialism and bureaucratic routine. Most important, the civil rights struggle began during this period, reminding Americans that all was not right in a nation where discrimination and prejudice against African Americans persisted. Conflicts continued— across the lines that separated parents and children, men and women, homosexuals and heterosexuals, African Americans and whites, rich and poor.

Despite these conflicts, politicians, businessmen, writers for the mass media, and some intellectuals celebrated the benefits of the American Way of Life. With varying degrees of exaggeration, they pictured a nation where Democratic Capitalism had produced ever-expanding prosperity, which in turn had brought about a harmonious and increasingly egalitarian society. Although many of the celebrants worried about the adverse effects of affluence, by and large they remained confident that the United States was the best place on earth. As workers joined the middle class, as expert managers replaced greedy capitalists, as the pot full of immigrants melted, and as poverty disappeared, these opinion makers confidently asserted, social divisions between classes and ethnic groups seemed to diminish. Unlike what had happened in the USSR, in America mediating institutions such as family, church, and voluntary association stood between the individual and the state. Many observers remained convinced that the limited welfare state, administered by experts, was beginning to solve many of the problems that Americans faced at home. Looking beyond the nation's borders, publicists of American exceptionalism were sure that, with God on their side, the American Dream would triumph over the Communist nightmare.[71]

As a writer in the late 1940s and early 1950s, Packard responded principally to what celebrants in the business community and the mass media were saying. Yet it is also important to understand him in relationship to American intellectuals, who varied in their stance toward this ideological consensus that shaped much of the nation's public discussions. Some, like Norman Mailer, Herbert Marcuse, C. Wright Mills, and Irving Howe, issued a vigorous dissent from consensus ideology and visions of a near-perfect America. However, many influential American writers—people such as David Riesman, Seymour Martin Lipset, Daniel Bell, Dwight Macdonald, Mary McCarthy, Reinhold Niebuhr, Lionel Trilling—approached American society with what one historian has characterized as a combination of "contentment and uneasiness."[72] Although they adopted many elements of consensus ideology and found much to admire in America, these liberal anticommunists offered what Richard H. Pells has described as a sophisticated critique of the impact of affluence on middle-class life. They paid relatively little attention to politics not only because they believed the New Deal's legacy had more or less permanently solved the problems the Depression had revealed but also because they thought the difficulties America faced would not be easily amenable to institutional solutions.

Accepting as givens the elimination of poverty and fundamental class divisions by a largely successful capitalism, they worried about the psychological and cultural strains that mass culture imposed on Americans, especially suburbanites. Moving away from the legacy of the 1930s, they focused not on injustice and economic exploitation but on the impersonality, uniformity, and manipulation that mass culture seemed to enforce. What bothered them was not poverty and discrimination; it was rather the moral issues raised by advertising, standardization, alienation, affluence, monotonous work, and bureaucratic boredom. As William H. Whyte, Jr.'s best-selling *Organization Man* (1956) and David Riesman's *Lonely Crowd* (1950) argued, middle-class Americans felt tremendous pressure to belong, to work together cooperatively, to curb their ambition and individualism, and to be sensitive to the opinions of others. Instead, liberal intellectuals urged Americans to take risks and to seek autonomy and identity. Their goals were not collective action but private fulfillment. In the 1950s the ideas of liberal intellectuals formed part of a broad consensus that avoided a direct attack on the social order. In the 1960s a new generation used this critique of modern culture to more radical ends.[73]

The World of Mass-Circulation Magazines

Though what Packard wrote responded to the Cold War consensus, the situation at *American Magazine* had more direct bearing on what and how he wrote. The periodical appealed to the broad middle of American society, to some extent transcending barriers of region, religion, class, and ethnicity.[74] Like other family publications, this one offered millions of Americans one of their last experiences with a common culture through the printed word, an accomplishment that more specialized magazines of a later generation would undermine. Participating in the consensus ideology of the Cold War, the mass-circulation magazines articulated a vision of America that was generally celebratory. Like its competitors—*Saturday Evening Post*, *Look*, and *Collier's*—*American Magazine* spoke in a voice that mixed realism and illusion, creating what one critic has called "an aura of legitimacy" through a combination of "authority, factuality, intimacy, and common sense." Often patronizing in a way that fostered the passivity of the spectator, the articles promoted the consumer culture that the magazine's advertisements hawked.[75] They turned the unfamiliar and unpredictable into the comfortable, regular, and recognizable. Romantic stories taught women to deal with humdrum routine, and how-to articles provided instruction about new goods and services. Experts offered uncertain readers advice on personal and public issues. Drawing on insider information and dramas that took place far from home, articles on political issues and famous personalities replaced the gossip of face-to-face communities.[76] *American Magazine* was, a colleague of Packard's later remarked, a "dinosaur-like monument to American culture."[77]

Human interest stories were one of the staples of *American Magazine*. To communicate the drama and meaning of lives and events, authors relied on attention-getting headlines, carefully selected details, the curiosity of readers, and the human angle. Always susceptible to cynicism or boredom, the successful writer had to approach each assignment freshly, carefully balancing involvement and detachment. The story's currency was fate, moral choice, human dilemma, and the conflict between the individual and society. Human interest articles offered instruction about traditional mores while they also helped an audience come to terms with new ideas and social forces. Feature stories thus led readers to shape new and disparate experiences into a comprehensive personal and social reality, addressing anxieties and yet resolving problematic situations in a reassuring manner.[78]

In memos written in 1946 and 1947, Packard spelled out his vision for *American Magazine*. In the process he revealed how well he understood the lingo of the world in which he labored and how far he had departed from the critique of journalism he had offered in the 1930s. He wanted to appeal to the nation's "Middle Millions," especially to "the whole family," by using the publication's "long-stressed optimism" to demonstrate its commitment to "ambition and individual success" and its "interest in the future and faith in America." Features would give "personal service to each reader," provide "guidance and relaxation," offer "the best thoughts of respected Big Names," and allow "intimate glimpses of people worth knowing." Americans who were "inclined to be worried, confused, restless, dissatisfied needed new ideals, new goals, new ambitions."[79] Packard called for features that had "adventure, nostalgia, earthiness—and most of all, surprise." Stories on celebrities, he wrote, should have "an angle, a little-known human interest sidelight," such as whether a famous man cooked "Sunday night spaghetti suppers for all his neighbors." Drawing on his work for the Boston newspaper, he also suggested pieces on "modern pioneers," "stirring achievement," individuals who made fortunes "out of screwy ideas," and "small people" who were helping "to promote tolerance or international understanding." He called for features that came "from deep within the country and awaken the nostalgia of readers" and for "more sentimental, heart-warming stories that make the readers exclaim 'Now there's a wonderful person.' "[80]

Packard's suggestions evoked a world where the public and the private were inextricably linked. He suggested a monthly profile on an individual who merited "special recognition for his unselfish, heart-warming service to fellow Americans." Stories could tell readers not only how they could derive "the most fun and satisfaction from their lives" but also how "to make their communities and their nation a finer place to live." Articles by famous people would "get Americans excited again in their own personal destinies" and demonstrate that the nation "was still the land of opportunity." A feature like "Big Thoughts of Big Americans on Today's World" could offer "readers sane, constructive slants" about how to make things better. As his example, Packard suggested that an article "might show not only why we must stop Russia but what we can do once we have stopped her." Only when Packard turned to the domestic scene did he suggest an approach that differed significantly from the course the magazine was taking, though in ways that remained sensitive to the largely white, middle-class majority that made up his audience. Packard thus called for "hard-hitting, constructive articles exposing national weaknesses or injustices" such as "depressing cities and the sad plight of our white collar workers."[81]

Packard's recommendations for *American Magazine* combined hype, a liberal perspective, and traditional values. He wanted to push the periodical in a direction that advanced the interests of the middle class, acknowledged some national weaknesses, and fostered both anti-Soviet feelings and humanitarianism. His proposals reflected his sensitivity to an audience of family-oriented middle-class Americans who lived away from the nation's most cosmopolitan centers. He skillfully mixed a flair for the dramatic with a preference for a vision of America that concentrated on both the unusual and the ordinary. Whatever his private opinions, the two memos demonstrated that, having understood the values of the medium for which he worked, he was aware of the importance of an emphasis on optimism, nostalgia, achievement, self-help, and relaxation.

In contrast to what he wrote in memos, in his diary Packard made it clear that he understood that the issues he faced as a writer were ideological. He confided that his editor would not let him write pieces on foreign affairs that Packard considered "constructive and provocative." The article that *American Magazine* actually published shows how unacceptable Packard's liberalism was to an editor who wanted to unleash attacks against internationalism and social reform. In a 1948 feature titled "Parasites of the United Nations," Jerome Beatty denounced some of those who worked for the United Nations as "swarming hordes of aggressive, articulate, and influential" people who planned to use the U.N. "to turn the world into a utopia." What the U.N. needed, he concluded, was "a house-cleaning by a ruthless hatchet man who will chop the heads off the parasites" and "block the noble but impractical endeavors of the professional do-gooders."[82] Given his liberalism and his strengths as a writer of human interest stories, Packard was under pressure to shift his attention from politics to features. His editor, Packard remarked at the time, asked others to prepare articles "very negative in tone pooh-poohing" aid to Western Europe. He then asked Packard to "do a story on the training of secretaries!" To add insult to injury, Packard had to attend "a command performance" at which the head of the firm that published *American Magazine* trumpeted his nationalism. Looking around at all the things about his situation that he found troubling, Packard concluded at the time, "I can find little to be cheerful about."[83]

The Medium Is the Message

American Magazine, 1942–1956

In his articles for *American Magazine*, Vance Packard constructed a vision of America in the postwar world. What he wrote ranged from boastful claims of American exceptionalism to mild critiques of suburban conformity, privatism, and materialism. When he had some freedom to write as he pleased, his embrace of consensus ideology paled in comparison with the celebratory expressions dominant in the worlds he knew best—where business publicists, advertising executives, and more conservative magazine writers held forth. Yet compared with the critique of America as a mass society launched by liberal intellectuals, the reservations Packard expressed seemed understated. Under pressure from advertisers, his editors controlled the topics and content of his articles. In the mid-1950s, when mass-circulation magazines faced intensified competition from television, Packard's autonomy was further diminished. Because he rarely had total freedom to say what he wanted to, it is not easy to distinguish between what he wrote and what he believed. Nonetheless, his work reveals that he was a person who loved to do research, who could turn out articles on a wide variety of subjects with considerable ease, and who learned to perfect the fast-paced feature. From the conditions under which he worked, over time he would develop familiarity with promotional skills, a desire to gain more freedom to express himself, and a sense of what his audience wanted. Once again his success at writing formulaic pieces advanced his career, made him restive about the restraints he faced, and intensified his ambivalence about the success he had achieved.

"Interesting People" and Ghost-written Articles

In his first years at *American Magazine* Packard's main contribution was Interesting People, a section that in many ways resembled his human interest stories for the *Boston Daily Record* and the Associated Press. The July 1943 issue, which featured a typical mix, told of Igor Sikorsky, "the shy, poetry-writing" helicopter entrepreneur; a Hollywood dancing star who had heroically overcome a childhood illness; and a winner of a science contest who had proved that "a young girl's education these days isn't finished when she learned to cook, sew, and dance a passable foxtrot." Also highlighted that month were a presidential adviser who "gives his time freely because he is a good American" and a man who was making a fortune by selling pincushions with Hitler's face on them so Americans could "stab Der Fuehrer where it hurts most."[1] Interesting People, Packard proudly wrote the Columbia dean in 1943, had the highest readership rating of any feature that appeared in ten major magazines.[2]

Success with Interesting People, on which Packard focused for more than two years beginning in the summer of 1942, led the editors to give him greater responsibility. He shifted from the monthly column to articles on public policy and then to human interest features. Most of the pieces he authored appeared under his own name, yet he also worked on more than eighty ghost-written or cooperatively written ones that carried someone else's byline.[3] Two kinds of articles fell into the latter category—those that editors assigned and those that Packard generated. In all of these cases, it is not always clear when Packard was speaking for himself and when for someone else.

With mortgage payments to make, a family to support, and ambition to feed, he could not turn down ghosted assignments, however much they might compromise his autonomy. Again and again, he later remarked, he held his nose when he wrote on behalf of people with whom he disagreed, such as conservative senators Homer Ferguson and Styles Bridges.[4] He also turned the public relations copy of politicians and businessmen into articles that defended corporations, attacked union corruption, and questioned the wisdom of federal programs.[5] With assigned pieces under someone else's byline, he had to deliver strong anti-Soviet rhetoric. In 1950 he wrote one in which a State Department official justified the efforts "to counteract the poison being injected into the minds of the Russian and satellite peoples" by "exposing the hypocrisy of the Soviet imperialists, their callousness, their failures, and their intrigues."[6]

In contrast, the political articles that Packard ghosted but generated himself were generally more liberal. His outlook reflected that of many people of his generation who had long since abandoned their unquestioning faith in the USSR, who had supported the war effort, and who now accepted America's new position in the world. He worried about the possibility of nuclear conflict, approved of the Marshall Plan, and had no fundamental disagreement with the policy of containing the USSR. Though he recalled that he believed "international Communism was a reasonable—if greatly overstated—concern during the 1945–47 period," what disturbed him was that in the late 1940s and early 1950s "it was increasingly exploited for political advantage" at home. He was outraged by loyalty oaths and believed that the purges of government security risks "got wildly out of hand."[7] Thus Packard felt that the fight against McCarthy was more urgent than opposing Communism. In contrast, he was distant from those who reversed that order and placed so much in American life in a favorable light.[8]

With shifts in Soviet-American relations influencing his articles on foreign policy, Packard's opinions ranged from mild anticommunism to a favorable view of life in the USSR. When he focused on the less-developed nations, he worried not about the spread of Communism but the possibility that the population explosion might cause "the descendants of our least intelligent and successful families" to become "*16 times* more numerous than" offspring of the most intelligent and successful ones.[9] The pieces that Packard generated on domestic issues represented the interests of the middle class. He worried that blue-collar workers earned more than white-collar ones, urged civic groups to make cities more livable, and advocated the rights of consumers.[10]

Most of the articles that Packard originated but that appeared under someone else's name focused on changes in American life. Among the pieces that most fully engaged his energies were ones for which he worked with a professor to explore the geographical, racial, psychological, and biological patterning of human affairs.[11] In some of his favorite articles, he urged Americans to live less materialistic, less selfish, and more fulfilling lives.[12] Under the title "It's No Fun to Be a Millionaire," he stated themes to which he often returned from the 1940s through the 1980s. In this case, a wealthy man argued that families with an income between five and ten thousand dollars a year "can live just about as comfortably and pleasurably as a millionaire" by serving others through philanthropy and by pursuing simple pleasures rather than luxury.[13] In 1948 Packard worked with a cardiologist to produce an article that warned Americans, men especially, that in order to reduce high blood pressure, they had to "learn the art of serene, leisurely living." Cut down on "aggressiveness, driving ambition, and gadding about," the physician warned, and seek instead "more rest and relaxation and vacations."[14] In the same year, he helped one of America's most successful African Americans attack the Russians for having said the United States was not a land of opportunity for its minority groups.[15] At moments Packard's celebrations of the American Dream pictured an abundance that was more spiritual than materialistic.[16] In other instances, his articles articulated the position that public policy could encourage "a fabulously rich material life" by wresting resources from nature. The keys to such economic expansion, wrote the head of the Brookings Institution in an article that Packard worked on, were *"the unfulfilled desires of the great bulk of the American population"* and "free enterprise," which despite its "imperfections," was the only system capable of helping America "realize its great potentialities."[17]

Packard's Portraits of the Postwar Generation

Most of what Packard authored at *American Magazine* appeared under his own name. His autonomy varied even when he developed these pieces. Some of the ideas were his own; others originated in response to pressure from advertisers and editors. Some of the leads he wanted to pursue did not get a green light from his superiors. Initial drafts of other pieces encountered such significant objections from editors that it is hard to distinguish what Packard wanted to write from what he put down on paper in order to keep his job.

The style of his stories reflected well-established traditions at mass-circulation magazines. A catchy title captured the reader's attention by suggesting the utility of practical advice, by conveying a sense of excitement, and by hinting at the drama to follow. Next came the subheadings, set in smaller type and offering a capsule version of the story to come— questions answered, adventures experienced, and dreams fulfilled. The accompanying drawings and pictures personalized the article's content. The beginning of the story—short paragraphs that used a personal drama,

Packard's own experience, or a question followed by an answer—quickly engaged the reader's attention. The body of the story was carefully constructed with a combination of personal and factual details that made it relevant to the reader's life. Timely and realistic, what he wrote established confidence by familiar techniques: an approach that was simultaneously personal and authoritative and made the ordinary event exciting. He usually ended on an upbeat note with the resolution of a problem and the hope of a brighter future.

Some of Packard's pieces seemed naive, overexcited, or too chatty.[18] When he had to soothe editors and advertisers, the result might come close to what Dwight Macdonald had said of features published by *Fortune* in the 1930s. They were written, he remarked, "in a slick, inflated, cheaply melodramatic style," with "their brilliance" having "the glossy shine of a new Buick" and "their logic" demonstrating "the verbal agility of the advertising copy-writer."[19] Yet when Packard was at his best, especially when he was bringing the scholarship of others to a wide audience or serving as a muckraker for the middle class, what he wrote was informative in its content, serious in its tone, and careful in its construction.

As Packard began to chronicle the lives of the generation that had seen victory in World War II and would experience prosperity in the ensuing years, his attention turned to subjects on which he would concentrate for much of the rest of his career. Many of his early articles focused on returning soldiers in the very years when Willard Waller was writing on the same subject for other mass-circulation magazines. Like his mentor, Packard stressed the importance of treating the veterans well. Yet if Packard tended to gloss over the bitterness of the returning vets and emphasize their optimism instead, Waller warned of the dire consequences of neglecting them and called on the United States to take positive steps to ease their adjustment to American life.[20]

The world Packard described in his postwar articles was peopled by white, middle-class, monogamous couples and their children. Bringing the advice of experts from the academy and business to a wide audience, he sought to teach the parents of the baby boom generation how to be good parents, spouses, suburbanites, workers, and consumers. Charting the mores and triumphs of a generation, he told his audience how to be modern without sacrificing traditional values, how to balance the claims of prosperity and family. With roots in an older America, Packard lived in a wealthy Connecticut community and preached small-town values to an audience of suburban, middle-class people. In 1954, for example, he described how his family left "the grim, workaday world of taxes, time clocks, and cold wars . . . a million leagues behind" to vacation in Nova Scotia, where they entered a "pastoral paradise" whose people were "'quaint' in their honest simplicity." The local folk worked, he remarked in a way that idealized the reality of life in places like Bradford County, "just as they have for centuries, in gentle leisure without hurry, without tension, without covetousness."[21]

Packard played on similarly nostalgic and patriotic themes, reminiscent of the way others defended Cold War America, when he celebrated the ingenuity and ambition of the nation's businessmen. In 1953, he told parents how a technical education would help their children bring new achievements to fruition—superhighways, plastics, wonder drugs, "electronic marvels," and "miracle fabrics." These young men and women, "in the front ranks of our pioneers," he commented, using the language of an older era, would help realize "the American dream of a bountiful and exciting future."[22]

Packard reacted against the conformity of the man in the gray flannel suit and the collectivism of totalitarian societies by celebrating American individualism. Writing in *Animal I.Q.*, when no zealous editor was looking over his shoulder, he noted that people did best not "under a herd society" but in an "individualistic society, such as is practiced or considered as ideal" in the United States. "The lesson of Nature," he concluded, "favors the rugged individual."[23] In an *American Magazine* piece titled "They Gambled on Greatness," he told the story of how Yankees baseball player Gil McDougald gave up a safe but unchallenging job so he "could take his chances in a notoriously hazardous and fiercely competitive field." Now his family had begun to enjoy the rewards of his selection as Rookie of the Year: an eight-room suburban house with its own lawn, a "'wonder' stove" with "'a million gadgets,'" and a new dress that made the wife feel "like Cinderella putting on a sparkling new gown." Americans should follow Thoreau's warning, Packard remarked, and not lead lives of quiet desperation. "Fate makes us clerks when we want to be cowboys," he commented to a generation whom the Depression had caused to value security over risk. Accepting the first job that came along, "we're afraid to change horses in midstream, so we stay where we are, square pegs in round holes." Perhaps reflecting his own sense of being trapped in a large corporation, Packard concluded that "there is no satisfaction in all the world quite like taking the big gamble—getting out of a humdrum routine—and making a success of the life you really like."[24]

Packard's stories often concerned a family-oriented man from a small town who, after having struggled during the Depression, made a fortune that he now used to help others and to lead an unpretentious life. In 1954, for example, he told of Jim Price, a Hoosier who "hit the jackpot" as a manufacturer. Packard remarked that Price "had served to enrich the life of his community and his country." He was not the "typical two-fisted business tycoon" but a quiet man who had married a hometown girl he had met at a church picnic. He had achieved financial success by following his father's advice that " 'nothing puts iron into a lad better than honest toil.' " By remaining in his hometown, Price had "built himself an enviable family life." Living modestly and sticking with his boyhood friends, he "never felt the loneliness that some wealthy executives complain of in big city penthouses or manicured suburban estates."[25]

Five years later, Packard returned to the same themes of hard work and simple living when he examined the lives of America's newest millionaires. The aspirations and living styles of these people paralleled Packard's own. Without inheritance, they had combined "imagination and foresight, willingness to take chances, . . . capacity for hard work, drive—and a rather disarming lack of pretentiousness." For example, "jewelry, yachts and riotous living" did not appeal to John D. MacArthur and his wife Catherine, later known for the foundation that bore their names. They lived in a "modest" home, had no chauffeur, were as likely to eat "hamburgers for dinner as *filet mignon*," and on Sunday afternoons could be found gardening in their yard. The successes of these and other entrepreneurs proved, Packard asserted, that America was "still the land of opportunity for the individualistic adventurer."[26]

When Packard turned his attention to politics, he articulated a postwar version of liberalism that kept alive an attenuated anticommunism, treated politics as a consumable item, and defined issues in middle-class terms. As had been true since the late 1930s, he worried more about the dangers of Communism in America than in the rest of the world. In 1947, as the Cold War intensified, he wrote an article titled "Hotbeds of Communism." Although he acknowledged that the Communist party appeared to be weak in the United States, he warned that small numbers were not necessarily an accurate gauge of true power. "Communists everywhere are so fanatical, so firmly disciplined, and so tightly organized," he remarked, "that they make themselves felt far beyond their numerical strength." Indeed, he noted at a time when unions were being purged of people considered subversive, in one American factory, party members "clung to the control of the union, even though outnumbered 40 to 1."[27]

Although Packard in the 1930s might have considered what he was now writing red-baiting, his two stories on the USSR itself evidenced little of the Cold War hysteria so prevalent in America in the late 1940s and early 1950s. The first article, one appearing when the United States and the USSR were still allies, saw the Soviet Union as an emerging power that wanted to defend itself against future assaults and then gain "windows on the world." The second, published in 1949 at the height of the Cold War and for which the Social Science Research Council commended him, drew on the work of academic Sovietologists. These articles offered a far-from-hysterical mixture that blended the boast of the United States as a successful consumer society, a picture of the USSR as more driven by historic traditions than by dangerous expansionary impulses, and a call on his own nation to meet its international challenges through moral and economic strength. Lacking the shrill anticommunism that others trumpeted, Packard's writing remained well within the consensus of the late 1940s and 1950s but distinct from its more strident version.[28]

A consumer orientation influenced Packard's treatment of domestic politics and in the process created a sense that conflict and ideology did not matter. When Dwight D. Eisenhower assumed the presidency, Packard spent almost a week inside the White House, "this fabulous $40,000,000 mansion." Like one of David Riesman's inside dopesters, Packard focused on how this "friendly, typical American family" adjusted to life "in this most exclusive and expensive residence in America," a place that had "more facilities for personal enjoyment and luxury than a billionaire's palace." Much of the article focused on the problems of everyday living that the couple faced. Packard depicted Mamie Eisenhower as just like any other American housewife, paying the bills, making ends meet, and re-decorating. His approach had all the earmarks of articles in similar magazines that gave readers a glimpse into how celebrities lived.[29] Cute and voyeuristic, he simultaneously let his middle-class readers know about an enviable style of life and offered assurances that the famous were not so different.

On the relatively rare occasions when Packard turned his attention to national policy, he drew on the producer ethic to provide grist for the mill of those who wanted to cut government subventions for special interests. Focusing on Maine potato growers, he argued in 1949 that recipients of federal funds indulged in luxurious consumption at the expense of the average member of the middle class. Farmers received subsidies "for helping to keep potato prices up at my wife's grocery," Packard commented in his first article that focused on the rights of consumers. Most potato growers, he wrote with the exaggeration that characterized this article, looked "more like suave businessmen than farmers." The latest appliances filled local stores, families lived in "stupendous white farmhouses," and "almost every barn" contained "one or two long, sleek limousines." Children went off to finishing schools for education and families to Florida for vacations. Especially galling to Packard was the sharp contrast between Granville Township early in the century and rural Maine in the 1950s: simplicity versus high living; independence versus government subsidies.[30]

What lay behind Packard's approach to politics was the vision of an abundant middle-class consumer society. Responding to the pressure put on his editors by advertisers, he provided Americans who came of age in the Depression with practical information on how to participate in the burgeoning consumer culture. In 1952, he discussed the meaning of common suburban experiences when he told how the acquisition of power tools transformed him from "the loneliest man in town" into one who benefited from the fellowship provided by "The Loyal Order of Sawdust Makers." Emphasizing the low cost and practicality of technological innovations, he described how he had changed from frightened novice to enthusiastic practitioner. Suggesting the democratic implications of new components of the American standard of living, his articles contained Cold War boasts about America. For example, when he mentioned how the rich and famous used things that ordinary Americans with modest incomes could afford, he told his readers it was incorrect to associate home movies with people who "collect jade and go grouse shooting in Scotland."[31]

Over time Packard shifted his perspective on changes in the American standard of living from that of an inside dopester to that of an advocate of consumers' rights. His early articles on consumer culture, which offered few hints of the antimaterialism or threats to individualism that ran through his later stories and books, lightheartedly combined information on how to consume, a look at what went on outside the buyer's view, and tales of business success. Beginning in 1949, Packard sought to educate consumers about their rights, in the process explaining how shoppers might resist sales pressure. These stories usually lacked villains and pictured the cautious and disciplined consumer as heroic. Packard carefully balanced appreciation for new elements of the standard package of consumer goods with mild cautions against excessive indulgence. On the one hand, he honored people who demonstrated self-restraint. On the other, his stories often told how families, having overcome the privations of the Depression, could now begin to enjoy the benefits that patience and hard work brought.[32]

In the 1950s, Packard celebrated the spread of affluence throughout America in a way that minimized the existence of poverty, highlighted the position of independent entrepreneurs, exaggerated the extent to which America had become a middle-class society, and emphasized the gains of some blue-collar workers. "The most important general fact," he wrote in 1956, is "that almost everybody except the farmer is making more money than ever before." With income distribution growing more equal, he argued, "a levelling is taking place, a shrinking at both ends of the income scale, with a great growth in middle incomes." Equally striking was "a remarkable sort of revolution," the emergence of a blue-collar middle class. People such as bricklayers, factory foremen, and truck drivers were "swiftly coming to dominate the middle position in our society," he wrote, making up a "clear majority" of households "in the middle-income ($4,000–$7,500) bracket." At the same time, *"many white-collar workers are feeling pinched and unappreciated,"* Packard emphasized, pointing to firemen, clergymen, bank tellers, and social workers.[33]

An article that Packard was unable to publish illustrates the extent to which he was capable, when not beholden to editors, of drawing a picture of America that was less bland and more conflict-laden. Right after World War II, he worked on a story about a Connecticut program, developed by émigré psychologist Kurt Lewin, that aimed to reduce tension among the state's ethnic groups. At a time when molders of public opinion were minimizing social divisions, it is not hard to see why Packard could not publish an article that began with the statement "No matter who you are—rich or poor, light complexioned or dark, Methodist or Mohammedan—there are probably quite a few people in your community who dislike the sight of you." Packard emphasized the pervasiveness of prejudice and the inadequacy of goodwill efforts like Brotherhood Week to overcome it. Without giving discrimination against African Americans any special valence, he focused on how both dominant and subordinate groups felt animosity toward outsiders. He especially attacked those who had "the upper hand" and erected barriers, preventing "individuals belonging to underdog groups from rising above a certain fixed level in the community, regardless of their personal ability." Such actions, he wrote, made "a farce of our profession of being the land of stubborn individuals who judge every man on his own merits."[34]

Although in this article Packard went against the grain of postwar consensus when he emphasized prejudice and tension, in other ways he relied on assumptions common in discussions of assimilation during the 1950s. He sympathetically embraced the view that if only "old-stock residents" made more effort to know newcomers and helped "them become part of their new American community," then they might no longer have "to preserve their own little cultures." However, when it came to marriage, Packard insisted on the importance of maintaining ethnic communities. In *How to Pick a Mate* (1946) he warned returning veterans and the women they courted to "beware of mixed marriages," because they involved differences "of culture or religious training," as well as those "of personality, of intelligence, of education, of race or nationality, of social culture or of economic status."[35]

Packard's Depiction of Family Life in Suburban America

More than any other topic, Packard focused on family life. This was among Waller's primary concerns, and it fit *American Magazine*'s strategy for developing reader loyalty. Compared with Waller's vision, Packard's view was more reverential and reassuring. Though he may have echoed some of his mentor's unease about new roles for men, Packard's stories lacked Waller's belief in the centrality of conflict within the family. Packard's own fascination with family life also stemmed from the sharp contrasts between the home in which he had grown up and the one in which he now lived, the somber and authoritarian versus the antic and more egalitarian. However distinctive his own household, his articles on family life created a picture that both accepted and mildly challenged the usual view of the domestic scene in the 1950s. Missing from his stories were not only women who conveyed a sense of their sexuality, single men and women, and people who lived outside traditional families but also overprotective women and feminized men.[36] "Living alone," he commented in *How to Pick a Mate*, "is an abnormal state for a woman."[37] His early writings took what a later generation would consider a chauvinistic position. Matrimony, he wrote in 1946, offered "a logical division of labor. Imagine," he continued, "how much more complicated and inconvenient life would be if men had to do their own cooking and sewing, and women—all women—had to compete with men for a livelihood!"[38] In 1948, he worried about how demotion to the "submissive role" was undermining "American husbandhood."[39] Three years later he described himself as a "gruff, reactionary old mossback" when it came to the duties of husband and father.[40]

Even though Packard evoked a world dominated by heterosexuality and nuclear families, he did offer a mild challenge to domesticity by showing husbands struggling to be more egalitarian and wives who moved beyond the confines of the home at the same time that they happily fulfilled their domestic duties. From 1945 through the late 1950s, Packard stressed the importance of modifying attitudes and practices in order to preserve the middle-class American family under new conditions. By the early 1950s, he began presenting himself as grudgingly egalitarian. In 1951, when Virginia participated in the Institute for Family Living at Vassar College, Vance reported that as a father he was learning to use "'nondirective guidance'" rather than the "undemocratic authoritarianism" he had expe-

At Vassar College: The author visits his wife, Virginia, and children, Randall, Cindy, and Vance

WILLIAM SEARS

I sent my wife to Vassar

Lend an ear to the sad, funny story of an old-fashioned husband. Since his spouse went to college and got the "new perspective" on domestic relations, his family life hasn't been the same. No longer can he "pressure" his children; he must cultivate "permissiveness" and "nondirective guidance"—with startling results

by Vance Packard

IF YOUR young son sticks his tongue out at you and calls you a nasty old stinkpot, don't slap him across the mouth. Instead, ignore the insult and rejoice secretly that you have such a fine, normal child! He is just channeling his aggressive, aggrieved feelings harmlessly by verbal projection.

I got that information straight out of the mouth of one of America's 116 most learned wives and mothers. I'm referring to my wife.

She became one of the 116 most learned wives and mothers by attending —along with 115 other wives from all parts of America—the Vassar College's unique Institute for Family Living at Poughkeepsie, N.Y., a few months ago. That's the special school held at Vassar, one of the world's leading women's colleges, where parents and their children can spend a month learning how to live a richer, more peaceable family life. On the teaching staff are some of America's leading child-guidance experts, educators, social workers, and homemaking and marriage experts.

Director of the institute is the famed expert on family relations, Dr. Mary Fisher Langmuir, who wrote the provocative article, *Wife Trouble? Get Her a Job!* for THE AMERICAN MAGAZINE last February. Some of the institute's teachers are men, but the majority are women.

Today, as a result of attending the institute, my wife is our neighborhood's expert on all problems of coping with children. Her opinions on the mysterious lore of child raising are eagerly sought by many of her neighbors. It is hard to realize that only a (*Continued on page* 117)

47

First page of a magazine article telling how Vance Packard, "an old-fashioned husband," obtained an education in "permissiveness" and "nondirective guidance." He sits at the center of the activity of members of his family. From left to right: *Randall, Virginia, Vance, Cindy, and Vance P. (From* American Magazine *151 [February 1951]: 47; used by permission of Vance Packard and Virginia M. Packard.)*

rienced in Granville Summit. With the help of experts on childrearing, he remarked with the exaggeration expected in a human interest story, his children had been transformed "almost beyond recognition"; they had become "more self-reliant, more friendly, more relaxed, and, for the most part, more civil to their daddy." Packard treated the situation (and his own response) with self-irony. He was thinking of corresponding with other men whose families had attended the institute in order to explore the possibility of establishing a "'Vassar Daddies Protective Association.'"[41]

In his pieces on family life, Packard emphasized the importance of traditional values such as hard work, faithfulness, community service, cooperation, adventure, and self-restraint in consumption. A 1955 article featured the president of the General Federation of Women's Clubs, a woman who raised hogs for a living and had organized "an enthusiastic, nationwide crusade to overhaul the way we Americans live as families" so that more people would live "in the rich, warm, close, old-fashioned way." Consequently she fought against "unwholesome influences" such as violence on television, "lewd and gruesome" comic books, and "growing experimentation with sex, dope, and liquor."[42] In another story, he breathlessly described a Mormon household of twelve as "a big, old-fashioned kind of family," whose "teamwork, enterprise, and joy of living make them an outstanding example." The wife had given birth to ten children in twelve years, helped finance her husband's medical education, and worked toward her own degree in child psychology. The children's self-reliance enabled the mother to go "through her day in a breeze." The father, Packard reported, believed that the people who built America "pioneered new frontiers because economic necessity drove them to put on their thinking caps and exert extra effort." The parents, he announced, were "getting more joy out of their children than they could possibly get from a fine house or sailboat, or fine furniture, or a mink coat alone."[43]

Packard's picture of the Mudds of Haverford, Pennsylvania, as "the most exciting family I have ever met" revealed his preference for marriages in which both partners pursued professional careers that enabled them to make contributions to society. They owned no television, preferring to be "explorers and adventurers," something that Packard felt gave every room of their house a feeling "as invigorating and stimulating as the brisk air of a mountaintop." Their exploration was not selfish. The husband, a noted scientist, was investigating the world revealed by the electron microscope, and the wife, a nationally known expert on marriage, was attempting "to find how people can live together in greater harmony in this era of mounting marital crack-ups."[44] In articles like these, Packard found heroes in what other writers considered suburban wastelands.

The Packards experience American prosperity as they "re-live their vacation on the screen, as real as life, in gorgeous color," with Vance as "Cecil B. de Mille." Around the projector, from left to right: Vance, Vance P., Virginia, Mabel Packard (Vance's mother), Randall (in the foreground), and Cindy; at the diving board: Vance Packard with his two sons. (From American Magazine *154 [October 1952]: 38, 39; used by permission of Vance Packard and Virginia M. Packard.)*

What appealed to him about the Mudds was precisely what liberal intellectuals felt middle-class Americans had lost—the capacity for meaningful work, restrained consumption, and risk taking.

Packard echoed other writers when he stated that the intervention of experts would strengthen American families. One of the central tasks of his articles was to inform his readers about the implications for their lives of the most recent research carried out in the academy and the business world. Yet if his stories combined inside dope and practical advice, they also thrived on his audience's titillation with what the magazine's examination of people's lives revealed.[45] Following the dictum that "where there is intimacy, the public print must confine itself to innocuous externals," what he said about his family's personal life was hardly revealing.[46] Writing about new kinds of leisure goods and services, he often used Virginia and the children as the focus of his stories that taught his fellow consumers about new elements in suburban living. At the suggestion of an editor at *Reader's Digest*, he authored an article on the impact on his family of his wife's enrollment in a course at a charm school that taught her how to be a success.[47] Packard paid for several summer family vacations in the 1950s by writing about them.[48] When he produced articles on family life in which his children played a role, they complained that their father was exploiting them.[49] Yet ironically, in view of the commercial use of his wife's and his children's experiences, even his articles on the household's vacations in remote places reiterated the importance of family values and wholesome fun.[50]

Like many contemporary writers, Packard emphasized togetherness of the suburban household, a common theme in women's magazines during the Eisenhower years. The families he described often pursued the companionate ideal without embracing equality. Moreover, he echoed what Barbara Ehrenreich has called the male revolt of the 1950s. Packard not only had written of the dangers that overweening ambition posed to a healthy heart but also had approached the idea of more egalitarian roles for husbands and fathers with some self-irony and discomfort.[51] His picture of American family life reflected the ways others linked domesticity and the Cold War.[52] Whether intentional on his part or not, it was possible to take his celebration of American family as a rebuke to the USSR. The suburban home—with its do-it-yourself workshop, new appliances, and harmonious family—was the chosen land.

Yet the vision that he offered did not always follow the portraits often assumed to have dominated women's magazines and television. His articles did not embrace most of the key elements that made up the feminine mystique. He did not write pieces that advised women to be either sexually submissive or alluring. He did not engage in the antifeminism offered by Philip Wylie in *Generation of Vipers* (1942) or by Marynia Farnham and Ferdinand Lundberg in *Modern Woman: The Lost Sex* (1947). Nor did he sing the praises of the mother who achieved fulfillment by changing diapers and keeping the kitchen spotless. He did not offer a picture of the Happy Housewife Heroine that Betty Friedan discussed in her 1963 book, drawn from stories in *Ladies' Home Journal*, *McCall's*, *Good Housekeeping*, and *Woman's Home Companion*.[53] After all, Virginia had serious professional commitments, as did many of the women Vance's stories described. The women he portrayed had little of the drive to dominate, and the families he wrote of possessed little of the anxiety other writers mentioned. Not only were his own children hardly conventional but the families his articles discussed were not as women- and child-centered as those pictured elsewhere. In addition, some of the households whose virtues his stories extolled, far from being totally encapsulated in suburban privacy, remained committed to community service. The husbands he pictured, like Packard himself, were more eccentric than conforming and generally not the typical breadwinner who worked as an organization man.

There were, however, limits to how far Packard went in adopting new views. Monogamy and heterosexuality were central to his vision. If he honored women who worked, he rarely wrote articles on unmarried or divorced women or even married ones with strong political commitments. Most of the time, his women entered the world outside the home mainly as an extension of their domesticity.[54] Packard's models were women who balanced career and family or those who were even more domestic in orientation.

Packard's Relationship to the Cold War Consensus

His articles on family life were but one of the topics that made it clear how Packard stood in an uneasy relationship to the celebratory consensus that dominated Cold War America. Although it is not always easy to separate what he believed from what editors wanted, his own political development, the pressure of editors, and the interests of the middle-class suburbanites who subscribed to *American Magazine* meant that his writings dovetailed with many of the claims of the Cold War consensus. Whether or how much he bit his tongue as he wrote these pieces, what appeared under Packard's byline celebrated the strengths of postwar America that others used to contrast with the weaknesses of the Soviet Union. He saw Communism as somewhat of a threat to America and a general interest version of New Deal liberalism as a positive good. From his articles emerged a picture of the United States as a place where opportunity abounded, affluence spread, the poor were disappearing, workers graduated from the working class, and the middle class triumphed. Minorities took advantage of unparalleled opportunity, families grew more democratic, the ambitious exercised their ingenuity, individualism remained strong, those who worked hard achieved success, and millionaires lived without ostentation. Most of his articles evoked a nation without class or ethnic divisions, with cameo appearances from only the most successful African Americans. Moreover, the photographs that accompanied what he wrote pictured what many social observers in the 1950s saw as prototypical Americans—white, middle-class, respectable, family-oriented suburban men and women.[55] Even though in 1955 *Look* covered the Emmett Till case and in the following year *Life* did a series on segregation, the world that Packard depicted was overwhelmingly white.[56]

To what extent Packard was responding during the early 1950s to McCarthyism specifically and to the Cold War more generally requires a complicated answer. He was quite aware of what he later called the "muffling effect" of wartime patriotism and postwar anticommunism.[57] It is not hard to see how, under somewhat different circumstances, Mc-Carthyism might have threatened him. After all, there was plenty in his life that had made him sensitive to the threat of persecution: against German American family members in World War I and against radicals in the 1930s. He knew people whose careers McCarthyism had ruined. Later he pointed back to the fact that he was "outraged" that both Eisenhower and the Senate tolerated McCarthy. At the time, he openly identified himself with Senator William Benton, one of McCarthy's enemies.[58] But neither Packard, his friends, nor his colleagues lived with the fear that the senator from Wisconsin or his allies might attack them.[59] The Red Scare threatened people's jobs in the magazine world less than it did in Hollywood or universities. Moreover, Packard had never made a commitment to radicalism, participated in suspect organizations, or sought to influence policy. *American Magazine* was the last place where even the most zealous might expect to turn up an ex–parlor pink. What did worry him, even into the 1960s, was that something he wrote might attract the attention of witch-hunters who would adversely affect his ability to use his pen to provide for his family.

In the best of his pieces, Packard offered an implicit critique of American society, putting some distance between himself and the fairyland picture of American life that dominated public discussions during these years. The evidence for his disagreement with some of his own words is clear: from what he said confidentially at the time, from what he has said since in retrospect, from what he wrote in the late 1950s once he had editorial freedom, and from his not having indulged in the more extreme forms of celebration and anticommunism. Yet there was often an ambivalence in his position. He loved gadgets, but he disliked celebrating ingenuity. New components of the American standard of living commanded his attention, but producer values were still important to him. He had a keen eye for the niceties of status, but he questioned the dream of success. He disliked celebrating opportunity and the self-made man, but he knew very well that these terms described the trajectory of his own life.

He articulated some of the themes that liberal intellectuals developed more fully and cogently. Like them, Packard experienced ambivalence toward the America that was emerging in the 1950s. He liked what he saw as the disappearance of poverty and the weakening of class divisions, but at the same time he had reservations about conformity and materialism. He celebrated professional achievement, individualism, and nonconformity. He honored entrepreneurship, but he also acknowledged the significance of nonmaterial values. People should take risks, he had written, not principally to make money but to find meaningful work. They should work hard, not to attain great wealth but to enjoy spiritual pleasures and contribute to their communities. Like other liberal writers during these years, Packard worried about the loss of individualism in a world dominated by corporate bureaucracies. Some of his heroes were pioneering entrepreneurs and self-made men who worked hard and lived simply. Like them and within limits, Packard stood against conformity and a too narrow sense of autonomy. As was true of Tom Rath in Sloan Wilson's *Man in the Gray Flannel Suit* (1955), Packard was skeptical of the wisdom of achieving ever-greater levels of material and occupational success by climbing up and up the corporate ladder. Like Rath, many of Packard's heroes could not accept the lot of the organization man keyed for success, choosing instead self-fulfillment achieved through family life and meaningful work whose importance was more socially than financially rewarding.[60]

While his heroes were in some ways lonely, they also reached beyond themselves to help others—not, to be sure, as social reformers but as men and women who had achieved enough themselves that they were willing to help others in more personal ways. Whatever its unintended implications, his individualism was not explicitly connected with the Cold War battle against the collectivism of 1930s America or 1950s Russia. Packard's model of an oppressive institution was not the Kremlin but the corporation that employed him. Unlike such people as Norman Vincent Peale and other advocates of mind power, Packard placed little emphasis on self-realization. Though at times he mentioned relaxation and serenity, for him these values remained subordinated to hard work and strong character. Packard balanced material and spiritual well-being, but his articles neither discussed success achieved through mind power nor emphasized the goals of psychic relaxation or personal self-actualization.

Moreover, Packard did not venture as far down the road to anticommunism or domestic celebration as did many of his peers in the media. Jewish intellectuals who had journeyed from Brooklyn to Manhattan by the mid-1950s came to feel that the United States was their country. Ironically, Packard, who had moved from all-American Pennsylvania through Manhattan to an idyllic place in Connecticut, responded to Eisenhower's America with considerable ambivalence. In a complacent era, he sustained some of the commitment of a liberal to the public good and his own sense of himself as a nonconforming individualist. He rarely celebrated free enterprise capitalism and remained critical of excessive materialism. Only occasionally did he use a Cold War framework in his treatment of foreign policy, domestic politics, or American life. Although he published one article that warned of the Red Menace in unions, privately he was an anticommunist who felt that McCarthyism was more dangerous than Communism. Publicly he offered views of the USSR that, under other conditions, have made overzealous anticommunists take notice.[61]

Deteriorating Conditions at *American Magazine*

Over time, Packard grew dissatisfied with the conditions under which he worked. The necessity to write articles whose content he could not control and about whose message he remained ambivalent was among the factors that made him restless.[62] At *American Magazine* he enjoyed neither the personal support he had had from his editor at the *Daily Record* nor the autonomy he had experienced at the Associated Press. The most powerful of his superiors was Sumner Blossom, a "rabid Republican" who kept everyone at a distance, grunting his responses and never deigning to be personable with the writers.[63]

As well as he could, Packard made the best of a difficult situation. He sought ways to keep his distance without jeopardizing his job. One contemporary remembered him as "careful, cautious in all dealings." Someone who was "definitely not a heckler," he kept to himself whatever objections he may have had to editorial policy.[64] Another colleague described him as "a nice, pleasant, likeable" person who "slouched around the office" and kept his opinions to himself. Consequently, fellow workers had no idea "that underneath a relatively unobtrusive, quiet, apparently egoless exterior lurked a terrific mind."[65] Blossom called him "the Professor," viewing him as a person whose interests, demeanor, and seriousness distinguished him from run-of-the-mill magazine authors. He did not involve himself in office politics and drew most of his friends from elsewhere. He did not discuss national politics with even his most trusted colleagues. Eventually Packard went into the office only once or twice a week, preferring instead to do his research at the New York Public Library and write in New Canaan.[66] As Alfred Kazin noted of writers who worked at *Time* and *Fortune* in the 1930s, Henry Luce "might own their typewriters, but he would never, never own their soul."[67]

At *American Magazine*, Packard recalled, he wanted freedom and his editors wanted set pieces. His situation differed from what Norman Podhoretz described as the cynicism and superiority that emerged from the tension between Art and Commerce experienced by liberal arts graduates of elite universities who worked in and around Madison Avenue but aspired to be writers. Packard had been a journalism major, not an English major; at Penn State, not at Harvard.[68] He did, however, face more direct pressure from advertisers and the same kind of persistent "warfare between editors and writing staff" that Dwight Macdonald had experienced at *Fortune* in the 1930s.[69] "The editors kept calling for fresh ideas," he remembered, "but in fact the magazine increasingly became a formula magazine emphasizing themes that would please advertisers." What he wrote had to pass through what he called "The Gauntlet." The board of editors, which had the right to reject articles or to insist on many rewrites, included one person claiming to speak for women, another for Roman Catholics, and a third for advertisers.[70] Sensitive about his independence from editors and formulas and harboring considerable ambition, Packard took his job as a writer more seriously than some of his peers who were glad merely to turn out another article and collect their paychecks.

"Having to please a series of editors," Packard later remarked, "had been a real gritty business when you had three kids."[71] Although during these years Packard earned a substantial income, obtaining it was not without complications. In 1946, he earned about $10,000 from the magazine. By the early 1950s, he could report that his annual income from writing was about $20,000, $16,000 of it from *American Magazine* and the rest from articles published elsewhere, royalties, and teaching. Translating that figure to 1994 dollars yields an income from professional work of approximately $112,000.[72] But the fact that he received no payment until the editors approved a particular article gave them additional power over him. The situation was especially galling to him because his articles were among the most heavily promoted and widely read.[73]

These pressures, present from the beginning, became especially intense in the mid-1950s.[74] He urged a friend who was an editor of *Woman's Home Companion* to hire him, noting that he could provide articles "that would make your women talk." He considered starting an agency that would match feature story writers with magazines. For several years he also tried to get a job on the staff of *Reader's Digest*, despite any reservations he may have harbored about that publication's conservative politics or set formula. It had accepted a considerable number of his pieces and had paid him well item by item.[75] Having articles published in other magazines caused tension between Packard and his editors. In 1954, Blossom reminded him and several of his colleagues that publishing elsewhere was a "privilege," not a "right."[76]

Eventually the situation at *American Magazine* became dire. For twenty years, beginning in the early 1930s, Crowell-Collier, *American Magazine*'s parent company, had reinvested few of its earnings, instead providing income for its absentee owners and thus cutting its periodicals off from the capital they needed to modernize and grow. By 1953, as television and special interest publications were diverting more advertising revenue away from *American Magazine* and similar periodicals, red ink covered the balance sheet of the publishing conglomerate. Those in control struggled for survival, pressuring writers to turn out articles that would enhance the sales of the consumer goods advertised in their pages.[77] "So the magazines began prostituting themselves to attract ads," Packard recalled. Every issue, he later remarked, "had to have a food article, a do-it-yourself article, a travel article, and a kiss-ass-with-big-business article because the advertising department told us we needed them."[78]

In his autobiography, Theodore H. White, who also worked for Crowell-Collier, described the atmosphere before the fall.[79] Above all, it was the connection between money, power, and writing that angered him. With "no other purpose than to make money," he wrote of *Collier's*, one of *American Magazine*'s sister publications, the editor could force a writer to take on "those stories dictated to him by the magazine's desperate need for advertising." Nonetheless, White believed, such stories, focusing as they did on the intersection of mass marketing and the lives of average Americans, brought him "closest to the appetite systems and social pressures" that were central to life in America. When *Collier's* failed in late 1956, he learned that an impersonal corporation had no concern for its laid-off employees. Like his colleagues, White had to rethink his career, an exercise that would result in his *Making of the President* series.[80] During the mid- to late 1950s, some magazine writers had taken another path and sought academic appointments, thus becoming freed, as one critic has written, of "the deep anxiety of selling their dreams to indifferent editors so as to eat and pay the rent." In 1958 Daniel Bell traded a position at *Fortune* for one at Columbia University. For most magazine writers, however, regular teaching positions were out of the question.[81] Despite the inspiration he drew from Waller, the pleasure he took from collaborating with academics, and his nickname "The Professor," Packard had no desire to enter the university.

Although neither White's experiences nor his perspectives exactly paralleled Packard's, his observations help illuminate the last years at *Ameri-*

can Magazine. Like his counterpart, Packard was in a perfect position to view the intersection of money, power, and writing and to learn from the resulting situation how little concern corporations had for the welfare of their customers and employees. However ambivalent Packard may have felt about writing stories of suburban life and new items in the consumer culture in a way that aided advertising, these assignments had placed him close to the center of American middle-class life. Working for owners who collected their dividends but demonstrated little concern for the magazine's long-term health left Packard with a sense of the danger posed by wealth unconnected to productivity or responsibility. Packard undertook the examination of advertising that would emerge as *Hidden Persuaders* at just the moment when advertising was interfering with his own journalistic freedom. His personal experience was bound to intensify his anger against the agencies that shaped mass culture and determined the fate of his career. Having to earn a living by writing assigned stories that would satisfy others was a situation perfectly calculated to turn a farm boy who had once celebrated rugged individualism into an advocate of humanistic self-determination.

Although as a writer working on a middlebrow magazine Packard doubtless developed some distance from and sense of superiority about the ordinary people whose lives he chronicled, unlike many writers he did not lose his country-boy sense of curiosity and wonder about what was happening to average middle-class Americans. In a 1954 talk at an advertising convention he emphasized how important it was for journalists not to isolate themselves from life by remaining in their offices in New York and their "upper middlebrow Westport homes." Of greatest impact were "the personal experience" stories "where I take the reader by the hand and help him live out with me a dramatic or exhilarating adventure." Successful pieces, like successful advertisements, he argued, relied on the "vividness" involved in actually doing what he wrote about; the "freshness" that came through "personal exploration of the subject"; and "believability," which evoked "greater enthusiasm and conviction."[82]

The years at *American Magazine* had given Packard an intuitive sense of what worked with the largely suburban, middle-class audience of his generation.[83] Early on, he learned the traits that Robert Darnton says newspaper writers assimilate from the ethos of their first jobs: "unflappability, accuracy, speed, shrewdness, toughness, earthiness, and hustle."[84] However, more than most writers, Packard worked alone. Not usually testing his ideas on others, he was unlike writers who rely on the people around them—fellow authors, editors, friends, and family—to mediate between themselves and their readers.[85] Though his editors had significant impact on what and how he wrote, the response of the audience to his articles was important to him in only the most remote of ways. Because he had the "detachment of an intelligent spectator" and was able to "constitute himself an average representative of the public," he had an uncanny ability to comprehend the world in the same way that his audience did.[86]

Packard's years at *American Magazine*, beginning as they did when he was twenty-eight and ending when he was forty-two, were critical in the formation of his adult identity and career goals. Working for a popular magazine sharpened his ability to write with extraordinary speed prose that was easily accessible to a broad range of middle-class readers. These years also made him a keen observer with an eye for telling details. He had benefited from the opportunity to read and write about subjects and themes on which he would draw for the rest of his years as an author. Moreover, working in New York on *American Magazine* had amply exposed him to the pressures of Madison Avenue. That world—with its hype, its emphasis on self-promotion, its sensitivity to the marketplace, and its focus on style—was a milieu that Packard both absorbed and disliked. Before he wrote *Hidden Persuaders*, Packard had often emphasized the importance of the independent individual but almost never the dangers of manipulation by outside forces. Beginning in 1957, he authored a series of books whose major theme was the manipulation of individuals by institutions, which his years at *American Magazine* had taught him well.

Whatever Packard's strengths as a writer for a general interest magazine, forces beyond his control were limiting his days as an employee of Crowell-Collier. The corporate survival strategies did not work, and with the August 1956 issue *American Magazine* ceased publication. Because of the effectiveness of his contribution to *American Magazine*, Packard was able to transfer to *Collier's*; he was the only person from the editorial section to do so.[87] On the day before Christmas 1956, that magazine too folded. What Packard had written about white-collar workers feeling pinched and unappreciated assumed a special poignancy for him: his article on that subject appeared in *Collier's* during the brief period when he worked for that publication.

Now Packard faced a critical situation. Unemployment was in the offing because television's situation comedies commanded larger audiences than human interest stories in magazines did. He knew that earlier he had lost his job as a cub reporter partly because radio drama was more compelling than newspaper features. This time he crossed his fingers and hoped that he could switch from periodicals to books. He had proved—to Virginia's mother, to Virginia, and to himself—that he could succeed and be a good provider. In early 1957 he was free of the strictures he had struggled against, but his ability to provide was threatened. A captive writer might lose his independence but gain success. An unemployed one had freedom but neither money nor status. Only a successful free-lancer could be both an individualist and a provider. For now, however, Packard's life seemed uncertain. In early 1957, he went on unemployment insurance as he tried to sustain himself as a free-lance writer.[88]

Making It

Three Best-sellers, 1957–1960

When Vance Packard lost his job late
in 1956, friends and family members recall his being "panicked," "in a state
of shock," "pretty desperate," and "very hungry."[1] A colleague remembered that Packard, upon hearing that his employment was ending, said,
"I'm going to lose my house, and my wife and kids are going to starve."[2]
The Packards met their financial obligations with Vance's severance pay
from Crowell-Collier, five unemployment checks, earnings from free-lance
writing, and Virginia's salary. Unsure of what to do next, he circulated a
résumé that listed subjects he wanted to focus on. He continued to think
about starting a company that would market feature stories. Early in 1957,
he was desperate enough to consider selling the New Canaan house. Of
some help was the advance of two thousand dollars for *Hidden Persuaders*, which was to be published on 29 April 1957. Packard figured that
even if the book were to sell twelve thousand copies, the highest number
he could imagine, he would still face an uncertain future.[3]

By the fall of 1960, when it became clear that he had produced three
best-sellers in a row, Packard had emerged as an immensely successful

author. *Hidden Persuaders* (1957), *Status Seekers* (1959), and *Waste Makers* (1960) brought together his life experiences—the lessons he learned from his youth on a farm and his young adulthood during the Depression, as well as the sociology he studied with Willard Waller. These books relied on the skills he had honed in the previous twenty years, as a keen observer of American life, a writer of human interest stories in mass-circulation magazines, an author fascinated with the social and behavioral sciences, and a man with an interest in developing a comprehensive picture of what he observed. Success as a free-lance writer also helped Packard begin to resolve the tension between the desires to be free from restraints and to be a good provider.

Scathing, nostalgic, humorous, moralistic, ambivalent, and influential—these books offered a critique of the way experts and powerful institutions manipulated Americans into pursuing false pleasures. Packard's mixed feelings about what he witnessed, which resembled the tensions that many in his audience shared with him, led him to express both fascination and horror with advertising, social status, and consumer culture. He advocated individualism, creativity, hard work, authentic relationships, and respect for the environment. His best-sellers were stronger on diagnosis than on strategies for change, and they assumed that affluence was more of a problem than poverty was. They awakened millions of Americans to the dangers of corporate power, the divisions between social groups, and the threats that economic growth posed to natural resources and national character.

Packard challenged what he called the "systematic optimism-generation" put forth by the business community and the mass media, as well as by some social scientists and intellectuals.[4] These celebrants claimed that the United States had entered a new era, characterized by advertising, consumer credit, product innovation, and a pleasure-seeking morality. They asserted that social differences were narrowing if not disappearing, poverty was all but vanishing, corporations managed their employees benevolently, and the existence of great wealth was increasingly irrelevant. The balance achieved by interest groups and labor unions, they argued, underwrote the smooth functioning of the political and economic order. These paeans to American achievement had a distinct Cold War flavor. By providing abundance for all, some argued, People's or Democratic Capitalism had fulfilled the goals of socialism and communism. Others asserted that the abundance and opportunity delivered by free enterprise contrasted sharply with the poverty and totalitarianism of the nations behind the Iron Curtain.[5] Having worked in Manhattan, where the loudest voices were those of business publicists, advertisers, and the mass media, Packard knew firsthand not only the strength and ubiquity of these celebrations but also their combination of fantasy and reality.

The Hidden Persuaders and the Critique of Advertising

While he was still at *American Magazine*, Packard first worked on the material from which *Hidden Persuaders* would emerge. Late in 1953, several editors at *Reader's Digest* read with interest an article in the *Reporter* that warned consumers about the uses of new psychological techniques in advertising.[6] In the fall of 1954, *Reader's Digest* gave him, Packard noted at the time, an assignment that "they apparently had laying around" on "the increased use of 'motivational research' by merchandisers."[7] Shortly after he finished writing his article, Packard learned that the magazine had broken its long-standing tradition and decided to begin carrying advertisements. Though *Reader's Digest* paid him, it did not print what he had written. His ire increased when he realized that there was a connection between the publication's decision not to publish his piece and its acceptance of advertising, the subject of his attack.[8]

Not surprisingly, Packard began to think about writing a book on the uses of the social and behavioral sciences in marketing. In 1955, Eleanor Rawson, who had worked with him on the Interesting People section at *American Magazine* and later served as fiction editor at *Collier's*, asked if he had any book-length projects in mind.[9] Now she was an editor at the David McKay Company, where she worked closely with Kennett Rawson, her husband and the publisher. Packard sent the Rawsons the rejected article, and they encouraged him to write a book on the subject.[10] By March 1956 he was far enough along to tell his editor at *American Magazine* that in his spare time he was pursuing "a semi-scholarly labor of love" that enabled him "to wallow to my heart's content" in the social and behavioral sciences. "The idea of getting a 'prestige' tome such as this off my chest," he commented as he revealed his own aspiration to publish a serious book, "has been percolating in my mind ever since you lightly began calling me 'Professor.'"[11] Once Packard completed the research, it took him less than two months to write the book. Around the time *American Magazine* folded, he sent off the manuscript.[12]

Hidden Persuaders answered those who claimed that advances in advertising were fundamental to national well-being. Expenditures on advertising in America grew from less than $2 billion in 1939 to nearly $12 billion by the late 1950s. With the increasing use of installment payments and credit cards, consumer debt grew at three times the rate of personal income. Ads had become more sophisticated, visual, and subtle in approach and more pervasive in reach, especially as practitioners learned how to take advantage of the new medium of television and the new methods developed by pollsters, psychologists, and social scientists. Agencies adopted new approaches, including motivational research (MR), which relied on intensive interviewing, psychoanalytic theory, and qualitative analysis.[13]

Until Packard's book was published, new techniques, though subject to debate within the advertising community, had remained largely immune to criticism in the postwar period. More than two decades had passed since any widely read books had set out to expose advertising: *Your Money's Worth: A Study in the Waste of the Consumer's Dollar* (1927), by Stuart Chase and F. J. Schlink; *100,000,000 Guinea Pigs: Dangers in Everyday Foods, Drugs, and Cosmetics* (1933), by Arthur Kallet and F. J. Schlink; and *Our Master's Voice: Advertising* (1934) by James Rorty had been the most recent treatments of the subject. As Max Lerner announced just before the impact of *Hidden Persuaders* became clear, "Periodically there used to be attacks from the Left upon advertising as an institution; it is a proof of the efficacy of advertising that these attacks have died down."[14]

In the dozen years before *Hidden Persuaders* appeared, a series of novels, some of them turned into movies, paved the way for Packard's nonfiction by depicting advertising executives as materialistic, status-conscious, immoral people who cynically manipulated the consumer's desires. Frederic Wakeman's 1946 number one best-seller, *The Hucksters*, set the tone for its successors. "We don't steal," remarked the central figure before his awakening to the sins of his trade, "probably because it's bad for business, but we sure as hell do everything else for clients."[15] By 1957, other novels elaborated on the formula—including Herman Wouk's *Aurora Dawn* (1947), Eric Hodgins's *Mr. Blandings Builds His Dream House* (1946), and Gerald Green's *Last Angry Man* (1956). "Now it's gotten out of hand," one observer noted, "if you want a villain in a novel, you make him an advertising man. He's the modern version of the horse-opera city slicker."[16]

In contrast, many contemporaries emphasized the importance of advertising. Salesmanship, noted Lerner in 1957, "is the core activity of the American economy, with technology, production, and financing all subsidiary to it."[17] In 1956 MR advocate Ernest Dichter announced: "Horatio Alger is dead. We do not any longer really believe that hard work and saving are the only desirable things in life; yet they remain subconscious criteria of our feeling of morality." The problem, Dichter asserted in a way that connected consumption with pleasure, was to "give people the sanction and justification to enjoy" prosperity by demonstrating that it was moral to approach life hedonistically.[18] In 1956 Robert Sarnoff, the head of the National Broadcasting Company, echoed a claim commonly heard from the business community when he remarked, "The reason we have such a high standard of living is because advertising has created an American frame of mind that makes people want more things, better things and newer things."[19]

Packard began *Hidden Persuaders* by warning against the implications of what he saw as ominous changes taking place in the United States. Calling on his sense of a better past, when producer values reigned, he argued that in the early 1950s corporate leaders had shifted "from being maker-minded to market-minded." As executives realized that there might be a limit to how much consumers would buy, they turned to advertising and market research for help. New kinds of appeals offered a way out of the dilemma caused by increased production and potentially stable demand. While at *American Magazine*, Packard had praised social and behavioral scientists who explored the mysteries of American life; now he criticized the methods they used to help business manipulate an unsuspecting public. With their aid, MR was developing techniques that promised to "channel our unthinking habits, our purchasing decisions, and our thought processes." By appealing to the fears of psychological obsolescence, sexual inadequacy, and loss of social status, Packard argued, advertisements were fundamentally reshaping everyday life and threatening to undermine individualism. At the heart of this assault on the psyche was an attempt by "depth merchandisers" to promote self-indulgence.[20]

Set within this larger framework, the great bulk of *Hidden Persuaders* relied on case studies to describe the new techniques that tempted Americans into consuming products. One particularly vivid example came from the Freudian-oriented Dichter. In his marketing study "Mistress versus Wife," carried out for the Chrysler Corporation, he had explored why men bought sedans even though they preferred sporty models. Drawn to showrooms by convertibles placed in windows to appeal to a sense of romance, Dichter's report suggested, a male customer actually purchased a less flashy automobile "just as he once married a plain girl." Dichter urged the auto maker to develop a hardtop, a car that combined the practical aspects men sought in a wife with the sense of adventure they imagined they would find in a mistress.[21]

Packard also warned of the consequences of the extension of new methods of persuasion into personnel management, public relations, and politics. Echoing David Riesman's *Lonely Crowd* (1950) and William H. Whyte, Jr.'s *Organization Man* (1956), he saw other-directed personalities and team players as threats to American individualism. Moreover, he resented corporate intrusion into the lives of executives and their wives. He warned against the use of public relations efforts aimed at "mind-molding on the grand scale." He also worried about the extension of MR methods into American politics. Warning his readers about threats to democracy, he noted the ways in which seekers of public office were appealing to the irrational, emphasizing the role of personality, and treating public issues like items in a supermarket.[22]

The use of MR, Packard asserted, relied on the exploitation of feelings below the conscious level. His ideal was not so much the success-oriented and plain-living type found in much of his magazine writing, but the growth-seeking, self-determined personality suggested by the humanistic psychologists he had been reading. Here he also drew on Riesman's argument in *Lonely Crowd* that Americans should resist adjustment and strive instead for autonomy.[23] Packard followed Riesman by lamenting the way Americans took their signals not from their sense of themselves but from the media. Driven by internal promptings more than by the opinion of others, he adopted a more thoroughgoing individualism than Riesman advocated. Packard defined nonconformity principally in terms of the desire to be free of restrictions and to be able to live apart from large bureaucratic institutions.

Packard feared that the hidden persuaders were moving America closer to the world that George Orwell had described in *Animal Farm* (1945) and *1984* (1949). Yet his interest in how society controlled the individual seemed sparked not at all by a haunting sense of the impact of totalitarianism or by the anti-Stalinism that others articulated during the 1950s. Drawing on his experience at *American Magazine*, Packard believed the danger was that Big Brother, represented by psychologists, market researchers, advertising agencies, and corporations, would invade privacy and erode self-determination. At one point, for example, he mentioned the way the business community simultaneously deplored "creeping socialism" and looked the other way when it came to industry's circumscription of freedom.[24]

Relying on the producer ethic, Packard expressed concern about the morality of a society built on happiness that was derived primarily from consumer goods. He bristled at Dichter's attempt to make hedonism moral by undermining the "old-fashioned puritanism of the average American" and by helping people overcome the guilt they felt when consuming conspicuously. Though he remained mute on the alternative to greater affluence, he took issue with the promotion of a growing GNP that rested on "a confidence-inspiring viewpoint, come hell or high water." He asserted that the broader question of the future of an economy based on consumerism was "destined to become one of the great moral issues of our times."[25]

In important ways, Packard dissented from the celebratory mood established by writers in the mass media, the business press, and some consensus intellectuals. What was responsible for the postwar's equation of spending and pleasure, he argued, was not irrational female consumers but the manipulative power of those who exploited the nation's fears and dreams.[26] Himself playing on what a critic called "overanxious fears of manipulation," Packard exaggerated the power of advertising, especially of MR.[27] He also overemphasized the degree to which ad agencies accepted MR, an approach that remained controversial in the industry. Taking the self-promoting claims of people like Dichter at face value and quickly passing over contradictory evidence, Packard could both criticize and unintentionally promote what they did. A Harvard professor of marketing stated in 1958 that though the "'hidden persuaders' in their exaggerated form are, in fact, made of straw," the most tangible result of Packard's book was "an increased and unrealistic demand for motivation research." Ironically, Packard's book allowed advertising agencies to complain bitterly about what he wrote and then call on people like Dichter to help them take advantage of the authority that *Hidden Persuaders* gave them.[28]

The ambiguity of Packard's book stemmed from a number of sources. *Hidden Persuaders* suffered from a tension between its critical framework and the often humorous stuff of its case studies. The larger argument sounded an alarm about the relationship between capitalism, individualism, and morality. When Packard focused on specific examples of how MR worked, however, he seemed more fascinated than alarmed. He almost fell off his chair laughing, he later remarked, when typing material for the book, a response that underscored his love of the preposterous.[29] He did not always make it clear if it was the means or the ends that were bad.[30] Although some read *Hidden Persuaders* as a sweeping attack on Madison Avenue, Packard had found fault mainly with those who exploited new manipulative approaches. "A great many" of those involved in advertising, he reported, "fill an important and constructive role in our society," by fostering economic growth and offering ads that were "tasteful, honest works of artistry."[31] In addition, the focus on MR underplayed the larger connections between the social sciences and advertising in the 1950s. Moreover, he offered few remedies for what he descried. His principal solution—greater consumer self-awareness—involved both demystification and self-help for the fascinated. An advertisement for the book suggested that reading it would provide answers to questions such as "WHY are little girls being psychoanalyzed by some firms who are trying to sell home permanents?"[32]

When *Hidden Persuaders* remained on the best-seller list month after month after month, Packard's career was at a critical juncture. He derived some satisfaction from the fact that *Reader's Digest* paid him twice for the same piece, this time as a reprint from *Harper's Bazaar*. But the real pleasure came from the income and sense of achievement that *Hidden Persuaders* brought. With a mixture of skill and luck, considerable but fluctuating royalties would govern the way he could choose to live. If he could sustain himself economically as a book author, a big *if* in 1957, attention-getting reviews and a place on the best-seller list might transform him from a relatively unknown but widely read journalist employed by a corporation into a nationally recognized free-lance author.

Although the success of the book was soon apparent, Packard continued to worry about his future. He was concerned that his attacks on advertising might scare editors off from accepting his articles.[33] "I still feel my head is very much out on the chopping block as a writer for magazines which depend on advertising," he remarked two months before the appearance of the book.[34] Writing to his publisher in May 1957 when sales began to take off, he identified "a special problem of a long-range kind developing" out of the book's promotion. He wondered "what kind of *image* (to use a M.R. phrase) is being created about *me*." Was he coming across, he asked people at McKay, in a way that reflected his concern about his book's being too adversarial, "as a perceptive and incisive observer of the contemporary scene, or . . . as a radical, arm-waving sensationalist?" Mixing irony and fear, he suggested that the fact that reviewers used words like "horror," "frightening," "Big Business," and "manipulation" might be having "the cumulative effect—or 'residual impression' to use another phrase from my book—of suggesting that I am pulling out all the stops to create a sensation."[35]

The public relations specialist at McKay responded to these expressions of doubt. "So, you're sitting on top of the world," Carolyn Anthony wrote, "and seeing nothing but ghosts." People are "looking at you as a *reporter*, not an ax-grinder," she remarked. Pointing to an author who had six related books published between 1936 and 1958 that had been best-sellers, she urged Packard to think about becoming "another John Gunther, . . . a reporter who becomes known for doing inside stories, and in an honest fashion."[36] In the summer of 1957, a friend from Packard's days at *American Magazine* encouraged him with the advice that "one more book in the field of sociological phenomenon ought to do the trick for you." He urged Packard to think about cultivating "the growing picture of Packard, the expert."[37]

The Status Seekers: Diminished Opportunity and Increased Anxiety in the Midst of Affluence

Although Packard continued to worry about his future, he was soon at work on his next project. Several months before *Hidden Persuaders* appeared, he had told his publisher that if it made a "sizeable public impression," then his next work would be "a kindred book taking another belt at some aspect of contemporary society." Inspired by the success of Whyte's *Organization Man*, he was looking for a subject that would touch the " 'national nerve' " by focusing on "how to achieve a creative life in these conforming times." Many Americans, he wrote his publisher, "resent the growing conformity and sterility of their life where they are left only with the roles of being consumers or spectators."[38]

By the summer of 1957 Packard had settled on an examination of status consciousness and social divisions in America.[39] In October, he signed a contract with McKay that provided for an advance of five thousand dollars.[40] Packard later termed *Status Seekers*, which appeared exactly two years after *Hidden Persuaders*, the "lightest" of any of the books he authored. Yet at the time he wrote that he hoped it would be "a contribution to scholarship," albeit "in compelling terms that will assure it a wide readership." Though this second of the three number one best-sellers drew on material in its predecessor, Packard's interest also stemmed from a marketing study that Eleanor Rawson brought to his attention, a study that explored the relationship between social class and patterns of consumption.[41]

Once he completed the research in the spring of 1958 and began writing, Packard traveled for several months in Europe, placing the material for the book in a trunk on the top of the car.[42] "While his seventeen-year-old son drove across the Alps last summer," a reporter noted, "author Vance Packard sat in the back seat peering over the preliminary notes" for the book. "As his family strolled leisurely through sunny Italian streets," the story continued, "Mr. Packard stayed in his hotel room correlating piles of sociological material. While they shopped and saw the sights, he delved deep into a stack of research data dealing with America's class structure."[43] Upon returning home, Packard completed the writing and sent the manuscript off by November 1958.[44]

In writing *Status Seekers*, Packard was reacting to claims that affluence was increasing social mobility in America and decreasing class and ethnic divisions. "Since writers, academics, and advertising executives came from the very segment of society making the most rapid gains," a historian has noted, "they found it easy to believe everyone was riding the same wave of prosperity."[45] The immediate context of Packard's response to the rosy picture of American society was an editorial in *Life* that, he later remarked, "exulted that the United States had finally achieved the 'most truly classless society in history.'"[46] Similarly, in 1955 the editors of *Fortune* hailed "the rise of the great mass into the new moneyed middle class," a change that was "erasing old class lines" and elevating "proletarians" into "America's booming new middle-income class." The lines between income groups were becoming "remarkably penetrable," "inconspicuous consumption" was making spending patterns more uniform, and people were trying "to keep *down* with the Joneses."[47] Pluralists argued, a historian has remarked, "that the commonality among ethnic Americans was greater and more powerful than their differences, which were vestigial and would soon disappear."[48] Claims such as these prompted one observer to comment that "there is subconscious agreement among the vast majority of Americans that the United States is not evolving *toward* socialism but *past* socialism."[49]

The question of whether postwar Americans had greater opportunities for social mobility than their ancestors or than contemporary Europeans evoked quite varied answers. While some social scientists argued that opportunity was diminishing, others emphasized the continuing uniqueness and openness of American society.[50] A distinguished anthropologist wrote, "Perhaps one should avoid the word 'class' with its misleading European connotations and speak of 'status groups.'"[51] There was some evidence to confirm the claims of celebrants of American opportunity.[52] Millions of people crossed the boundary from manual to nonmanual work, more of them going upward than downward. Many workers, especially unionized ones, put poverty behind them. Postwar economic and social changes confounded older hierarchies of class and status. Skilled and unionized factory laborers began to earn more income than teachers and social workers.

However, paradise was not quite at hand. Discrimination and segregation sustained divisions between African Americans and whites. Women faced hostility as they tried to remain in the work force and improve their positions. The working class hardly disappeared. Though some laborers "acquired the trappings of middle-class life," a historian noted, they did so "while inwardly retaining their working-class identity."[53] Clear fissures persisted between skilled and unskilled workers; and, in the middle class, between managers and clerks. Suburban development drew only on the upper 40 percent of the population, especially families headed by managers and professionals. Given the combination of prosperity and uncertainty, people grew increasingly preoccupied with symbols of status. In suburbs and office buildings, minor distinctions in style produced exaggerated differences in status. By 1960, the distribution of income was not substantially different from what it had been in 1945. In 1960 the top 5 percent of the population controlled more than half of the nation's wealth, while the bottom 20 percent held only a twentieth. As many as one in four Americans lived in poverty—African Americans and Puerto Ricans in inner cities; whites in Appalachia; African Americans, whites, Indians, and Chicanos in rural areas; the elderly and single mothers across the nation.

Against this background, Packard argued in *Status Seekers* that the nation's "fantastic" extent of affluence, by strengthening the "barriers and humiliating distinctions of social class," was intensifying status striving.[54] Because he saw America's problems coming from those who tried to manipulate consumers, Packard did not direct his work toward the debate over the dangers of a mass culture. Where liberal intellectuals traced the origins of the problem of mass society to mindless consumers, Packard blamed consumer culture developed by capitalists. Advertisers, he wrote, wanted "to put some sizzle into their messages by stirring up our status consciousness" and "sometimes playfully call themselves 'merchants of discontent.'" Unless people could look forward to the possibility of upward social mobility, he cautioned, a "prolonged recession" might rub off "the patina of prosperity," put Americans "in an ugly mood," and make the "new stratifications . . . uncomfortably apparent and embarrassing." For the time being, clear distinctions among classes had diminished, he argued, as more and more people enjoyed larger incomes that enabled them to own "one-time upper-class symbols" such as powerboats and mink coats. Such evidence made it possible for some to promote what Packard saw as the incorrect belief that prosperity was helping America achieve the dream of an egalitarian society. He thus questioned the conclusion, common among market researchers and even among those intellectuals who celebrated the results of prosperity, that sustained economic growth was turning the nation into a classless society. Rather, he asserted, "under its gloss of prosperity" the nation was becoming more socially divided as people scrambled "to find new ways to draw lines that will separate the elect from the non-elect."[55]

At the heart of the book was evidence, drawn mainly from market researchers and social scientists, on the relationship between consumption and status. Here Packard displayed his eye for what he found fascinating and preposterous. He drew upon Thorstein Veblen's *Theory of the Leisure Class* (1899) in a number of ways: by preferring practical engineers over wasteful executives; by contrasting real work with false consumption; and by exploring the hidden significance of everyday items, especially the true meaning lurking behind the pretensions of the wealthy. Packard's commitment to producer values came through in his preference for workmanship and his hostility to status based on materialism. *Status Seekers* also provided readers with material they could use in their own quest for higher status. "If we aspire to rise in the world but fail to take on the coloration of the group we aspire to . . ." Packard noted, "our chances of success are diminished." He educated his readers about the occupations that provided the greatest financial rewards and offered ways they could gauge their own social position.[56]

Nowhere was his material more vivid than in the chapter titled "Snob Appeal = Today's Home Sweet Home." There Packard chronicled the marks used to distinguish homes: keywords such as "estate," "exclusive," and "executive" and symbolic touches like gas lanterns and colonial decor suggesting that the occupants had roots in the nation's past. Top executives lived on estates, "beautifully manicured on the outside, highly polished on the inside," with period furniture, family portraits, books bound in leather, and a paneled den with leather chairs and old sporting prints. Houses for those who lacked money but not aspirations displayed air conditioners, television aerials, monogrammed towels, antiques, and classical records.[57]

Turning "from the horizontal social-class grouping to the vertical ethnic-class" ones, a shift he made without successfully grappling with the relationships between the two types of classification, Packard focused on other marks of difference. Real estate developers learned that people of British ancestry preferred an early American motif. In contrast, market researchers revealed that Italian Americans looked for what one builder called "'lots of goop,'" such as marble and stucco. Polish Americans chose what a developer labeled decoration that was "'very garish, with loud, screaming colors.'" Jews wanted houses on small lots so they could more easily chat with their neighbors and so the husbands, who had neither "the temperament nor the know-how" of the do-it-yourselfer, would not have to care for a large yard. What Packard had learned as a young farm boy—that a home should not be a badge of social position—made him feel offended by what he saw in the American suburbs. Now an exurbanite very much shaped by his own situation and by the 1950s, he asserted that home was to be "a private and very individual haven" where people turned "inward rather than outward for inspiration in the creation of one's homestead."[58]

A series of factors, he argued, had transformed American society. With work in large national corporations increasingly fragmented and impersonal, employees derived less social prestige, job satisfaction, and self-esteem from their labor. As stepping-stones disappeared, skill levels increased, management grew more isolated, and unions discouraged extra effort, Americans lost their ambition and initiative. Similar changes had sharply downgraded "the amount of skill and dignity" of millions of white-collar workers, something Packard well understood from his experience with corporations. Bigness and impersonality also characterized labor unions, military organizations, educational institutions, and government bureaucracies.[59] In developing these points, Packard was following other writers in the 1950s who worried that changes in postwar America were undermining traditions of independence, autonomy, and individualism. But he did so as someone who took his bearings from an earlier America.

With opportunity blocked and status striving exaggerated, Packard argued, millions of Americans were suffering emotionally, frightened "by the anxieties, inferiority feelings, and straining generated by this unending process of rating and status striving." Americans, he wrote in a way that expanded upon rating schemes Willard Waller had noted in American dating patterns twenty years previously, were constantly trying "to surround themselves with visible evidence of the superior ranking they are claiming." Perhaps reflecting upon the experience of European totalitarianism during the 1930s, Packard wrote that with status intensifying and social boundaries getting more rigid, an economic setback might increase the frustration of those "frozen into the lower layers" and thus fuel "a movement for the nationalization of industry."[60]

Shut off from social advancement, bored with their jobs, and lacking the "pride of initiative or creativity," blue-collar and white-collar workers could feel they were getting somewhere by increasing material consumption. Like writers such as Daniel Bell, Packard believed that consumption became compensation for the loss of meaningful work.[61] Consequently, people consumed "flamboyantly, much as the restless Roman masses found diversion in circuses thoughtfully provided by the emperors." Advertisers and market researchers were foremost among the villains who persuaded people to seek satisfaction through consumer goods, not jobs. Advertisers had intensified feeling about status by encouraging the achievement of success and status through self-indulgence. At the same time that they promoted the vision of a classless society, he noted, advertisers exaggerated the importance of specific ways of identifying status.[62]

Like the historian David M. Potter in *People of Plenty: Economic Abundance and the American Character* (1954), Packard emphasized the costs of mobility and explored the benefits of a more integrated and stable life. Potter had hoped that abundance might make it possible to "relax the tensions of mobility, keeping it as an instrument for the self-fulfillment of the individual but dispensing with it as a social imperative."[63] What Potter took from his origins as a Southern gentleman, Packard derived from his evocation of the farm and small town where he had grown up before World War II. Unlike Potter, Packard embraced the fullest measure of social mobility. He spoke out against a social system based on "ascribed status" because it ran counter to American ideals and to his own preference for the status earned in a society that encouraged new talent.[64]

Packard worried that a decline in social mobility might undermine what he saw as the American Dream of abundant opportunity. The United States, he wrote, was no longer a unique society; even some European nations had developed a more "open-class system, where the poor but talented young can rise on their merits." Although he divided people into five social classes, he saw the real chasm between the Diploma Elite and the Supporting Classes. It was becoming increasingly difficult for a person to rise in larger businesses without an education beyond high school. He cautioned against exaggerating the extent to which members of the working class had entered the middle class, noting how "many of the new white-collar jobs are essentially manual or require little skill." Yet he remained worried about how blue-collar workers, especially union members, had gained in income or social position. "The better-paid blue-collar working people such as craftsmen and foreman," he argued, "are coming to dominate the middle-class positions in our society." He reserved some of his ire for organization men "who have successfully shed their rough edges of individualism," and especially for those who "manage to become rebels at night," turning into people who were "wicked wits and flaming liberals in the safety of their patios and favorite bars."[65]

Packard's critique of a status-driven present rested on a naive vision of a better past. The book appeared before historians discovered that rates of social mobility in the United States had not changed dramatically over time. His argument went against the grain of those who celebrated the openness of the American system. From his childhood experiences on a farm watching cows establish a pecking order and from his studies of animal behavior, he had concluded that a hierarchy was natural. No nation, the USSR included, had succeeded in building a truly classless society. Packard commented that perhaps America around 1870, with its frontier still open and its industry still undeveloped, came "closest to a genuine system of equality of opportunity." Even before 1940, he argued, the chances for social mobility and social intercourse were more prevalent than in the 1950s, an observation that rested on the perspective of a white Protestant male from small-town America and that minimized the limitations people had faced because of their gender, ethnicity, and race. He recalled his own experiences as a child "attending Protestant churches that drew their congregation from virtually the entire community." He remembered a time when neighbors knew each other well enough so they "could be judged for their personal worth rather than by the trappings of status they exhibited." In contrast, most contemporary suburbs lacked class and ethnic diversity and instead had a "synthetic, manipulated quality of community life." He also regretted that large organizations lacked the "democratic custom" of an earlier day.[66]

Packard's nostalgia emerged in other ways. He rejected the way contemporaries judged each other by "the trappings of status they exhibited." The danger of a status-driven society was that, by "conspiring to squeeze individuality and spontaneity from us," it undermined the power and prevalence of the independent and self-respecting individual. Perhaps recalling the pain his father had suffered when he switched from yeoman farmer to state employee, Packard lamented the replacement of a "true middle class" of "small entrepreneurs and self-employed people" by organization men. He looked back to a day when men without college educations had grounds for believing they could rise within the society, something that was still possible on Main Street and "with a small or pioneering producing firm," and, he might have added, for his father. *Status Seekers* thus echoed a theme of Packard's pre-1957 magazine writing, that America was still an open society for entrepreneurs who stayed in small towns. Feeling his own emancipation from bureaucratic captivity, he criticized "the withering of individuality of the 'teammates'" and celebrated the "lone wolves." In a 1959 article in *Ladies' Home Journal*, he honored Americans who earned fortunes through risk taking, hard work, and imagination and yet "feel no desire to impress the world with their wealth." Such examples proved that America was "still a land of opportunity for the individualistic adventurer."[67]

One of his principal solutions to the problems of a status-conscious society was to enhance the understanding of one group by another. By comprehending the entire society and not just their particular place in it, Americans might "lead more effective lives, and quite probably more serene ones." Packard's second solution was opening up opportunity. He criticized college-educated and economically comfortable Protestant men, who he believed should have had the least cause for concern about social position, for erecting barriers against Jews in corporations, clubs, and neighborhoods. Packard's solution to the problems of blocked mobility was to make class distinctions less burdensome by ensuring that the society discovered people of real talent and then helped them reach their potential. He advocated open access to higher education, especially for "all of high native ability" and for those discouraged by the high cost or by "an environment of resignation, ostracism, and hedonism."[68]

Unlike others who argued that America's actual achievements were a foil for the USSR's weaknesses, Packard insisted that only by overcoming problems could American exceptionalism, based on the restoration of a better past, be a true counter to the Soviet Union's example. Yet he still worked within a Cold War framework. He argued that opportunity was important because America needed all of the talent available to meet the challenges it faced, including dealing with "the state of precarious adjustment in our relations with other major societies (notably Russia's)." He found it "most disheartening" that "the nation that poses as a model for the democratic world," through decisions that excluded outsiders from clubs, neighborhoods, and jobs, was erecting invidious barriers to advancement up the ladder to social success. "In this time of transcendent challenge and danger to our way of life," he wrote at the end of the book, doubtlessly with the struggle between the United States and the USSR in mind, America could "endure and prevail only if" most citizens had confidence that "our system" offered "fairer rewards and opportunities for the fulfillment of human aspirations than any other."[69]

Status Seekers was better at synthesizing the work of others than it was at striking out on an original path. Virtually everything Packard said, contemporary authors had said before. Packard acknowledged that he had relied on others for the central ideas of the book. His contribution was in assembling the data and ideas that others had developed and then making that information more accessible to a lay audience. The originality came when he supported his arguments against the benefits of classlessness and affluence with data on how advertisers were trying to increase status identification and thereby class division. What spurred him on was that advertisers were accentuating divisions even while the business community was emphasizing the rise of America as a classless society. In addition, much that can be said in criticism of *Hidden Persuaders* applies also to the second of his best-sellers. Here again, Packard confused what marketers said with what people actually did and felt. *Status Seekers*, like its predecessor, combined horror and fascination. Packard continued to evoke an American past where all was well. Moreover, as much as it was a book of social criticism, it also offered practical self-help to the perplexed. Not very rigorous in its handling of tough theoretical issues, the book tended to fudge critical distinctions between class, status, and ethnicity.

Still, *Status Seekers* was important because it challenged the celebrations of American exceptionalism. Reflecting the liberal feminism of the late 1950s, Packard discussed the feminization of the lower echelons of white-collar workers, decried job discrimination against women, and bemoaned the way corporations treated the wives of their male executives. He recognized the real problems that workers faced, pointing out that those "in the bottom class" encountered "the most severe strain." He acknowledged the existence of a true lower class, made up largely of African Americans, that lived in inner cities and lacked steady employment. He recognized the force of residential segregation in housing and remained hopeful that integration would help the nation achieve racial balance in cities and suburbs.[70]

Yet as was true in most social analyses of the decade, the problems faced by women, African Americans, and the poor were not among Packard's principal concerns. Despite the ways in which he challenged the placid consensus of the 1950s, his book's central focus was the plight of the middle-class male who lived in a suburb and worked in a large organization. As he had in his magazine articles, Packard tended to exaggerate the degree to which working-class and lower-middle-class Americans could participate in the affluent society, stating at one point that prosperity allowed "plumbers to drive limousines." To a middle-class audience anxious about its status, Packard continued to sound a note of alarm when he wrote that the earnings of blue-collar workers were growing relative to those of white-collar employees.[71] As in his *American Magazine* story on Maine farmers who were living the life of luxury with the aid of government subsidies, in *Status Seekers* Packard seemed most fearful about the impact of economic and social changes on members of the middle class who had no powerful institutions to protect them. Worried about blocked opportunity, he did not focus on prejudice against African Americans. Indeed, reflecting commonly held ideas of the 1950s, in one instance he pointed favorably to S. I. Hayakawa's advice that African Americans could gain acceptance by "acting naturally" and forgetting "as far as possible that one is Negro."[72] Rather, drawing on firsthand fieldwork in Rochester, New York, he reserved his sharpest words for the anti-Semitism of white upper-class men who excluded Jews from major institutions. This focus, though admirable, underscored the way he worried about the social problems of the affluent more than about the difficulties facing those in poverty.

Packard's definition of America's problems reflected his own social isolation and underscored his tendency to confuse trivial and genuine solutions. Antiurban and yet lamenting the deteriorating conditions of inner cities, he hoped to bring heterogeneity to suburbs. Reflecting the Exciting Lives he wrote about in his Boston days, Packard said that people who lived only among their own kind would "never know the exhilaration and fascination of having as friends such colorful and often wonderfully articulate people as clam diggers, house movers, volunteer fire chiefs."[73] Shortly after the book's publication, in a way that reflected a nostalgia tinged with primitivism, he wrote of watching a movie "about life in a Samoan village," which reminded him of the "wonderful 'socials'" of Bradford County that had been open to everyone "regardless of age or economic status." He talked about a repairman he had known who turned out to be a part-time artist, short story writer, and world traveler. Packard concluded from these encounters that it was important to take "affirmative action" to break out of social isolation. When having a party, he recommended inviting school-teachers from underprivileged sections of the city, exchange students, African Americans, and commercial fishermen. He also suggested taking a vacation in a place where people would be "altogether different from yourself," holding up as an example a friend of his who went native in a New England fishing village. Finally, he suggested that his readers get involved in projects, such as town politics, that crossed status lines. He knew many wives, he remarked, who volunteered in order to "broaden their personal horizons."[74]

Obviously, there were limits to how effectively his suggestions could help Americans overcome social isolation, let alone solve social problems. Inviting a handyman to a party or getting involved in New Canaan politics could go only so far. Packard himself lacked social pretentiousness. Yet as one contemporary critic noted, "I suspect Mr. Packard of feeling that he ought to find his clam diggers and volunteer fire chiefs fascinating, but really prefers other writers, artists, and professional folk."[75]

The comparison of *Status Seekers* with other influential or popular analyses of American society published during the 1950s underscores the strengths and weaknesses of Packard's approach. Contemporaries often mentioned this book in the same breath as Riesman's *Lonely Crowd* (1950), Whyte's *Organization Man* (1956), and C. Wright Mills's *Power Elite* (1956), all works on which Packard drew.[76] Thus in 1957, an editorial in *Life* remarked that "some of our recent books have been scaring the pizazz out of us with the notion of a Lonely Crowd . . . bossed by a Power Elite . . . flim-flammed by Hidden Persuaders and emasculated into a neuter drone called the Organization Man."[77] All these authors worried about the autonomy of middle-class men who worked in bureaucracies and lived in suburbs. Packard shared with these writers an emphasis on the costs of affluence, the dangers of conformity, and the problems of personal autonomy. Like Riesman and Whyte, he rejected both nineteenth-century individualism and 1930s communitarianism, focusing instead on how to achieve self-determined individualism within the existing social order. The books of Whyte, Riesman, and Packard provided data and strategies that would enable readers to demystify society's codes in order to achieve greater personal freedom. The three authors tended to psychologize social and cultural phenomena rather than to embrace programs for fundamental transformation of the social order. None of them really grappled with political solutions to the problems that their analyses revealed.[78]

Though Packard shared much with Riesman and Whyte, he also differed from them in important ways. Compared with *Organization Man* and *Lonely Crowd, Status Seekers* was more accessible, derivative, and nostalgic, as well as less subtle, sophisticated, well crafted, and measured. More critical of capitalism than Riesman or Whyte and lacking Riesman's faith in the pluralism that resulted from the competition of veto groups, Packard went beyond emphasis on the power that the corporate world had to shape the individual's psyche to focus, more than Riesman or Whyte, on the ability of big business to influence politics and society. Despite his concentration on the psychological and despite the degree to which his critique echoed theirs, Packard asserted, albeit tentatively and sometimes vaguely, that public policy provided legitimate ways of addressing social grievances. Whatever his equivocations, Packard also went farther in asking his readers to question basic assumptions about the beneficence of American society and economy. His emphasis on blocked mobility, discrimination, and social divisions gave his analysis of society a critical edge and a breadth that the other analyses sometimes lacked.

The comparison of *Status Seekers* with Mills's *Power Elite* and *White Collar* (1951) places Packard's work in a more problematic light. To be sure, some similarities were evident. He drew on Mills (and others) for key notions such as blocked opportunity, status panic, social conflict, alienated work, the moral vacuity of consumption, and the role of higher education in social mobility. Packard replaced the optimism of his magazine articles with concern, at times even alarm, which he shared with the Columbia sociologist, about the gap between American ideals and realities. Here the similarities ended. Unlike Riesman, Whyte, or Packard, Mills successfully linked private and public issues. Focusing principally on the middle class, Packard lacked Mills's penetrating analysis of the way interlocking elites dominated society. Mills's critique of the 1950s consensus was more serious, sustained, far-reaching, and probing than Packard's. Through simplification, Packard could take the troublesome questions Mills raised and tame them, making them more fascinating than challenging.[79] In short, Packard lacked Mills's sweep and critical edge.[80]

In writing *Status Seekers*, Packard was operating on the border between human interest journalism and the social sciences. As a work of observation from the hand of a magazine writer, Packard's book compared favorably with John Keats's *Crack in the Picture Window* (1956) and *Insolent Chariots* (1958); Russell Lynes's *Snobs* (1950) and *Surfeit of Honey* (1957); and A. C. Spectorsky's *Exurbanites* (1955). Packard shared with these journalists-turned-social-commentators an ability to mix a sense of humor, a keen eye for detail, and observation of the way manners reflected the forces transforming American life. However, Packard tested the limits of the genre they developed. More social criticism and muckraking, and less social satire, his trilogy included translations of academic research and offered a more biting and comprehensive critique of the whole society.

The success of *Status Seekers* began to transform Packard's self-definition and the way others saw him. In the short period between 1957 and 1960, most reviewers stopped calling him a journalist or magazine writer and began to identify him as a social critic.[81] In the spring of 1959, he wrote his publisher that he hoped "to establish a beachhead as a 'social critic'—as I'm now widely being described—and not have to go back to the magazine writing business."[82] Recognizing the importance of the new label, Packard encouraged its use. "Asked to define himself," a reporter remarked in May 1959, "Packard paused lengthily as though he had never before considered either the question or the answer." He then replied, saying, "'I don't know what I am,'... 'They've been using the word 'social critic' and I guess that's all right with me.'"[83] Packard bristled whenever someone suggested he was merely a popularizer. "I see myself as a social critic rather than a bringer of the social sciences to the public," he remarked to an audience of social scientists in 1965. Even as late as 1980, he cautioned against the use of the "denigrating label 'pop sociologist.'" Arguing that he covered "a far broader range of human affairs than the sociologist, pop or otherwise," he wanted to replace this term "with something such as 'author' or 'social critic' or 'social observer.'"[84] The decision to call himself a social critic was a fateful one. In many ways, he approached these three books as he did magazine pieces, as assignments to do before moving on to the next task. He did not yet take himself absolutely seriously as an author.[85] Now, however, reviewers were judging him as an analyst and critic. Unaware of the consequences of his decision, he set himself up to be evaluated by new standards, standards commonly applied to public intellectuals, standards that were hard to live up to.

The Waste Makers: The World of Planned Obsolescence

Although he was still not sure his career as book author was secure, by the time *Status Seekers* appeared Packard was at work on *Waste Makers*.[86] On 23 December 1959, he signed a four-book contract with McKay. For each book, the publisher promised $10,000 for hardback and $50,000 for paperback. Packard insisted on a clause in the contract stating that although McKay had the right to decline to publish what he wrote, the subject matter and content was "within the sole discretion of the Author." Henceforth, he later commented, after the acceptance of the general theme and format of the work, only illegibility of the manuscript or statements that raised legal issues could prevent publication.[87] Such an acceptability clause was unusual; it was important to Packard because it confirmed his freedom as a writer and minimized the power of the publisher to control what he said.

At the same time, Packard also formalized the arrangements for representation of his interests with publishers that would last until the early 1990s. For *Hidden Persuaders*, he had used a literary agent. Dissatisfied that he was not available at a critical moment, with *Status Seekers* Packard changed to another. In both instances, he used agents to handle business issues, not as sounding boards for his ideas. Though he continued to rely on an agent for foreign sales until the early 1970s, with *Status Seekers* Harriet F. Pilpel took over the job of negotiating and overseeing his contracts, an association that continued until her death in 1991.[88] A distinguished lawyer who specialized in cases involving civil liberties and women's rights, Pilpel read book proposals, drafts of some manuscripts, and, more generally, offered the aid and comfort of a friend.

Scarcely before the ink was dry on the contract, Packard faced an unexpected emergency when on Christmas Eve of 1959 a fire raged through the New Canaan house. "Sparks from the Packards' roaring Yuletide log rose up the chimney," *Time* reported, and "removed all chance of a visit from Santa by setting fire to the wood-shingled roof." With its usual jibes at Packard's symbols of status, the Luce publication went on to say that "in the best Early American tradition, the Packards retrieved their Christmas present packages, opened them the next day in their Federalist garage apartment."[89] For Packard, this was no time for humor. "The problems of rebuilding my house after that damned fire," he wrote a few months later, "have slowed me up a couple of weeks."[90]

Nonetheless, work on the book proceeded, if anything too quickly. Because the time between the publication of *Status Seekers* and *Waste Makers* would be only about seventeen months, Packard wondered if a complication might arise "if it *seems* short to critics and the public." After all, he wrote his publisher, "the impression we create is a tricky business."[91] Worrying about "the hazards of over-exposure," he was justifiably nervous that reviewers might recognize the consequences his pace had for the quality of his prose and argument.[92] Yet in 1959 Packard had reason not to delay, a reason that would affect the pace of his work in the future as well. He learned in the summer of that year that someone was writing a book that would compete with his. So he sped up his timetable, sending the family home early from Chappaquiddick and completing his book with dispatch.[93]

In the fall of 1960 *Waste Makers* appeared, the third of the number one best-sellers that established Packard's reputation as a social critic. Although in *Hidden Persuaders* he had touched on some of the issues he now raised, the more immediate origin of the project lay elsewhere. In the spring of 1957, William Zabel, a Princeton undergraduate, had written a long paper on planned obsolescence in a course taught by H. H. Wilson, a professor who was skeptical of the claims that big business was benevolent—a perspective that influenced a number of his students, including Ralph Nader. When Packard came to Princeton to deliver a talk, Zabel approached him and mentioned the subject of his paper. Packard hired Zabel, paying him a lump sum for summer research and for the right to use his paper. When he published *Waste Makers*, Packard acknowledged the student's contribution and drew on his case studies and his exploration of planned obsolescence.[94] Packard knew the book would be "highly provocative," "extraordinarily timely," and might "touch off some violent denunciations."[95]

With *Waste Makers*, Packard was responding to a series of changes in postwar America, especially the increasing pace of technological innovation and the rapid shifts in styles. Though these were hardly new phenomena, Packard correctly understood that manufacturers and advertisers had devised strategies to tempt consumers to buy products they wanted but did not necessarily need. "The challenge to business," remarked the editors of *Fortune* in 1955, "is to keep up with the market's potentialities not only by making and selling more of everything but by improving, varying, and adorning everything—by blurring still further the already blurred line that distinguishes Americans' luxuries and Americans' necessities."[96] The automobile industry set the pace by introducing a wide range of options: power accessories, air-conditioning, a full pallet of colors and body styles, and a cornucopia of gadgets. Americans traded in and traded up, with these choices tempting them to equate the new with the better.[97] In 1950, a retailing executive argued that "basic utility cannot be the foundation of a prosperous apparel industry. We must accelerate obsolescence."[98]

Packard was not the first person to take up the issue of economic waste. In 1925, in *The Tragedy of Waste*, the technocratic progressive Stuart Chase had explored some of the questions Packard now considered. Though Packard and Chase shared a number of approaches, their perspectives also differed. If Chase concentrated on the wastefulness of capitalist production, Packard riveted on the excesses generated by Madison Avenue's tactics. Chase's solution, national economic planning that relied on a union of a technical elite and the working class, was more radical than Packard's. In addition, where Chase worried that inefficiency hurt the poor economically, Packard's concern was that wastefulness hurt the middle class psychologically.[99] More recently, John Kenneth Galbraith, in the best-selling *Affluent Society* (1958), had turned the nation's attention to the contrast between the private opulence of tail-finned cars and the public poverty of the national transportation system.

With *Waste Makers*, Packard offered his most thoroughgoing critique of America as an affluent society. He argued that the nation's enormous productivity had forced the business community to invent new methods to sustain the economy. The result was a widespread commitment to use an increasing GNP as the mark of national success. Employing a metaphor that had some resonance for him, Packard hoped that America could "thrive reasonably well without force feeding." Dedicated to his parents, who, Packard wrote, "have never confused the possession of goods with the good life," *Waste Makers* argued that the United States faced the problem not of scarcity but of overabundance. Regardless of whether they really needed these goods, Americans had learned that continual prosperity demanded that they must consume more and more. Although he acknowledged that millions of American families lacked adequate food, clothing, and shelter, he nonetheless concentrated on the way prosperity seemed "to spill over into the aisles of stores, spread along the highways, and bulge out the doors, windows, and attics of houses." Though hardly blind to the Soviet Union's faults, Packard dissented from the way the media, politicians, and members of the business community used competition with the USSR to justify more rapid economic growth, a focus that he felt distracted the United States from grappling with issues more central to the quality of life.[100]

Though at the outset Packard stated that "if I can help it, there will be no villains in this book," in fact he lay blame at the feet of boastful businessmen, laborers who lacked a sense of workmanship, and politicians like President Dwight D. Eisenhower who implored people to help the nation buy its way out of a recession. Packard was especially critical of conniving market researchers and advertising executives. Market researchers, he argued, systematically developed techniques to transform millions of Americans "into voracious, wasteful, compulsive consumers."[101] Packard devoted almost half of the book to an examination of newly developed strategies, gleaning his information from reading trade journals, interviewing product designers, and attending industry meetings. Corporations encouraged people to buy more goods or goods with frills and accessories when simple items sufficed. They promoted planned obsolescence by introducing products that broke down easily or whose style became quickly outmoded. In addition, the business community used installment debt to enable consumers to pay for present purchases with future income, packaged goods in a wasteful manner, and encouraged a hedonism that undermined the commitment to hard work and self-restraint.

Experts dreamed of a utopian "Cornucopia City" where buildings were made of papier-mâché, where every week a rocket would be launched into outer space, where the military could dump excess goods into the ocean, and where it would be "unpatriotic" for home owners "even to look inside an ailing appliance that is more than two years old." This future was a place where citizens could pass "their lifetime electronic credit cards in front of a recording eye" to facilitate their purchases in a "titanic push-button super mart built to simulate a fairyland," a place "where all the people spend many happy hours a week strolling and buying to their heart's content." Succumbing to the campaigns of marketing experts who had promoted a morality of hedonistic consumption, people spent more on "frivolous or playful or whimsical" private goods than on worthwhile public ones. Americans, increasingly seeking "their main life satisfaction" as consumers rather than producers, were becoming pleasure-minded, self-indulgent, materialistic, and passive.[102] Although in his earlier books Packard blamed advertisers and market researchers for foisting goods upon an innocent public, in *Waste Makers* he argued that consumers were culprits as well.

Packard went against the grain of the 1950s celebrations of prosperity built on rapid innovation and changes in taste. He picked up on the late 1950s concern about national purpose, arguing that the implications of affluence for American society were portentous. Excessive fascination with consumer goods had begun "*to make Americans look a bit fatuous in the eyes of the world,*" with the Soviets, for example, puzzled by the sense of values of a nation that placed so little emphasis on education and health care. By concentrating on obsolescence, marketing, and advertising rather than on technology, skills, and resources, Packard perspicaciously warned, the nation had begun to lose its competitive edge, thus opening itself to a flood of goods from abroad. Moreover, reflecting the producer ethic and the hostility to larger corporations that he had absorbed during his childhood, he argued that increasing attention to promotion and display encouraged *"the rise of business oligarchies."* The affluence that marketers promoted threatened to bring a real decline in the quality of American life, a judgment that reflected his concern that many middle-class Americans were losing the ability to resist consumer culture.[103]

Other consequences of economic growth were troublesome to Packard as well. The combination of more consumption and more people, he asserted, was forcing America to exhaust vital resources. Moreover, in its search for raw materials abroad, the United States was colonizing other countries and helping to develop friction among nations. He also lamented the way the commercialization of American life was "becoming so all-pervasive that at times it seems to be getting into the air the public breathes," causing "an unprecedented saturation of American life with pleas, hints, and other inducements to buy." His analysis of the impact of these changes on women, primarily those in the upper reaches of the working class and the lower reaches of the middle class, was especially telling of both his commitment to traditional roles for women and his ability to spot major social trends. The purchase of household appliances and prepared meals, he wrote, "tends to disenfranchise the wife by depriving her of many traditional, time-consuming homemaking functions." Pinched budgets and the diminished domestic challenges, Packard concluded with regret, "tend to send the wife out looking for a job."[104]

Above all, the waste makers threatened to change American character, undermining what Packard saw as values that had long stood the nation in good stead. Americans used to think of themselves "as a frugal, hard-working, God-fearing people making sacrifices for the long haul." Early in the nation's history, "puritanical traits" were essential to "settlers struggling to convert forest and prairie into a national homeland." In the nineteenth century, however, as greater numbers of Americans settled in urban areas, "hedonism as a guiding philosophy of life gained more and more disciples." Packard noted that "quite possibly, the environment of thickly settled areas brought a lessening of serenity and a feeling of being swallowed up that impelled people to strive for distinctive emblems and gratification through consumption." Greater concentrations of population, Packard argued in a way that reflected his antiurban bias, meant crowds, ugliness, noise, pollution, and threats to individual liberty. He wanted to attack urban blight, "the growing sleaziness, dirtiness, and chaos of the nation's great exploding metropolitan areas."[105]

When he turned to solutions to the problems that the new affluence caused, Packard warned that over the long run Americans had to balance the importance of a "satisfying way of life" with the preservation of "a reasonably thriving economy." He opposed what he saw as the two alternatives that dominated American politics: the "business-Republican-conservative" emphasis on increased population and the "liberal-Democratic-labor" commitment to economic growth. He called on Americans to seek other choices besides these. To begin with, they had to take "pride in prudent buying." They should follow the advice of Consumers Union and become self-respecting shoppers by demanding to "be approached on a rational basis, and protest" when they are not. Selecting plain and functional items, avoiding the new and fashionable, buying generic drugs, and learning how to repair broken items would help "restore today's consumer-citizen to this sovereignty he has lost." Packard also hoped manufacturers would once again emphasize quality and resist the guidance of marketers who promoted gimmicks and evanescent fashion.[106]

Beyond these methods, Packard called for even more fundamental changes. By curbing population growth, recycling materials, changing the tax laws, and rejecting planned obsolescence, the nation could begin to restore the balance between growing population and diminishing natural resources. With considerable accuracy he predicted that America would experience an oil shortage in 1973. He tempered his advocacy of shorter hours of work because he feared that people might use the time released to consume more. "In terms of life satisfaction," he warned, "acts of consumption are no adequate substitute for acts of individual productivity." Packard also toyed with the idea of having the nation "tune down the economy somewhat, even if it meant settling for a more modest level of living." He encouraged his readers to avoid changes in living standards that were superficial, such as buying multiple items of clothing when one would do or frequently trading in automobiles. He urged the nation to work instead toward historic innovations, such as the automobile, radio, refrigerator, and jet airplane, that "would fill a genuine need and represent a real breakthrough for technology." Finally, Packard hailed the coming dominance of a service economy because, unlike mining and manufacturing, "travel, cultural, or educational activities" made only a "modest" claim on natural resources and were "capable of greater reasonable expansion."[107]

Ultimately Packard's vision of a better society rested on a restoration of the balance between public and private needs and the enhanced opportunity for individual fulfillment through nonmaterial pleasures. Drawing on producer values and on the writings of Reinhold Niebuhr, Arthur M. Schlesinger, Jr., and Galbraith, he called for a reversal of the trend toward "private opulence amid public poverty." He hoped that the reduced commitment to unnecessary goods and services would enable the nation to devote more of its "creative energy" to improving the quality of life. Though he remained skeptical about the benefits of economic growth, much of what he wrote paralleled a liberal consensus emerging in the late 1950s concerning the agenda of American politics. Packard mentioned some of what in the early 1960s would become essential elements of the New Frontier and the Great Society. He focused on air pollution, conservation, urban slums, education, health care, public amenities, and the elderly. The problem, he realized, was that people did not like paying higher taxes. He recognized that "the opprobrium generally attached to taxes does not apply to taxes spent to build military barracks in North Carolina or maintain garrisons in Morocco." Packard joined others in calling for a turn away from military expenditures, which were an example of what he considered government prodigality. Beyond that, the solution was "a more mature citizenry" and a "more painless" way of getting taxes, such as through payroll deductions before the taxpayer saw the income.[108]

At the end of the book, Packard looked forward to a time when Americans would find new kinds of pleasures. The benefits of "ardent materialism" and "superabundance" had reached their limits. To encourage "self-respect, serenity, and individual fulfillment," it would be necessary to lift "the all-pervading smog of commercialism." He called on Americans to counter the pressure to define life satisfactions in terms of material possessions and develop opposition to merchants of discontent. In the construction of urban cultural centers and especially in the grass roots revival of music, art, and reading, he found signs of "a cultural renaissance in America." He believed that "such reflective, private pursuits . . . may help Americans gain a new perspective on their possessions in relation to other life satisfactions." He hoped that greater numbers of Americans would come "to see that cherished values and integrity of the soul have more to do with a well-spent life than self-indulgence." He admitted that he felt "a freshening of the spirit" whenever he would stroll "about the tree-shaded village green, peer into the lovely old spired, clean-lined churches, visit the still picturesque stores, chat with the natives, and walk among their two-century-old homes." Contemporary marketers, "with all their huffing and puffing to sell their packaged dream communities," had not been able to match the "spiritual and political environment" of these small New England villages.[109]

In the final analysis, Packard's solution to the problems of affluence in *Waste Makers* was more personal than political. He offered no legislative agenda, and his solutions relied as much on individual effort and the work of nonprofit organizations as on government action. At the end of *Waste Makers*, he recalled "one of the wisest, gayest, most inspiring, and most courageous" people he had ever met, an elderly woman who lived adjacent to his property on Chappaquiddick "in a lonely New England cottage" by the sea. She earned a "very modest income" by selling individualized greeting cards made from sea mosses placed on paper. Knowing a person such as this woman made him think many Americans would achieve greater satisfactions if they lived by a creed that emphasized nonmaterial pleasures, including "at least occasional dedication to the problems" of others, "a judicious attitude toward the values receivable from personal possessions," and "strongly held personal standards" on what constitutes good and evil, success and failure. Perhaps adversity, Packard speculated, would be necessary to bring Americans to appreciate these values. "The central challenge," he wrote in the book's last sentence, was that "Americans must learn to live with their abundance without being forced to impoverish their spirit by being damned fools about it."[110]

A comprehensive examination of America as it entered the 1960s, this last book of the trilogy was a forthright statement of Packard's faith. Though not without equivocation, it vigorously exposed some of the worst excesses of American industry and then called on the public to respond in a variety of constructive ways. As was true in *Status Seekers*, in this book also Packard exaggerated affluence and minimized poverty. "Haunting anxiety about where one's next meal or pair of shoes is coming from," he commented, "has become but a memory for all but a small proportion of the population that is unemployed or lives in rural slums or is engaged in migratory work." In the next sentence he offered an example that was as illustrative of his confidence in America as it was of his naiveté. "A Negro bootblack in Oklahoma," he noted, "proudly showed me his pair of thirty-dollar cowboy boots." He remained ambivalent toward the products of affluence. Though he extolled the simple life, he hailed the invention of jet planes. Similarly, in a way that reflected his fascination with new technologies and his ambivalence toward abundance, he recommended helping other countries develop nuclear energy as one way of enabling "the people of friendly nations [to] enjoy a little more of the fabulous abundance attained in the United States."[111]

As social criticism, the book relied on the new moralism, a righteous critique of the pursuit by middle-class Americans of the materialistic pleasures foisted upon the nation by corporations and professionals.[112] Even more so than in the first two books, Packard here equated what market researchers attempted to do with how consumers felt and behaved. Like its predecessors, this book was derivative, hasty, and exaggerated. He again articulated his vision of an America composed of independent individuals free from manipulation by outside and highly organized forces. Hailing efforts to "scrub up" the central cities, his discussions of what he and others called urban blight revealed his antiurban bias, his nostalgia, and his preference for distinctive contemporary suburbs.[113] This attitude toward cities, common to 1950s liberals before the publication of Jane Jacobs's *Death and Life of Great American Cities* in 1961, minimized the vitality of neighborhood life and the diversity of cosmopolitan centers.

More so than in the two previous books, in *Waste Makers* Packard recommended how to change the world for the better. He admitted that it was easier to diagnose than to suggest remedies, but what he wrote nonetheless more fully explored public solutions to the problems people faced than had his earlier books.[114] Yet, as was true in his other writings, at critical moments he often undercut his own recommendations. "Perhaps the United States has no acceptable alternative to ever-rising and wasteful consumption," he noted at one point and then went on to say that "this viewpoint deserves respect" though it was a position with which he did not agree. Elsewhere, having built up his case against the false pleasures of consumption, he stated, "Whether this trend to hedonism represents regress or progress may be arguable." He toyed with using advertising practices to achieve his goals, at one point suggesting that "the federal government should imitate private industry and offer projects requiring public consent to the public with such appeals as 'ONLY 3% (a month)' or 'ONLY $20 (down),'" with the parenthetical words in much smaller type. He had a tendency to consider solutions and then discard them. Characteristically, just at the moment when he seemed to be building to a crescendo of analysis and recommendation, he would fail to deliver a strong punch line and would instead move on to a new topic. Finally, Packard seemed unwilling to answer the question of how to provide "a sane, intelligent and satisfying way of life while preserving a reasonably thriving economy."[115]

The comparison of *Waste Makers* with Galbraith's *Affluent Society* reveals a good deal about Packard's strengths and weaknesses. Though his style was no match for Galbraith's, Packard drew on the economist's work, especially for ideas about the wastefulness of capitalism, the artificial creation of consumer demands, and the imbalance between private wealth and public constraints. They shared a skepticism about the equation of more consumer goods with a higher standard of living. Differences were nonetheless marked. Though they both saw affluence as a central social issue, Galbraith recognized poverty as a problem that society had to solve.

Nor was *Waste Makers* as bold in its political position as *Affluent Society*. Packard's psychological critique and often individualistic focus contrasted with Galbraith's emphasis on politics and economics and especially with his call for a more equitable distribution of income.

Whatever the strengths and weaknesses of *Hidden Persuaders*, *Status Seekers*, and *Waste Makers*, their publication solidified Packard's position as a free-lance writer of books and an influential social critic. They catapulted Packard out of his career as a journalist for magazines whose audience was shrinking and into the national limelight as a widely read author. By providing him with a steady income for the foreseeable future, the commercial success of these books transformed his career. As one contemporary commented, three best-sellers in a row was "'the kind of parlay both a horse player and an author can dream about but almost never experience.'"[116]

Marginal Man

The Emergence of an American Social Critic

The book-buying public rushed to read what Packard had written, in the process transforming his career. In less-tangible ways, the trilogy also helped to transform American life. A number of factors account for the popularity and impact of his three books. They appeared at a critical time in American life—after the most chilling effects of the Cold War and McCarthyism had begun to diminish, but before the new political agendas of the 1960s coalesced. Packard's works influenced Americans in a number of ways, not the least of which was the support they built for emerging social movements and, more generally, for the shift from a complacent 1950s to the more questioning mood of the 1960s. Packard articulated what many Americans sensed but had been unable to express, as he explained changes in the United States that excited and frightened those in the audience. His moral tone and ambivalent attitude toward consumer culture appealed to people who felt that something was wrong with affluent America but nonetheless enjoyed comforts that their parents had been unable to afford. Now a social critic, Packard also wore the hats of a journalist, a writer on the social and behavioral sciences, and a public intellectual. What some critics saw as weaknesses of the books—their ambivalence, nostalgia, moralism, and slickness—also helped account for their sales and impact.

Three Number One Best-sellers

Each of these books reached the number one position on the list of nonfiction best-sellers. *Hidden Persuaders*, which stayed at the top for a year, had the greatest sales, with almost three million copies in print by 1975.[1] *Status Seekers* remained at number one for more than four months and on the list for a year.[2] Although *Waste Makers* remained at the top for only a few weeks, it was on the list for about six months.[3] The American Library Association reported that in 1963 Packard was one of America's most widely read nonfiction writers.[4] With these three books Packard achieved what few if any other American nonfiction authors have done before or since—had three different books in the number one position on the bestseller list within four years.

These books launched Packard's career as a celebrity. He appeared on major television shows. Penn State honored him with its Distinguished Alumni Award in 1961 and Columbia's Graduate School of Journalism gave him two awards, one in 1958 and the second five years later.[5] During 1961, he held the most important leadership position of his life, the presidency of the Society of Magazine Writers, welcome recognition for someone whose peers had not chosen him to head the *Collegian* a quarter of a century earlier.[6] Business concerns took out advertisements answering his criticisms. As would happen with the language of women's liberation twenty years later, ads used Packard's catchwords to hawk goods. Cartoonists had a field day, especially with *Status Seekers*. So pervasive was the notoriety of these books that their titles earned a place on the list of phrases—like "1984," "future shock," and "feminine mystique"—that entered the language at home and abroad.

Packard's audience was exceptionally broad. Translated into more than a dozen foreign languages, his books were read by millions of people around the world.[7] Of the three, *Hidden Persuaders* had the largest foreign sales, and Germany made the greatest contribution to Packard's royalties.[8] At home, Packard benefited from the postwar boom in paperbacks on serious topics, which was fed in turn by professors' assignment of his works to be read in college courses. His audience ranged from the famous, people such as the Soviet writer Boris Pasternak and President Harry S. Truman, to the ordinary. Once a police officer stopped a car in

Photographed by Steve D'Arazien
AUTHOR AND ARTIST: Vance Packard and his wife, Mamie, in their New Canaan home. Mrs. Packard sold her painting, on easel in background, for $300.

Vance Packard and Virginia M. Packard at home in 1959, preparing for the CBS television show Person to Person. *(Used by permission of Vance Packard and Virginia M. Packard.)*

which Packard was a passenger and, upon hearing that the author was in the back seat, did not issue a ticket for a traffic violation.[9] In the 1960s a tool and die maker, who read and reread *Status Seekers* and *Hidden Persuaders*, quoted Packard extensively in conversations, making special note of what he had written, his daughter recollected, "on how automobile makers win customers through subtle seduction rather than solid engineering."[10] A novelist recalled poring over a copy of *Status Seekers* as a young man, thinking that "whatever he meant it to be," Packard had

In one of many examples of the way businesses drew on Packard's critique of advertisers for using sexual suggestions to sell their products, a New York store promotes "'The Hidden Persuaders,' perfumes that gratify a lady and her 'id.'" (From the New York Times, *22 December 1957.)*

provided "the perfect guide for social climbers." People read it "not to deplore the class problem but to solve it by changing classes."[11]

Catapulting Packard out of his career as a journalist for a genre of magazines whose audience was shrinking and into the national limelight as a widely read author, these books provided him with a steady income for the foreseeable future. Over the course of his life, *Hidden Persuaders* earned Packard about $350,000, with half of that coming in the first year and the rest spread unevenly over the rest of his life. *Status Seekers* brought in $240,000 and *Waste Makers* $100,000, with most of these funds coming in within a year or so of publication.[12] In the five years beginning in 1957, Packard earned, in 1994 dollars, roughly $2,600,000 from these three books. In the early 1960s, McKay agreed to spread payments forward over the years, a form of "forced savings," Packard noted in 1964, that was his "only hope for a comfortable old age." He could be reasonably sure of an annual income for ten years of between $62,500 and $125,000 in 1994 figures, solely from royalties from the trilogy. The household also had income from Virginia's teaching and painting and from Vance's lecturing, as well as from rentals of their properties in New Canaan and Chappaquiddick. The funds held by McKay were not depleted as quickly as anticipated. In the late 1960s more than $300,000 was still due the author; even as late as 1972, more than $250,000 remained on account at the publisher.[13]

If before the appearance of *Hidden Persuaders* in the spring of 1957 Packard had worried about having enough to live on, three and a half years

Like other corporations, a liquor company in 1962 turns the critique in Status Seekers *to its own advantage, linking its brand with foreign cars, French restaurants, and custom clothes as items that are "something special for status seekers." (From the* New Yorker, *10 November 1962.)*

later, when the income from these books confirmed his role as a good provider, his concerns about money diminished significantly. Packard did not suffer the fate of other writers for whom a rapid improvement in notoriety and income proved to be a mixed blessing. For him, success did not lead to difficulties with Virginia or with friends. Nor did it produce writer's block. In important ways, life remained the same. Packard continued to drive "clunker cars" and dress unpretentiously.[14] He was not in danger, as Sloan Wilson reported of himself, of having the appearance of "becoming more of a personage and less of an individual."[15] Packard was in an enviable position. He had status, Cindy later noted, "was fascinated by it and could snub his nose at it."[16] Virginia, Packard himself reported in the mid-1960s, "is amused when reporters interviewing me have noted that I

the waist makers

Restaurants catering to business men have never heard of a diet. Or else, to them, it is a dirty word which they are careful never to utter. All the medical talk about the dire consequences of overweight has never penetrated to their kitchens and they still serve executives with portions suitable for longshoremen, with calorific desserts and side dishes of cholesterol.

The man who is concerned about his intake must either go to his club, suffer a drugstore sandwich in his office or sneak into a woman's restaurant for a salad and hide behind a newspaper.

Things are different in the tailoring trade where a man's height and waistline are the longitude and latitude of the business. When men are trenchermen, their clothes are designed to drape their avoirdupois. And when they start reducing, their pants fall down.

Right now, at Wallachs, for every three pairs of trousers that we have to let out at the waist, we have to take in seven. And we are glad to do it. If the doctors are right, proper weight promotes longevity and we want all our customers to live as long and as happily as possible.

P.S. For those who want to take an notch in their belts, we keep a specia in each of our stores.

Using a homonym in a newspaper advertisement, a men's clothing store in New York offers an ironic play on the title of Waste Makers *to call attention to the importance of tailoring that recognizes that "a man's height and waistline are the longitude and latitude of the business." (From the* New York Times, *ca. 1960.)*

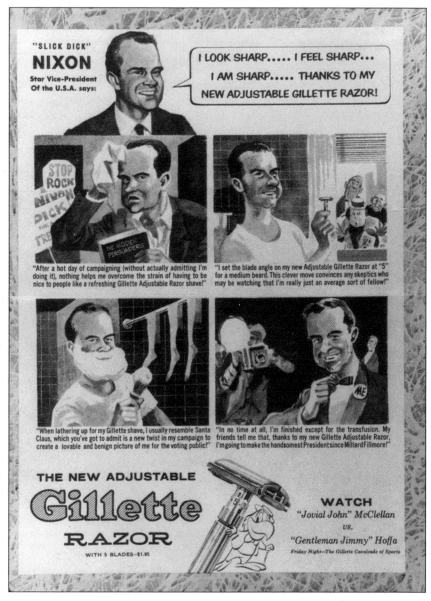

Vice President Richard M. Nixon, pictured in Mad Magazine *during the 1960 presidential campaign, as he remakes his image with the benefit of a copy of* Hidden Persuaders *and a Gillette razor. (Used by permission of* Mad Magazine; © *1960 E. C. Publications, Inc.)*

"*If there's one thing I can't abide, it's an out-and-out status seeker.*"

A drawing by James Stevenson depicts the one-upmanship of a status-seeking commuter arriving at a suburban railroad station. (From the New Yorker, 22 August 1959. © 1959, 1987 The New Yorker Magazine, Inc.; used by permission.)

seem unaffected by whatever success I've had as an author." Vance continued, "She knows that I wouldn't dare to take on airs and still live with her."[17] "Success," his wife recalled, "never went to his head."[18] Packard was "diffident" and "self-deprecating" about his triumph, a friend later remembered.[19]

In some ways, however, life at the Packard house changed significantly. As Wilson remarked of the dramatic increase in his income with the publication of *Man in the Gray Flannel Suit* in 1955, at a time "when Americans were much criticized for being materialists, I suddenly had the means to buy almost anything material I wanted."[20] Royalties made it possible for Virginia to resign her position in the Darien school system around 1960 and pursue her career as an artist.[21] The children no longer heard arguments about money problems in the house. "Life became magical," recalled Vance P. of the late 1950s.[22] Whatever quest for the simple life Packard expressed in his writings, his impulse was not puritanical. Cindy had a horse and Vance P., an Alpha Romeo. The family frequently went into New York to see Broadway shows.[23] As Vance Packard had noted in *Hidden Persuaders*, people who felt secure in their elevated social

"*Maybe at future parties you'll leave it to Vance Packard to tell people what strata they belong to.*"

Another Stevenson drawing dramatizes the danger of using Status
Seekers *to describe the social position of people at a cocktail party.
(From the* New Yorker, *8 August 1959. © 1959, 1987 The New
Yorker Magazine, Inc.; used by permission.)*

position engaged in "deliberate downgrading," a demonstration of their
superiority by showing their indifference to status.[24] Once, he remarked in
1959, "I used to worry as much as anybody about who we were having to
parties, who could help us out." In contrast, "now it's an exhilarating
feeling to know you can—you want—to live your own life. . . . I could walk
down the street with my pants off and not worry about my status as a
result." Pondering his good fortune, he concluded by saying, "It is a less
troubled life now, freed from deadlines, editors and advertisers, freed for
further reporting on the contemporary scene."[25]

A less troubled life perhaps, but he did worry about the future—remem-
bering what it felt like to be unemployed, possessing an ambition to
succeed and provide, and knowing how fickle the reading public could be.
In his magazine articles, he had advised others to relax, citing studies of
people with type A behavior and responding to the appeal of humanistic
psychology. Yet he did not follow the advice that he issued in his pieces.
Even as he embraced the ethic of self-realization, he remained committed
to hard work and driven to continued success as a writer. In 1960, he knew
he had to pay for the college education of three children before the decade

"*The Junior League is coming over this afternoon, Fred. Don't leave our copy of* The Status Seekers *lying around.*"

Cartoonist William F. Brown warns social climbers not to let people know they rely on Status Seekers *for how-to information. (From William F. Brown,* Girl in the Freudian Slip *[New York: New American Library of World Literature, 1959]. © William F. Brown; used by permission.)*

Playing on a Cold War theme, in a Grin and Bear It *cartoon dated 26 March 1961 George Lichty has a Soviet "hero" tell a "comrade 'status seeker' peasant" to stop acting "like you were official big shot with money to buy car." (Reprinted with special permission of King Features Syndicate.)*

ended. The properties in New Canaan and Chappaquiddick had to be managed and maintained. He knew that he had to capitalize on fame that would eventually fade. So he embarked on a frenetic lecture schedule in the early 1960s. He used his speaking tours to do some of his research and to identify professors and students who would administer surveys for him. In the early 1960s, he gave about sixty lectures a year across the nation, mostly on college campuses and at conventions.[26] In a ten-month period in 1961 he delivered forty-seven lectures, an activity that, after expenses, gave him almost $15,000 in income.[27]

The Craft of Writing: From Magazines to Books

In working on these three books, Packard was developing the methods of research and writing that enabled him to sustain such a prodigious output over so long a period of time. The Rawsons credited Packard's achievement to his "hard work and wonderful intellectual curiosity."[28] To that one would have to add his ambition and his ability to write with dispatch. He was an avid reader of contemporary fiction and nonfiction, a practice that kept him in touch with what intrigued the reading public. His familiarity with works by social scientists and journalists who reached a wide audience kept his eyes on topics that had contemporary currency. Virginia Packard was also of inestimable importance. On a practical level, she ran

Charles M. Schulz has Charlie Brown learn different ways to become a status seeker, ca. 1959. (© United Feature Syndicate; used by permission.)

the household so that her husband could devote his full attention to his work. Less tangible but more important, on some level he was writing for Virginia, as a way of paying homage or justifying himself to her.

By the late 1950s, Packard was beginning to master ways of developing a book that he would rely on for the rest of his career. Eleanor Rawson noted his skills as an investigative reporter and his ability to decide on the structure of a book early and then set up a filing system.[29] Except when commitments to promotional efforts intruded, by the time one book was in press he had begun to work on the next. Drawing on files containing his ideas for projects, Packard would take several weeks to generate three or four possibilities in detail. After getting reactions from family members, friends, and people at McKay, he would settle on his next topic. Because the publisher had to accept the book as submitted, the proposals were often twenty to thirty pages.[30]

As he developed interest in a specific topic, Packard stuffed files with clippings from newspapers, popular magazines, government studies, academic journals, trade publications, and notes he had taken while reading and thinking. Whatever sense of distraction he conveyed as a person, once he settled on a subject he was able to focus on it with rapt attention. His voraciousness as a researcher meant that he was more interested in absorbing, assimilating, and synthesizing than in generating new concepts and formulations. "I'll keep adding and adding and adding" to folders, he later commented, in a way that reflected habits of work characteristic of a person whose boyhood had instilled in him a sense of both deprivation and the wonder of discovery. "It's awfully difficult, you know, to end research. You can say to yourself, 'Stop. I have enough now,' and start organizing, but all the time that you're organizing, you're seeing new things."[31] Once he had accumulated enough information, he went through the folders. As he noted in 1982 concerning a later project, he would spend a considerable amount of time reading what he had collected, "first looking for interrela-

"Do you know who I'd like to see mayor of this town? Vance Packard!"

Soon after the publication of Waste Makers, *a cartoon depicts a park cleaner who believes that Packard would reduce waste if he were mayor. (From* Saturday Review of Literature, *21 January 1961; used by permission of* Omni Publications International, Ltd.*)*

tionships and things that seemed of particular interest for making some point or other. Then I went back and did it all over again to shape the surviving material into chapters," developing a "flow" for each section.[32]

During his career, Packard relied on a number of research strategies. For *Status Seekers* he did fieldwork, carrying out eight "informal" but "intensive" investigations.[33] In addition, he went to Rochester, New York, for several weeks to examine patterns of leadership and discrimination.[34] In other instances, he traveled to conventions of home builders and advertising executives, where he listened to speeches and interviewed people. Packard's appearance, that of an "earnest, Four Square American,"

INTERNATIONAL

Mao Tse-tung at Peking victory parade in October 1949: Stronger and more influential in 1964

Mao Now—Successful Status Seeker

The Chinese have always had a flair for pageantry and now their Communist masters seem to have made a science of it. Every year since Mao Tse-tung proclaimed the establishment "satellite," was there as well, a telling symbol of the unsettling role China's continued ideological warfare with Russia is playing in Eastern Europe. And from Africa, where Chinese subversion about to explode its first nuclear device. Curiously, the stories were first given international prominence by Secretary of State Dean Rusk. Seemingly anxious to obviate any Republican charges that

Five years after the publication of Status Seekers, *a headline in* Newsweek *underscores how the media confirmed the entrance of Packard's words into common language, even in unexpected contexts. (From* Newsweek, *12 October 1964; headline and text used by permission of* Newsweek.)

proved to be an asset in getting unsuspecting people to talk with him.[35] After his success in the late 1950s, he increasingly employed secretarial and research assistance. He also spoke with academics who were experts on some aspect of his study, professionals (usually in the employ of corporations) who were trying to reshape the world, and people in public-interest organizations such as Consumers Union. When he went on the college lecture circuit during the 1960s, he built a network of sociologists and their students who later carried out surveys for him.[36] Though there was no one with whom he discussed the content of his books in a sustained way, he tried out his ideas and solicited readings of his manuscripts from a number of people: Virginia and, when they had come of age, Cindy and Randall; the Rawsons; Harriet Pilpel; and friends such as Charles Saxon, Middy Darrow, and Whitney Darrow, Jr.

The strengths and weaknesses of Packard's style linked the magazine articles to the best-selling books. To be sure there were important differences—the books were similar to the more serious of Packard's articles, and they also developed arguments with greater thoroughness and complexity than was possible in shorter pieces. Yet Packard's debt to his years as a journalist was considerable. At *American Magazine* he had learned to be a trend watcher, someone who could draw from one source ideas that would capture what was transforming America.[37] Producing three books in four years meant writing with great speed, a skill for which his experience as a journalist trained him and which made him prolific and his prose breezy. In the 1940s and early 1950s, he had learned how to turn the research and ideas of academic social and behavioral scientists into highly accessible prose, and he did so now as he drew on the work not only of David Riesman, William H. Whyte, Jr., John Kenneth Galbraith, and C. Wright Mills but also of professors whose style made it difficult for their work to reach a wide audience. As he worked both sides of the border that usually divided journalists from academics, his books, like his articles, relied on an instinctive sense of audience, the importance of personally relevant details, an evocation of wonder, and relatively little attention to solutions.

In significant ways, Packard's style blunted his critical edge. Chapter headings from the three books—"RX for Our Secret Distresses," "Behavior That Gives Us Away," "How to Outmode a $4,000 Vehicle in Two Years"—sounded like titles of magazine pieces as well. The book chapters were often like expanded articles, blending as they did a carefully structured mixture of the opinions of experts, stories about individual lives, and a combination of dire warnings and inspiring conclusions. At key moments he could record a stunning incident and then extrapolate from it to prove a point or demarcate a significant trend. He managed to use the anecdotal to persuade his readers that his evidence was more than anecdotal, that it provided the foundation for social criticism. Like the articles, the books played on the tensions in a series of opposites: fascination and horror, a sense of shock and calm reassurances, seriousness and lightheartedness, the personal and the authoritative, the ordinary and the unusual. Packard's books used a technique that one critic has noted was common in mass-circulation magazines—an apparently realistic voice that was "colloquial, forceful, direct, and seemingly personal," a stance that, by combining the familiar and the terrifying, both frightened and reassured. At moments, his style, relying on the clever turn of phrase and the dramatic verbal picture, made him complicit in the very consumer culture he was criticizing. What Christopher Wilson said of early twentieth-century magazines also applies to Packard's approach. It evoked "the pathos of the modern consumer: endlessly enticed and dissatisfied, reminded of one's shortcomings, set 'free'—and yet guided by a 'pseudo-conscience.' "[38]

His style was often that of a crusading journalist, relying as it did on a combination of exposure and controlled moral outrage. At their worst his writings, rushed and excited, involved the stringing together of one example after another drawn from a variety of sources. As one sympathetic critic remarked, Packard hits his readers "with such a barrage of anecdotes, casual observations, memories, statistics, and reports on academic studies that sometimes it is hard to tell what he considers important and what trivial."[39] His writing often lacked the critical sense that would have enabled him to resolve contradictions. The genre he had perfected as a magazine writer, like the books he now produced, was longer on human interest and dramatic detail than it was on sustained and carefully-thought-out discussions of remedies. Yet Packard was doing what mass-circulation periodicals had accomplished in an earlier time but had been unable to do well enough in the 1950s to remain commercially viable—spark interest in issues that were at once personal and political and that would appeal to a broad range of Americans. Packard's sense of timing and audience were so sharp in part because as a journalist at *American Magazine*, he was at a critical juncture where writing and capitalism met in a world dominated by television, advertising, and public relations.

The Impact of the Trilogy on American Society and Politics

However much Packard's practice of his craft enhanced his influence, it is also possible to understand his contribution in terms of the changing mood of Americans. Packard's best-sellers appeared at a time when a series of events had begun to undermine the complacency that shaped American politics for many of the years after World War II. In 1957, the battle over school integration in Little Rock and the Soviets' launching of *Sputnik* called into question two tenets of the 1950s consensus—that opportunity had eliminated social conflict and that Democratic Capitalism had given America unquestioned technological supremacy. Disquieting events followed in the rest of the decade: a serious recession, revelations of corruption in the White House and in television game shows, anti-Americanism among Latin Americans, and the shooting down of a U.S. spy plane over the USSR.

In response to these events, during the late 1950s there emerged a debate about national purpose in which many writers, even those who had celebrated America's present, now raised questions about the nation's future.[40] What, asked a series of studies commissioned by the Rockefeller Brothers Fund, was the *Prospect for America*? What, wondered the authors of a report issued by the Presidential Commission on National Goals, were *Goals for Americans*? A number of themes dominated these debates. Sluggish economic growth and competition with the USSR prompted writers to talk of a renewed commitment to national greatness. People wondered whether abundance and materialism were enough and spoke of a qualitative liberalism that involved a healthier balance between public and private needs. Worried that the Soviets were gaining on America, commentators looked for solutions in renewed commitments to education and scientific research. Intellectuals also joined in the reexamination of American life. With the waning of the Cold War, they became more aware of the problems and injustices of American society.[41]

Many of the differences between what Packard wrote during his stint at *American Magazine* and what he wrote after that underscore the fact that in the very late 1950s there was an extraordinary and in some ways fortuitous fit between the man and his times. The changes from what he had written before 1957 were due not just to the freedom he experienced as a free-lance writer but also to shifts in the national mood. Several of the distinctions between his articles and his books reflected the new mood— the shift from entrepreneurship to self-fulfillment, the questioning of materialism, the worry about forces that were manipulating Americans, the new balancing of interest in individual and social change, the move from celebration to critique of America, the change from individual to political solutions, and the diminished hold of the Cold War outlook.

Though Packard may have been the right man at the right moment, his notoriety is easier to prove than his influence. The impact of his writing was less direct and tangible than that of Betty Friedan's *Feminine Mystique* (1963) or Ralph Nader's *Unsafe at Any Speed* (1965). Nonetheless, there is evidence that Packard's books were among the forces that shaped political discussions in the United States in the late 1950s and early 1960s, as the nation shifted from the quiescent politics of one decade to the more active and reform-minded public life of the next. *Hidden Persuaders* affected attitudes toward advertising and helped prompt the federal government to curb the use of subliminal messages, a practice that Packard brought to the attention of a wide audience although he wrote relatively little about that particular technique.[42] Editorial writers and columnists made it clear that he demonstrated the need for protection of the individual from motivational research, invasion of privacy, and pressures for conformity.[43] A 1963 study gave ample testimony to the impact of Packard's books. Twenty-nine percent of the community leaders surveyed said they had read what he had written on advertising and consumer culture. They were twice as likely to "remember reading Vance Packard," the survey concluded, "as they do newspaper reports about advertising and its role in our society." By a margin of three to one, they agreed with his argument that advertising prompted people to spend wastefully.[44]

When a reporter later discussed the factors that "helped to make consumerism a household word" beginning in the late 1960s, he included Packard's writings.[45] More specifically, *Hidden Persuaders* and *Waste Makers* were among the many factors that persuaded President John F. Kennedy to create an office of the Consumer Council.[46] Among government officials and shapers of public opinion, Packard's exposé intensified interest in curbing excessive advertising and materialism, in protecting the environment, and in redressing the imbalance between public squalor and private wealth.[47] All three books, but especially *Waste Makers*, taught consumers how to buy wisely and how to protest the actions of corporations.[48] Some corporations became more sensitive on issues involving planned obsolescence. The book also awakened popular consciousness to the world population crisis and to the threat that excessive consumption posed to our natural resources.[49] *Waste Makers* reflected the transition that Americans had begun to make after 1945 from conservation to environmentalism—from a focus on production, work, and the efficient use of resources to consumption, leisure, and the enjoyment of nature.[50] Packard's concern for the environment rested both on the implications of profligacy for the nation's long-term industrial well-being and on the definition of personal pleasure. Along with others, he was coaxing his readers to think in terms not of possessions but of a clean environment and mental health achieved through experience with nature.

As did the proponents of the environmental movement that emerged in the 1970s, Packard spoke of a way of life that was decentralized and small in scale. Along with environmentalists, he believed that natural resources were finite. He differed from those who would follow in that he seemed relatively mute on the issue of the impact of pollution on people and nature.[51] Like Rachel Carson's *Silent Spring* (1962), *Waste Makers* evoked an earlier idyllic America; but unlike Carson, Packard paid relatively little attention to the impact of human action on the natural world.[52] Like others who fought to protect the environment, he allied with the Left in his attack on big business, but he also searched for human meaning in nature. A sense of place and the experience of nature were important to him, and he expressed that in his writings and in his life.[53] Packard used his pen to attack billboard advertising, junkyards, and polluted rivers.[54] Yet to him, communing with nature was to a very great extent a private matter, best achieved near the waterfall across the road from his house in New Canaan and on the beaches in Chappaquiddick—not by fighting publicly to preserve as assets for the nation the country's wetlands, national parks, and wilderness areas.[55]

Whatever the contribution of Packard's trilogy to specific causes, more generally these books helped to shape the transition from the 1950s to the 1960s. Like others, Packard served as a scout or negotiator in this important shift.[56] In the late 1950s, the Beat Generation and the civil rights movement questioned the extent of the nation's commitments to justice, equality, and authenticity. Books such as Mills's *Power Elite* (1956), John Keats's *Crack in the Picture Window* (1957), Galbraith's *Affluent Society* (1958), and Paul Goodman's *Growing Up Absurd* (1960) taunted the complacent to examine their apathy. Compared with works by intellectuals, such as Daniel Bell and Seymour Martin Lipset, these more popular books reached an extensive audience.[57]

Though presidential adviser Arthur M. Schlesinger, Jr., could not recall "an actual instance" in which people in the White House mentioned Vance Packard's name or his books, he nevertheless felt that Packard "was one of those irreverent writers of the 1950s who helped shape the intellectual mood in which the Kennedy administration operated."[58] In 1961 the historian Eric F. Goldman listed *Hidden Persuaders, Lonely Crowd, Organization Man,* and *White Collar* as being among the books that made Americans "highly critical of the condition of our own country, particularly when a long period of suffocation has been with us."[59] Packard's books reflected the tone of social criticism of the 1950s at the same time that they heralded and influenced the bolder politics of the 1960s. In its earliest stages, during the late 1950s, this renascent sense of social responsibility often lacked specific programmatic content, and thus it dovetailed well with Packard's approach. His politics appealed to readers who were dissatisfied with the complacency of the 1950s but unsure of how to achieve a better society. Yet it is important to recognize that Packard's critique of the 1950s, which helped to undermine that decade's celebration, came from someone who had participated in the period's most characteristic and central experiences.

Packard's books were also among the many sources that influenced radicals of the 1960s. Jules Henry's *Culture against Man* (1963), one of the key texts in the counterculture, drew on *Waste Makers*' critique of the misuse of scientists and engineers.[60] In September 1960, Tom Hayden, a founder of Students for a Democratic Society (SDS), wrote that the emergent generation could not "avoid reading criticism of itself and its fathers; indeed," he noted, "the media have flooded the market with inexpensive paperbacks such as 'The Lonely Crowd,' 'The Hidden Persuaders,' 'The Organization Man.'"[61] In 1963, the Port Huron Statement, the key document of the early New Left, acknowledged the contribution of Packard and others when it noted that college students paid too much attention "to social status" when they decided what to wear, whom to befriend, and whom to marry; how the Americans' "nagging incentive to 'keep up' makes them continually dissatisfied with their possessions"; the economy's reliance on "'market research' techniques to deliberately create pseudoneeds in consumers"; and the introduction of "wasteful 'planned obsolescence' as a permanent feature of business strategy."[62] Todd Gitlin, one of the founders of SDS, retrospectively identified *Hidden Persuaders* as one of many books by "popular social critics" whose works were "lying on the coffee tables of many a curious adolescent" during the 1950s.[63] In the late 1960s, Herbert Marcuse, an émigré from Nazi Germany whom radical students considered one of their most influential intellectual mentors, assigned *Naked Society* to be read for his course in order to suggest to students that what had happened in Nazi Germany could also happen in the United States—the total domination of the public arena by powerful forces.[64] When Ellen Willis evaluated the 1960s after they ended, she remarked that "perhaps the most widely accepted tenet of the movement ideology . . . is the idea that we are psychically manipulated by the mass media to crave more and more consumer goods," a view that Willis identified with Marcuse but one that, another scholar noted, "received its most celebrated formulation" in *Hidden Persuaders*.[65]

Without Packard's books, SDS, the New Frontier, and the Great Society would have been no different, and the late 1950s and early 1960s would have turned out the way they did. Packard's trilogy lacked the focused impact on public discourse of Galbraith's *Affluent Society* (1956). Unlike Michael Harrington's *Other America* (1962), Carson's *Silent Spring*, and Nader's *Unsafe at Any Speed*, Packard's writing did not directly change public policy. Nor could hundreds of thousands of people say, as they did of Friedan's *Feminine Mystique*, that reading Packard's books transformed their lives. Neither did Packard's books have an impact on a new generation of activists similar to that of Marcuse's *Eros and Civilization* (1955), Goodman's *Growing Up Absurd*, Norman O. Brown's *Life against Death* (1959), or Mills's *Power Elite*.

However, from the pages of these three books millions of college students and members of the general reading public came to understand the imbalance between public and private needs, the value of self-realization, and the evils of advertising. Packard promoted an animus against experts, attacked unquestioned growth, and emphasized the social and psychological costs of status and class. His writings stressed the quest for meaningful work and for a more democratic workplace, addressed the perils of conformity in corporations and suburbs, questioned discrimination based on ethnicity, advocated consumer rights, and expressed concern for ecological balance and natural resources.[66]

Nor did the impact of these three books end with the 1960s, though to a considerable extent what persisted had more to do with key phrases and the concepts they embodied than with public policy, conceptual break-throughs, or central arguments. Of the three books, the influence of *Hidden Persuaders*, which remains in print, was the most sustained.[67] In 1985, a British executive, writing in the cover story of *Marketing Week*, called *Hidden Persuaders* "probably the most famous book about advertising ever written."[68] Someone familiar with the advertising business in the early 1990s commented that the idea of hidden persuaders has remained the public's definition, a view to which people in the field "adapt and rebel against."[69] The book is often remembered for its dramatic data. In the summer of 1976, for example, after reading *Hidden Persuaders* a group of high school students in a summer honors program began to examine advertisements for subliminal messages, especially sexual ones. "I know that I still cannot look at a glass in a liquor ad with ice cubes," one participant remembered, "and not let my eyes wander in search of subliminal sex."[70] In the mid-1980s, a group of high school students in California, having read Packard's book, searched through magazine advertisements for hidden persuaders.[71]

More than three decades after publication of the second book in the trilogy, the notion of status seeking still served as a reference point for discussions of social striving in America.[72] In 1991 an African American woman journalist told Packard that thirty years earlier, her mother, who had a "keen interest in class," read *Status Seekers*, "most likely for pointers."[73] In 1980, an article in *Time* referred to *Waste Makers*, by "Social Critic Vance Packard." Almost a quarter of a century after the third book's appearance, *Consumer Reports* remarked that "Vance Packard hadn't seen anything yet" when it surveyed the spread of commercialism.[74] *Webster's Third New International Dictionary* used Packard's prose to illustrate more than two dozen entries.[75] An examination of scholarly references to his work recorded on standard data bases reveals hundreds of citations over more than three decades and in a wide range of fields—especially market research, consumer affairs, and advertising but also geography, sociology, journalism, political psychology, history, law, and planning.[76]

Vance Packard and the Canon of Social Critics

Scholars' evaluations of Packard's contribution vary considerably. In 1990 a historian spoke of a new book that "will fuel controversy in the tradition

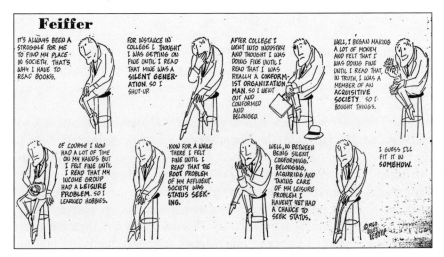

Jules Feiffer explores how readers used books—including Status Seekers, Organization Man, *and* Affluent Society—*to wrestle with problems of identity and conformity. (From the* Washington Daily News, *20 April 1960. FEIFFER © Jules Feiffer; reprinted with permission of Universal Press Syndicate. All rights reserved.)*

of Lewis Mumford, Walter Benjamin, C. Wright Mills, Marshall McLuhan, Vance Packard, and Daniel J. Boorstin."[77] Others have acknowledged Packard as a social commentator whose works were influential in the late 1950s and early 1960s, at times placing him in a canon of social critics.[78] However, many observers believe that Packard's works did not have the conceptual power to withstand the test of time. Ironically, if in the late 1950s and early 1960s critics and admirers spoke of Packard, Mills, Riesman, and Whyte in the same breath, by the 1980s the common practice among historians was to neglect Packard but focus on the others.[79] The reputations of suburban and exurban intellectuals did not fare well after the 1950s. Generally speaking, New York intellectuals were over-appreciated, partly because of the cultural power of the city.[80] Looking back on the late 1950s and early 1960s, some scholars, especially those who have placed Mills, Riesman, and New York intellectuals in the canon of influential social thinkers, have minimized or neglected Packard's role in shaping public consciousness in the late 1950s and early 1960s.[81] By and large, historians have tended to draw on Packard's works more as evidence for what happened in the past than as books responsible for breakthroughs to new ideas. In developing a canon of significant intellectual contributions, scholars have valued sustained originality more than immediate impact and popularity.

Nor did Packard's name appear in a 1992 study that listed the works of the previous fifty years that "most profoundly affected the thoughts and actions of humankind." A panel that included Russell Baker, William Sloane Coffin, Jr., Maxine Hong Kingston, and George F. Will listed forty-three books, with Carson's *Silent Spring* coming in first and Benjamin Spock's *Baby and Child Care* and Friedan's *Feminine Mystique* tied for second. The absence of Packard's works was notable given the prominence of books on the list that the historian of the project described as "a literature of warning" that was "part of a progressive, muckraking journalism and scholarship" that explored the abuse of power by powerful institutions. A number of factors explain Packard's absence. Prominent among the books included were ones that focused on gender and race, issues not central to Packard's trilogy. Moreover, the list included many books directly linked to social movements—not only feminism and environmentalism but also civil rights and Black Power.[82] Packard's writings, laced with the preposterous and the ironical, lacked the unambiguous urgency of many of the books on the list, such as Frances FitzGerald's *Fire in the Lake* (1972) or Friedrich A. von Hayek's *Road to Serfdom* (1944).

Whether Packard belongs in some pantheon of American social critics is not easily resolved and depends in part on what the term "social critics" means. Certainly neither New York intellectuals at the time nor most historians since then have so admitted him. He is admissible if the term refers to a critic of society who had considerable influence. Packard's journey from journalist to public intellectual was incomplete. He ended up in the middle of debates that he did not really construct or intend to focus on over the long haul. Unlike those who gave sustained attention to key problems, Packard typically focused intently on one issue and then moved on to another. What also set him apart from others who more successfully entered the ranks of public intellectuals was that Packard did not provide extended engagement with theoretical issues.

Packard operated at the intersections between a number of worlds. During the 1950s, American intellectuals worried about their place in society, especially as free-lance writers entered the academy. Packard, who began to make the transition from journalism to public intellectual but who never earned great respect from academics, was ambivalent about the world of professors—especially given their scientific claims, their desire to exclude the uncertified, and their drive to specialization. He never wanted to be a professor himself, but he certainly desired to gain their respect. Being someone who brought university research to a wide audience should not disqualify him from being taken seriously, especially in light of his impact. To be sure, Packard's work did not have the intellectual force that came from Mills's analysis of power, Marcuse's combination of Karl Marx and Sigmund Freud, or Bell's penetrating discussion of key institutions. Yet Packard's notions of hidden persuasion, status seeking, and planned obsolescence earned a place in the lexicon of phrases along with Riesman's inner direction, Galbraith's affluent society, Whyte's organization man, and Friedan's feminine mystique. As he neared the realm reserved for public intellectuals, Packard faced a situation that Whyte and Friedan encountered but Riesman and Galbraith did not. Typically, academics entered the public arena from the lofty position of the university, not from the more ambiguous position in the cultural hierarchy of the lucrative heights a journalist could reach on the best-seller list.

Vance Packard was both a border crosser and a marginal man. He emerged as a social critic when he did partly because, for a variety of reasons, a number of roles for writers had become problematic in the late 1950s and early 1960s. He wrote at a time when most academic social scientists had left the field of comprehensive and provocative social analysis to nonacademics. The independent cultural critic, free of academic affiliation, exemplified by such people as Edmund Wilson and Lewis Mumford, was waning. The man of letters was already gone. Trilling was among the last of the literary critics of his generation who, seeking to address a wider audience, mediated between the university and the public. More and more, free-lance public intellectuals were entering the academy at the same time that television had made free-lance writing more problematic. Crusading journalists were few and far between in a time generally skeptical of crusades, and the New Journalists had not yet emerged.

The term "social critic" thus only partially described Packard's position as a man who straddled several worlds. A journalist who no longer wrote primarily for newspapers or magazines, he had a voracious interest in the social and behavioral sciences, even though many professionals in those fields did not take his work very seriously. Packard brought together two traditions, a maverick sociology sparked by the work of Willard Waller and a crusading journalism inspired by the muckrakers of the Progressive period. *American Magazine* and its companions had failed in the 1950s for a number of reasons. One of the factors was that they had lost their ability to find an appropriate crusade. Armed with data and ideas that academics had developed, Packard used the style of these magazines to uncover the ills besetting American society. Although his life experiences often cast him as an outsider, he was nevertheless a success—not only in terms of impact but also as a self-made and self-realized individual.

Packard was hardly alone in being an outsider. Many major texts of social criticism of the 1950s and early 1960s came from people who found themselves between worlds. European émigrés like Marcuse were *in* America but not fully *of* it. Riesman was a sociologist without a degree in sociology. Mills was not only a Texan on Morningside Heights but also a sociologist who went against the grain of his discipline. Galbraith was a Canadian and an economist neglected by professional economists. Somewhat similar patterns obtained among nonacademics. Until the 1960s, Goodman's writings and way of life placed him on the fringes of American life.

Packard was a transitional figure who occupied territory between modes of social criticism. On one side stood the 1950s observers of the national malaise: Riesman, Whyte, A. C. Spectorsky, Keats—people who offered analysis but whose books rarely suggested any political way out. On the other side stood the New Journalists and Nader, Harrington, and Carson: people who wrote the more-political best-sellers of the 1960s, which saw something wrong and explained how to make it right. The early 1960s were, one observer noted later, "a time when books became banners for causes."[83] Somewhat unwittingly, Packard's books became banners for a number of causes—campaigns against advertising, social exclusion, and destruction of the environment. In the late 1950s, when Friedan was finding it difficult to get her controversial articles published in mass-circulation periodicals, she listened as Packard talked about how he, faced with a similar situation, decided to write a book; she realized she too could turn her interest into a book, and that project became *Feminine Mystique*.[84] In the late 1950s and early 1960s, Packard and Friedan stretched the limits of the genre that had its origins in magazine journalism. The two shared familiarity with 1930s radicalism, journalism careers, and books whose titles became meaningful phrases in the American language. Packard and Friedan offered their works at a special moment, when the audience for mass-circulation magazines still existed and when the basis for reform movements was just beginning to form.

To state the situation in another way, the works of Packard's most obvious predecessors—Keats, Spectorsky, Riesman, and Whyte—underscored the mood of the 1950s but did little to fan the flames that swept across America in the next decade. Packard's work, and more dramatically that of Friedan, helped to underwrite the social movements and changes of the 1960s. *Hidden Persuaders*, *Status Seekers*, *Waste Makers*, and *Feminine Mystique* offered a social criticism that grew out of a genre, one that combined journalism, the social and behavioral sciences, self-help, and human interest, but only hinted at means of political recourse. The failure of many of the leading mass-circulation magazines in the years around 1956 let loose a huge audience still attuned to their style of writing.

Writers now faced a crossroad in their careers. Thousands of them had dreamed of success as free-lancers, but in only a few cases did achievement match ambition. Among those who entered the marketplace with all the skills and drive that they brought to periodicals like *American Magazine*, *Collier's*, and *Ladies' Home Journal* were Cornelius Ryan, Pierre Salinger, Theodore White, Irving Wallace, Kurt Vonnegut, Stephen Birmingham, Peter Maas, Robert Massie, "Adam Smith" (George Goodman), Alvin Toffler, Friedan, and Packard—writers whose works would rise to the top of the charts for a generation.[85]

Yet the placement of Packard's best-sellers in their historic moment gets us back to their ambivalence—the ambivalence within his books, in their impact, and within the early moments of the reform movements that emerged from them. That virtually no newspaper reviewers seconded the diatribes from the business community makes it clear that by the late 1950s millions of Americans, however ambivalent they were about affluence, were tired of mindless celebrations of materialism and yearned instead for the reemergence of social criticism, even if at times that criticism allowed them to deplore what they secretly craved. The social critic, Michael Walzer has written, has "a kind of antagonistic connection" to the society, "a passionate commitment to cultural values hypocritically defended at the center, cynically disregarded at the margins." He noted further that "his fiercest criticism is often aimed at those individuals and groups to whom he feels closest, who are most likely to disappoint him."[86] These characteristics help to explain Packard. His life's "twin pulls" placed him in precisely such an antagonistic position—willing to attack the excesses of advertising but also stating that he saw nothing fundamentally wrong with most of what Madison Avenue did; critical of wastefulness but fascinated with gadgets; lamenting the costs of status striving but finding fascination in its mystifications. Packard stood apart from at least three groups: celebrants of American life who defended success, affluence, and individualism; sociologists whose work was less accessible; and cosmopolitan intellectuals who could not understand how a better future might be grounded in a vision of an earlier America.

The Lonely Crowd

Readers Respond to *The Hidden Persuaders*,
The Status Seekers, and *The Waste Makers*

Understanding how readers respond
to what an author writes is no easy matter. What helps in this process with
Vance Packard's best-sellers are the hundreds of letters that people sent
him, letters that are moving, humorous, and revealing.[1] Reader-response
theory, by exploring the complex relationship between the intentions of
the author and the interpretations of the audience, helps illuminate the
reasons for Packard's popularity. Most scholarly attention has focused not
on empirical data about audience reaction but on literary texts themselves. As suggestive as reader-response criticism is, rarely if ever has
anyone applied it to popular nonfiction.

Shaping an Audience's Expectations

Janice A. Radway's *Reading the Romance: Women, Patriarchy, and Popular Literature* (1984) offers a framework for understanding the letters

that readers sent to Packard.[2] Admittedly, there are significant differences between the Harlequin Romances that she studied and the social criticism Packard wrote. Moreover, Radway had the advantage of asking questions of actual readers. Nonetheless, her approach remains helpful. A text, Radway argues, is not a fixed entity whose meaning only a skilled critic can explicate. Readers, even those who repeatedly devour formulaic works, actively create meaning. The way they make sense of what they read depends on a number of factors: the nature of the writing, the social context of the production and promotion of the book, and the circumstances in which they find themselves. Literary codes learned from cultural authorities and from previous experiences with a genre are also influential. Consumers take from a book not only the interpretations the author intended but also those they generate from their own situation.

If millions of people read *Hidden Persuaders*, *Status Seekers*, and *Waste Makers*, fewer than a thousand wrote to Packard. Loneliness, the need for help, strongly held convictions, the desire for reassurance or self-expression, and the dramatic impact of a book are among the reasons that a reader turned to pen or typewriter. The statistical exceptionality of the act calls for caution in claiming that the views of those who wrote closely paralleled the opinions of those who did not. Nonetheless, an examination of the letters helps to illuminate the impact of the books.

How Packard addressed his readers at the beginning of his books established expectations about what followed. Like many journalists of his generation, he opened with an approach that, though informal, was not personal.[3] In both *Status Seekers* and *Waste Makers*, he quickly established his authority by emphasizing the extensiveness of his research and the expertise of the scholars on whom he relied.[4] Even more prominent in the beginning of all three books was the invitation to the reader to embark with the author on the quest for answers to critical issues, a quest that promised revelations vital for individual self-awareness and national well-being. For example, *Waste Makers* started with an invitation to ponder the intriguing issue "What will the world of tomorrow be like?" Then, having raised a series of "momentous questions," Packard promised an exploration of them "with all the compassion and forbearance we can muster."[5]

The books' covers, press releases, and advertisements also shaped expectations. With *Hidden Persuaders*, the dust jacket undermined Packard's aura as a serious social critic by pointing to pages on which the book answered the question "WHY are women in supermarkets attracted to items wrapped in red?" Mixed in were suggestions of horrible and fascinating things to come, with the jacket stating that "this book is your eye opener, your guide to the Age of Manipulation."[6] An advertisement for the second book announced: "Reading THE STATUS SEEKERS will ease the pressures of your social and business life. Try It." Another ad noted: "MERCHANTS are learning how 'status seeking' influences national tastes, fads, fashions among different economic and national groups." The cover of *Status Seekers* suggested how the book "will jolt the complacent" and marshaled pairs of mutually exclusive words such as "witty" and "dismaying." It also conveyed the sense of Packard as a well-known authority, invoking the fame he had achieved with *Hidden Persuaders* and speaking of how he had introduced new phrases into the American language.[7] With *Waste Makers*, advertisements took advantage of the way the book was "disconcerting the business community." Public relations copy also connected the book with emerging public issues. On the eve of the 1960 presidential election, a press release trumpeted that the book offered "a positive action program for tomorrow, a tomorrow in which America and Americans can once more represent to themselves and to the rest of the world the strength and the leadership that is the tradition of this country." Finally, by suggesting that with *Waste Makers* Packard was continuing the search begun with its two predecessors, the publicists built on the momentum created by previous successes.[8]

Like the author's initial statements and the promotional material, reviews also shaped the readers' experiences. The unfavorable responses to Packard's best-sellers derived their importance from the cultural authority of those who wrote them. The favorable ones, much greater in number and with a wider audience, usually appeared in newspapers from small and less cosmopolitan cities, in middlebrow magazines, and in periodicals for libraries and the book trade. The combination of fascination and horror that Packard conveyed about what he discovered struck a responsive chord among commentators.[9] In describing what his best-sellers revealed, the favorable reviews used contrasting words like "humor and horror," "entertaining but serious," "funny and depressing."[10] Another notable characteristic of these reviews was their attention to the stuff of the books—the tricks advertisers used to entice customers, the inside information on the status meaning of consumer goods that market researchers developed, and the methods merchandisers employed to get buyers to spend their money wastefully.[11]

Especially with the first two books, reviewers revealed the ambiguous and opposite ways that audiences might use what Packard had written. One remarked how *Hidden Persuaders* would enable the professionals Packard criticized to sharpen their skills.[12] Another observer compared the appeal of *Status Seekers* to that of a Dale Carnegie publication; a second said that Packard had invented "a sociological parlor game" that might augment the book's sales; and a third talked of the work's usefulness as gossip and as instruction for the socially mobile.[13] In addition, the favorable reviews focused on Packard's analysis but paid minimal attention to his recommendations. "Exhortations to virtue," as one observer commented, "are seldom as interesting—(or, that matter, as useful)—as examinations of vice."[14] Again and again, however, they congratulated him for dealing with important issues that deserved attention, although they asserted that what he had provided was not adequate to the task at hand.[15] Sympathetic observers hailed the power of these books to awaken an apathetic public to urgent issues.[16] They also spoke of Packard's impact as an earlier generation might have described a religious experience, using phrases like "astonished gaze," "wake up," and "eye-opening."[17]

The Hidden Persuaders: Help Seekers, True Believers, Challengers, and the Converted

The letters in response to *Hidden Persuaders* show the myriad ways in which people read, used, valued, and criticized a best-selling book. The writers fall into four overlapping categories: help seekers, true believers, challengers, and the converted. Somewhat more than half who wrote were help seekers, most of whom contacted Packard for very particular reasons, such as inviting him to speak at a meeting, obtaining assistance with class assignments, and seeking symbolic contact with the writer of a best-seller.[18] Many help seekers turned to Packard because they wanted to know more about the methods that *Hidden Persuaders* described. Of these, only two joined the battle against new advertising techniques: the managing director of a credit union sought aid in exposing efforts to undermine nonprofit financial institutions, and a public relations expert in the temperance department of a church wanted to know how to "warn the members of our organization against the subtleties of the advertisers."[19]

Ironically and revealingly, the overwhelming majority of those who turned to Packard for more information on advertising did so because they wanted to embrace the practices *Hidden Persuaders* decried. Some of the requests were relatively benign. People sought assistance in promoting projects whose goals Packard may well have deemed admirable, such as gaining support for refugees who had broken through the Iron Curtain or learning how to promote physical fitness.[20] Someone recalled that reading *Hidden Persuaders* led him to avoid advertising as a career and decide instead to become an artist.[21]

Even more striking, though, is that so many people asked for assistance along lines that Packard opposed. Readers wanted to obtain information that would help them use new techniques in pharmaceutical advertising, increase sales of real estate and stocks, and bring American marketing methods to Europe and Mexico. A reading of *Hidden Persuaders* aided others in finding in the fields Packard was attacking a career they wished to pursue. Many of the readers were persuaders themselves, people involved in sales, public relations, or advertising—and some of these turned to the book because it would improve their ability to write copy.[22] A sociologist wrote Packard that though 10 percent of his students gained much from *Hidden Persuaders*, "I'm afraid 50 percent [will] decide on motivational research" for a career.[23] The way readers used Packard's writings in support of methods he had attacked underscores his own ambivalence to the material he covered. *Hidden Persuaders*, a Connecticut lawyer wrote, "sparked ... an enthusiasm not usual for me." He asked Packard to suggest the name of "some adventurous friend in MR who would give me a try." Packard answered that he could not be of any help because he was "not on the best of terms with" motivational researchers.[24] Packard's response was revealing and disingenuous. In several instances he had given people information on how to reach prominent people in MR. Moreover, in 1958 Ernest Dichter wrote a "Dear Vance" letter thanking him for the jobs that had come to him because the attacks on his work had made "the whole world motivation research conscious."[25] Another told Packard he had "done a great job" making MR intelligible to the average reader. A year later, writing about the possibility of scheduling a debate between the two of them, he told Packard, "We will plan to have dinner together before the 'combat.' "[26]

If more than half of the correspondents turned to Packard for help, often in a way that went against the grain of what he had written, then the rest of those who sent letters did so to discuss substantive issues. Many of these letters were routine or perfunctory, but all were all revealing. These respondents fall into three broad categories: ten true believers, who contacted Packard because his work provoked them to articulate a system of beliefs to which they were already fully committed; the thirty-nine converted, to whom *Hidden Persuaders* had revealed or made articulate a way of looking at the world with which they agreed; and the six challengers, who pressed the author on critical issues.[27]

The true believers wrote not to change Packard's mind but to express their own strong convictions. Among those in this group were people who believed that the Bible or the spiritualist P. D. Ouspensky provided answers to the dilemmas of the modern world or who felt that psychiatrists were the real hidden persuaders. Several of the true believers were quite political. A man from a Midwestern suburb wrote to warn of "The Hidden Dictatorship" that had set out to "condition" him and a few of his friends by "behind-the-scenes 'scientific' management" when they were growing up and now sought to extend their control "to the political-social-economic and personal spheres." These people, he remarked, "had almost unlimited power over my life for over forty years" and "can and do bring crushing pressures to bear on me."[28] Doubtless Packard took more seriously the letter of a man who, working on a construction project in eastern Connecticut, wrote in 1958 of his fear of "the hydrogen bomb in the hands of hysterical men" and of the decline of American prestige "because our economy is propped up by war spending."[29]

The strongest response from a true believer came from the anti-communist Right. A man from a Southern city suggested that Packard write a book revealing "how the Communists are using PSYCHOLOGY in their strategy to conquer the United States and the Free World" as well as how America could fight back by using fire to fight fire. He revamped the paperback cover of *Hidden Persuaders*, mixing Packard's words with his own and stating on the redesigned cover: "In this book you'll discover a world of psychology professors turned CRUSADERS. You'll learn how they operate, what they know about you and your neighbors and how they are using that knowledge TO PROVIDE THE PSYCHOLOGICAL IN-FORMATION NEEDED BY THE FREE WORLD TO SUCCESS-FULLY DEFEND OURSELVES AGAINST THE COMMUNIST AF-FRONT TO OUR WAY OF LIFE." He also penned one final question to Packard. "Why," he wrote, "are Teenagers such willing tools of the Communists; i.e. student riots, snake dances, etc.?"[30]

The converted found that a reading of *Hidden Persuaders* shaped or confirmed their outlook, but their reaction was less ideological or passionate than that of the true believers. Inspired by something Packard had written, many of these letters, which usually asked for no response, were ruminations, sometimes meandering and sometimes focused. Many people wrote to thank the author, establish symbolic contact with a famous person, or offer evidence that bolstered his arguments. They enclosed information on reviews and sermons, or they forwarded advertisements whose content Packard's analysis illuminated. Some of these correspondents seemed to be testing their wings as writers in the presence of a professional.[31] Readers were grateful to Packard for making them realize the adverse impact of advertising. "It was one of those books which put into words ideas and thoughts which I have had," a man from Detroit wrote, "but have never been able to express so well."[32] "Little people like us," said a woman who doubtless reflected the views of many others, "need big people like you to open our eyes ears and understanding."[33] One high school student from rural Ohio revealed the power of Packard's mixture of the familiar and the authoritative when he mentioned the impact of "personal viewpoints along with statements from the higher authorities."[34]

Cautious spenders responded positively to what Packard had written. Articulating the religious perspective of many in his audience, a Massachusetts couple remarked that reading the book provided "renewal of faith in mankind" about "the situation which almost brainwashed some citizens into a stupor of a constant state of consumption of consumer goods." The " 'Babylon' of Madison Avenue," they continued, "has peddled its devilish gospel, but a modern miracle has occurred because the false god of *making* and *adoring* money has not engulfed all of us."[35] A man from Long Island wrote that "we live in the very modest circumstances our means allow, and truly hate and fear the things we see going on," such as child neglect, invasion of privacy, and "foolish spending of taxpayers' money."[36]

In the late 1950s, many people were beginning to articulate their own strategies for withstanding the pressures of aggressive advertising, an endeavor for which Packard's book gave them support. A housewife from Kentucky expressed "indignation" at the MR men who, "with dollar signs instead of hearts," believed women's eyes glazed over when they entered supermarkets because they were hypnotized and tempted by what they saw. If women had a glazed look, she wrote, it was because they were tired of doing housework and of planning a week's menu while staying within their family budget at the same time that they were struggling to keep young children under control in supermarkets.[37] Similarly, a woman from a Boston suburb wrote that, "as one of the common garden-variety housewives," she was "having long-overdue second thoughts on a way of life that expects us to spend all our time, effort and profits on the acquisition of more material things."[38]

In addition to the true believers and the converted, a handful of challengers wrote Packard, pressing him on critical issues. Two people urged him to provide leadership in the fight against MR. Especially telling was a letter written in the fall of 1957 by a woman who lived on New York's Upper East Side. A marriage counselor, she had believed for much of her adulthood that therapy "was the only sure, visible way of being a do-gooder" because "large movements are too obscure for one to be certain whether the end result was for better or for worse." However, at moments she wondered if Packard's revelations did not force him and his audience to take a political stance. Might they not lead "to some action beyond reporting and clarifying," she asked in a way that made it unclear whether she was figuring out the situation for herself or calling on him to assume the mantle of a leader. In response, Packard begged the question, saying that though he wished he "could suggest some good answers" to her inquiry, "a simple awareness of the techniques being used, I suspect, could do a lot."[39]

In only two cases did challengers offer sustained and unequivocal criticisms. From Philadelphia came a letter that challenged Packard's assertion that most Americans had no unfulfilled real needs, stating that it was "the most idiotic statement since Marie Antoinette said 'let them eat cake'" and reflected the perspective of someone who lived in a wealthy community and overlooked the extent of poverty.[40] A Danish man took Packard to task for leaving his own position "a little vague" and being ambivalent about what he described. "It seems to me as if you yourself are a little fascinated among all the vast million-dollar-figures," he noted, "just like most of the gangster-movies in spite of the gangster's violent death provides most youngsters with a feeling that the gangsterism is a hell of a exciting way to live."[41]

Previous books of social criticism prepared several readers to respond favorably to what Packard wrote. "If I had my way," said a woman from Colorado, "'The Lonely Crowd,' 'The Organization Man' and 'The Hidden Persuaders' would be made required reading for every American mother. They should think about these books for the sake of their children, if they won't for their own."[42] Another person wrote that *Hidden Persuaders*, along with *Organization Man* and *Lonely Crowd*, "provide a tripod perspective from which to see and appreciate the depth meanings of our culture."[43] The books by David Riesman and William H. Whyte, Jr., by creating expectations that Packard could now fulfill, had established for his audience the definition of a particular kind of social criticism.

Other responses help explain additional dimensions of Packard's popularity. A high school senior from Omaha perceptively noted Packard's accessible prose. She liked to read books like his, she told Packard, but "usually they are so complex that I can't finish them. Yours was easy for me to understand, and informative as well."[44] Several of the letters echoed the contrasting emotions that appeared in many of the reviews. Thank you, wrote a woman from Missouri, for a million "chuckles—and your gospel truth!"[45] Some of the information "made me want to cry," remarked someone else, "some of it gave me a hearty laugh, but *all* of it set me to thinking."[46] One especially probing letter used material in the book to suggest reasons for its popularity. What needs did *Hidden Persuaders* meet that made it so successful, asked a man from a suburb in Kentucky? Some, he responded, bought it just because it was a best-seller, while others were "curious to know the answers to some of the questions appearing on" the paperback's cover. Then, reminding Packard that the book argued that overt reasons are not the true ones, he went on to explore the possibility that the book's popularity stemmed from the satisfaction of hidden needs. He perceptively noted how books relieved anxiety by making readers feel they had an ally in their fight against the pressures of advertising. "Does your book sell emotional security," he challenged Packard, by letting "the reader feel that he is 'above' or 'safe from' these marketing pressures now that he has read about them?" Or does the "book sell ego-satisfaction," he continued, "in that it gives the reader a sense of superiority to the mass man who 'falls for' depth marketing?"[47]

The Status Seekers: Letter Writers and Status Anxieties

With *Status Seekers*, people wrote to brag about, decipher, or puzzle over their own position in American society.[48] A clear majority of the help seekers, comprising a substantial number of the correspondents, turned to Packard to increase their own status or to figure out problematic issues in their social situation. These responses ranged from the mundane and blatant to the moving and perplexed. In a few instances a reader clearly went against the book's attack on ill-considered striving. Thus a student at an Ivy League university asked Packard for the address of a store he had mentioned that sold "Brooks-type clothing" at discount prices. "I haven't turned into a status seeker yet," the young man wrote, "but I do have a millionaire's taste without the money to indulge it."[49] In contrast was a letter from a Jewish steelworker from Baltimore who agreed with the book's explicit message. He revealed this by hailing Walter Reuther as "the lone hold-out against opulence among the labor leaders" and by speculating on how "people seek power through things." In the end, he too turned to Packard for help, but of a kind more meaningful than how to dress inexpensively and still look like an Ivy Leaguer. Not having the "courage" to write for money, he sent off letters to newspaper editors, and he enclosed some of these missives in the hope that Packard might read them.[50]

With an even greater sense of urgency and of the problematic nature of status came a letter from a woman in a Midwestern industrial city. Married to an owner of a barbershop, having a son in a private boarding school in New York, and being a public school teacher herself, she found her family in the anomalous position of having more income than status. People, she observed, responded in two distinctive ways: some pigeonholed them as

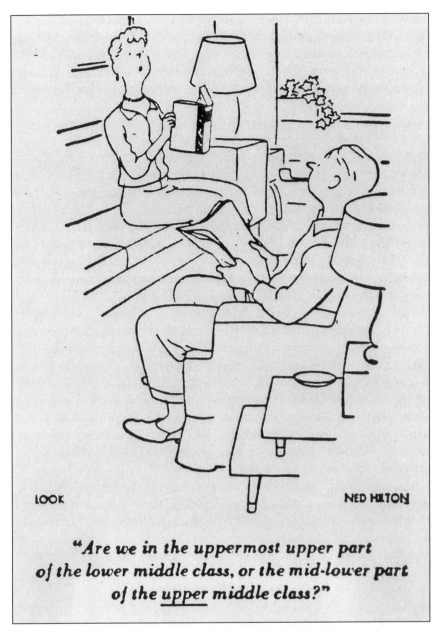

"Are we in the uppermost upper part of the lower middle class, or the mid-lower part of the upper middle class?"

In a Ned Hilton cartoon, a woman looks up from reading Status Seekers *and asks her husband about their social position.*
(From Look, *August 1959; used by permission.)*

"'rich'" "'four-flushers' and 'fakers,'" while others snubbed them because "we 'ain't got nothin','" but act like 'big shots.'" Turning to Packard for help and denying that they were "'climbers,'" she asked how she and her husband might meet "a couple or two with whom we feel congenial, with whom we can exchange visits occasionally without this underlying feeling of animosity, or rivalry."[51]

Remarkably few true believers wrote in response to *Status Seekers*. Only two correspondents tried to convert Packard to their own deeply held position. A woman from Memphis spoke of the American Medical Association as "a powerful trade protection union" designed to enhance the incomes of doctors and to make the public believe they were scientists, not quacks.[52] In addition, someone wrote from Idaho to convince Packard that Technocracy provided the solution to America's problems.[53] The nature of the response from challengers to *Status Seekers* was also different from their response to *Hidden Persuaders*. Only two fit into this category, and both of them offered critiques that were more friendly and less political than had obtained with the first of the best-sellers.[54]

With *Status Seekers*, by far the largest batch of letters came from the converted, people who agreed with Packard. Most of these responses were routine—writers passed along confirming evidence or acknowledged the author's contribution. However, some went beyond the obvious and helped to illuminate reasons for the book's impact that had not been factors before. "I have followed your writings almost religiously," a man wrote from a Baptist church in a Southern city, revealing how each new book augmented Packard's following, "and look forward to a new book from you like a kid looks for Christmas. I have a reserve in the local book store for the first copy of any new book that you publish."[55]

The success of *Status Seekers* also underscored the vacuum created by developments in academic sociology. A doctor from Connecticut remarked that the book left him "spellbound." Usually he found "the perusal of a sociological tract an onerous and emotionally unrewarding business." In contrast, Packard's work "sparkles with wit, abounds with timely anecdote, and is packed full of instructive and valuable facts." Were "more treatises on sociology" well written, he concluded, "there would be a much wider audience for publications in the field."[56] Others agreed that the book was superior to academic sociology: an insurance agent from Indiana called it "the most fascinating social study I've read since the Lynds' 'Middletown'"; a disk jockey from New Bedford, Massachusetts, said Packard's two best-sellers had given him "more insight into the social sphere than all of my social textbooks in college"; and a man from New

Orleans congratulated him for not hiding "behind a lot of high-sounding sociological phrases."[57]

Equally telling was the correspondence from a high school teacher from a small city in the Midwest. In 1960, he thanked Packard for writing books that, compared with "Talcott Parsons' dense volumes," were readable and personal. "Those in the sociological field," he remarked, "may not think too highly of you for putting your personal self in the book since [sociologists] seem to think that sociological research and communication must be as impersonal as a washing machine." A friend of his who taught high school sociology had told him that Packard was a "popularizer" who lacked depth and had "the nasty habit of dashing in where even fools would fear to tread" and that he was "really not in sociology," by which he meant that he was "not a full professor at a big, high status university." Five years later, this teacher wrote Packard again. After remarking that he appreciated Packard's books because they told "truths that most 'good' people would just as soon ignore," he noted that "the 'experts' in sociology apparently have little use for you or your wares." In a class the teacher had taken during the summer, a sociologist at a university had said that Packard's work was "not a 'safe' or 'reliable' or 'scholarly' source." His guess was that "these boys are jealous of you—of your fame or notoriety and of the great amount of money you make" out of what academics felt was "'phony'" scholarship and "'glib'" judgments.[58]

Several letters revealed the tremendous impact the book had on some readers. The most dramatic came from a nurse. "There are two or three situations," she remarked, "resulting in a release of joy normally attributable to orgasm—a new idea, a phrase that writes itself, or a *real* feeling of accomplishment. It is with this feeling I finished your book."[59] More typically, the testimonials to the book's impact came from people who prided themselves on their avoidance of status seeking. A person from Chicago reported staying awake until five o'clock in the morning to finish *Status Seekers*. "I feel that my life has been immeasurably enriched by reading and understanding your book." Long fearful of articulating the ideas that Packard now expressed, this person was grateful that "there are men such as you to bring these truths to the attention of the world."[60] An African American woman from a city in the Midwest talked of how "intensely" the study had held her interest, attacked people for spending and not saving, and hoped that what Packard wrote "will awaken and enlighten the masses about some of the true values of life which seem lost."[61] Somewhat similar was the response of a woman from Florida who, noting that "if you do regard people for their personal worth, then you are an odd-ball," confessed to being "the rebel."[62] Probably with unintended irony, an antiques dealer from Pennsylvania asserted that America was "doomed" because the entire economy, based "on trying to get others to covet things which they do not even need," violated one of the Ten Commandments.[63]

As profound as the impact was on some of the converted, for others the book served as a manual for evaluating or displaying status. A woman from a distinguished Southern family commented that she "subscribed to the American Heritage and owned the eleventh edition of the Encyclopedia Britannica and was once invited to Newport but couldn't go" and asked Packard, "Will that do?"[64] An army officer from Pennsylvania thanked him for providing "excellent background data in dealing with my associates both in business and socially."[65] Although a number of people talked about their social position in terms of how the book illuminated their understanding, to the converted the book served as a self-help manual for social climbers less frequently than was true with *Hidden Persuaders*. When most people among the converted turned to *Status Seekers* to place themselves on the pecking order, they usually did so more playfully than seriously.

Moreover, there is considerable evidence that the book had special appeal to people concerned about prejudice and limited opportunity. Several Jews wrote Packard to discuss discrimination.[66] He also heard from people who were downwardly mobile, without college degrees, aspiring but fearful, or worried about the implications of blocked social mobility. Remarked a woman from Pennsylvania who considered herself to have "a high degree of intelligence but without the advantages of college and 'good background,'" the book had given her "hope that the need for seeking out the above-average intelligent student for guidance and additional education has been recognized."[67]

An especially poignant example of someone who wrote because she believed Packard was sympathetic to the plight of people whom America might push aside came from a woman in the state of Washington. The wife of a farm laborer who was "white of Latin heritage" proudly described how frugally the family lived. They did not drink alcohol, and they drove a nine-year-old automobile, "for transportation, not show." Every day she read to her two young daughters, choosing such authors as Charles Darwin, Thomas Mann, and Carl Jung. How many people of higher social status, she asked Packard rhetorically, read books by writers such as these? How many members of the Junior League, Episcopal church, and Rotary Club "want their children to become understanding, educated ladies and gentlemen?" She hoped her daughters would "attend a good college," become "ladies, not women," and "marry educated non-conforming gentlemen, not college men." Ending the letter, she said, "I remain a friend," as if to tell Packard how important it was to have the ear of a sympathetic and authoritative person who wanted to strengthen America's commitment to equal opportunity.[68]

One final characteristic of the response to *Status Seekers* is worth mentioning. A significant number of letters from the converted, help seekers, and challengers sought to establish contact with someone who was famous. To some extent this had been true with *Hidden Persuaders*; with the new book, contact-seeking had greater frequency and, at times, a sense of urgency. Packard was emerging as a celebrity. One best-seller had made him widely read; two, famous. Hopeful authors wrote to obtain real or symbolic help. For example, a personnel manager from New Jersey, who considered writing his "avocation," asked Packard what he thought of a paper he had done in graduate school seven years previously. "When I find somebody else thinking the same way I think," he commented, "[I have] to add my two cents' worth."[69]

In other cases, people seemed to be reaching out to someone who was prominent or who they thought understood their perspective. With *Status Seekers* Upton Sinclair did what famous writers rarely did with the books of others: he expressed his pleasure with Packard's work.[70] People whom Packard had no reason to be interested in meeting presumed upon his friendship. A couple from New Mexico invited him to be their guest. "September might be a nice time to travel," they said, "but any time would be fine."[71] Wrote a man from California who asked for an autograph: "It is indeed an honor to know you are taking time to read my letter," as if to reassure himself that he would receive personal attention.[72] Not in a way that was intended to start long correspondence or even in the expectation of a reply, people appreciated having the opportunity to try expressing their ideas.[73]

The Waste Makers: The Growth of Political Consciousness

With the third of the best-sellers, the letters reveal major changes in readers' responses to Packard's writings.[74] This time, no correspondents sought to use the material in the book in a way that conflicted with its message. Although Packard's attitude toward affluence may have been somewhat ambivalent, the information on planned obsolescence and the importance of natural resources pointed mainly in the direction of careful shopping and sensitivity to the environment. Moreover, although with the earlier books men had been more likely to write than women, with *Waste*

Makers the numbers were almost equal. The principal reason for this shift was that in readers' responses to the earlier books, men greatly outnumbered women among the help seekers; now there was near equivalence in that category. The feminization of help seekers may have stemmed from greater self-confidence among women in the early 1960s. Also, *Waste Makers*, unlike the earlier books, offered information more pertinent to households run by women than to professions dominated by men.

As had been true with *Status Seekers*, the number of true believers was quite small, with only two people fitting this category. A magazine editor who accused Consumers Union of trying "to put small retailers out of business" was less ideological and more self-interested than most other true believers, and a man from Boston sent a long letter on the credit system. He asserted that a change in monetary arrangements from the present "500-year-old feudal handicraft scarcity antique sleight-of-hand" would solve the nation's economic problems and protect America from the Communists.[75]

In addition, only two challengers contacted Packard. A man from the Los Angeles area expressed agreement with Packard's description of "the foibles of American society" but took issue with his proposals for government intervention because they might "be destructive of the very freedoms on which genuine progress depends!" He asserted that "nations that have sacrificed private freedom to the 'public interest' (or the 'State,' or the 'Fatherland') have lived to regret it."[76] More hostile and threatening was a letter from a reader who was involved in advertising. "As long as you continue to take fragments of truth, and then build upon them vast edifices of deception and untruth," he warned, "we will continue to mount a campaign to expose your motives, your techniques, and your lack of documentation." He also accused Packard of having unrealistic notions of how the American economy worked and of pandering "to the underlying guilt feelings of a Puritan-oriented population whose philosophy hasn't caught up with their physical demands for high standard of living." Eventually, he concluded, "someone is going to find an emotional, popular way of telling people that it is not immoral to consume—and then where will your market be?"[77]

By far the largest group of respondents were the converted, representing more than 70 percent of the total. Some offered comments on Packard's writing that help explain the effectiveness of all three books. As a woman from Denver noted, "I like your terse, no-nonsense style and I am even more impressed by your meticulous research."[78] As had been true with the previous works, people sensed that Packard was saying what they had always felt but had been unable to express. "Thank you," remarked a woman from Connecticut, for confirming "what I have been vaguely aware of from daily experience for a long time."[79]

Waste Makers, more than did *Hidden Persuaders* and *Status Seekers*, elicited boasts from people who felt that they heroically resisted the temptations of materialism. A wealthy woman from North Carolina wrote of how others succumbed to "persuasive purveyors of the newest, unnecessary models of everything" because "they lack the inner resources which a stable background, a good education, a tradition of morality and gentility" provided.[80] From a different background came a similar testimony to prudence. A working-class woman who lived in an area outside Cleveland "overrun by Suburbia," drove a Volkswagen, and paid cash for her purchases, told Packard that "most of your revelations are only what my husband and I have been saying for the last ten years."[81] Similarly, a Denver woman claimed that she and her husband "live a life completely untouched by the glittering copy dreamed up by ad-men." They drove a ten-year-old car with 131,756 miles, ate no TV dinners, had few appliances, and would get rid of a television set if someone gave them one. "We aren't beating our brains out to keep up with anybody," she said proudly, "— we're too busy fishing or writing or walking in the forest or reading our books." She concluded by remarking, "The American public is fully as soft, as decadent, as irresponsible and as stupid as our enemies have painted us."[82] Reading Packard's book made others feel reassured. "I continue to cling to my old-fashioned notions and values," remarked one letter writer, "—even though it sometimes makes us appear as 'odd-balls.'"[83] Another said it was necessary to "relearn the old ideals of moderation, work, and looking forward to unknown territories, the 'territories' are no longer lands, but men's minds."[84]

Even more so than with the two previous books, readers unequivocally embraced Packard's message. While reading *Waste Makers*, one man reported, he "was shouting hooray on almost every page" because "you had the courage to speak out."[85] A number of people offered testimony about things they bought that did not last. Others congratulated the author for fighting against shoddy goods. "Planned obsolescence and the 'brainwashing' techniques of Madison Avenue," remarked a woman from a small city in Massachusetts, "are not only economically bad, but morally evil."[86] In addition, some picked up on Packard's concern about the exhaustion of natural resources, with one woman expressing her fear of the "effect on character of waste and materialism."[87]

If *Hidden Persuaders* and *Status Seekers* prompted few people to contemplate political action, *Waste Makers* had a very different effect. Critical to an understanding of the book's impact was the sense that Packard was helping people overcome political lethargy in affluent America. "We are all too self-satisfied and comfortable," commented a reader.[88] Yet to some extent, the book's politics were sufficiently ambiguous so that people of various persuasions felt that it confirmed their views. One woman asserted that planned obsolescence fostered "the drift toward socialism and national bankruptcy." Another, an advocate of Technocracy who had written a true believer letter in response to an earlier book, now hailed this one as "helping to make the public mind aware of the elements which are causing our dilemma."[89] A woman from Colorado perfectly caught the ambivalence of many Americans who felt something was wrong but remained uncertain of what to do. On the one hand, she advocated good government, wilderness legislation, and cleaning up urban blight. On the other hand, she emphasized that she did not "want to see us expect the Federal government to do everything for us" because the nation's greatness rested on the "continued character of its people." Perhaps responding to the moral tone of Packard's book, yet uneasy with its political implications, she concluded by saying that "spiritual and moral values," best inculcated in the home, "are the very basis of the American way."[90]

Despite such responses, *Waste Makers* made people consider political action in part because, unlike the earlier books, it attained a better balance between criticism and solutions. As one reader commented, "I think you have tempered the harsh and critical realities with an outline of potentially constructive hope."[91] The book provoked a number of people to think seriously about acting on what they had learned. Thanking him for mentioning "practical suggestions," a woman from a city in Iowa noted that Packard's writings "make people uncomfortable and thoughtful. Some *may* even try to *do* something about the problems."[92] Similarly, another woman testified that "you have really reinforced my determination to do my small part in the struggle against . . . materialism."[93] Some reported that they followed Packard's suggestion of "writing complaining letters by the carloads" to heads of corporations, while others said they had now subscribed to *Consumer Reports*.[94]

Some people even went so far as to offer Packard their pledge of loyalty. "If you ever seek political office," wrote a man from San Diego, "I would certainly offer my support."[95] Another correspondent suggested a different form of action, but one that gave testimony to the power of writers like Packard. He called on him to join with fellow nonfiction authors John Keats and Whyte to write a book that would "diagnose properly our civilization" and "prescribe some sort of cure for the illness whatever it may be."[96] In addition, one person connected Packard's writings with the renewed interest in social reform of the early 1960s. "More people are beginning to think in 1964 as you did in 1960," noted a woman from North Carolina, and so the proposals made in the book "are being realized" in the administrations of John F. Kennedy and Lyndon B. Johnson.[97]

Though Packard had worried that his books sounded too critical of the United States, they did not elicit charges from readers that he was subversive or unpatriotic. Even the two challengers from the Right quoted above did not raise such a possibility. In fact, the few correspondents who used a Cold War framework made it clear that the danger to America came not from Packard's pen but from the excesses he exposed. A U.S. citizen living abroad remarked that *Waste Makers* would help the nation avert 1984 and expressed surprise "that on publication of this book, you weren't hauled up before an Un-American activities committee!"[98] Commented another reader who raised issues in a way that supported Packard rather than accused him of subversiveness: "We Americans scorn Communism because it disregards the rights of the individual, yet we seem to care nothing" about the millions society turns its back on, "those who, through no fault of their own are excluded from the main stream and flow of our economic currents."[99]

Although the response of readers to Packard's three books showed considerable consistency, there were also important changes. From the first book to the third, the percentage of help seekers, true believers, and challengers fell dramatically. At the same time, the proportion of converted more than doubled. The fact that the material in *Hidden Persuaders* and *Status Seekers* was more personal helps account for the decrease in the proportion of help seekers. As reform politics came to the fore between 1957 and 1960, some people in Packard's audience shifted their attention from the private to the public. The diminished presence of the true believers and challengers also came about because the conspiratorial tone of *Hidden Persuaders* was more apt to elicit letters from people who not only felt that they had the truth but also believed that hidden forces were working against them. The proportion of the converted may have increased because Packard's growing reputation as an authority attracted letter writers who already agreed with him.

The Development of an Audience for Social Criticism

These shifts reveal the changing reaction to Packard's books, but they only begin to answer questions about the popularity and impact of his writing. The hundreds of letters Packard received point to both the patterns and the particularities of the responses. Certain themes appear over and over again, reminding us of the way texts, reviews, promotional materials, cultural conventions, and social conditions shape reactions. Yet the uniqueness of many of the responses is also striking. People read the books in relationship to very particular aspects of their situation. Many readers derived from the books what their previous experiences, idiosyncratic reactions, and social situation fostered. In most cases, members of the audience discovered what they already knew; in others, the books served as revelation. Packard's audience read extensively rather than intensively—very few reported reading the books over and over, and many made it clear that absorption of these books was part of their experience with a broad range of reading material.[100] Although readers shared intimate thoughts, Packard, unlike some other authors, did not expect, encourage, or receive many intensely personal responses that tried to eliminate barriers between him and his audience.[101] Yet some did respond out of profound or superficial psychological need, using the text to reaffirm or shape their identity.

A number of factors were especially influential in determining how people read these books. Whether coincidental or causal, the parallels among text, public relations efforts, reviews, and reader response are striking—especially the importance of self-help themes in the first two books, the nascent political vision in the third, and the tension between shock and reassurance in all three. In most instances there was a reciprocal relationship between Packard's intentions and the reader's response. At times, Packard's ambivalence made possible a range of readings. Unlike what some literary critics have led us to expect, only in the most exceptional cases did readers create *de novo*, shaping a vision that emerged from their own psyche and not from the text. These books of social criticism were more accessible and the interpretation of them more bound by culture and society than might be true of a complicated poem or novel.

What governed many of the readings was membership in an interpretative community created by mass-circulation magazines and popular social criticism.[102] The letters demonstrate that previous works by Packard himself, as well as by such writers as Rachel Carson, Stuart Chase, Keats, Riesman, and Whyte led many in the audience to respond in patterned ways. Although no one mentioned to Packard that they had read his earlier articles, people in his audience who were inveterate readers of family-oriented magazines had extensive experience with the stylistic conventions upon which Packard's books relied. The magazine pieces had accustomed the audience to a narrative structure and style that was built upon ordinary words and syntax, familiar detail, and personal drama.

Packard's colloquial style and tone helped readers believe that he described a world they inhabited. Just as romances offered their readers a sense of connection with fine literature, so Packard's books drew on the words of experts from business and the academy to offer the reader a sense of connection with authoritative expertise. As the letters testify, many in his audience respected his diligent research and the sense he conveyed that he really knew his subject matter. Moreover, the books used an easily comprehended universe of goods and experiences to enable the members of the audience to see the familiar in a new context.[103]

By leading readers from problems to solutions without insisting on a strong commitment to work actively for a specific solution, the books sustained a community of concern. For the members of that community, reading may have been as important as political action. For some, reading one or more of these books served a function similar to the reading of a romantic novel: it enabled "them to deal with the particular pressures and tensions encountered in their daily round of activities." Moreover, it is possible that the books' realism, combined with their evocation of a more perfect world in the past, did for readers what other forms of popular culture have done: it simultaneously projected and undercut a utopian vision, in the process leaving "unchallenged the very system of social relations whose faults and imperfections gave rise" to the social critique in the first place. In the end, at least for some, the process of reading Packard's books offered an experience analogous to that of the female romance reader, "a strategy for making her present situation more comfortable without substantive reordering of its structure rather than a comprehensive program for reorganizing her life in such a way that all needs might be met."[104]

As useful as this line of analysis is, however, the response to *Hidden Persuaders*, *Status Seekers*, and *Waste Makers* poses distinctive problems of interpretation. To begin with, the letters reveal that many in Packard's audience shared his ambivalence with regard to affluence, success, and political action. The contradictory impulses held by members of his audience made it possible for them to use the books in ways that went against the grain of the explicit message they offered. Some could turn to what Packard wrote for self-help that ultimately led in divergent directions because the books themselves, like their author, were ambivalent about what he saw. Yet, however much Packard and members of his audience shared this ambivalence, the letters nonetheless brought to the surface a considerable number of puritanically minded people who stood against the tide of America's growing affluence. Letters from the proudly prudential who thought that affluence was undermining America's traditional values provide evidence that many in the audience shared Packard's commitment to key elements of the producer ethic.

The response to his books revealed the ironies of a therapeutic culture for which an emphasis on personality was central. The letters make clear that many Americans were already establishing an antagonistic relationship to postwar consumer culture. Yet by focusing on his audience's awareness of the problems that people encountered in social situations, Packard could both mollify and intensify the anxieties they faced in their daily lives as they came to terms with affluence. Reliance on others, including experts like himself, was the key to self-awareness. The road to the restoration of a world where hard work, character, and self-reliance reigned was paved with the good intentions of the educated shopper.[105]

Finally, insofar as these letters are representative of the reaction of a wider range of readers, they uncover the loneliness of the American crowd. For a significant percentage of the respondents, letter writing was an act of reaching out to someone who seemed sympathetic with their personal and social situation. The urge to seek contact was powerful—among the abstemious who had felt odd in an affluent society, writers who needed encouragement, individuals who wanted to touch someone famous, people with ideas they had long held but been unable to express. Changes in postwar American society prepared the ground for the reception of Packard's books—changes that made people uneasy not only with affluence, advertising, and the destruction of natural resources but also with the emergence of an increasingly impersonal society. Ironically, books shaped by Packard's experience as a writer for the mass media touched thousands, if not millions, of Americans in the most personal of ways.

The Crack in the Picture Window

The Response of Critics to the Trilogy

Packard's books mobilized critics. Members of the business community launched a full-scale attack on *Hidden Persuaders* and *Waste Makers*. Especially with *Status Seekers*, sociologists responded in ways that revealed much about the nature of their discipline and the heritage of Willard Waller. New York intellectuals offered a thoroughgoing critique that underscored the similarities and differences between Packard and the writers who set the terms of serious public discourse in the 1950s and early 1960s. Reviewers in national magazines and big-city newspapers criticized Packard for pandering to mass taste. Conservatives took issue with his skepticism about the benefits of affluence and free enterprise. Those to the left of Packard joined others in questioning his moralism, nostalgia, and ambivalence. Critics also raised issues about the cogency of his analysis, the power of his solutions to set things right, and the contradictions between his medium and his message.

Attacks from the Business Community

The most coordinated and vituperative critiques, ones that made most others pale by comparison, came from the business community. Admen, market researchers, corporate executives, and writers in the business press had much to worry about at a time when observers of the American scene were beginning to raise questions about America's national purpose.[1] People in advertising are particularly sensitive to images—not only the ones they create but also the ones others offer of them. Except in novels and movies, since World War II they had remained relatively immune to public criticism. With the publication of *Hidden Persuaders*, they felt that they had come under attack and that they could never be sure that their profits or prestige would remain strong enough to protect them from government regulation or business skepticism. Packard had divulged trade secrets but, more important, he had divulged them to a wide and responsive audience. He had used preposterous examples and dramatic prose to cast doubts on the claim that American capitalism was efficient and moral. The USSR may have had its state planning, but he showed that American corporations had planned obsolescence. Similarly, market research and subliminal messages seemed ominously like the tools of the Soviet Big Brother.

Packard's trial by fire occurred early. In the fall of 1957, during a debate between Packard and an agency executive, his opponent administered what *Advertising Age* called a "tongue-lashing." He denounced Packard for writing "a malicious book" that held the field responsible for "many callously powerful schemes and tactics." He attacked Packard for using innuendo to make motivational researchers seem like "a cross between Harold Lloyd and the witch in Walt Disney's 'Snow White.'" Like other critics, he argued that Packard had exaggerated the power, newness, and evil of advertisements. Displaying his own ability to manipulate symbols, he reminded his audience that hidden persuasion, clearly preferable to "the cave man's club, or the concentration camps or banishment to Siberia," was one of the main things that differentiated people from animals. Finally, he turned the tables on Packard by remarking that more dangerous than the work of Madison Avenue was the "propaganda that walks around hidden in the trusted and respected apparel of a book."[2]

Packard was caught off guard. Soon after, he confided to a friend that he had been subjected to "an ambush" when his opponent offered a "personal attack upon me and a bitter, sneering literary criticism of my book."[3] Packard's naiveté, his antagonist's geniality at the lunch preceding the debate, and early reviews in the business press encouraged him to expect temperate treatment from those he had exposed.[4] Counting admen among his acquaintances and believing that many people in the field did good work, he felt that his critique was aimed at MR, not at all advertising. He was, he believed, talking "not about villains but rather about historical forces."[5]

In response to what Packard and other critics said, people who supported the advertising industry had reason to be nervous. A report sponsored by the American Association of Advertising Agencies in 1968 noticed that "a new peak in concern over advertising's social malfeasance erupted after" the appearance of *Hidden Persuaders*, a book described as "a diatribe against the unseen (although perhaps nonexistent) manipulators of our national consumer behavior." In the late 1950s and early 1960s, the business community answered Packard's attack with a concerted public relations campaign.[6] The response that attracted the most attention came in 1963 with David Ogilvy's *Confessions of an Advertising Man*, a widely read book by an agency executive renowned for his inventive strategies. Although Ogilvy did not mention Packard, much of his effort went to counter the picture of the dark side of the business. In contrast, he discussed advertising campaigns as acts of creativity and imagination.[7]

As strong as was the response from the business community to *Hidden Persuaders*, the reaction to *Waste Makers* was even more forceful and ill-tempered. Under the headline "Is 'The Waste Makers' a Hoax?" *Printers' Ink* led the counterattack with a seven-page cover story, followed a few weeks later by an article titled "Packard Hoodwinks Most Reviewers," and then concluded five months after that with an editorial whose title asked "Has Packard Flipped?"[8] Pointing to what they characterized as "inflammatory language," "half-truths, distorted facts, and twisted ideas," the editors cast doubts on Packard's motives and criticized him for writing a book that reviled "an economic system which, for all its shortcomings," had given America "the world's highest standard of living."[9]

The criticism of *Waste Makers* came from a broad range of people within the business community.[10] Relying on the language of progress, free enterprise, and need fulfillment, writers took issue with what they perceived as Packard's attacks on affluence and the American economic system.[11] Ernest Dichter wrote that Packard and other critics were "morality hucksters" who pound "their royalty-stuffed chests and weep bitter tears over tailfins, then step into their sports cars and roar out to their Connecticut homes to cool off with a drink iced from a 1961 refrigerator engineered by waste makers."[12] Dichter defended MR on the grounds that it provided "an invitation to new experiences, to a more creative and more fulfilled life."[13] Executives at General Motors criticized Packard's emphasis on

The Un-hidden persuaders

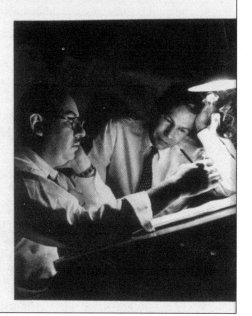

If you draw your conclusions from the self-styled experts in the field these days, advertising and selling are pretty sneaky stuff.

To hear these boys talk, you'd think advertising was one part psychiatry to two parts brainwashing, with a couple dashes of henbane and dragonwort thrown in.

We happen to think that most people buy things because they need, want, and can use them.

And that these people, regardless of their libidos or ids, like the kind of advertising that shows arresting pictures of these products and delivers fresh, truthful, interesting words about them.

Thank heavens, that's the kind of advertising our clients seem to like, too.

Advertisement by leading ad agency, in response to Hidden Persuaders. *(From the trade journal* Tide, *13 June 1958, p. 12.* © *Leo Burnett Co., Inc.; used by permission.)*

planned obsolescence, preferring instead to call frequent model changes "dynamic obsolescence," something "for the customer's own good" that created jobs, improved products, and enabled customers to keep up with the Joneses.[14]

Business representatives also took issue with Packard's politics. Some disagreed with what he wrote about the imbalance between public and private spending. "If there wasn't a whale of a lot of spending on such baubles as lemon drops and diamond bracelets, not to mention convert-

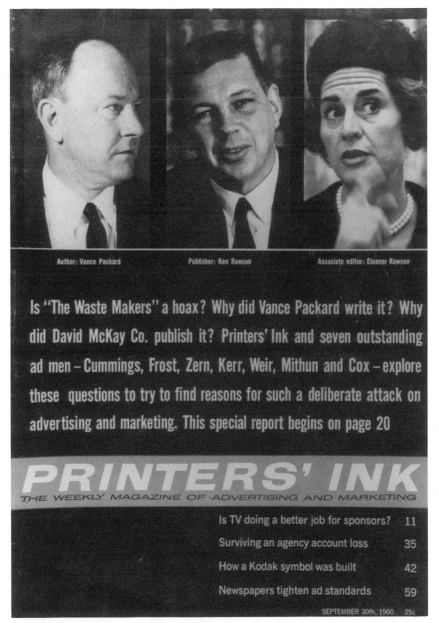

The cover of a weekly trade magazine of the advertising and marketing industries illustrates the attack by the business community against Waste Makers. *(From* Printers' Ink, *30 September 1960.)*

ibles with all the extras," commented one advocate of private enterprise, "there could not be research and scholarship on the scale we enjoy—if at all."[15] For others the problem was that Packard had too much confidence in the ability of wasteful and "paternalistic government" to "shield the American commonalty from its own follies."[16] On relatively rare occasions, business representatives participated in red-baiting Packard by couching their objections in Cold War terms. A public relations executive remarked that what Packard wrote was both "puritanical" and "socialistic."[17] The head of General Foods said that Communist governments, by restricting choice, were "doing precisely what some are advocating for America." Degrading political freedom by conflating it with consumer choice, he contrasted this with the American Way—freedom of choice, consumption, progress, and competition—all of which were set in motion by "aggressive persuasion . . . utilized by business to accelerate our free enterprise machine."[18]

Although the initial attack from the business community may have

Referring to Affluent Society, Status Seekers, *and most pointedly to* Waste Makers, *E. I. du Pont de Nemours and Co. adds its voice to the corporate attack on Packard's critique of the excesses of affluence. Celebrating "self-criticism" as "a luxury which only a very successful society can afford," the newspaper advertisement asserts that turning aside "the better, the less costly, or the safer . . . would relegate progress itself to the scrap-basket." (From the* New York Herald Tribune, *8 January 1961.)*

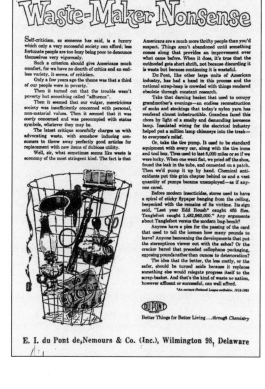

stung Packard, at least in public he came to accept and even appreciate what he thought of as the ill-founded hostility of these critics. Years later he remarked, "When you're in the business of throwing stones, you're not surprised if stones come back at you."[19] At the time he explained that "good enemies 'are those who are so obviously prejudiced that their criticisms mean nothing.'" Extending the maxim that any publicity is good, he commented, "'The best thing for an author, next to being banned in Boston, is to be blasted on Madison Avenue.'"[20] Indeed, as one of his best friends remarked, the "assault" in *Printers' Ink* "delighted" both Packard and the people at McKay. "In terms of lineage," he wrote, "it was book advertising no publisher could afford to buy."[21]

Sociologists Draw the Line

If the business community took issue with Packard's work, sociologists unleashed a barrage of criticisms, especially of *Status Seekers*.[22] Packard had his admirers within the field, and many professors assigned his books. Yet by and large, sociologists paid attention to his work mainly when they criticized it or when, having read and absorbed it, they denied reading it in the first place.[23] The attacks threatened to undermine Packard's claims of expertise. As a colleague reported later, Packard was "very ambitious to be taken seriously as a sociologist."[24] Although much of the questioning of Packard's work echoed themes found elsewhere, the criticism by sociologists was distinctive because it focused on issues of class, status, and opportunity. Sociologists asserted that Packard was wrong when he argued that American society was becoming more rigid and social mobility more difficult to achieve.[25] Moreover, academics wondered if in fact status seeking was either on the rise or necessarily bad.[26] They questioned Packard's belief in a connection between increased status seeking and changes in class relationships.[27] Furthermore, professors found his stance on class and status equivocal. One observer remarked that Packard wavered between a "realistic" acceptance of class distinctions and a "fanciful" dream of a classless society.[28]

Several responses by academics deserve particular attention because of the issues they raise about Packard and sociology. In the *American Sociological Review*, William Petersen, after noting reluctantly that his peers held "popularization in contempt," attacked Packard's book on several grounds. Like others, he questioned the idealization of an earlier day as well as the "doleful picture of America's class system."[29] Moreover, he asserted that Packard combined "a monumental arrogance with an obsequious deference to authority or money." *Status Seekers* was a success, he commented, in part because its appeal lay "in the social climber's ambivalent stance toward social climbing." Packard provided a formula "that had been perfected long since in moral tracts against pornography." First came "up-to-date Emily Post," a detailed description of the tricks by which one could achieve new status. There followed the denunciation of "statusseekers as an unworthy lot." He concluded that "such careful catering to a widespread need suggests that the author is a good businessman."[30]

Writing in *Partisan Review*, sociologist Lewis Coser launched an equally acerbic critique. He saw the book as an example of "*Kitsch* sociology," a "spurious reproduction" that reshaped scholarship in a way that eliminated all nuances. Packard, Coser wrote, frightened "the jaded reader," then aroused his "guilt and anxiety," and finally reassured him with homilies about the possibilities of individual happiness. Coser ascribed the book's success to Packard's skill in having correctly "sensed the drift of the *Zeitgeist*" when he cleverly exploited people's status anxieties. Not informed "by a scholar's concern or a reformer's zeal," *Status Seekers* was "anchored in nothing more substantial than a guilty nostalgia for a supposedly less status-conscious and hence less anxiety-ridden past." In the end the criticism Packard offered was harmless, Coser wrote, because it set out "to afford its audience the pleasure of deploring a state of affairs which it secretly craves." Flattering the reader, the book made it possible for "him to compensate for his guilt in condoning a meretricious reality by the fake catharsis of verbal condemnation," which was "designed to reconcile him to his role as a part of that reality."[31]

More extensive and persistent was the critique by sociologist Seymour Martin Lipset. His 1959 essay on *Status Seekers* in the *Reporter* started off by emphasizing the barriers between academics and nonacademics. Pointing to the statement on the dust jacket that Packard was an associate member of the American Sociological Association, Lipset informed "all intellectual status seekers" that for a fee of twenty dollars they too could claim such membership. Relying on overconfident positivist assumptions, Lipset asserted that the basic problem with the book was that it misused "scientific evidence to construct a prejudiced and partisan case" that wrongly argued that the United States was becoming less egalitarian. Lipset cited studies demonstrating that Americans were satisfied with their work, that rates of social mobility and opportunity were steady if not improving, and that access to higher education was enhancing opportunity.[32]

In response to *Waste Makers* Lipset offered two essays—one in *Commentary* and the other in the *Progressive*. He congratulated Packard for having set out to reach a broad reading public, a task that most of those in

American sociology, perhaps too "anxious about its status as a science," refused to undertake. Lipset pointed to the contradiction between what was apparently a "radical polemic against the traditional American way of life" and the fact that Packard's "books are largely bought by those whose behavior they seem most violently to be attacking." Far from having a genuine concern with changing things, he argued, the book created "a more sophisticated status symbol than those it opposes." Packard, Lipset remarked, refused to consider the possibility that what he described might "be inherent in *institutions* based on American democratic values." He also found fault with Packard's remedies. Refusing to accept government planning or ownership, Packard proposed "no serious institutional reforms . . . because essentially he is an old-fashioned conservative."[33] What was needed, Lipset argued, was "radical thinking about what Twenty-first Century America should look like, not . . . nostalgia about how good it is to be able to live in a Vermont farmhouse without central heating, running water, or electric lighting."[34]

Lipset asserted that Packard's work represented a new kind of cultural criticism that saw affluence as a problem. Americans, he remarked, "seem to love to hear how corrupt, wasteful, status-seeking, and conformist they are."[35] He argued that Packard's analysis relied on the "nostalgia of the wealthy ex-urbanite for a world in which he does not live; and who, further, though he feels guilty about all the abundance he shares, is still determined to keep it." Although Lipset believed that Packard probably thought of himself as a "rebel" who embraced some liberal or even radical action, in fact he was a conformist who managed to hide his nonconformity in a book that combined "a critique of commercialism with an espousal of the verities advocated by Herbert Hoover." This, the sociologist remarked, was a "foolproof combination that sells books."[36] In the end, Americans devoured books that let them "have their cake and eat it too, to indulge in all the activities" that Packard "morally condemns, secure in the belief that the good society lies in the American past." *Waste Makers* was "like a good sermon"; it was something that could "make you feel better, more moral, personally above the crass world which you can enjoy, but for which you are not responsible."[37]

Even after Packard's popularity peaked in the early 1960s, social scientists continued to question his work. In 1965, in *Trans-Action*, a periodical edited by sociologists who had roots in 1930s radicalism and who were trying to reach readers outside universities, a writer said that Packard posed a "dilemma" for many academics because he had brought their findings to a larger audience and yet had not convinced them that he had a firm grasp of the field.[38]

In response to the attack from social scientists, Packard proved he could give as well as take. He thought about writing a reply to Lipset, but in the end decided not to, because "only teams in the second division blast the umpire."[39] This sentiment did not prevent him from answering Petersen in print, characterizing his review as "a highly emotional sputter" that was "a good example of status protection in action by a member of an in-group. Strike down the impertinent outsider who pretends to have assimilated some of the secret lore of the insiders!"[40] In 1970, Packard wrote caustically about *Trans-Action*'s "long campaign to establish that it is the only proper medium for making facts about human behavior known to the world outside Science."[41] He defended himself against charges of saying nothing new, researching sloppily, simplifying, misrepresenting, being naive, and putting forth conspiracy theories.[42] He also answered the criticism that he was an old-fashioned conservative by pointing out how President Lyndon B. Johnson's Great Society embodied many of the recommendations he made in *Waste Makers*. Against those who sought to explain away his popularity with general audiences, he argued that people read his books principally because they wanted to learn how to deal more intelligently with the changes in society that they found swirling about them.[43] In the end, he asked to be judged on the issue of whether his work was "essentially useful, essentially useless, or essentially harmful."[44]

On some issues, the attacks from sociologists were on the mark. They effectively captured Packard's nostalgia, ambivalence, moralism, and naiveté. They understood the contradictory ways in which readers could use his books, even to the point of undermining what at first appeared to be the radical nature of their message. Packard was proud of how quickly he could turn out a book, but he did not come to terms with the costs of his speed. Nonsociologists had noted some of the worst features of his writing when they remarked that these books were "slapdash," exaggerated, "unnecessarily hectic," unsophisticated, "pedestrian," "glib and facile."[45] Packard composed more accessible prose than academics did, wrote books quicker than they could produce articles, and had an ability to absorb what more cautious writers would have struggled to resolve or qualify. What he gained in impact, productivity, and accessibility, he lost in originality and subtlety.

Yet whatever the accuracy of the sociologists' criticisms, the tone, themes, and persistence of their response call for explanation. In 1963, a college student wrote Packard of an incident in the classroom that underscores the vehemence of their reaction. Having reported that reading *Status Seekers* "changed my desires, outlook and conduct of life," he called Packard his "patron saint" who had inspired him to resume his college education after twenty-eight years away from the classroom. When he mentioned Packard's work in a sociology class, he noted, "one would have thought I dropped a bomb in our midst." The teacher "stalked out of the classroom," returned with an uncomplimentary report, and then launched into a "dissertation about what a faker, charlatan etc etc V. Packard was."[46]

Like this teacher, critical reviewers tried to draw clear lines between academics and others in a way that suggested the importance they attached to protecting turf.[47] Indeed, a number of contemporaries joined Packard in pointing out that professors, with their limited readership, pressure to specialize, and jargon-filled prose, were envious of someone who had the freedom to write on a wide range of subjects, a huge following, and the royalties that such a readership brought.[48] "Professional sociologists need not be astonished that Mr. Packard has filled a void," remarked Robert Lekachman, an economist who wrote for lay audiences. Though he agreed with the criticisms the sociologists launched, he also acknowledged that if they "want responsible versions of their findings to be read by publics wider than their colleagues, they had better write them."[49]

During the period of Packard's greatest popularity, the discipline, under the influence of Robert K. Merton, Paul Lazarsfeld, and Talcott Parsons, was in the process of transforming itself into a specialized, theoretical, and quantitative field that aspired to scientific status and had primary responsibility to a professional audience. Skeptical of approaches that were adversarial, humanistic, moral, or historical, mainline sociologists usually emphasized the integration of elements within a smoothly functioning system and laid claim to an objectivity that often proved illusory.[50] What came before this priestly approach—and in some ways would return later—was a sociology that was prophetic, adversarial, qualitative, and accessible to a general public: books like Robert S. Lynd and Helen M. Lynd's *Middletown* (1929), Harvey W. Zorbaugh's *Gold Coast and Slum* (1929), and Paul G. Cressey's *Taxi-Dance Hall* (1932).[51] The ascendant group in the late 1950s worried about the danger that sociology, made fashionable by best-selling journalists, might lose its scientific status.[52] These academics offered a view of American society consistent with the liberal consensus—one in which stratification was defused, social mobility celebrated, and conflict minimized.[53] This celebration appeared with abundant clarity in a 1953 article that Petersen published in *Commentary*. American life, he wrote, was "based on the same essential factors—the enormous industrial production, the high and widely distributed income, the general distribution of equalitarian cultural values—that any socialist culture would rest on."[54]

Especially revealing is the fact that many of the strongest attacks on

Packard came not from Parsons, Merton, or Lazarsfeld but from Coser, Lipset, and the editors of *Trans-Action*. These scholars were to the left of the mainstream and were themselves striving to make contributions as both public intellectuals and specialized professionals. As academics striving to reach a wider audience, they were making it clear that professors could enter the arena of intellectual discourse from above but most journalists could not do so from below. They had every reason to exclude someone like Packard in order to affirm their own professional respectability. For all of these reasons, they had to draw lines between the kosher and the traif. When these sociologists questioned the value of Packard's work, they were worried about their standing among New York intellectuals. Coser, Lipset, and Petersen published their attacks in journals that this audience respected: *Commentary, Reporter, Partisan Review, Progressive, Dissent*. Thus they had to make their opposition to Packard clear to both scientific sociologists and anti-Stalinist intellectuals.

Coser, an émigré from Germany and a student of Merton, was, like Lipset and Petersen, a Trotskyist in the 1930s and an anti-Stalinist in the 1950s.[55] Like other sociologists, such as Daniel Bell, who were identified as New York intellectuals, Coser was a broad-ranging writer who drew on a copious knowledge of literature, philosophy, and social theory. In important ways during the 1950s he challenged the mainstream of sociology and, more generally, the way intellectuals celebrated American life in the Eisenhower years. A founder of *Dissent* in the early 1950s, he defined himself as a socialist and paid more attention than Packard did to poverty and to the struggle for civil rights. He was among those who began the attack on the dominance and ideas of Parsons with a 1956 book that stressed conflict, called for recognition of materialistic forces, and expressed skepticism of the view that the United States was a smoothly functioning society. Yet, as Lipset noted in 1961, Coser occupied "a mixed position"; he was "impatient with 'functionalist' analysis" but nonetheless used "many of the functionalist assumptions and methods in demonstrating the importance of conflict in society."[56]

Lipset, a student of both Merton and Lazarsfeld, shared with Coser a desire to find a middle ground between Parsonian sociology and his own interests in "social change and historical specificity."[57] Lipset was closer to the political center than Coser was. His own path-breaking work on social mobility, Lipset argued in an article published in *Commentary* in 1954, demonstrated that what made America distinct from Europe was not only the widespread commitment to "egalitarianism" but also "the greater economic productivity and more equal distribution of income and prestige symbols."[58] In *Political Man* (1960), he announced, "The fundamental political problems of the industrial revolution have been solved." He emphasized the persistence of "the democratic class struggle" in "stable and affluent democracies," yet noted that it would be fought "without ideologies, without red flags, without May Day parades." He reminded his readers that "many of the disagreeable aspects of American society which are now regarded as the results of an affluent and bureaucratic society may be recurring elements inherent in an equalitarian and democratic society." Not unlike Petersen, he concluded that *"the values of socialism and Americanism are similar."*[59]

Given the sharpness of the attacks by Coser and Lipset, it was surprising how many beliefs they shared with Packard. Like Packard, Coser stated that the issues facing America were not so much the standard of living as "the standard and quality of life." Even though "immediate material problems may be near solution," Coser wrote, "with each apparent material improvement there has been a severe social and psychological problem."[60] Like Packard, Lipset remained fascinated by the anxieties of social status. To varying degrees, Coser, Lipset, and Packard were anti-Stalinists who remained skeptical about the celebratory mood that dominated American intellectual life in the 1950s.[61] Yet there were also significant differences between Packard and his sharpest academic critics. Coser, clearly to Packard's left, shared with Lipset a grounding in the democratic socialist tradition. The two sociologists were also more rigorous, original, and sophisticated than Packard. To them, familiarity with Aristotle, Friedrich Nietzsche, Alexis de Tocqueville, and Karl Marx served as a counter to the mediocrity of mass media that they believed threatened American culture.

Drawing lines between the respectable and the unacceptable was an issue for Lipset especially. In 1961, he had optimistically sung the praises of advances that had "culminated in a sociology which is more consciously oriented toward the objective of building a science of society." He hailed Parsons and Lazarsfeld as "pacesetters in this new scientific sociology." In contrast stood the radicals C. Wright Mills and Barrington Moore, for whom the dominant approach was but "an empty body of study whose primary task is to deflect possible sources of intellectual criticism of society."[62] Ultimately Lipset cast his lot with those who, he argued, were secularizing sociology against those who, he thought, were clinging to an older, moral, and nonscientific tradition. In the controversies over the discipline, he wrote in 1961, "most of the vitriol comes from the side of people who incline toward political sensitivity and broad moral concerns, who see sociology becoming less problem-oriented, less vital, less concerned, less committed, less historical, less humanistic, more sterile, and more conservative politically." In contrast were "those identified with the more scientific side of sociology," people who "have tended more to 'go about their business'; they have been (at least in public) much less defensive, aggressive, and vigorous on their side of the controversy."[63]

Precisely at the time when he was defending the reasonableness of his allies and attacking Packard, Lipset led the effort to place Mills beyond the pale. He asserted that the Columbia professor had "little importance for contemporary American sociology." Using words whose unintended irony the future would make clear, he argued that Mills, by not teaching graduate students, had cut "himself off from the sociology fraternity" and "deliberately" rejected the chance "to affect the work of a large number of the future sociologists of America." Lipset noted, as "a further indicator of Mr. Mills' alienation from academic sociology," the fact that he recommended as "the best books available in 'sociology'" those that he himself had written, works "by non-sociologists," and an anthology of the writings of Marx and Friedrich Engels. Nonetheless, Lipset stressed, in words that also reflected part of what must have bothered him about Packard, Mills "retains important outlets of expression in the more popular and commercial media, and thus manages to influence the outside world's image of sociology."[64] There was much to differentiate the radical Mills from the debunking Packard—*Status Seekers* was no match for the reach, critical edge, and originality of *Power Elite* (1956) and *Sociological Imagination* (1959). Yet among the things that Packard and Mills shared were critiques of the 1950s celebration, antagonism from sociologists, and success in reaching an audience outside the academy. After all, the best-selling social critics of the 1950s were not New York intellectuals like Lipset and Bell but people like Packard.[65]

By the 1970s, some social scientists offered a new appreciation of Packard's accomplishments. Looking back at the battle between Packard and the sociologists, a political scientist in 1978 criticized Packard's adversaries for "building walls of linguistic and statistical density around their subject areas, heaping invective on those so foolish as to try to enter without the proper advanced degrees." He hailed Packard as "one of the few writers around who has made a point of challenging social scientists for their turf," who "translated their research into English," and who studied "social problems they should have been looking at but were not." He then listed all the things Packard saw that "only years later would be hailed as revealed knowledge"—that prosperity hardened social divisions; that America had a real lower class; that there was reason to support greater democracy in the workplace; and that unrelenting growth had an adverse impact on the environment.[66]

This favorable assessment was possible because the 1960s had challenged consensus social science and brought about a heightened appreciation of writers who addressed a larger public. The New Journalists—represented by Tom Wolfe, David Halberstam, Joan Didion, and J. Anthony Lukas—offered books marked by personal engagement and jargon-free writing. A new generation of sociologists, for whom the 1960s were formative, responded to Packard's work very differently than had their mentors. In 1990, Barbara Ehrenreich, though lamenting the way *Status Seekers* had too quickly turned from class to status, remembered Packard as "one of the few dissenters from the dogma of American classlessness."[67] Another sociologist later reported that he read *Status Seekers* just before he graduated college in 1960 and before he encountered the writings of Mills. The book helped radicalize him, Gary T. Marx recalled, opening his mind "to alternative perspectives." Though he found Packard's book useful for its "status-enhancing quality" with left-leaning women who might see him carrying it, he also believed it provided him with the intellectual tools with which to criticize society. Packard, he remembered, was a social critic who "helped him interpret and channel the socially critical themes that were simmering just below the surface in the late 1950s." As a young man whose familial milieu was pressuring him to pursue a business career, Marx was encouraged by *Status Seekers* to see the ways in which materialism and the American dream could be "corrupting." The book supported his intellectual aspirations, and he was as yet unaware that it was tainted. When Marx arrived in Berkeley to begin graduate school, however, Lipset clearly communicated the failings of *Status Seekers*.[68]

The sociologists shaped by the 1960s produced work that was somewhat similar to and yet strikingly different from Packard's, a point that Marx made clear when he wrote the introduction to *Muckraking Sociology: Research as Social Criticism* (1972). Marx acknowledged the influence on his generation of the social movements of the 1960s and of writers whom academic sociologists had marginalized—not only Mills but also Packard's fellow journalists William H. Whyte, Jr., and Charles Silberman, both of whom wrote for *Fortune* and authored influential books of social observation and criticism. Muckraking sociology, as Marx defined it, had some resemblance to Packard's work. The scholarship that came out of the 1960s was "at once more critical, . . . concerned with studying immediate human problems [and with] reaching a wide audience." The work of a new generation documented "conditions that clash[ed] with basic values" and was "capable of generating moral outrage." In other ways, however, the scholarship that Marx and his generation produced was light-years away from what *Status Seekers* offered. The work that Marx's cohort wrote was less equivocal in "questioning established orthodoxies," more determined to fix responsibility on dominant groups for their treatment of subordinate groups, and committed to "social upheaval and questioning." The new generations of sociologists held to the optimistic belief that they could have it both ways: By doing good social science, they could also bring about social change. Above all, whereas Packard concentrated on the suburban middle class, the new sociology used concepts of oppression, sexism, and racism as it turned its attention to "ignored and powerless groups" such as prostitutes, African Americans, prisoners, and migrant workers.[69]

Further evidence that Packard is a connecting link, albeit a tenuous one, between the prophetic and qualitative sociology of the 1930s and the late 1960s comes from a comparison of his work with Waller's. The similarities between teacher and mentor are significant. They both embraced a realistic sociology, used a nontechnical style, and emphasized social conflict. They shared a flair for the dramatic. They wrote about society in an ironic, demystifying, and often impressionistic manner. Gestalt psychology prompted them to stress wholeness and patterns. Politically Waller and Packard were both mavericks and moralists. Neither demonstrated much interest in political structures, yet they fully acknowledged the power of such basic American mores as the family, individualism, and private property. Consequently, they sounded more like reformers than they actually were. If "one side of Waller was the sociologist concerned about the scientific reputation of his work," David Tyack has noted in words that could also apply to Packard, another side "was the writer and former journalist who wanted to shock people."[70] What sociologists in 1970 said of Waller's popular writings, they also wrote of Packard—"adequate as journalism," it was "diffuse and intellectually superficial" and "hardly" added to the "fund of sociological knowledge."[71] An untimely death at age forty-five made it impossible for Waller to fulfill his dream of continuing to write popular sociology; his student carried on the tradition and ran into the same response from mainline academics that Waller had encountered.[72]

To be sure, not only is the direct influence of mentor on student difficult to track but there were significant differences between them. Packard was a good synthesizer but Waller sustained himself as a writer of great originality. Packard evidenced minimal interest in the sociology of education, a central preoccupation of his mentor, and Waller paid little attention to social divisions based on class and ethnicity. Their views of the family diverged considerably. Moreover, Waller maintained an interest in social interaction on the micro level while Packard gravitated to the national scene. Packard demonstrated none of Waller's fascination with psychological interaction and symbolic analysis. Waller's determinism contrasted with Packard's sense of possibility. Although they were both ironic, Waller's writings exhibited a number of qualities that Packard's lacked—a sardonic tone, anger, and brashness. Nonetheless, the similarities are great enough to underscore the ways in which Packard both tamed and carried on Waller's legacy. The parallels also suggest that Packard's sensitivity to the criticisms of academic sociologists derived in part from the fact that on some level he felt the academy denied him respect from the world to which his mentor had introduced him.

New York Intellectuals: Cultural Hierarchy and Identity

Like sociologists and members of the business community, New York intellectuals criticized Packard's works. Among his sharpest and most penetrating adversaries, to a considerable extent they shaped the contexts in which most academics and intellectuals would interpret and locate Packard. If many readers had responded to Packard because his writings reminded them of the critiques of Thorstein Veblen, the muckrakers, H. L. Mencken, and Stuart Chase, for comparative purposes it is also important to consider Packard alongside the New York intellectuals, the most influential group of writers in the postwar period. They were like gatekeepers, a literary critic has noted in a different context, whose approval was necessary for a book "to remain in the universe of cultural discourse, once past the notoriety of best-sellerdom."[73] Like sociologists, New York intellectuals used the language of purity and danger to separate themselves from Packard.

The way in which Packard was caught in the cross fire of 1950s debates on mass culture begins to suggest the fundamental differences between him and his most articulate opponents. In his classic 1960 essay that warned of the threat that "masscult" and "midcult" posed to high culture, Dwight Macdonald with some accuracy wrote of Packard as "an enterprising journalist" who had "manufactured two best sellers by summarizing the more sensational findings of the academic sociologists, garnering the results with solemn moralizings, and serving it up under catchy titles." Middlebrow culture—a category in which he included *Saturday Review of Literature*, John Hersey, the Book-of-the-Month Club, the musical *South Pacific*, and Packard—was "a peculiar hybrid" that resulted from the "unnatural intercourse" of High Culture with Masscult. In the process mass culture pretended "to respect the standards of High Culture while in fact it waters them down and vulgarizes them."[74] Similarly, Mary McCarthy, a writer prominent among New York intellectuals who in the 1950s to some extent had participated in the celebration of America, remarked that books on "mass culture for the mass audience," such as *Status Seekers* and *Organization Man*, "had become the latest form of pornography—'the mirror on the ceiling of the whorehouse.'"[75]

The cultural critic Harold Rosenberg provided a thoroughgoing attack on Packard's work. Writing before the appearance of *Status Seekers* and *Waste Makers*, he linked *Hidden Persuaders* to A. C. Spectorsky's *Exurbanites*, Whyte's *Organization Man*, Mills's *White Collar*, and David Riesman's *Lonely Crowd*. To Rosenberg these books made up the "new American sociology," which turned away from the issues raised by radicals during the Depression and offered a self-absorbed picture of suburban America. Rosenberg scolded these writers for describing America as a place where alienation and loss of identity were the chief problems, a society in which "everyone has won a fairytale luxury and lost himself." Consequently their world was without conflict or fundamental social issues. They presented problems "in a perspective that denudes them of radical implications" and in a "tone . . . of injury but of injury unsuffered." They failed to recognize social ills that existed outside suburbs, such as urban decay. Packard and his peers were "inspired not by a passion for social correction but by nostalgia."[76]

Rosenberg argued that the ideology offered by Riesman, Packard, Whyte, Mills, and Spectorsky was a "projection of the fate they have chosen for themselves." Representing "the new post-War employed intelligentsia, the post-radical critic suffers also a nostalgia for himself as an independent individual. For his former abstract sympathy with a nominal working class," Rosenberg continued, "the intellectual of this decade has substituted an examination in the mirror of his own social double as insider of The Organization and The Community." As both the manipulator and the manipulated, "the 'organized' professional cannot escape a conviction of guilt for his part in depriving others of their individuality." Depressed about situations that reflected more about themselves than about reality, they could not become "a force against a more radical and realistic understanding of American society."[77]

What Rosenberg wrote was more provocative and artful than accurate. To be sure, he caught some of the issues raised by Packard's type of social analysis—especially its suburban orientation, its nostalgia, and its unwillingness to grapple with issues of social conflict. There is certainly no gainsaying that the dominant social criticism of the 1950s differed from that of the Depression. Yet Rosenberg ignored evidence that would have undermined his case. He did not discuss the two books by Mills that ranged beyond a consideration of the new middle class—*The New Men of Power* and *Power Elite*. He neglected Packard's arguments that motivational research was a symptom of a crisis in capitalism. Protecting the realm of public intellectuals from entrée by a journalist from below, he did not see that Packard's switch from the captivity of corporate employment to the role of independent social critic was among the factors that undergirded his analysis and his individualism.

Those who felt Packard produced masscult or midcult correctly saw his work as patterned and derivative rather than idiosyncratic or original, soothing as much as adversarial. Unlike his detractors among the New York intellectuals, Packard did not believe that the avant-garde provided a compelling alternative to the world of advertising and mass consumption. It was hard for people who thought that the power of mass culture was a symptom of much that was wrong with America to see how someone could use middlebrow appeals and commercial techniques to raise consciousness about the dangers of excessive materialism. The view of Packard as someone who wrote *Kitsch* relied on the trope of 1950s critics, on a sense of a clearly defined hierarchy that placed on a lower part of the totem pole articles in *Readers' Digest* or *American Magazine* along with books that reached the best-seller list. As Norman Podhoretz has noted, in an effort to convince themselves that they were not fighting "a battle for the soul of America which had a chance of eventually being won," the group of New York intellectuals "devoted much of its energy to protecting itself against contaminating influences from the surrounding American world: from *Kitsch*, from middlebrowism, from commercialism, from mass culture, from academicism, from populism, from liberalism, from Stalinism."[78]

There was at least one irony in the situation: Intellectuals were demeaning Packard's work as kitsch when he himself was protesting the spread of mass culture throughout American society, albeit in a manner that they felt resembled kitsch. If they blamed the producers and audience of middlebrow culture, he blamed experts and the economic system they served. Unlike those who worried about the threat that a debased mass and middlebrow culture posed to elite Culture, Packard pointed to how powerful corporations and their hired hands on Madison Avenue undermined the autonomy of ordinary Americans.[79] For example, testifying before Congress in 1958, he ascribed the "gross degradation in the quality of music supplied to the public" to the ties between broadcasting stations and recording companies.[80] Such a statement distinguished him from most prominent intellectuals, who tended to hold the consumers responsible for what they saw as the dangerous tendencies of mass culture. To a greater extent than was true of many others, he balanced hopes of individual rebirth and social regeneration.[81]

Packard's writings bear comparison not only with the products of those who attacked him in print but also with a wider range of authors who were active in the late 1950s and early 1960s: certainly McCarthy, Macdonald, and Rosenberg but writers such as Bell, Sidney Hook, Reinhold Niebuhr, Riesman, and Trilling as well. That both groups were sophisticated and original while Packard was popular and derivative was bound to create disagreements. They insisted on their superiority to middlebrow culture and to adversarial positions not based on literary modernism. It was not simply that their view of Packard was distinct and in some ways on the mark; what was also important was that it was their opinion that dominated intellectual life—both at that moment and over the course of time. They had the power to establish borders and to exclude people whose work they considered to be of a lower order, a power that enshrined the values of their own work and careers.[82] Intellectuals serving as cultural experts, Andrew Ross has written, are people "who patrol the ever shifting borders of popular and legitimate taste, who supervise the passports, the temporary visas, the cultural identities, the threatening 'alien' elements, and the deportation orders, and who occasionally make their own adventurist forays across the border." The language of contamination that the New York intellectuals used against Packard served to contain Packard and his influence.[83]

Despite the very considerable differences that separated Packard from many of the most prominent intellectuals, he had much in common with them. He dissented not from liberals in the intellectual community but from writers in the mass media and the business community whose celebrations of American life he considered extravagant. Packard and his detractors often approached social issues with a sense of irony and indirection. Moreover, what Podhoretz said about his peers found similar expression in Packard's comment about life's twin pulls: noticing the pressure for success and the charge of corruption, the editor of *Commentary* spoke of "the curiously contradictory feelings our culture instills in us toward the ambition for success."[84] Packard and his adversaries, both ambivalent about what they saw in post–World War II America, combined criticism and accommodation. What the historian Richard Pells said of writers who dominated public discourse also applied in some ways to Packard: "a mixture of contentment and uneasiness with the organization and values of contemporary American society."[85] To varying degrees, the liberals among them, like Packard at *American Magazine*, participated in the 1950s celebration of American life and in what Irving Howe called "the constantly growing industries of pseudo-culture."[86]

Like many intellectuals, Packard assumed that the problems America faced stemmed from affluence, not poverty. All of these writers focused principally on the middle class, especially the moral dilemmas raised by success, affluence, and mass consumption. They did not think that it was possible to solve the problems by fundamental restructuring of institutions or by collective political action. Rather they called for individual resistance to the pressures of affluence and conformity. Concentrating on the dangers posed by materialism, bureaucracies, and standardization, Packard and his contemporaries replaced the pursuit of communitarian solidarity with an emphasis on privacy, individual self-fulfillment, and identity. They saw the problems as psychological, sociological, and cultural—not political or economic. In the late 1950s, his perspective, as did that of the liberal intellectuals, became increasingly critical.[87]

The rough similarity of the political journeys of Packard and many New York intellectuals—fascination with radicalism in the 1930s, deradicalization around World War II, ambivalence in the 1950s—cannot conceal important differences. Packard lacked key elements that had been part of the experiences of New York intellectuals in the 1930s: a radical past, a sharp break with youthful ideological commitments, suffering during the Depression, and an appreciation for proletarians. What shaped Packard's adversarial position was his connection to an American tradition grounded in the producer ethic. The centrists among the New York intellectuals were liberal anticommunists who felt that the USSR posed the greatest threat to America. Packard was closer to anti-anticommunists—people committed to civil liberties who believed that McCarthy, not Stalin, was the problem.[88] To him, but not to many of them, the Cold War was relatively peripheral. Moreover, Packard was critical of America in ways that were unacceptable to the more centrist of the intellectuals. He did not believe in classlessness, social equilibrium, or democratic capitalism. Though they both focused on those who created mass culture, Packard also paid attention to the economic forces that lay behind the emergence of motivational research, status seeking, and planned obsolescence.

Packard and the New York intellectuals also had different perspectives on the heritage of the 1930s. The dominant critique of Packard came from anti-Stalinists, who, with the emergence of the Popular Front in 1935, had turned away from mass culture and toward modernism. New York intellectuals may have seen in him the ghosts of the 1930s Popular Front: a critique of capitalism, a hint of a conspiracy theory of history, a highly moral view of the world, the use of the techniques of mass culture, and an emphasis on social divisions. Packard's adversaries may have seen in his colloquial style and evocation of a simpler America the memories of the sentimental egalitarianism of the 1930s.[89]

There were other important differences. Packard lacked what even the social scientists among the New York intellectuals had: a thorough grounding in and an affirmation of Culture. He lacked the commitment of his adversaries to stylistic grace and subtlety. Without an attachment to literary modernism or a tough-minded Niebuhrian skepticism, Packard was in many ways a sentimental moralist. Complexity and ambiguity were not the most prominent features of his writings. Unlike his critics, Packard, far from being disputatious, disliked combat in speech and in print. He had none of the "free-lance dash, peacock strut" that Irving Howe ascribed to his contemporaries.[90]

Packard was neither a Jew, a city dweller, nor, in any strict sense of the word, an intellectual. Unlike the New York intellectuals, many of whom were Jews, Packard overlooked the positive elements of urban life and celebrated an America of farms and small towns. He did not orient his life as a writer around the editorial boards of journals, the meetings of political organizations, or the conversations at faculty clubs and coffeehouses. Though personally sociable, as a writer he worked alone—without sustained intellectual relationships with anyone.

In 1967 Podhoretz stated that the Jews among the New York intellectuals *"did not feel that they belonged to America or that America belonged to them."*[91] In contrast, Packard believed he belonged to America but that the nation had forsaken its heritage. Called the Professor by his editor at *American Magazine* but sustaining an ambivalent distance from academic life, Packard stood in sharp contrast to the New York intellectuals who in the late 1950s were making the switch from free-lance writers to tenured professors, a change that meant acceptance in American society. Perhaps Packard and his Jewish contemporaries all felt alienated; however, it is one thing to have arrived at that stance on the way from Brooklyn to prestigious universities and quite another to have done so en route from Granville Summit to New Canaan. As Podhoretz remarked, before the 1940s New York intellectuals had criticized America for its materialism; now, in the 1950s, experiencing acceptance, securing an audience, and obtaining jobs, they celebrated an America that welcomed them.[92] Success, combined with the childhoods of "economic deprivation and cultural estrangement," frequently resulted, as Russell Jacoby noted, in "an identification, and overidentification, with the dominant culture."[93] Thus Alfred Kazin recalled that *"Omaha* was the most beautiful word I had ever heard, *homestead* almost as beautiful." He remembered a moment in his Brooklyn youth when "every image I had of peace, of quiet shaded streets in some old small-town America I had seen dreaming over the ads in the *Saturday Evening Post.*"[94]

However much Packard felt he was an outsider, the very real ways in which many of the New York writers had once experienced rejection by mainstream America shaped their reaction to this true American who derided what some of them were struggling to affirm. What Podhoretz said about non-Jews among this group of intellectuals was partially applicable to Packard. They believed, he noted, "that they *did* belong to America, that it indeed rightfully belonged to them, and that it might perhaps even belong to them again some day as it had belonged to their grandfathers before being stolen away by the forces of mammon."[95] Though Packard may have felt marginal, a perception that emerged from his sense of himself as an observer, he was in fact all-American, as his affectionate use of terms like "frontier," "pioneer," and "homestead" proved. Yet Packard's experiences differed from those of the non-Jews among the New York intellectuals, such as Macdonald and McCarthy, whose backgrounds were more elite than Packard's and who had had experiences that stood in contrast with his rapid upward social mobility. In some ways, what separated Packard from his most articulate opponents was a series of issues concerning the meaning of America. Many of them were embracing America, while Packard, a true native, was asking unsettling questions. Key elements that drew on his all-American background provided him with the sources of his ambivalence—a vision of a past that was better than the present, a commitment to a producer ethic, and the moral power of Methodism.

Cosmopolitan Reviewers Respond to a Suburban Social Critic

Reviewers, especially those for big-city newspapers and national periodicals, echoed some of the issues raised by the business community, sociologists, and New York intellectuals. A considerable number of observers took issue with what they saw as Packard's naiveté and excessive moralism. They called his "a shocked gee-whiz" approach, characterized his tone as that of an "innocent who has just discovered the prevalence of sin," and said that what filled his work were "eternal verities about truth, prudence and saving."[96] Others, opposing the religious undertone of his writing, used phrases such as "homilies," "hodgepodge jeremiad," "somber earnestness," and "swollen with righteousness."[97] In a somewhat similar vein, one reviewer remarked that Packard was an "egalitarian snob" whose "cloak of classless virtue covers a patronizing attitude."[98]

Critics who looked at the relationship between Packard's writings and his life probed for contradictions of an even more personal nature. In

typically caustic fashion, *Time* ended its story on *Status Seekers* by pointing out that the author lived "in New Canaan, Conn., in a twelve-room
house (white frame), and has a Weimaraner, just about the highest-status
dog available." Writing in the *Wall Street Journal*, John Chamberlain, a
radical anti-Stalinist turned conservative, remarked ironically that "if Mr.
Packard really wants to prove his sincerity about his thesis he will have to
sell that home in New Canaan and go back to living in a cave."[99]

More common was the assertion of contradictions of a different sort.
Critics echoed what sociologists had said when they held that Packard
himself continually used the very methods that his books attacked—hidden persuasion, status appeal, and wastefulness. The conservative Ernest
Van Den Haag suggested that in order to increase sales, Packard, "by
instinct or perhaps by 'motivational research,'" had employed the kind of
appeal to unconscious motivations that the first book in the trilogy questioned.[100] In a review of *Status Seekers*, Richard C. Kostelanetz, then an
undergraduate at Brown and later an influential cultural critic, noted
Packard's use of a "'shock-and-soothe'" technique: He began chapters
with a tale of horror and then reassured the reader with "cliched homilies."[101] Similarly, the British cultural critic Richard Hoggart saw *Waste
Makers* as "a symptom of the ills it describes. It is a concocted, a gimmick,
book—to be consumed while its theme is fashionable and then discarded,
like last week's Kleenex packet."[102] Looking back on all three books, a
historian turned the tables on Packard. "His sprawling audience—the
persuaded, seeking, and wasters—" he commented in 1961, "has agreed to
read about its slick, adman, production-by-formula society in Mr. Packard's three slick, adman, production-by-formula books."[103]

Finally, in response to all three books, reviewers from a wide range of
ideological perspectives raised legitimate questions about Packard's politics.[104] Writing in *Encounter* about *Hidden Persuaders*, Irving Kristol,
who would later emerge as a leading neoconservative, argued that "if
Americans are credulous enough to think that the Good Life consists of
lots of manufactured things, all of which can be bought, then only a
misanthrope would begrudge them the accompanying titillations of the
spree while it lasts."[105] Aldous Huxley echoed others when, catching a
central tension in Packard's books, he said that people reading *Hidden
Persuaders* were "more amused than horrified, more resigned than indignant."[106] The conservative *National Review* took Packard to task for his
"materialist's eye," his "Marxian assumptions," and his belief in equality.
In a *Wall Street Journal* book review that stood next to an editorial
attacking Packard, Chamberlain caught the ambivalence of *Waste Makers*,
a book, he wrote, that was "afflicted with Galbraithitis, which is a modern

form of commercial puritanism" and yet one that "plunges on to advocate a world of two-seater helicopters, gas-turbined motor cars, 'picture telephones,' and ultrasonic devices to clean fabrics and cooking utensils." In an essay that reflected his preference for a tough-minded liberalism, the theologian Reinhold Niebuhr took issue with Packard's "rather doctrinaire egalitarianism."[107]

Critics on the left took Packard to task for emphasizing small-town values, celebrating American ideals, and oversentimentalizing the past. The most sustained argument along these lines came in 1961 from Loren Baritz, a historian influenced by C. Wright Mills; Baritz in turn influenced the New Left. He had just completed a book in which he opposed the way professionals in industry had become servants of power, a project that made him sensitive to social science writing that was not sufficiently adversarial. He had begun to write another book that explored major American thinkers' struggles with national myths, an effort that underscored for him how Packard's invocation of American dreams seemed superficial at best.[108] Writing in the *Nation*, he compared Packard with other backward-looking reformers. Baritz pointed to the references in Packard's writings to suburban houses as homesteads, to self-sufficiency, to individualism, and to New England villages, all of which conjured up a "notion of the nineteenth-century pastoral as the measure of our degeneration." Baritz saw Packard as a person who was "still a spiritual citizen" of the nineteenth-century small town, whose "self-appointed task is to convince those Americans most committed to the twentieth century to become villagers too." Consequently, Baritz incisively noted, although Packard criticized "industrialism and—even—capitalism," he nonetheless accepted "the situation which gave rise to the things he now finds unpleasant." Baritz asserted that Packard shied away from the realization that waste, economic growth, rising profits, and a cornucopia of consumer goods were essential to the American economy. Packard, he stated, was a proponent of a "nostalgic" or "anachronistic liberalism" whose solutions of "pious wishing and wet hankies" relied on the ignorance of "considerations of power."[109]

Herbert Marcuse offered a more balanced evaluation. In *One Dimensional Man* (1964), he included Packard's works among the sources that he had found useful for their discussions "of the familiar tendencies of advanced industrial civilization." He emphasized "the vital importance of the work of C. Wright Mills, and of studies which are frequently frowned upon because of simplification, overstatement, or journalistic ease," including Packard's three best-sellers, Whyte's *Organization Man*, and Fred J. Cook's *Warfare State*. "To be sure," he continued, "the lack of theoretical analysis in these works leaves the roots of the described conditions covered and protected, but left to speak for themselves, the conditions speak loudly enough."[110]

Marcuse's carefully phrased evaluation caught the contributions and limitations of Packard's works. He used a crucial comma to separate Packard from Mills. In associating Packard's works with those of Whyte and Cook, he recognized the importance of journalism's contribution to public consciousness. Marcuse clearly disapproved of the way in which Packard's books were "frequently frowned upon," yet at best he remained neutral on issues of "simplification, overstatement, or journalistic ease." He recognized how Packard's lack of interest in theoretical dimensions of fundamental social forces left them "covered and protected." Finally, though he appreciated that Packard's muckraking revealed unjust conditions, he implied that Packard had been only a handmaiden, since he had left them "to speak for themselves."

In a rare public response Packard answered some of the issues his critics raised. The occasion came when the *New York Post* published a review by a journalist who attacked him for being little more than an unoriginal thinker who expanded "slick" magazine articles into thin books. Years of writing for periodicals, the reviewer had commented, had trained Packard to speak on any subject at the drop of a royalty check. He believed that the reader had every right to expect more than the combination of "surface profundity and cliché rediscovery" that came from the pen of "a popularizer and an organizer of other people's thoughts and theories."[111] In a letter to James Wechsler, the newspaper's editor and a man known as a passionate liberal, Packard responded. Although his reply had a specific target, it is possible to read it as an retort to left-wing critics. Far from taking the easy way out, he noted, he had written *Hidden Persuaders* "at considerable personal risk myself as a writer for magazines carrying advertising." He emphasized that the main purpose of the book was to warn his audience about "slickness coming over American life" and about how conservative forces used psychological techniques to advance their goals. Because he had directed the book "at the liberal conscience," he had assumed that the Right would attack it. In fact, he noted, the skeptics came more from the Left than the Right. Moreover, Packard complained, confusing political positions with the larger questions raised by critics, that he was "denounced and spat upon for writing the book in the style of a magazine pro." He asked rhetorically, "And what is so bad about that?"[112]

By 1960, reviewers were becoming important to Packard's further development as a writer. The list of those who had responded to his books demonstrated that in some way Packard had to come terms with the views of people as important as Lipset, Coser, Lekachman, McCarthy, Rosen-berg, Kristol, Hoggart, Niebuhr, Marcuse, and Huxley. Editors did not control his writing as they had in the days at *American Magazine*. Pack-ard's audience influenced him only indirectly, and then principally through sales. In many ways, his new masters were the reviewers—both those who spurred sales and those who offered criticism. The critical review-ers, whose authority he well understood, were offering him instructions on how to become a writer who took himself with greater seriousness. Though the results would not be apparent until the late 1960s, at some level Packard was deciding to seek the respect of academics and intellec-tuals. If he still saw books as sources of royalties and as assignments to complete before proceeding to the next project, as a social critic he would come to feel that he had to be more disciplined and serious.

A Station Wagon Driver
in the Suburb

Moralism and Its Contradictions

Reviewers raised a number of issues about Packard's trilogy that deserve extended examination. To begin with, they correctly pointed out his moralism, but only rarely saw this quality in historical or cultural terms. Critics underscored Packard's admiration of an idealized past. They also stressed a number of factors that made his politics problematic, including his ambivalence about what he witnessed and his greater attention to analysis than to solutions. Two kinds of contradictions captured the attention of Packard-watchers: the discrepancy between the way he lived and the values he espoused, as well as the disparity between the ends he embraced and the means he used to promote them. Also of note was Packard's reworking of American individualism. Finally, there is the issue of Packard's complicated response to the celebratory consensus.[1]

Locating Packard in Traditions of Social Criticism

Written by a "modern Isaiah crying out in the wilderness of tail fins," Packard's books were in many ways jeremiads that celebrated virtue and lamented corruption, that warned Americans that they had departed from the moral path on which their forebears had walked and then called on them to repent.[2] The three books appealed simultaneously to individuals who feared losing their self-sufficiency and to citizens who worried about the erosion of their nation's exceptionalism. They connected symbols of social change with such emotionally charged aspects of American life as home, frontier, and opportunity. Locating Packard's work within a tradition of jeremiads underscores his distance from urbane writers for whom old-fashioned moral righteousness was anathema. Like many in his audience, Packard reasserted the primacy of individual responsibility and remained connected with the biblical and reform traditions whose advocates had responded with a sense of shock when they discovered wrongdoing.[3]

A number of parallels exist between Packard and previous generations of social critics, muckrakers especially. Packard used gossip, anecdote, and the inside story to help Americans focus vague discontent on specific grievances. Like journalists in the Progressive period, Packard had a greater impact on people's view of their society than on the nation's legislative agenda. In important ways, however, Packard differed from muckrakers. The Protestant sense of responsibility was more attenuated for him in the 1950s than it was for those who had come before him. If muckrakers fixed responsibility for deplorable conditions on businessmen, Packard was more equivocal in assessing blame. Humor more than guilt, fascination more than outrage, characterized his response to the wrongdoing he saw. The reality he disclosed was not as much sordid as it was preposterous.

Above all, Packard was linked to previous reform movements by an analysis that relied on producer values; yet he relocated the focus of journalistic exposés. The excesses of capitalism, he argued, were corrupting Americans, eroding the work ethic, and threatening the moral basis of the economic order. He did for suburban America what an earlier generation had done for cities. By asserting the appropriateness of producer values for places like New Canaan, he blunted the edge of the critical perspective that reformers had earlier offered.[4] Packard did not concentrate on the adverse effects of immoral activity by the rich and powerful upon the poor and helpless. Although he had some sense of the systemic origins of social problems, he zeroed in on the ways professionals shaped the lives of middle-class consumers. In the process, the sins of consumption—advertising, affluence, and status seeking—replaced the sins of production—child labor, harmful working conditions, and manipulation of capital.[5] In the late 1950s and early 1960s, Packard identified as one of the instruments of social change Consumers Union, whose audience was middle class and whose most common solution was the individualistic one of informed shopping.[6]

Placing Packard in a tradition of moral reform brings us back to his espousal of a secularized version of his childhood Methodism. He did not share his mother's equation of alcohol with sin, but he did interpret the world in categories that would have been familiar to people in Bradford County. With *Hidden Persuaders*, the effort to control the abuses of advertising took on many of the qualities that Prohibition had had for his parents. Moral and prophetic, his vision relied on the ability of an aroused social conscience to reshape society. Casting the consumer as the drunkard and MR as the Liquor Interests, Packard attacked the way commercialism, corporate power, and city vices threatened family life, democracy, and self-control. His work drew on an impulse described by Frederic C. Howe, a muckraker who had also grown up in a Methodist household in Pennsylvania. "Early assumptions as to virtue and vice, goodness and evil," Howe wrote, "remained in my mind long after I had tried to discard them."[7] Self-restraint, hard work, anticommercialism, and simplicity were values that connected the successful author with his origins as a child raised in a rural community by a religious mother and a farmer father.

Throughout his life, Packard projected the image of himself as a farm boy. Former president Harry S. Truman, glancing at a copy of *Waste Makers* on his desk, relied on an old adage when he told a visitor that Packard's writings reminded him that you could take the boy out of the country but you couldn't take the country out of the boy. "Americans traditionally have liked to think of themselves," Packard wrote in 1960 in a statement that reflected the values his parents exemplified, "as frugal, hard-working, God-fearing people making sacrifices for the long haul."[8] Later, he used irony when he expressed concern that an inquiring biographer might uncover evidence that destroyed "the decades I have spent trying to create an image of myself as still basically a farmboy."[9]

In the fall of 1960, John Keats, author of an exposé of suburban life called *The Crack in the Picture Window* (1957), wrote Packard a revealing letter that, though it may not have fully reflected the views of its recipient, nonetheless made clear the contexts of his values. Keats believed that what corporate life lacked was a morality that sprang from "common decency, and a regard for our fellow man, and for excellence in choice." The basic "appeal of socialism, or communism," he continued at the same time that he expressed reservations about the actual working of the Communist state, "is its essential *morality*."[10] Keats and Packard shared a number of experiences. They had roots in small-town America, as well as parents who were Republicans and evangelicals. They had worked for publications in which journalism and capitalism met, and they continued to live in a world where people they knew defended the practices of corporate America in moral terms. Both wrote muckraking jeremiads that attacked contemporary patterns of consumption from an ethical perspective.[11]

If critics bridled at Packard's moral vision, they also saw him as a backward-looking reformer. At times his preference for the old days reinforced the blinders that life in New Canaan engendered.[12] His evocation of a better time appealed to those in his audience who, feeling uneasy with the changes sweeping across America, took their bearings from a rose-colored picture of life on farms and in small towns. Yet the fact that Packard looked backward was hardly unusual: Reformers and even revolutionaries have often taken their bearings from evocations of a past to which they hoped society would return in the future.[13] More specifically, what one scholar has called the "innovative nostalgia" of the turn-of-the-century Progressives has been a critical element in American reform movements.[14] Whatever its resonance, Packard's nostalgia was troublesome: It exaggerated the appeal of the past at the same time that it distorted his analysis of the present.

Problematic Elements in Packard's Politics

Critics also identified troublesome aspects of Packard's politics. To begin with, they asserted that his analysis betrayed an ambivalence about contemporary America.[15] In fact, he was both a child of the 1930s and a product of the postwar consensus. The tension between his drive for success and his disdain for status adversely affected his analysis at critical points. Even as he offered a telling critique of affluence, he continued to express appreciation for growth, the American economic system, and a high standard of living. Both horror and fascination suffused his portraits of consumer culture. Like many popular social critics of the 1950s, Packard had a constricted sense of the choices available to Americans about their future. "The uncomfortably challenging point," he wrote in 1960, was "that perhaps the United States has no acceptable alternative to ever-rising and wasteful consumption."[16]

Packard's politics are revealing in other ways. The fact that his outlook did not really fit the terms conventionally used to describe positions on public policy underscores the complex elements of his own vision. The insufficiency of his proposals to set things right meant that he resembled an earlier generation of muckraking journalists who, as historian Richard Hofstadter noted, exposed wrongdoing within American society but "were themselves moderate men who intended to propose no radical remedies."[17] He used producer values to suggest solutions that were moral rather than statist, relying as they did more on control by the individual and community than on legislation passed by distant governments. He did not believe that the problems of the American economy could be solved by frontal attacks on capitalism or by government intervention. As his son Randall later remarked, Vance, who believed the purpose of government was to serve and not to line the pockets of officials or citizens, was "critical of capitalism in its foibles and not in its heart."[18]

Being better at describing social problems than at offering solutions was a limitation that was not his alone. The most radical social criticism of the 1950s, such as Herbert Marcuse's *Eros and Civilization* (1955) and C. Wright Mills's *Power Elite* (1956), did not contain very clear guidelines for action. Like the two most popular analyses of the 1950s, David Riesman's *Lonely Crowd* and William H. Whyte, Jr.'s *Organization Man,* Packard's books lacked sustained discussion of proposals for the future that rose above the personal level. Like many of his contemporaries, Packard also paid little attention to people for whom the American standard of living was elusive. Although all three books acknowledged the existence of poverty, like John Kenneth Galbraith's *Affluent Society* (1958), they defined affluence as the problem.

The gap between problem and solution stemmed partly from Packard's commitment to the power of the individual. Characteristically, having spent more than sixty pages in *Waste Makers* on possible courses of action, he concluded with the story of the woman who lived near him on Chappaquiddick and made greeting cards from natural products, a response that could not encompass many Americans. Packard's reluctance to make his remedies fit his diagnosis brings us back to what Willard Waller once said. "Until the humanitarian," he wrote in 1936, "is willing to give up his allegiance to the organizational mores," such as private property, individualism, monogamy, and nationalism, "he must continue to treat symptoms without removing their causes." Like Waller's humanitarian, Packard did not confront "the fact that he does not really want what he says he wants. The difficulty which an individual faces," Packard's sociology teacher had written in the year his student graduated from college, "is that the human misery which he deplores is a necessary part of a social order which seems to him good."[19]

There was an additional element in Packard's political situation. As a person who had admired the USSR in the 1930s, who abhorred Senator Joseph R. McCarthy, and who knew the business community's anticommunism firsthand, Packard remained concerned that critics would accuse him of being un-American. Several years after the publication of *Hidden Persuaders*, he learned that a leading advertising agency had tried unsuccessfully to turn up damaging evidence by hiring "detectives to see if there were any Communist leanings in my background."[20] Yet when the salvos from the business community appeared in print, they were often defensive and narrowly self-interested. Moreover, despite his fears, reviewers in conservative newspapers almost never leveled the charge of subversiveness.[21] Only on rare occasions did someone use a Cold War framework to criticize Packard for stressing what was wrong with America.[22] More typically, reviewers used the language of un-Americanness to congratulate Packard by indicating that it was now patriotic to criticize the nation for its shortcomings. Some warned that American corporations, like Communist states, were willing to engage in thought control, bringing 1984 to America via Madison Avenue more than a quarter of a century earlier than the title of George Orwell's book predicted.[23]

To some observers, Packard's angry prose seemed at odds with his mild manner and conventional looks. Thus one woman, when she met him on his arrival at a lecture in the late 1950s, remarked " 'My, you don't look a bit ferocious!' " As a reporter noted later, Packard was "a ruddy-cheeked, soft-spoken man" who "gives an impression of shyness and hesitancy hardly in keeping with his reputation as a hard-hitting journalist specializing in books of expose."[24] In 1960, he wrote about his friend, *New Yorker* cartoonist Charles Saxon, in a way that described himself as well. Saxon, Packard noted, was a master of "satiric social comment" who enabled people to laugh at themselves. The cartoonist "has diagnosed what ails modern Americans" in an amiable manner. "The nation," Packard observed, "does not listen to an angry man." Yet Packard said of himself that though America had been good to him and he was "by nature amiable," his "personal contentment" did not "change the hard facts about the relentless drift of our society."[25]

With the publication of *Waste Makers*, Packard's fears of being accused of subversiveness resurfaced. A review of the book in the *El Paso Times* made him realize that people might serve up "some ugly comments of a comfort-to-our-enemies type."[26] No one worth worrying about, Carolyn Anthony reassured him, would describe him as subversive. Because he cared for America, the publicist at McKay remarked, "any suggestion of a non-patriotic attitude, subversion or what-have-you" was "only for those oddballs way out in right field."[27] Two weeks later the same issue cropped up again when someone noted that " 'by indirection the work constitutes an indictment of Capitalism and could be used by Communist propagandists with considerable effect.' " Don't worry, his publisher remarked, Packard had offered "constructive criticism" in a society "which no responsible social philosopher has ever claimed is perfect." America's "very fluidity and constant exposure to internal criticism are among its greatest strengths."[28]

The fear of such accusations, as well as the anti-Stalinism he had been developing since the late 1930s, made Packard worry about even the appearance of any connection with Communists or radicals.[29] Ironically, the FBI did not open a file on him until 1964, when the publicist at McKay sent J. Edgar Hoover a copy of *Naked Society* in the hope that he might write a book review. Although the staff at the bureau noted that their files "contain numerous references" to Packard that stemmed from "citizens' inquiries," the agency could uncover "no derogatory information on him."[30] In fact, in most imaginable situations Packard had little cause for concern. "After 1938," he later remarked, "I had no serious association that I know of with Communists and did not attend the kind of meetings that would warrant entry in a file."[31] Nonetheless, well into the 1960s Packard was concerned about attacks from the Right or association with the Left, principally because he worried—perhaps not without justification, given what happened under McCarthyism—that any red-baiting might adversely affect his popularity and the sales of his books.

Simple Virtues and a Complicated Life

Observers also explored the contradictions between a writer who preached simplicity and a person who lived comfortably in a wealthy community. The tension between these two identifying characteristics underscored Packard's espousal, from a privileged social position, of a producer ethic usually identified with people of a more modest social position. After the publication of *Waste Makers*, when a reporter asked Packard how he lived, he replied that he owned "four houses containing a total of nine bathrooms, three cars, a refrigerator, automatic clothes washer and dishwasher, a 20-foot deep-freeze, a TV set, hi-fi, a motor boat, a dictating machine and three typewriters." Then he went on to point out that he used the freezer for storing notes and worked "at a drafting table bought second-hand fifteen years ago." His response conveyed his sense of irony about his situation:

surrounded by the symbols of affluence, he was also proud of how he used them unconventionally and how he mixed luxury with simplicity. The reporter overcame her initial assumption that Packard did not practice what he preached. She noted that the houses were "merely a studied investment" bought when they were in terrible condition and that the Packards then proceeded to fix them up. Vance, she concluded, using a familiar cliché, lives "much as we do."[32]

Packard could convince others that he practiced what he preached. His eccentricity enabled him to eschew social pretension. He told the host of a television show that his New Canaan house was "not new enough or old enough to be fashionable," that he bought his suits at discount stores, and that he was unaware of fashion.[33] Another observer remarked that the author, who drove a six-year-old Chevrolet with 86,000 miles and a second motor, "lives his philosophy," as someone not "swayed by commercials with snob or economy appeal."[34] Another journalist commented, however, that Packard acknowledged "frankly that his own home bulges with faulty appliances and that, despite his written words, his wife is a confirmed impulse buyer."[35] His research, he remarked in 1960, "helped me bring pressure on my family to be a little more prudent. We've always been pretty impulsive, careless and haphazard."[36] Even when success brought greatly increased income, the household continued to be overextended financially. In 1964 he wrote Harriet Pilpel that if his family received more income, "we probably wouldn't invest it anyhow. We would spend it. That, at least, is alas the way it has always worked out. We are always close to being broke."[37] The household continually pushed the limits of its means. As he told a reporter in 1960, "There's no way a writer can bookkeep, we're always spending on the anticipation of selling."[38]

The truth of the matter was that Packard lived a life that most of his readers might dream of but could hardly afford. Despite evidence to the contrary, he talked poor and did not think of himself as rich.[39] He was anxious about being a good provider and kept his eyes on those above him: corporate executives and heirs to fortunes in both New Canaan and Chappaquiddick. He worried that spreading affluence was enabling workers in the upper ranks of the blue-collar class and the lower rungs of white-collar occupations to undermine the status of an older middle class and, in relative terms, the position of the yeoman writer.[40] Even though finances remained stretched, the family's situation had changed. As Virginia noted at the time, her husband, who used to write success stories in a Boston newspaper, was now the subject of them.[41] Yet Packard remained ambivalent about his situation. "Insecure and diffident," as one friend remarked years later, he did not feel he belonged in a world of style and sophistication.[42] Though he had three number one best-sellers in a row, success did not go to his head. He remained "a Pennsylvania farm boy who was goggle-eyed about the world."[43]

Packard's combination of anxiety and simplicity came through again and again. After an appearance on television where he was noticeably awkward, he told how he had resorted to name-dropping on the show when faced with a socially difficult situation. Vance Packard the sociologist, he commented soon after, watched Vance Packard the social striver "with a sort of fascinated horror."[44] Such a remark reminds us of the honesty of his own self-perception in describing himself as "always an observer" and as someone torn between life's "twin pulls" of concern with status and "scorn for Success." His response to these contradictions came through in other ways also. One interviewer in 1959 observed that "one can imagine how Mr. Packard—especially when having made no secret of his disapproval at status-seeking—must constantly feel tempted to live up to his beliefs, or, in this instance to 'live down.'" Despite the house they lived in, she noted, the Packards "'live down' very nicely," something proven by the fact that Vance had a modest wardrobe and that he seemed "not far removed from his Pennsylvania-farmer forebears."[45] Yet the way the Packards lived could be a source of embarrassment. After all, in *Waste Makers*, he had pointed to second homes as an example of new needs invented by market researchers.[46] If he could not change where he lived, in order to avoid charges of hypocrisy he could emphasize some of the elements of how he lived. More than twenty-five years later, recalling how college students asked him what kind of car he drove, he ended an interview by pointing with pride to a well-worn and ordinary-looking Chevrolet.[47]

If there was some truth to the charge of a tension between what Packard wrote and how he lived, even more problematic was the possibility of a contradiction between the values he espoused and the ways he developed and promoted his books. Packard may have experienced the evils and pressures of advertising during the 1940s and 1950s, but he had also assimilated techniques from the worlds of Madison Avenue, New York publishing, and mass-circulation magazines. He did things that would have confirmed the suspicions of his critics. He worried about the image advertisements would create, working to make sure that he would seem less intemperate and more respectable.[48] At one point, he asked his publisher to use quotes from trade magazines that had hailed *Hidden Persuaders* for its documentation and thoughtfulness; this would, he commented, not only demonstrate the solidity of the book but also show "admen (all 60,000 of them) that it is safe for them to be seen in their office with the book without being considered the office radical."[49] Even after the book's publication, Packard developed doubts about the image that was being projected. Though he wanted to promote the book by stressing its "frightening" quality and the "fascinating insight-into-self and the humor of it all," he knew that ads which "exuded solidity, authority and restraint" were more likely to attract serious readers. Similarly, when the paperback included a tear-out advertisement, he wrote his agent that "it cheapens the book immeasurably and puts me in the position of being a hypocrite. The book itself is about advertising abuses and deplores over-commercialization."[50]

The promotional efforts for these three books did play upon themes that critics found troublesome, and at times Packard complied with questionable promotions, making suggestions that McKay often adopted.[51] Before the publication of *Hidden Persuaders*, he recommended using "provocative questions for teasers on the jacket" that would tempt readers by hinting that the book would help them understand things like why "middle-aged ladies prefer DeSotos."[52] He suggested using phrases like "HOW TO BE A SOCIAL SUCCESS for $3.75" as a "stopper" of "a selling line." Such a strategy, he wrote, would tempt consumers to buy the book so they could "enthrall the people at the party with some of the nuggets of preposterous information." It was more likely, he remarked, that people could be "hooked by the fascination and entertainment appeal of the book than" by suggestions about how they were being manipulated. Appeal along this more serious line, he concluded, "could be mentioned in passing."[53]

At another point, he suggested a strategy because it sounded "a lot more sinister and exciting."[54] When Packard saw the jacket cover for *Hidden Persuaders*, he called it "a masterpiece" that was "an interesting study in depth persuasion," with color and graphics that made "it all seem nicely sinister." Expressing some reservations about "a shocker" of a "hard-sell slogan," he wondered if "a softer sell might be advisable, at least at the start." Reviewers would be "more apt to 'discover' the book and get excited about their find if," like *Organization Man*, "it is initially promoted to them in an objective, urbane vein." As for readers, he predicted that at first it would "appeal most to people who like to think they are in the know—and to the curious persuaders themselves." Once these "opinion-formers" began talking about it, "then perhaps you can turn to selling to the sheep themselves—all 170,000,000 of them—and use a harder sell."[55] He encouraged Kennett Rawson to balance what people saw as "a grim anti-advertising tone" with "quotes suggesting the fascination and entertainment values of the book."[56]

With *Status Seekers*, Packard hoped to capitalize on the lessons taught by the success of the previous book. He saw this work as "another appeal-

A Station Wagon Driver in the Suburb

Status seeking, the big ploy of the 1950's, is practiced by **Art Carney** in sincere gray flannel. Essentials for the hard life of the soft sell: a bone-dry martini, tranquilizer pills, pedestal furniture, attaché case, mobile, the "think" book of the moment.

Art Carney surrounds himself with "essentials for the hard life of the soft sell: a bone-dry martini, tranquilizer pills, pedestal furniture, attaché case, mobile, [and] the 'think' book of the moment," Status Seekers. *(From* Look, *February 1960; used by permission.)*

ing and startling dissection of the American social scene," able to draw on the "residual impact" of its predecessor. Moreover, he hoped that the promotional efforts could use the word "hidden," in part because such a repetition had served John Gunther so well in his "Inside" books, which established his career as a serial best seller, a path that Packard hoped to follow.[57] Anxious not to seem too radical, he preferred to avoid the term "hidden class barriers" in publicity because it had "a Marxian ring."[58] After the book's publication, he found it not at all "objectionable" that reviewers emphasized the "'How Do You Rate?' theme," which he knew was "one of the major mass appeals of the book," but he worried that the use of this approach on the paperback jacket would have "its hazards for the long run."[59]

Stung by some of the negative reviews of the first book, concerned with the staying power of his reputation, and eager for approval by academics, Packard sometimes hoped his publisher would take the high road. Although he was willing to use "sophisticated provocativeness" in the promotion of the book, he wanted to tone down the "harder-selling line" and avoid "eye-stopping headlines," for it was important to be careful, he told his publisher, with the image created. "Who," he asked rhetorically, "would want to leave a book sold in such a manner on the living room table for guests to see and admire." In addition, he worried that the "impression" that his work offered "a 'sensational' treatment" would frighten off the college audience. Nothing would adversely affect the response of critics to future books more, he warned, than the creation "of the impression that we are mass-merchandisers out for the buck."[60] The promotion for *Status Seekers* did reflect a balance among the serious, the sensational, and the personal. In the prospectus, Packard talked of the book as a "genial but blunt, bold and provocative" dissection that would provide people with "insight into themselves and their status in their community" and "a new inside look" at the society.[61] Although the press release did focus heavily on public issues of social class, opportunity, and American ideals, at moments the promotional campaign followed personalized, self-help paths.[62] One advertisement quoted from reviews that recommended the book "'if you want to be in the conversational swim this summer'" or if you did not want to "'risk being a cultural laggard.'"[63]

Partly because *Waste Makers* lacked the self-help dimension of the two earlier books and partly because author and publisher wanted to strengthen Packard's reputation as a serious social critic, its promotion generally took the high road, emphasizing the seriousness of the issues raised.[64] To be sure, old patterns persisted. In thinking about a title, Packard wanted to build on the earlier successes by developing advertisements that, he wrote his publisher, "used the 'You' appeal" as much as possible, referring to "people in an invidious way" and involving "a phrase that has the potential of becoming a part of the American language."[65] Yet the questions the advertisements now asked rhetorically were not about the meaning of brand names or how to find one's place on the social ladder; rather, they were about the exhaustion of natural resources and the threat of population growth. Bringing the book out in late 1960, just as the Nixon-Kennedy campaign was focusing attention on public issues, the author and publisher knew, to quote Sylvia Porter in the ads, that " 'Packard's sense of timing is breathtaking. He has caught a national trend in the making.' "[66]

Moral Individualism and the Critique of the American Consensus

Though critics raised serious issues about Packard's life and work, with *Hidden Persuaders, Status Seekers,* and *Waste Makers* he was at last free to express his skepticism about the American exceptionalism he had earlier cheered in his articles. With the simultaneous calls for social action and reassertions of individualism in his books, Packard's own ambivalence fit in well with the mood of a nation that enjoyed new levels of affluence and yet recoiled from some of the implications it had for social relations, the environment, and national self-definition. His appeal also stemmed from the way that he combined the traditional values of the hardworking and self-reliant individual with a more modern sense of the troubled relationship between the self and society in a world of bureaucratic employment and commercial consumption.[67] Along with many of those who read his books, Packard was in the process of making the shift from a belief in success marked by material achievement to one that relied on a vision of psychological or spiritual self-fulfillment.[68]

In his earlier writings Packard had been, to a considerable extent, complicit with what he now denounced. Whereas he had once promoted President Dwight D. Eisenhower and political questions as consumer goods, he now warned that the focus on personality and the use of political advertising hindered serious attention to public policy. Having revealed to readers the private lives of his subjects, including his own, he now worried about threats to privacy. The way his earlier articles had persuaded Americans to buy more stood in sharp contrast with what he now wrote. Experts, whose advice Packard had once eagerly conveyed to readers, were now people whose influence he often denounced. Ironically, of course, Packard attacked experts at the same time that he adopted the role of Packard the expert.

His articles and books embodied many of the key elements of what Barbara Ehrenreich has described as the male revolt of the 1950s that preceded the movement for women's liberation of the 1960s.[69] At *American Magazine* Packard had written of the dangers of stressful work and expressed a restlessness with the more democratic role for fathers and husbands. He had opposed the strictures of the life of the organization man and praised the virtues of relaxation and self-fulfillment. A hint of the appeal to men who were quietly in revolt came when *Playboy*, the principal postwar platform for the liberation of suburban males who worked in large bureaucracies, welcomed *Hidden Persuaders* by asserting that motivational research "molds you into a docile Organization Man, persuades you of the logic of mortgaging your future to buy things you don't need."[70]

An overriding concentration on the individual had replaced Packard's earlier focus on the family and gender relationships, in good measure because he was no longer writing for a family magazine. Yet something else was at work too. Packard had often felt a tension between individualism and family obligations—the restrictions he faced as a child had made him a fighter for independence, but he also wanted to reaffirm the importance of the nurturing family. Now financial and editorial conditions made it possible for him to know that he was supporting his family at the same time that he was feeling a great sense of freedom. Moreover, in his books Packard was continuing to shift his attention from character to personality, from the rugged individual to the self-fulfilling one.[71] About the same time that he was emerging as a book author, attitudes toward success in popular American novels changed from an emphasis on work, material rewards, and unlimited opportunity to a more bounded outlook: worldly success became problematic, the integration of work, family life, and public life became desirable, and self-fulfillment became a goal.[72] Two bestselling works of fiction published in 1955—Sloan Wilson's *Man in the Gray Flannel Suit* and Herman Wouk's *Marjorie Morningstar*—heralded the changed attitude toward success. As others in Packard's generation recognized, the forces that brought about affluence threatened the entrepreneurship on which one version of the American Dream had rested.

To some extent, especially in *Status Seekers*, Packard saw the individual as the rugged pioneer and ambitious small businessman of his earlier writings. But his vision increasingly came to rest on a different goal. In *Hidden Persuaders*, he celebrated the self-guiding person who cherished freedom and impulsiveness. In the next book, he honored the independent and self-respecting individual who resisted the traps set by the status system. Similarly, *Waste Makers* ended with praise for the lone person who sought nonmaterialistic pleasures. In place of the self-made, opportunity-seeking entrepreneur, humanistic psychology's self-determined person who sought growth and resisted social pressures was coming to stand as his ideal. Though later critics would see narcissism in this new psychology, during the 1950s and 1960s it enabled some people, including Packard and Betty Friedan, to connect nonconformity with social criticism. In fact, Packard saw the pursuit of pleasure as bad when it came to materialistic things, in 1961 attacking people who "seek their main satisfactions in life from often narcissistic self-indulgence."[73]

An examination of what Packard was reading and experiencing helps explain his shifting view of individualism, or perhaps his greater freedom as a writer made it possible for him to articulate what his reading confirmed. He absorbed the works of humanistic psychologists—Kurt Lewin during the late 1940s and later Carl Rogers and Abraham Maslow as well. Riesman's *Lonely Crowd* had underscored the importance of autonomy and self-actualization. That his editors at *American Magazine* encouraged him to emphasize worldly success and entrepreneurial individualism increased his interest in writers who celebrated the autonomy that his occupational situation had prevented him from fully achieving. From the 1930s to well into the 1950s, Packard sang the praises of the self-made man. Now that he was one himself, having accomplished it through writing and real estate investments, he was defining life's goals less in terms of worldly gain and more in terms of self-realization.[74]

Being a successful free-lance writer, he had begun to resolve the conflict between his desire for independence and his ambition to provide for his family. For a man who actualized himself as an independent writer, humanistic psychology provided the vehicle of revolt against the life of the organization man. His own achievement, based in part on books that attacked status seeking and excessive materialism, reduced the tension that he had long felt between love of status and scorn for success. Packard's discovery of humanistic psychology exposed him to a set of ideas that some writers used as a basis for an adversarial position, others for a soothing affirmation of an American way of life. Packard's version was certainly not part of the mellifluous refrain of a Norman Vincent Peale. Rather, though he tended to undercut his own critical edge, Packard used the emphasis on self-realization to critique the institutions and forces that, he argued, prevented people from fulfilling themselves.

Vance Packard was both a creator of and in unique ways a dissenter from consensus ideology. He was skeptical as to whether corporations were as benevolent and responsible as those who spoke for them claimed they were. To Packard, America was not a consumer paradise inhabited by a contented and growing middle class but a society divided by social fissures that marketers did their best to exploit. Rather than seeing the United States as living proof of the failure of the Soviet experiment, he saw competition with the USSR as a goad to make America come to terms with its own problems. He hardly believed that America had moved beyond socialism and embraced People's Capitalism. However, though Packard did dissent from the celebration, he did so selectively and, at key moments, halfheartedly. Crucial experiences in his life made him shape an outlook that was both soothing and unsettling. His evaluation of affluence, which he saw as "fantastic" and frightening, though more critical than what he had written before 1957, was nonetheless mixed. He criticized MR but found most advertising acceptable. A notion of simple living still attracted him, and status seeking both fascinated and frightened him. He attacked materialistic excesses but saw atomic power and jet airplanes as genuine advances.

Above all, his was a suburban vision: He minimized the extent of poverty and discrimination and exaggerated the degree to which America was a middle-class society. His sense of a better America in the past allowed him to block out the full diversity of American life. Calling attention to the problems of discrimination and technological unemployment, in 1961 Packard acknowledged that "islands of poverty remain, but," he added in a way that limited the force of his recognition, "they are usually special circumstances."[75] Affluence was a convenient object of attack. "If the problem had been described as wealth," and not the generalized condition of affluence, one critic of 1950s social analysis remarked, "one would have had to specify *whose* wealth."[76]

In the end, what made his critique distinctive was his reliance on the producer values and the Methodism he had learned in Bradford County, however vitiated they became in their translation to a suburban and mid-century setting. This heritage undergirded his opposition to what he saw as the excesses of affluence and tempered his commitment to government action. Like others who came to an appreciation of what they saw as the authentic values of a producer tradition through experience with the inauthentic world of advertising and white collars, Packard relied on what Jackson Lears has called a vision of "pastoral harmony."[77] All three books took their power from Packard's moral outrage, and that in turn stemmed from a sense of an America disappearing because of evil done secretly and in high places. His youth on a farm made him especially sensitive to the threat posed to the environment by unbridled growth. Packard questioned the wisdom of the kind of economic growth that emphasized the false values of display, disposability, and salesmanship and that too easily connected an increase in the GNP with greater personal and social happiness.

He remained skeptical of middlemen, preferred hard work and simple living, and expressed hostility toward large and distant organizations. Manipulative advertising, status seeking, and force-fed waste making angered him because they challenged essential elements of democratic individualism, especially the belief in free will and individual responsibility. By basing a critique of contemporary America on traditional values, Packard enabled many of his readers to find their bearings between past and present.

Future Shock, 1960–1968

The Pyramid Climbers, The Naked Society,
and *The Sexual Wilderness*

In the 1960s, with his liberal politics and traditional values, Vance Packard faced a dramatically changing world. *Pyramid Climbers* (1962) and *Naked Society* (1964) reverberated with familiar issues—the impact of change on the individual, a sense of moral outrage, a commitment to the values exemplified by a vision of a better past, and a tension between analysis and solution. *Sexual Wilderness* (1968) marked transitions in his career and demonstrated the persistent dilemmas of Packard's liberalism. This was the first of his books that did not make it to the best-seller list. By the mid-1960s, Packard was determined to gain respect from the academic community, and his style grew more ponderous as the amount of research he carried out increased, he said, "exponentially."[1] Struggling to come to terms with the tumultuous 1960s, he shifted his emphasis from individual rights to social responsibility. Like other influential writers who shaped the 1960s, he dissented from what he saw as the excesses of that decade. Though he opposed

American policy in Vietnam, he took offense at the manners, dress, and sexual expressiveness of participants in the counterculture. He also worried that women's liberation threatened men and the traditional family. Although these themes paralleled what many leading intellectuals of his generation articulated, Packard's position remained distinctive.

Aspiring Executives Meet a New Frontier

Pyramid Climbers was a natural extension of the concerns Packard had articulated in his trilogy. He was trying to find the right mix of practical information, "unblinking exploration," and "constructive" social criticism. He struggled to come up with a title that referred to people "in a rather invidious or ominous way" and that used a phrase that might "become an everyday expression." McGraw Hill, known for its books aimed at the business community, published *Pyramid Climbers*. Packard hoped it might have the synergy of *Hidden Persuaders* and reach a general audience by sounding "like something that a social critic" would write.[2]

Focusing on the methods used to recruit, train, and evaluate aspiring executives, Packard reiterated many of the themes of his earlier works. He continued to question the belief that American capitalism was benevolent to employees. Unlike William H. Whyte, Jr., in *The Organization Man* (1956), he did not describe bureaucracies committed to belongingness and togetherness.[3] Medium and large corporations, he argued, were manipulating the white-collar employees who worked at the upper levels. Packard criticized the "lean, earnest, handsome, constrained, doggedly friendly" conformists in their gray flannel suits. In contrast, he celebrated the "outspoken, colorful crowd" of buccaneers in smaller and family-owned firms who achieved the American Dream. In a passage that underscored his preference for an earlier America and for entrepreneurial success, he noted that few of America's postwar corporate leaders resembled "such of their memorable professional forebears" as Andrew Carnegie, William Randolph Hearst, and Henry Ford.[4]

Packard's social vision was both broad and narrow. His inattention to what blue-collar workers faced and his characterization of pyramid climbers as the most "exploited steady job-holders" made it clear that he continued to focus on the plight of white, middle-class men who worked in large bureaucracies and lived in suburbs. Yet he disliked the exclusion from managerial positions of nonwhites, Catholics, Jews, and those without college degrees. Reflecting the liberal feminism of the early 1960s, he lamented the exploitative treatment of corporate wives and showed a

"*Let me put it this way, Saunders. We feel you might be happier climbing some other pyramid.*"

James Stevenson cartoon playing off a theme of Pyramid Climbers.
(From the New Yorker, *12 January 1963. © 1963, 1991*
The New Yorker Magazine, Inc.; used by permission.)

sensitivity to the relationship between gender and language. Offended by the corporate violation of the principle of equal opportunity, he called women "perhaps the most discriminated-against of all minority groups in industry."[5] Such a statement reflected his lack of direct experience with the lives of African Americans. It also drew on his own relationships with professional women of his generation who were married, had children, and had achieved professional success—his lawyer Harriet Pilpel, his editor Eleanor Rawson, his publicist Carolyn Anthony, and his wife Virginia.

Central to his solutions was a style of management that he called Relaxed Autonomy.[6] Here he relied on the work of Chris Argyris, then a professor of industrial administration at Yale who, drawing on humanistic psychology, stressed the importance of group dynamics and widely shared responsibility for decision making. Packard argued that diminishing the authoritarian nature of hierarchical institutions would increase the potential for human growth within the organization.[7] To Argyris's social science, Packard added moral passion and a commitment to what he saw as the values of a better past.

The public received *Pyramid Climbers* more as a guide for rising business executives than as a book of social criticism. It was not as comprehensive as *Organization Man*, which discussed (as Packard did not) the executive's education, life in suburbia, and religious experiences. *Pyramid Climbers* was an insider's guide, reviewers pointed out when they noted that Packard was following the path taken by John Gunther.[8] Although he wanted the publicity to emphasize how he was serving as the conscience of the nation, the reviews tended to echo the advertisements' promotion of the book as one about businessmen.[9] When sales lagged, he asked his publisher to place a band around the jacket, heralding the book as offering "SECRETS of THE WINNERS IN MANAGEMENT."[10]

Pyramid Climbers sold well, at one point making it to the number eight position on the best-seller list and bringing in about $80,000, mostly in the first year or two, an amount equal to almost $400,000 in 1994 dollars.[11] This level of success was no match for that of the trilogy, but it was a significant amount of money in the early 1960s for a book that took about two years to complete. "Professional pyramid climbers will buy it—Narcissus must be indulged," one observer remarked. "Mr. Packard will, for a fourth time, cry all the way to the bank." However, if with his earlier books Packard had demonstrated an extraordinary sense of timing, with this one he seemed out of sync with what was going on in society. As one reviewer remarked, *Pyramid Climbers* was "less original and lack[ed] the excitement and novelty, the impact of new facts and new insights that hitherto have been Packard specialties."[12]

Packard seemed stuck in a late 1950s frame of reference with a book that merely reviewed familiar issues. *Pyramid Climbers* received remarkably little attention from the broader intellectual community, which was now beginning to deal with questions raised by the civil rights movement.[13] As conflict between African Americans and whites intensified, Packard focused on the psychological tensions that executives were feeling. As Martin Luther King, Jr., and John F. Kennedy were redefining leadership in America, he wrote that business executives were "seen as our foremost social models if not our leading heroes." When young radicals were struggling to come to terms with capitalism, Packard did not ask about the larger social and economic processes that explained what was happening. "The private corporation," he wrote in 1962, only a few years after he had exposed the way the economic and social system promoted hidden persuasion, status seeking, and planned obsolescence, "is unquestionably the best institution yet devised for filling the material wants and needs" of an affluent society.[14]

Privacy and Individualism

Naked Society, with its focus on threats to privacy, was one of Packard's most path-breaking works. Two problems plagued him as he worked on the book that would appear in March 1964. The first involved his relationship to a private investigator named Guenther Reinhardt. A shadowy figure, Reinhardt had a tendency to cross the line between legal and illegal activity as he tracked down controversial information for the FBI, the House Un-American Activities Committee, insurance companies, and advertising agencies.[15] Then in April 1963 a story broke in the New York papers that, Packard worried, could seriously injure his own reputation. Reinhardt was arraigned for having tried to sell to undercover police officers materials he had acquired in a questionable manner but that had no relationship to the research into contemporary investigative techniques that he had done for Packard. The investigative reporters who broke the story mentioned in an article in the *New York Post* that Reinhardt had recently worked for Packard.[16] For Packard, the situation was "a nightmare."[17] He was anxious to keep the subject of his next book secret and worried that Reinhardt might go public about the nature of the investigations he had done for him. Moreover, Packard did not want to be connected with a person that he later called "a jailbird." Threatening what Packard considered "blackmail," Reinhardt wanted his contribution prominently recognized. At a tense meeting in mid-1963, Kennett Rawson negotiated a settlement in which Reinhardt received cash in exchange for agreeing to accept a brief acknowledgment of his contribution when the book appeared.[18]

Early in 1964, a second problem emerged when Packard learned that Myron Brenton was also working on a book on privacy. As had been the case with *Waste Makers* and would be true again with *Sexual Wilderness*, Packard worried that a competing book would steal some of his thunder and sales. Goaded by the news that Brenton's publisher had pushed back the date of publication when they learned of Packard's book, he rushed to bring his own out first.[19] Also annoying was that they changed the title of the competing book to *The Privacy Invaders*, which, Packard noted, "has a McKay-Packard ring if I ever heard one."[20] In the end, *Naked Society* appeared first and overshadowed its competitor. "Vance Packard has not only gotten there first," noted the influential Kirkus review, "but with the most."[21] Nonetheless, the competition took its toll. It exacerbated the tension connected with health problems that Packard was beginning to experience. *Privacy Invaders* probably did cut into Packard's sales, and it ended the string of titles that Packard had come to feel were like a "talisman."[22] With each book, Packard placed scores of possibilities for titles on cards, showed them to family members, the mail carrier, and friends, and then kept a tally of the reactions. Although he would return to the formula with *People Shapers*, *Naked Society* ended a string of similar titles. The British sexologist Alex Comfort captured the flavor of the situation when he suggested *"Organ Grinders"* as an alternative to *Sexual Wilderness*.[23]

Using the familiar mixture of the frightening and the fascinating, in *Naked Society* Packard continued to emphasize the manipulation of the individual by outside forces. He exposed the "recent enormous growth in methods for observing, examining, controlling, and exchanging information about people." He argued that government, corporations, and schools were using new technologies to curb freedom and manipulate minds. Packard aligned himself with the nation's historic pursuit of liberty, whose dimensions he exaggerated as he evoked the vision of an older America filled with freewheeling people. In ways that were noticeably less hedged than in his previous books, he openly attacked efforts to persecute those accused of having unfashionable opinions or subversive pasts. He reminded his readers that antifascists, "misguided and often duped," in the late 1930s and early 1940s "became fully, partially, or innocently involved with Communism for reasons other than a desire to overthrow the U.S. form of government."[24]

Packard offered a number of remedies for the ills he exposed. He applauded the efforts of the American Civil Liberties Union and called on the nation to rally around the Bill of Rights.[25] He spoke before a congressional subcommittee against the increased role of the federal government in data collection, helping to stall the establishment of a national data bank.[26] He urged leaders of institutions to respect people's rights and offered citizens a series of practical measures with which to protect themselves. Yet at moments there remained a familiar gap between problem and solution. Near the end of the book, he wrote: "The most important thing that every American can do to protect his heritage of a right to privacy is to see that the right is respected in his own home." In the next sentence Packard stated: "This means that parents should knock or call before they enter the room of a child who [has] his door closed."[27]

Often more implicitly than explicitly, he protested the way McCarthyism invaded privacy and threatened individual rights. More sensitive to the power of McCarthyism than Brenton's book was, *Naked Society* discussed government snooping. A revealing series of incidents made clear Packard's fear of McCarthyism, as well as his distance from radicalism. In 1962, accompanying an article in the *Saturday Evening Post* was a photograph that showed books on a table in a store that was, the caption noted, "the country's main outlet for Communist" material. Prominently displayed were studies of Fidel Castro's Cuba by C. Wright Mills and Jean-Paul Sartre. Much less visible in the picture, indeed not noticeable unless one looked very carefully, was a copy of *Waste Makers*. Packard's attorney, Harriet Pilpel, informed the magazine that Packard "has suffered embarrassment as a result of the appearance" of his book in the picture.[28] In addition, he worried about the tone of the advertisements for *Naked Society* because he was "sensitive about stirring up the FBI."[29] Then in 1964, when he was invited to speak to the Emergency Civil Liberties Committee, Packard tried to find out if the committee was on the attorney general's list of subversive organizations. He was concerned, he wrote, about appearing before a "quite left wing organization" that counted among its leaders I. F. Stone and Corliss Lamont, both "long associated with far left wing causes."[30] Though there was not anything in Packard's past that was subversive, given what is now known of the FBI's methods, it is not impossible to imagine a scenario that could have caused him considerable harm. Indeed, on occasion he did receive accusing letters. In 1964, a dentist from Southern California suggested that he should have titled his book *A Pinko's Views of the American Scene*.[31]

Naked Society warned of the threats that powerful technologies and institutions posed to privacy. Until 1964, privacy issues, largely the ken of legal scholars, had reached only specialized audiences.[32] Columbia University professor Alan F. Westin, whose seminal and monumental *Privacy and Freedom* (1967) established his reputation as America's foremost scholar in the field, both acknowledged Packard's importance and made clear the differences between popular and academic treatments. He credited Packard (and Brenton) with having sounded "a full-scale alarm" about threats to privacy, thus helping to make 1964 a year that marked "a new state of public awareness and concern." Yet he also wrote of Packard's "angry, social muckrake" approach. A comparison of Packard's career trajectory with Westin's is instructive. Even before he completed *Naked Society*, Packard was moving on to another subject; in contrast, Westin stayed with the topic, using university, foundation, and government resources to build his career and expand the scholarship on privacy. After 1968, what had been a trickle of books on threats to privacy turned into a torrent. Many of those who now entered the field struck a greater balance between the individual's rights and society's claims than Packard had. The growing body of scholarship followed many of the trails he had blazed—warnings of the invasion of privacy, the evocation of technology's nightmarish consequences, and the call for restraint on intrusions by business and government. Over time, however, Packard's contribution by and large faded from view among those who wrote on the subject.[33]

Naked Society sold relatively well, making it to the number two position on the best-seller list.[34] The book earned Packard about $50,000 in royalties, then a not inconsiderable amount for what was less than two years of work.[35] Shortly after its publication, Packard signed a contract with Pocket Books that guaranteed $300,000 for the paperback rights to *Naked Society* and his next two works.[36] Despite the book's commercial success and often favorable reviews, Packard remained sensitive to the charges that intellectuals continued to levy against him. Daniel Aaron, director of the American Studies program at Smith College, remarked that Packard had turned what could have been a serious project into *"Reader's Digest* pap." When Packard saw the review, he circled the name of the popular periodical and wrote "wouldn't touch!" He did this even though he had published articles there as recently as 1963 and would do so again in 1966, with a title of "Seven Steps to Greater Personal Freedom."[37]

Naked Society was problematic in a number of ways. It suffered from its presentation of a litany of dangers without enough of a connecting argument. Written in haste, this book and *Pyramid Climbers* showed some evidence of the worst of Packard's 1950s writing—paragraphs hastily strung together, example following example, and statements that were more sweeping than precise. In addition, its politics were ambiguous. "I've been called both a left-winger and a right-winger," he remarked in 1964, taking a certain pleasure in being attacked from opposite directions. Moreover, at moments Packard had difficulty in distinguishing between threats to privacy that were well intentioned and arguably warranted and others that were more questionable—for example, between census takers who collected information on households and corporations that secretly investigated the private lives of their employees. A friend had warned him on this issue, pointing out Packard's "youthful resentment" at controls "without any examination of the necessity for them."[38] With what a British reviewer called "an intransigently libertarian viewpoint," Packard had opposed the invasion of privacy from whatever source and for whatever purpose.[39] Nor did he wrestle with the problem of conflicting rights, such as those of the celebrity to be left alone, the reporter to investigate, and the public to know.

Packard's emphasis on rights represented a temporary break with his commitment to producer values, for that tradition had remained suspicious of the way that excessive regard for the self threatened communal obligation. Privacy and restraint were long-standing issues in Packard's life, going back to his childhood and reinforced during his years at *American Magazine*. Though he would soon turn away from such an archly individualistic position, in the early 1960s privacy was central to his definition of the autonomous person and his celebration of nonconformity in behavior and beliefs. Together with *Pyramid Climbers, Naked Society* played out his declaration of independence from the forces that he felt had restrained him as an adult—editors, McCarthyism, and life in a bureaucratic corporation. With these books, Packard completed projects begun in the 1950s. He was eager to finish these two books quickly, striking while the iron of his reputation was still hot. Yet by the mid-1960s, with his income and freedom relatively secure, Packard was on his way to putting behind him the tension between being a good provider and being independent. At last he was coming to terms with life's "twin pulls" of desire for success and scorn for status. With *Pyramid Climbers*, he announced that he had ascended to a high point in American society without climbing the corporate ladder. With *Naked Society*, he celebrated his individualistic self-actualization and lamented the invasion of his privacy as a celebrity.

Respectability and the Sexual Revolution

The publication of *Sexual Wilderness* in 1968 marked a turning point in Packard's career and revealed continuity in his outlook. With this book, Packard ended his challenge to the 1950s consensus and shifted his focus from people in his own age cohort to their children, albeit from the perspective of his generation. Like other writers his age, he witnessed the disquieting results that occurred when younger people took his advice seriously, rejecting materialism and embracing self-expression. With *Sexual Wilderness*, Packard returned to his long-standing reliance on the producer tradition and the Methodism he had absorbed in his youth as well as the liberalism he had developed in the 1930s. Determined to write a book that academics would appreciate, he produced one whose seriousness

Vance Packard in his New Canaan study in 1967, surrounded by piles of material on which he drew when he wrote Sexual Wilderness.
(Used by permission of Vance Packard.)

and traditionalism proved problematic in a rapidly changing market for books on sex.

Packard struggled with how to win over an academic audience without losing popularity among a more general readership. His research for this volume was more extensive than that for any of his previous works. He talked and corresponded with experts in the United States and two dozen nations abroad. He went to conventions and campuses. The published material that he consulted, he noted, "if put in one stack" would "rise 30 feet in the air." He took great pride in a detailed survey of sexual behavior and attitudes through which he collected data on several thousand students at five foreign universities and at twenty-one American colleges and universities.[40] "As far as I can find," he wrote in 1967, "it is the only survey making comparisons of samples from several different countries ever undertaken. And in the U.S. it is the largest national sampling undertaken in more than 20 years."[41] To gain academic legitimacy and access to computers, Packard worked with two university researchers. On the top of a reprint of a journal article written by his collaborators, he wrote, with a combination of confidence and uncertainty, "closest to professional recognition, probably."[42] Packard commented that a leader in the field told him that his study " 'has the makings of a first rate contribution to the literature. The findings could be relevant to the most sophisticated sociologist.' "[43]

Yet Packard recognized the flip side of the respect he hoped to earn from professors. Especially given the "careful, sober, comprehensive" treatment that they expected, he wrote in 1966, he was not certain that he could satisfy them and, at the same time, his "own usual book readers. . . . It is all very perplexing."[44] Working "to win respect for my research from academicians" might conflict with his desire to be readable.[45] A lot was riding on Packard's reach for validation. In doing a book on sex, family, and marriage, he was working in the same territory in which Willard Waller had first made his reputation. Closer at hand, Packard at last had a chance to respond to academics who had criticized his earlier works, especially *Status Seekers*.

Sexual Wilderness focused on the changes that young people, mostly college students, were experiencing in their intimate relationships. He explored how they came of age in a world where, he argued, traditional morality was weakening and the media were bombarding the young with sensual images. He discussed shifting patterns of premarital relationships, how young men and women met one another, and the conditions that shaped their marriages. He also speculated on the future of sexuality and marriage.

Although Packard recognized multiple answers to complex questions, the emotional core of his book was clear. With old standards "in disarray," he found especially distasteful the changes he saw taking place in gender roles. Though he thought it was possible to be feminine and a feminist, he pictured many women nonetheless at sea "because of all the uncertainties, guilt, and frustration" they felt when faced with new opportunities. Packard believed that many young men were having a difficult time adjusting to women's demands, losing their sense of manliness in bed and on the job. For men, he wrote, "one of the most deflating of all findings" of William H. Masters and Virginia E. Johnson was that women had better orgasms through masturbation than intercourse. He also lamented the "disillusionment with what modern homemaking today offers as a full career." He longed for a society in which men and women were equal but different. Pointing to women who wore pants and men who wore their hair long, he, like Waller, regretted the diminishing differentiation between the sexes. "The world will be more ugly and less charming," he remarked, "if each of the two sexes cannot enjoy the special attractiveness of the other." If men and women insisted on emphasizing their similarities, he wrote, "there would be a loss of enchantment in both camps, a loss of gallantry, for example, among men and a loss of appreciativeness among women."[46]

Packard used the word "wilderness" in the title quite intentionally. "Bewilderment and normlessness," he believed, made the contemporary situation one in which experts could not agree, with a picture "too chaotic and varied" to be called a sexual revolution. What intensified uncertainty, he argued, was the "many young rebels, such as those in the hippie movement" who questioned "just about everything assumed about appropriate male-female roles." Connecting excessive sexual expressiveness to the demise of civilizations, he wrote that "it seems plausible that any society that is preoccupied with play—sexual or otherwise—to the point that it neglects social well-being for the long term is not likely to be a forward-moving society."[47]

If in earlier books Packard had argued that rapid social change was creating status seeking, wastefulness, and the invasion of privacy, he now explored the ways in which many of the same forces were ripping the nation from its moorings and producing moral confusion. As evidence he pointed to changing technology (especially the Pill), the alienation found in cities and large organizations, and the waning of religion and traditional families. He also discussed forces as diverse as the entrance of women into the work force, the rise of hedonistic affluence promoted by industry, the increased emphasis on equality, and even the promotion of "living for the moment" that he believed the social security system and affluence encouraged. "Carried to its logical extreme," wrote the man who four years earlier, in *Naked Society*, had bristled at any evidence that society was infringing on personal freedoms, "this enthronement of the individual tends to undermine group norms and even implies a kind of anarchy as an ideal." Americans were "wary when free-wheeling, hard-driving private entrepreneurs advance under the banner of rugged individualism," he noted, but then he went on to wonder about the younger generation's neglect of injury to society when they agreed with "amatory adventurers who argue that anything goes as long as the sexual partner does not get 'hurt.'"[48]

In assessing the causes of what was happening to American morals, Packard paid little attention to the larger context of the rebellion of the young—relations between African Americans and whites, the use of drugs, the impact of music, discrimination against women, and the protests against the war in Vietnam. He yearned for an older world where the young respected their elders and women did not assert their interests against men. As Allan Bloom would do in *The Closing of the American Mind* (1987), Packard attacked feminism, excoriated the decorum of the young, and found rock and roll "abrasive," a phenomenon that conveyed the "defiance of adult control." By "permitting monogamy to be optional," Packard noted in a way that paralleled the link Bloom saw between the erosion of the family and the threat to cherished values, "we might well be undermining the advance of Western civilization."[49] Packard celebrated monogamy as the solution to moral uncertainty and social upheaval. As was true for many contemporary observers, homosexuality and single-parent families generally remained beyond his purview. Like many of the middle-class, heterosexual men who dominated the field of sexual surveys, Packard linked traditional marriage and nuclear families with social well-being.[50]

At the end of the book, he recommended the adoption of codes of behavior that might foster individual fulfillment, integrity, social stability, enduring companionship, and assurance that only children who were wanted would enter the world. In a way that reflected the side of the generation gap on which he stood, as well as his view of sex as recreation rather than a sacrament, he wrote that he wanted society to "declare premarital coitus out-of-bounds for most unmarried adolescents" because it was a "form of play that can best be appreciated by people who were adults, or close to it." He also proposed that the first two years of a marriage be viewed as a confirmation period, after which the commitment would become final. This was neither a trial marriage nor a sexual experiment; rather, its purpose was to strengthen the emotional bonds that made a relationship enduring. "Participating in this process of fulfilling, unifying, and recreating remains, for most of us," he said in the book's last sentence, "still the ultimate of attainment in this or any century."[51]

As Packard worked on how to promote the book, he came up against a dilemma: whether to emphasize sexuality or to stress his commitment to traditional values. To some extent this involved questions of audience. He believed a title "less sensual in its overtones" would ensure "greater friendliness by reviewers, academicians and the kind of people who usually buy my hard-cover books." He also hoped the book would appeal to the young. "I have been told," he said, referring to college students just before he would learn how quickly the situation changed, "that they trust me and come to my lectures in heartening numbers at colleges because they believe I do tell it like it is."[52] His publicist Carolyn Anthony wrote him that McKay did not want *Sexual Wilderness* to be "an old folks' book. . . . How about letting me use more sexy questions and get the kids excited."[53] When he saw the cover of the paperback, which featured a scantily clad couple, he told his publisher that he would have preferred a picture that did "not put the emphasis of the book so solidly on the intimacy aspect." He suggested making "the nipple area not quite so explicitly highlighted." As it stood, he noted, the couple on the cover "quite clearly have been having a nude romp."[54]

When the book appeared, expectations were high. *Publishers' Weekly* predicted that Packard's latest effort might outsell any of his previous ones.[55] "Undoubtedly the most successful book he has done," announced the prepublication Kirkus review, "instant best sellership assured."[56] Advance praise from the academic community was also fulsome. "We academicians," wrote a sociologist in a quote on the book jacket, "can never get over the skill with which a man like Mr. Packard can put together relevant research and come up with stimulating and exciting new insight."[57] About a month after the book appeared, Packard realized that he did not have a smashing success on his hands. "People looking for simple wickedness would rather get it under some vague title such as *Myra Breckinridge*," he wrote, referring to a popular 1968 novel by Gore Vidal that included transsexuality and ritual humiliation. On the other hand, he believed that people who did not know that *Sexual Wilderness* contained "useful information are nervous about leaving it around the livingroom although there isn't a leer or even a four-letter word in it. Oh well."[58] In the end, Packard was not able to satisfy all his audiences: academics who wanted solid social science, the young who presumably wanted a book offering both practical advice and sexually suggestive material, and adults who, Packard assumed, sought help with their children.

Although *Sexual Wilderness* was the first of Packard's books since the late 1950s not to ascend to best-seller status, he remained in a strong position financially. The book earned about $160,000, equivalent to almost $700,000 in 1994 terms, a good payoff for four years of effort.[59] In the fall of 1968, Packard asked Pilpel to begin to work on a revision of the 1959 agreement with McKay. When he had signed that contract, he noted, no one would have imagined that nine years later there would still be $312,000 remaining in his account. Now Packard knew that rising interest rates and inflation meant that McKay was earning a healthy income on his money at the same time that the real value of his account was diminishing.[60] As John O'Hara wrote Bennett Cerf in 1961 about the issue of who kept the interest earned on an author's funds, the publisher "is getting rich on my money, and I am *not* getting rich on my money."[61] The revised agreement, signed in late 1968, increased the takeout from the accumulated royalties if the balance was more than $300,000. It also provided that the payments for expenses increase to $5,000 a year and that McKay pay Packard an annual consultant's fee of $6,500.[62]

The response by reviewers to *Sexual Wilderness* was disappointing.

Though some were enthusiastically complimentary, others discerned that Packard had identified problems that he failed to resolve in the book. One observer noted that the book "stretches the reader's tolerance of boredom to the limit."[63] Not surprisingly, *Playboy* noted that one result of Packard's "hyperdiligence is that all work and no play makes Vance a dull boy," a person whose reliance on empirical data transformed "the mating dance into a parade of wooden soldiers."[64] Because of his shock at the sexuality of the young and because he had decided to prove he could write a serious book, Packard had tamed a controversial topic in the heady days of the late 1960s. "Mr. Packard is a Mr. Sobersides throughout," remarked a reviewer, and he had written "an entangled mishmash" that lacked "the intense focus and sense of timely exposé and urgency" of his earlier best-sellers.[65]

The style of *Sexual Wilderness* was central to Packard's expectations and his audience's reaction. Though as a writer he was free from the control of magazine editors, he had to deal with the less direct influence of publishers, readers, and reviewers. Stung by what some of the most influential reviewers for his earlier books had said about how his fast pace and lack of originality undercut the seriousness of his arguments, he worked on making the book more solid, sober, and original. Proving that he was the social critic that people called him, he was also trying to become the social scientist that academics had accused him of failing to be. The result was an unsatisfactory compromise. The book lacked the familiar style of his *American Magazine* articles and possessed trappings of scholarship that could be distracting. As Packard worked his way through the welter of methodological questions and reviewed inconclusive debates on controversial issues, he lost readers who were impatient to get to the punch line. The fascination with the preposterous that filled his earlier books here turned to moral offense.

Appearing as it did at a critical moment in American encounters with sexuality, the book soon seemed old-fashioned, especially to many in his audience who had made his previous ones so popular. What Packard saw as a wilderness—a sense of being lost—seemed to others like a revolution, with purpose and direction. In 1962, Illinois became the first of many states to end criminal sanctions against all types of sexual activity between consenting adults. In the mid-1960s Rudi Gernreich designed the topless bathing suit. By the time Packard's book appeared in 1968, hundreds of colleges were giving up their attempts to control students' private lives.[66] Millions of Americans were experimenting with new forms of sexual expression and emotional commitment.

By the late 1960s, the study of sexuality was changing in ways that left Packard behind.[67] As one professor remarked in the year that *Sexual*

Wilderness appeared, "The enormous public interest in sex seems to have been matched by moralizing and reticence in scholarly research—a situation that has only recently begun to be corrected."[68] Packard certainly did not follow the humanistic psychologists whom he admired in equating self-realization with intensified erotic experiences. Academic researchers, such as John H. Gagnon and William Simon, were placing the experiences of gays, lesbians, prostitutes, swingers, and prisoners at the center of their analysis.[69] Feminist Kate Millett and others attacked patriarchy and used a feminist perspective to explore the nature of sexual politics in her book of that title, published in 1970. Packard hoped to produce a book that was both scientific and popular, just as Alfred Kinsey had done with *Sexual Behavior in the Human Male* (1948) and *Sexual Behavior in the Human Female* (1953)—though the range of sexual experiences that he explored was markedly narrower than Kinsey's.[70] Masters and Johnson's *Human Sexual Response* (1966) was just such a crossover book. Their effort succeeded where Packard's failed because their scientism barely cloaked their titillating data.

Packard was determined to write a scientific book that emphasized the nonphysical dimensions of heterosexual relationships and that was more about moral confusion than sexual ecstasy.[71] Yet this was a time when popular discussion was changing dramatically. Boston Women's Health Course Collective's *Our Bodies, Our Selves* (1971) encouraged women to recognize the political dimensions of their sexual relationships with men and celebrate their own sexuality. *The Hite Report* (1976) countered the notion of a standard way to sexual pleasure by offering vivid accounts of masturbation, orgasm, lesbianism, and sexual slavery. Moreover, feminism suffused Shere Hite's study. Determined to free sexual surveys from the dominance of male expertise, she relied on extensive quotations from women themselves, focused on feeling rather than action, emphasized pleasures other than those achieved through vaginal orgasm, stressed the political nature of sexual experiences, and gave ample evidence of male insensitivity and brutality.[72] In *Open Marriage* (1972), Nena O'Neill and George O'Neill advocated self-realization through alternatives to traditional marriages.[73] A host of immensely popular books of the late 1960s and early 1970s—including those by David Reuben, Alex Comfort, and Marabel Morgan—demonstrated the appetite for advice and titillation that Packard had been so leery of satisfying.

Neither did Packard have unqualified success with academics, some of whom found problematic his methods of collecting and analyzing data—especially his sampling techniques and his lack of control groups.[74] Simon and Gagnon, who were working on what Packard thought of as a competing book, offered sharp criticisms.[75] Writing in the *American Sociological Review*, Simon asserted that Packard's book "reads very much like a rewrite of the best of *Cosmopolitan*." Moreover, he remarked, "worse than he who panders to the young is he who uses the young to pander to those no longer younger." Acknowledging that "the social sciences appear somewhat defensive before pop writers like Packard," he nonetheless suggested that only Packard's banker could really discern "to whom a writer is responsible."[76] In *Trans-Action*, Gagnon continued the attack. He identified Packard's book as "midcult behavioral science," insisting that "as a translation of social science knowledge for general consumption, this volume is a disaster." Recognizing, as Seymour M. Lipset had in the 1950s, that social scientists had failed to reach a wide audience, Gagnon warned, "To leave this task to the Vance Packards . . . of the world while we maintain our academic purity is to abandon what is, perhaps, social sciences' most important subgenre to the wolves of commercialism."[77]

In response, Packard met fire with fire. In a letter to the *American Sociological Review* that he sent but that the editor refused to publish, Packard said that Simon had made "libelous attacks upon me personally" in his "totally generalized exercise in hatchery." He called into question the objectivity of a reviewer who had a stake in a competing book. Moreover, he said that a reader of the review would not know that "a number of the most respected figures in family sociology . . . made generally admiring or friendly comments" or that his collaborators' article appeared in a scholarly journal.[78] In a letter that *Trans-Action* did publish, Packard asserted that the journal had again offered its "readers an entertainment that many low-level social scientists seem always to relish: the spectacle of the brash outsider—always pictured as a mercenary—who is caught trespassing and is properly punished by a public thrashing." To spend more than four years on his book, Packard concluded, was "just dumb, not mercenary."[79]

For Packard, much was at stake in his battle with academics. When one observer called him "the USA's resident sociologist," Packard placed a star in the margin of his copy of the review.[80] Reflecting his concerns about crossing the boundaries of both decency and scholarship, he contacted Raymond Mack, an old friend and a professor of sociology at Northwestern University, to ask him if the reason he had not written in a while was that "the area of my inquiry was too sensitive or elusive to be probing" and had therefore "offended you, or sociologists you know." Mack responded reassuringly: "Your book did not offend me, but the reviews of it by Simon or Gagnon certainly did. When I read them, I was reminded again of the Lipset review of *The Status Seekers*. Your treatment at the hands of what

I hope is not a random sample of the fraternity has certainly fallen short of scholarly objectivity. 'Intemperate' is putting it mildly."[81]

Vance Packard and the Crisis of American Liberalism

Sexual Wilderness marked a number of changes in Packard's outlook. He paid relatively little attention to the ways in which powerful institutions were manipulating people's lives. He now blamed self-indulgence and extravagance on the excesses of feminism and the counterculture, not on corporations and professionals.[82] The vision of a past that had undergirded his attacks on excessive consumption he now applied to excessive sexuality. The reviewer in *Life* described "the middle-class farm boy from Pennsylvania—Babbitt come of age—who can't stop talking about sex" as someone who had written "an extraordinary modern-morality lecture." Confronted "with Sweden, homosexuality, career women and other terrors of the times," Packard was beating "a strategic retreat prudently disguised as a liberal."[83] The mid- to late 1960s was a period when the world seemed to be changing with exceptional rapidity. As Alex Comfort pointed out, Packard "is as confused as the rest of us," and his book was "likely to leave us, as it leaves the author, worried because it seems something important is going on in our society which we don't quite understand."[84]

The assertive individualism and sexuality of a younger generation awakened Packard to the dangers of the extreme individualism that he had embraced in *Naked Society*.[85] "The whole damn complex of what is going on in our society today," he said just before the book appeared, "is that so many kids want independence without responsibility."[86] He remarked about a younger generation in language that could have applied to him several years before, "Perhaps the more the individual feels hemmed in and threatened by the pressures of large organizations and prolonged dependency, the more he reacts by asserting that only the individual counts."[87] If in earlier books he had balked at the invasion of privacy, with *Sexual Wilderness* he displayed no such reluctance on his own part. Now the world of Granville Summit that he had lost impelled him to celebrate not frontier individualism but the traditional family. Self-realization came not through entrepreneurship or humanistic psychology but through a reciprocally satisfying marriage.

The book marked a turning point in Packard's relationship with college students, and his growing audience outside the United States began to replace that age group in his readership as foreigners became fascinated with the implications of America's experience for their own situation. Until the mid-1960s, he had served as a guru for a new generation, with his central message, if not his underlying values, in harmony with those on college campuses who read what he wrote and attended his lectures. To a considerable extent Packard was naive and prudish about sex, especially in its more varied and public forms.[88] Because of his moralistic beliefs on the subject, friends tried to talk him out of doing this book. "Straitlaced," as friends recalled, Packard was fascinated, shocked, and indignant at things that affronted conventional morality.[89] When he spoke on campuses in the late 1960s, he later reported, students would make a statement and then walk out of the auditorium, which he viewed as an example of their bad manners.[90] Young women, he remembered, got angry when he began talking about the importance of motherhood or when he insisted that men and women had different aptitudes.[91]

Packard resembled other writers of his generation who, having shaped the 1960s, late in that decade found abhorrent what their words had wrought. In the 1960s the chasm was opening between mentors such as Packard, Paul Goodman, and Irving Howe and their more adversarial college readers. Packard's reaction did not stem from familial experience. His own children, who were teenagers and young adults during the 1960s, were not involved in the countercultural excesses that their father found abhorrent.[92] Yet, like some other writers of his generation, Packard saw a new generation both affirm and overturn what he had long advocated. In seeking self-fulfillment and rejecting materialism, the counterculture appeared to be doing what Packard had earlier recommended. At their best moments, like Packard, they loved nature and hated pretense, materialism, technology, and large organizations.[93] They offended him, however, on issues involving manners, respect, and marriage. He himself had emphasized self-expression, but now he objected to the way in which members of a younger generation adopted an "anti-achievement orientation."[94]

By insisting on equal opportunity, women were doing what he had long advocated, but Packard now faced the radicalism of feminists who challenged patriarchy. When he began to work on *Sexual Wilderness* in 1964, Betty Friedan's *Feminine Mystique* had been out for a year. Though it sparked the insurgent feminism of the 1960s, in the context of 1968 Friedan's book was relatively tame. Sexism, patriarchy, and clitoral orgasm were absent from its pages. Instead Friedan, like Packard indebted to Kurt Lewin and other humanistic psychologists, emphasized self-realization, continuing education, and career exploration for married middle-class women who did not work outside the home.

Though race was a more minor note in his 1960s writing, Packard nonetheless experienced the shifting tides of racial politics in ways similar to some in his generation. In the 1950s, his was a liberal's faith. His daughter remembered her parents' bending over backwards to make it clear that all children were equal and that the facts of birth were accidental.[95] Vance P. recalled that he and his siblings "grew up without prejudice or exposure to Blacks." He never heard his parents make any negative references to a group, except Republicans.[96] In the spring of 1964, as Civil Rights was giving way to Black Power, Vance made it clear that he was unhappy about what he saw as the emergence of "antisocial personalities" who were "pushing too hard" and "scaring off moderate and liberal white sympathizers." A newspaper reported his saying that "he believes the Negro is closer to attaining total victory in his drive for 'equality now' than he knows." Sympathetic to the civil rights movement in its integrationist phase, he now noted that this was a time "when the extraordinary gains of the last ten years should be consolidated," an achievement that "extremists" threatened.[97]

With respect to women and African Americans, Packard's situation resembled the experiences of many other liberals of his generation as they confronted the late 1960s. "Brotherhood," "opportunity," "integration," and "prejudice" were the words that marked his commitments. Sisterhood, separatism, institutional racism, and sexism were the new issues to which he responded uneasily. Whether Packard abandoned the movements for social justice or they abandoned people like him is a moot point; by the late 1960s, he had stayed the same while many in the nation had changed.

"I have tried to figure out what your politics are," wrote a Chicago high school senior in 1965, "and every time I think I have it figured out I read something that changes my mind. I would like to know, what side of the fence do you stand on?"[98] Though this student was right to recognize that Packard did not always fit into obvious categories, his books did take strong positions on controversial issues, and he made his commitments clear in other ways. In the early 1960s, he served as a sponsor of the Fairfield County Committee for a Sane Nuclear Policy.[99] With the publication of *Naked Society*, he spoke out publicly for the American Civil Liberties Union.[100] In the mid-1960s, he lent his support to the efforts of Jewish groups to fight anti-Semitism.[101] Yet Packard's stand on specific political issues often remained best known to his family and friends. Consistent with his desires for privacy and commercial success, in the 1982 edition of *Contemporary Authors*, he listed his politics as "my own."[102]

In fact, Packard had strong likes and dislikes. He opposed President John F. Kennedy's "promotion of an economy of force-fed abundance." He dissented from what he saw as JFK's "confrontational style," which, he believed, led America into the Cuban missile crisis, slowed the end of the Cold War, and increased the nation's level of intervention in Vietnam.[103] He valued President Lyndon B. Johnson's Great Society but dissented from his foreign policy in Vietnam. He hated President Richard M. Nixon.[104] More generally, he resented government officials who used their position to line their pockets, and he often made comments about how stupid politicians were.[105] His first response was not how government action could solve problems but how individuals and communities could improve their own situation.[106] He advocated protection of consumers and opposed excessive defense spending.[107] In his "sole adventure into political activism," he supported Senator Eugene McCarthy's presidential campaign in 1968 because of their shared opposition to the war in Vietnam.[108] Packard gave about ten talks on behalf of McCarthy in places around the nation where his lecturing took him.[109] This experience marked the end of Packard's concern about being attacked for being subversive.

Packard's faith remained that of an American liberal of his generation, a faith that the late 1960s seriously tested. His opposition to the war in Vietnam sprang not from a sense that something was fundamentally wrong with the nation but from a belief that the nation had to live up to its ideals. 1968 was an especially perilous year for a book to appear from a writer with liberal credentials and traditional values. Among the events that preceded the publication of *Sexual Wilderness* in August were the Tet offensive in January, the assassinations of Martin Luther King, Jr., in April and of Robert Kennedy in June, the student rebellion at Columbia University in April, the opening of *Hair* on Broadway the same month, and the Poor People's March on Washington in June. A few days after the book's appearance, violence exploded outside the Democratic National Convention in Chicago. The reaction to *Sexual Wilderness* was one of the prices he paid for sticking both to his liberal faith and to the vision of America that his life experiences sustained at an extraordinarily tumultuous time in its history.

The Cultural Contradictions of Capitalism, 1969–1984

A Nation of Strangers, The People Shapers,
and *Our Endangered Children*

From the late 1960s on, Vance Packard faced a number of critical turning points in his life. With children out of the house and his career as a writer well established, Vance and Virginia diminished their ties to New Canaan and began to spend their time in three different residences each year. By 1975, having ended his connection with the Rawsons and McKay, he signed on with Little, Brown and Company. These changes, along with health problems, affected his writing. At the same time, the New Journalism, television documentaries, and the performance of authors as celebrities posed new challenges. Moving between the poles of rights and responsibilities, in the 1970s and early 1980s he remained committed to traditional values. With *Nation of Strangers* (1972), *People Shapers* (1977), and *Our Endangered Children* (1983),

Packard began to mute his critical edge, modify his liberalism, and write at a less hectic pace.

A Critique of American Rootlessness

Nation of Strangers explored the rootlessness and loneliness of contemporary Americans and advocated a return to a sense of community. At the heart of the book was an examination of corporation nomads, migrant workers and soldiers, people who lived in trailers, students and senior citizens who inhabited age-specific communities, and citizens who, fleeing racially divided cities, sought refuge in homogeneous suburbs. After briefly considering the benefits of uprooting, Packard concentrated on its costs—urban sprawl, crime, divorce, and alcoholism. Finally, he suggested strategies to enhance community stability, including changes in corporate transfer policies, summer homes for people who had to change their principal residences, racial integration so whites would not move merely to flee African Americans, improvements in welfare programs and minimum-wage laws to reduce the incentives for migration, and programs to enable the poor to buy homes and settle down.

He continued his search, first visible in *Sexual Wilderness*, for sources of stability and responsibility in American life. In a speech in the early 1970s, he confessed that his books "may have contributed" to a mood that overemphasized individualism. Reacting against selfishness and attacks on the "so-called establishments," he wanted to connect self-realization with being "a reasonably responsible citizen." Packard admired contemporary communes, the revival of urban areas, and planned communities that focused on neighborhoods and were committed to racial integration. As a counter to the decay of cities and the sprawl of suburbs, he lauded "the natural human community," characterized by small-scale, shared experiences, citizen control, and a sense of identity. Together, he said at the very end of the book, these could provide conditions that fostered "personal serenity."[1]

With reviews ranging across the whole spectrum from enthusiastically appreciative to caustically critical, *Nation of Strangers* sold reasonably well, making it to the number seven position on the nonfiction best-seller list and bringing in an income of approximately $70,000, which equaled $250,000 in 1994 dollars.[2] Yet there were worrisome signs. The royalties were for four years of work, unlike the two years it had taken a decade before. In real dollars, the income was less than that for *Sexual Wilder-*

ness. "People are exhausted from the Vietnam War, assassinations, busing and radical changes," he wrote. They wanted "to be reassured, tranquilized—not a book that tells them what is wrong with this country."[3] Packard was right. In the year that *Nation of Strangers* appeared, Kenneth Taylor's *Living Bible* and Thomas Harris's *I'm O.K., You're O.K.* topped the best-seller list.

Packard had some success in gaining respect from academics. Recognition came from Morris Janowitz, the head of the department of sociology at the University of Chicago and a person whose commitment to the civic and moral role of the sociologist as public intellectual stood in sharp contrast to Talcott Parsons's more professionalized orientation. Despite the "bitter" attacks by sociologists, Janowitz remarked, Packard in fact commanded "wide audiences because he was able to touch a sensitive American nerve" and because he offered "an intriguing message." Not blind to the book's shortcomings, Janowitz correctly predicted that once again academics would criticize Packard.[4] The *American Journal of Sociology* ran not one review but three, all of them critical but nonetheless lacking the edge of Seymour Martin Lipset's response fifteen years before. And actually, these academics gave Packard more ground than had their predecessors. They acknowledged that he had grappled with important issues. One of them recognized that "the concreteness" of Packard's analysis made him easier to understand than academics whose writing was abstract. "Maybe the problem," the largely negative review concluded, "is not that there is no one out there listening, but that we are mumbling."[5]

With *Nation of Strangers*, the criticism that stung came from Herbert Gans, a sociologist who had reached a general public by not mumbling.[6] Once again, Packard faced an academic who was also a public intellectual, though in this instance it was someone who remained left of center and was doing the kind of qualitative, accessible sociology that Waller would have approved of. Gans's work raised important theoretical issues but never lost hold of the concreteness of the situations he studied. With *The Levittowners* (1967), he had decried "upper middle class ethnocentrism," questioning those who saw suburbanites as conspicuous consumers and conformists living in a mass society. Gans argued that the inhabitants of the lower-middle-class suburb that he studied adhered to "traditional virtues" such as "individual honesty, thrift, religiously inspired morality, Franklin-esque individualism, and Victorian prudery."[7]

In reviewing *Nation of Strangers* in *Psychology Today*, a magazine that broadcast the results of scholarly research to a wide audience, Gans argued that Packard was "a sociology-using preacher" who offered sermons on how corporations, technology, and suburbs were destroying an older

*Sign outside a motel in Lawton, Oklahoma, welcomes the traveling lecturer
Vance Packard and confers a doctorate on him as well, early 1960s.
(Used by permission of Vance Packard.)*

America of stable and authentic communities filled with individualists committed to traditional American values. This was, he argued, "an ancient and hackneyed" lament, now put forth by "nostalgic Americans of rural origin." Yet Gans paid Packard a compliment and acknowledged the limits of academic sociology when he said that no professor "has carried out as broad and wide-ranging a study as Packard, and none can really offer final proof that Packard is wrong."[8] In a letter to the editor published in *Psychology Today*, Packard displayed some of the touchiness he felt when sociologists criticized him. What Gans said, he commented, was "not only unfair but extremely damaging both to my reputation and to my book." He believed that the review "far exceeded the bounds of fair comment since it both misrepresented and maligned me." Calling it an "exercise in hatchetry," Packard went on to say that Gans had set out "to flog me properly—as many but not all card-carrying sociologists seem to feel they must."[9]

Despite their differences, Gans and Packard shared more than the disagreement revealed. They both wanted America to live up to its commitment to equality of opportunity. They desired to open up the suburbs to the poor and to nonwhites. What stood between author and reviewer was the difference between the research strategies of a journalist and those of an ethnographer. Also at issue was the distance between a New Canaan resident who had grown up on a farm and an academic who had emigrated to America as a child and had lived much of his life in cities. There were ironic elements to the exchange. Gans appreciated middlebrow and popular culture but in this case took on the nation's leading popular middlebrow social observer.[10] Moreover, the producer values that Gans found among the Levittowners bore a striking resemblance to what Packard absorbed as a farm boy and advocated as an adult. Failing to discover these in contemporary America, Packard had used them to criticize the communities that Gans celebrated.

The disagreement was also between two people who approached the realm of public intellectuals from opposite directions. Unlike other academic critics of *Status Seekers*, Gans did not taunt Packard with a line drawn between professors and free-lancers. Yet because he based his judgments on scholarly standards that Packard did not claim he had tried to meet, in some sense what was involved was the clash of discourses. Still and all, Gans stayed well within the bounds of scholarly reviews, and Packard overreacted, as if he saw in Gans the ghosts of Lipset, Coser, and Petersen. Packard had done his best to respond to his critics in *Nation of Strangers*. He avoided the ponderous scholarly apparatus of *Sexual Wilderness* and worked to make his style less frenetic and anecdotal. He made fewer romantic references to an earlier America and made it clear that he did not want to return to the world that had vanished after World War II. He felt frustrated that, try as he might to get respect from academics, the attacks continued along what he saw as the old lines. Yet he missed the compliment that Gans, like Janowitz, had paid him.

"To my mind," Packard later commented, *Nation of Strangers* "was the best book I ever wrote."[11] It is not hard to see why he felt that way. There was nothing that competed with it in scope and popularity. Packard combined two topics that had usually been considered separately. Social and behavioral scientists had focused on loneliness, but rarely had they explored its social dimensions or gained a significant audience. Far from sharing Packard's view of mobility as problematic, social scientists usually linked movement to equality, democracy, and freedom.[12] In this book Packard fully indulged his penchant for finding the unusual in unexpected places. He derived great pleasure from carrying out research in the field among ordinary people, reaching beyond his usual middle-class territory to talk with Mexican migratory workers in Texas and factory workers in Akron. The writing here was tighter than in some of his earlier books, less structured around a string of anecdotes and quotes. Using a style accessible to multiple audiences, he achieved the kind of balance between the serious and the fascinating that was his hallmark. He offered some imaginative solutions that got at the nexus between public policy and social welfare. He made clear his commitment to a racially integrated society and lambasted "panic-peddling realtors" who made that goal hard to achieve.[13] Above all, Packard gave testimony to the commitments from which he never wavered: family life, small communities, the natural environment, anticommercialism, and social justice.

Yet the book was not without its problems. Packard failed to engage the emerging scholarship on mobility, which suggested that an earlier America had been no heaven of stable communities.[14] At moments he relied on omnivorously gathered research, sweeping through his findings and piling up one piece of evidence on top of another.[15] Try as he might not to romanticize an earlier America, nonetheless his sense of loss did influence his analysis. Such nostalgia for the past was also evident in some of the academic writing of the period, such as John Demos's *Little Commonwealth* (1970) and Peter Laslett's *The World We Have Lost* (1965). At the beginning of the book Packard contrasted the vital and charming "footlooseness" of pioneers with the alarming and "accelerating rootlessness" that he saw in contemporary America.[16]

Aware that the new generation of writers gathered interviews from ordinary folk, he seemed unable to turn vivid firsthand testimony into compelling copy.[17] One reviewer pointed out how Packard missed the boat by not employing the approaches developed by Oscar Lewis in *La Vida* (1966).[18] His work among the poor, Lewis once remarked, "involved the establishment of deep personal ties" between researchers and subjects, a result that Packard's usually brief site visits made impossible. While Packard relied on techniques he had developed at *American Magazine*, Lewis carried out fieldwork over several years and made people come alive as he combined the approaches of anthropologist, oral historian, and novelist.[19] In other ways also, Packard seemed isolated from important trends that were transforming American society. He overlooked the complexity of race relations when he asserted that integration of working-class neighborhoods could be made easier if "responsible blacks" would fulfill their "moral duty to condemn and help to combat predatory and vengeful attitudes that a small but conspicuous segment of blacks have toward whites in the cities." Such a statement caused one reviewer to remark that Packard offered a "child's primer on racial tolerance that makes one wonder where he has been living for the past 20 years."[20]

In a book that asserted that America was "a society that is coming apart at the seams," Packard paid hardly any attention to some of the most powerful forces that were creating a nation of strangers—the war in

Vietnam and the backlash against the assertiveness of women and African Americans.[21] Philip E. Slater's widely read *Pursuit of Loneliness* (1970) did offer a penetrating analysis that connected loneliness to many of these events. Though Packard had the evidence to do so, he was reluctant to lay the blame for rootlessness at the feet of the economic system. In *Nation of Strangers*, remarked one observer, "Packard simply did not want to deal with the big business and corporate mentality that causes so much" of the fragmentation and rootlessness he lamented.[22] Perhaps, another reviewer suggested, "Packard had been too isolated from the mainstream of American life in his own affluent New Canaan."[23]

Racism and Environmentalism

A "blunt, constructive book" on race that Packard considered but never wrote underscores this isolation. The proposal neglected inner city poverty and focused on the contacts between whites and middle-class African Americans, emphasizing what worked in reducing tensions and overcoming prejudice. He suggested that he would use some of the newer approaches to journalism and meet criticism of those who might see him as a white from New Canaan writing about blacks. He would hire African Americans "to probe black feelings and pose" questions to whites. He would incorporate a dialogue across racial lines by including a critique of each of his own sections by a black writer. If that person "blisters me," he remarked, "that would be all right." Packard revealed a liberalism at bay and his distance from the forces transforming America. He optimistically believed that most Americans wanted to cooperate when it came to economic relationships but to be apart socially. Like many upper-middle-class whites, he underestimated the force of the reaction against African Americans that President Richard Nixon encouraged white ethnics to express. He demonstrated little understanding of the impulse behind the ideology that black was beautiful. Partly, he remarked in a way that psychologized the social situations faced by African Americans in the 1970s, the preference by blacks to be "with their 'own kind'" stemmed from "the uneasiness of dark Americans as they grope toward more confidence, independence and self-reliance."[24]

Had the Rawsons not encouraged Packard to pursue a different project, he would have focused in this proposed book on the issue of race more directly and fully than he ever did in his career. A lot had happened since his first encounter with a black person at a county fair where whites paid to dunk an African American in a tub of water. During the postwar period, he had celebrated the success of black entrepreneurs and watched appreciatively as Kurt Lewin worked for racial understanding. In *Status Seekers* and *Pyramid Climbers*, he had paid some attention to issues of race, though he had viewed Jews and women as the groups most discriminated against. With *Sexual Wilderness*, he had not followed Eleanor Rawson's suggestion that he focus more on Africans Americans partly because, he wrote at the time, "in these days of riot and talk of possible black-white apartheid I confess I felt uneasy on black-white differences."[25] In *Nation of Strangers* he explored the racial dimension of the shifting relationships among racial and ethnic groups. The proposed book relied less on the conflict of cultures and ideologies than on what he called color aversion. The emphasis reflected his own childhood sense of shock at hearing about people with darker skins and then, upon actually seeing them, discovering that they were not so different.[26] Thinking about "We're All Colored" as a title reflected his commitment to a liberal's notion of prejudice and the faith that skin color should not matter.[27]

If in the early 1970s Packard did not find his issue with race, the energy crisis provided him with a moment when his long-standing concerns had great currency.[28] He gave speeches on environmentalism and eventually served on the boards of the Center for the Study of Commercialism and the Population Resource Center. He made clear his opposition to excessive growth of population and the economy, his love of nature, and his distaste for the manner in which malls and suburban sprawl were transforming America.[29] Once again in the vanguard, he continued the attack on waste and imbalance that he had begun in the late 1950s. He lamented that Americans, at a time when people around the world were starving, were increasingly getting their "main satisfactions from consuming rather than from creating," thus denying themselves "a valid means of achieving self-actualization." He continued to attack market researchers for devising strategies to encourage people to spend. Returning to the gulf between public shortages and private opulence, he remarked, "You can't go to the store and buy a better school system, or clean water, or clean air, or a lovely city to live in." Calling on the government to develop strategies for conservation and exploration of energy modeled on the space program, he urged the nation to avoid profligacy.[30]

Change and Continuity in the Packards' Lives

For Packard, the most harrowing times he faced in the 1970s stemmed from health problems.[31] In the early 1960s, he experienced his first serious problem with heart disease.[32] He mistook the symptoms "for death rattles," he wrote at the time, remarking that "this impression turned out to be premature." He might have recalled the advice that he had conveyed in a ghost-written article in 1948: Cut down on "aggressiveness, driving ambition, and gadding about" and instead "learn the art of serene, leisurely living." His doctor told him, he reported, that he "had been pressing too hard at work by day—and boozing too hard to relax at night."[33] After he again had trouble in 1964, his doctor urged him to cut back as far as he could on "situations involving prolonged tension."[34] In the following years, Packard was not particularly careful: He maintained a vigorous travel schedule, and by the late 1960s his frame of about five feet nine inches carried almost two hundred pounds. His writing in the 1960s had begun to shift from advocating hard work to emphasizing self-realization; in his life he remained more driven than relaxed.

In 1970, at age fifty-five, he suffered a heart attack. In March, while on a research trip, he woke up shaking one morning and ended up in the hospital for about seven weeks. When he returned to New Canaan, he began to take the warning signs more seriously.[35] Throughout the following year, a friend noted a "scared look on his face," as Packard constantly took his pulse. Until the heart attack, he had been physically venturesome and vigorous, always assuming that he could do anything. Now for the first time, he had to come to terms with the realization that he could not go on forever doing all the things he had always enjoyed. Yet, with resilience and thoroughness, he committed himself to diet and exercise, forging "ahead with his usual gusto and enthusiasm as though nothing had happened."[36] By the early 1970s, he decided to be more selective about speaking engagements. Lost luggage, missed connections, adverse weather, and a grueling pace had often made Packard's life as a lecturer trying. His doctors, he wrote Carolyn Anthony, told him "the main reason I blew my gasket" was that he had been pushing himself "too hard for two months trying to combine lecture travel with research travel."[37] During the 1960s, he had given up to sixty talks a year; in the 1970s he reduced this number to about twenty. By 1984 he retired from the lecture circuit. Over the course of his life, Packard had appeared on about eight hundred radio or television shows and had lectured at about five hundred colleges and universities.[38]

During the 1970s, Vance and Virginia made major shifts in the way they lived, changes that cast light on his endorsement of the simple life and eventually had considerable impact on his writing. By 1970 the Packards had an empty nest. When Cindy finished college that spring, her father breathed a sigh of relief at the release from the obligation to pay for the undergraduate educations of three children.[39] By the early 1970s, the world the Packards had known since the late 1940s was disappearing. Their circle of friends was breaking up, as couples divorced, friends died, some moved, and others began to spend part of the year elsewhere. Traffic congestion, increasing population, and new residential and commercial developments were fundamentally altering Fairfield County, making the towns seem less like the idyllic settings of the earlier America that Packard remembered from his childhood. "Virginia and I," he concluded, "feel increasingly isolated."[40] Other changes made it possible for Packard to write even though he and Virginia lived in three different places. Improvements in transportation and communication, new methods of reproducing research materials, greater reliance on the researchers he hired, longer periods between books, and the diminished dependence on income from speaking meant it was not as important as it had once been for Packard to be in one place, close to libraries, and within striking distance of New York.

To some extent the Packards were able to find in San Miguel de Allende in Mexico the sense of community they had lost in New Canaan. Beginning in 1971, they went there almost every winter for more than a decade.[41] They lived in a walled villa, organized around a beautiful courtyard filled with fountains, tiles, and flowers. A 1983 article in *Town and Country* featuring a picture of the Packards described "the pale pink beauty" of the Mexican town, "a small, charming wonder" that was "just inaccessible enough . . . to attract painters, scholars, writers and a small group of attractive social personae who honestly like to get away from it all."[42] In truth, the social situation was more complicated. The Packards socialized not only with people they knew from the United States but also with members of the Mexican elite. Yet poverty was all around them. Despite the luxuriousness of their immediate setting, this third home was a bargain. The income from the rental of their New Canaan home offset the costs of travel to and from Mexico, of the advantageous lease they had signed, and of the inexpensive help they employed.[43]

The third major change in their dwelling places came on Chappaquiddick. Beginning in the late 1950s, Packard did what he had earlier done in Fairfield County as he used his energy and ingenuity to fix up his properties. Around 1958, he put together outbuildings moved from various parts of the acreage to form the Studio House. Around 1960, the Packards built the Tower House on a high point of their land. In addition, in the mid-1970s, they created the Beach House, their principal summer residence, by expanding a small dwelling that they acquired. The previous occupant was the elderly woman whose simple life Packard had celebrated at the end of

*Vance Packard and Virginia M. Packard in 1983, "enjoying their rooftop
sunshine" in San Miguel de Allende several months before the publication of*
Our Endangered Children. *(From* Town and Country, *February 1983.
Photograph by Robert Phillips; reproduced with the permission of
Fitzgerald Associates International, Inc.)*

Vance Packard, with dog named Storm, in front of the house on Chappaquiddick, 1970s. (Courtesy of Cindy Packard; reproduced with the permission of Women's Wear Daily.)

Waste Makers. On Martha's Vineyard Virginia found the most compelling subjects for her paintings and the best market for them. In addition to being a place where Packard could play golf with friends, many of them richer than his New Canaan friends, Chappaquiddick provided an ideal mixture of natural beauty and small-scale community. "There are still," he wrote in 1974, "thrilling, unspoiled vistas of sand, sea and sky peopled only by" birds. Here Vance and Virginia felt at home "emotionally," a place clearly preferable to a "suburb or high-rise apartment."[44]

Shortly after Packard had described America as a society of uprooted people in *Nation of Strangers*, he and Virginia were dividing their time among three locations in what he later called "our now triangular nomadic movement": winter and early spring in Mexico; late spring, summer, and early fall on Chappaquiddick; and then late fall, Christmas, and New Year's in New Canaan. Packard felt that their "experience of mounting isolation and family fragmentation" was "mild indeed compared with" that of others because "we at least have a home base, and we don't have to keep moving."[45] The operative phrase was "don't have to"—no one was forcing them to move.

More and more, the changes in Packard's life insulated him from what his books set out to describe. He was now living, more than had been true earlier, among well-to-do and famous people. He encountered poor people more in San Miguel than in the United States. His direct contact with his audience through his lectures and on-site research diminished. In 1954, he had written of magazine writers who isolated themselves "from life here in our New York offices and in our upper middlebrow Westport homes" and through research carried out by reading rather than experience. In contrast, as a journalist he once had "to *live* an article before" he began to consider how to write it. Twenty years later, no longer was it necessary, as he said in 1954, "to sweat for his money."[46]

Also shaping the conditions under which he worked were corporate mergers and acquisitions that transformed the publishing industry during the 1970s and 1980s. Executives with their eyes on balance sheets took over, pressuring editors for blockbusters that would turn handsome profits through paperback sales, serialization in magazines, deals with book clubs and movie studios. The squeeze was on middle-range books that would sell tens but not hundreds of thousands of copies. Within weeks of publication, publishers often made the decision whether to back a book with intensified promotional efforts or to let it sink or swim on its own.[47] In this context, the author's celebrity status was critical, with a premium on writers whose force of personality could captivate a television audience.

These changes provided the background for the amicable parting of the ways in 1975 between Packard and the Rawsons. In 1957 when he started with McKay, Packard was a virtually unknown book author. If by 1960 his trilogy had helped transform McKay, ten years later he was no longer as central to the house's future. The sales of *Sexual Wilderness* and *Nation of Strangers* had been disappointing. In contrast, in the early 1970s the Rawsons had a string of successes, including the Fodor travel guides, Robert L. Atkins's *Dr. Atkins' Diet Revolution* (1972), Herman Tarnower's *Complete Scarsdale Medical Diet* (1979), and two books by David Reuben—*Everything You Always Wanted to Know about Sex* (1970) and *Any Woman Can!* (1971). At the same time that Eleanor Rawson was working on *Sexual Wilderness*, she was also editing *Born Female* (1968), by Caroline Bird, whose feminism stood in sharp contrast with the content of Packard's book.

From Packard's perspective there was reason to think about moving elsewhere. Several publishers had courted him and would no doubt have been proud to add him to their roster, but in early January 1973 he had signed a contract with McKay for the next three books. Then in December a British firm announced the purchase of McKay. Packard's contract provided that he could leave McKay when Kennett Rawson was no longer in charge, and in December 1974 the Rawsons, citing "irreconcilable policy differences," announced that they were leaving. These events made Packard understandably nervous. He worried about the safety of the nearly $250,000 in his account, an amount that represented as much as three quarters of McKay's liquid assets and, aside from real estate, "the great bulk" of the Packards' net worth.[48] Eleanor, Packard wrote shortly after, reported that the situation in the final days at McKay had "terrified" her and "reminded her of the gradual Crowell-Collier collapse in the 50s," which both she and Vance had experienced.[49] During the period when he was leaving McKay, a friend recalled, Packard was "full of anxiety," worried that no other house would publish his next book.[50]

By the summer of 1975, Packard was free to leave McKay. Though he eventually received the funds in his account, the situation was troublesome. The protracted negotiations had involved considerable fees for lawyers and accountants. The separation from McKay ended the annual payments for consulting and expenses.[51] What revived painful memories of the demise of Crowell-Collier for Eleanor Rawson had reverberations for Packard as well. This was not the first time that he had been torn between being free and being able to provide. Not as rooted in New Canaan, he was now also cut off from the people at McKay who had been so critical to his career—the husband-and-wife team of publisher and editor, as well as his skilled and reassuring publicist, Carolyn Anthony.

By the end of July 1975, Packard had completed the shift to a new publisher. In the early 1970s, on Martha's Vineyard he had met Arthur Thornhill, Jr., who in 1962 had succeeded his father as head of Little, Brown and six years later oversaw its acquisition by Time Inc. Now Packard signaled to Thornhill that he was ready to discuss a switch. The move meant going from the medium-sized McKay, with special strengths in self-help and travel books, to a more venerable and prestigious house, whose list stretched back to Francis Parkman and forward to William Shirer and Frances FitzGerald. Packard was also changing from a publishing house whose success his books had helped create to one where he was but one of a large number of authors and where, he later remarked, "relationships were substantially more formal." The contract that Packard signed covered his next two works. At Packard's insistence, it contained the acceptability clause. At McKay, though he always put forth several possibilities for projects that he might work on, contractually he had sole discretion to pick the topic of his books. At Little, Brown, beginning with the second book, author and publisher were to come to mutual agreement on the subject. Little, Brown guaranteed Packard $80,000 against earnings for *People Shapers* and an equal amount, this time adjusted for inflation, for what would become *Our Endangered Children*.[52]

Despite the major changes brought by success, movement among several residences, and a shift to a new publisher, as a person Packard remained relatively unchanged. Though he had had a formal religious affiliation throughout much of his life, Packard had never tolerated religious pronouncements, and in the 1970s he only very rarely went to church.[53] Even when his success and fame were at their height, he showed no touch of pomposity, immodesty, or vanity, although his bravado did show through at moments and he appreciated his notoriety.[54] In 1988, a reporter noted that Packard was "a paradox in many ways, an intriguing mix of country boy, critic, sophisticate, and mellow family man."[55] He was, remarked a sculptor who was also a good friend, someone he would portray "with hands folded modestly with a sort of stoop."[56] "Bumbling and hesitant" in speech, over the years he had overcome most of his social diffidence. An "avid party-goer" and a generous person, Packard delighted in "the role of expansive host" at "lavish" dinner parties. He and Virginia maintained an active social schedule and a large circle of friends, many of them writers, cartoonists, and artists.[57]

People who knew him well continued to note, as one of them put it, the contrast between his single-mindedness at work and his absentmindedness at play.[58] "One Vance is a pit bull of a journalist," a colleague remarked, "who sinks his teeth into a subject and doesn't let go until he's devoured it, and the other is a quiet, humble, rather eccentric and delightful character."[59] He almost never took a vacation and felt naked without a pen. As his younger son remarked, " 'his antennas are always up,' " on the lookout for information he could incorporate into his writings. His children told a reporter in 1983 that he cared "deeply about the subjects he writes about, although it isn't always apparent." Though " 'it *looks* like nothing affects him, except golf and the stock market,' " Cindy remarked, " 'he's always trying to change the world.' "[60] Whatever edge he expressed in his writing he did not display as a person. "I don't think he's ever been mad about anything," a close friend remarked in the late 1980s.[61] Rather, what came through to those who knew him was his seemingly boundless fascination and curiosity and an almost childlike enthusiasm.[62] He would talk about his work with his friends, but only if they prodded him and even then not extensively.[63] He almost never appeared to be depressed. Those who knew him well saw him as "amiable, soft spoken, unpretentious," and "serene."[64] They understood that there were moments when his insecurity broke through—about how people felt about him and about dangers he might face; yet to everyone, including himself, he seemed to be a happy person who took events in stride.

Events in the Packard family continued to command his attention. Both sons divorced and then remarried. Packard's children came to terms with the challenges of balancing careers and marriage, with Cindy and Randall taking on the additional responsibility of parenting two children each. Packard's children could convey to their father what it meant to have a commuting marriage or one shaped by the trials of corporate relocation. Packard certainly had every reason to be proud of his children's achievements. Cindy worked in publishing and then authored two novels—*Hell's Bells* (1983) and *The Mother Lode* (1986). Vance P., after earning a master's degree in anthropology, worked for the Pennsylvania Historical and Museum Commission, eventually directing its Division of Industrial Sites. After serving in the Peace Corps and earning his Ph.D., Randall went on to a career as a historian of Africa, first at Tufts and later at Emory.

Vance also had ample reason to be proud of Virginia, who juggled the demands of career and family with great skill and panache. Pursuing her career full time beginning in the early 1960s, by the early 1970s she began, according to her husband, "devoting herself exclusively to capturing on canvas mood scenes of her great love: the sea, sand, sky and beach flora of Martha's Vineyard." She built a strong reputation as a painter, and her canvases of Martha's Vineyard scenes commanded considerable prices and admiration. Shows on Martha's Vineyard and Nantucket, as well as in Connecticut, New York City, and State College, helped place her works in over two hundred private collections.[65]

The Reshaping of Human Nature

Before Packard settled on what he would do after *Nation of Strangers*, he explored the possibility of breaking away from the genre that had engaged his efforts since the late 1950s. He proposed writing "a tongue-in-cheek report" on technological innovations, "seen through the enthusiastic eyes of a single-minded" figure "modelled vaguely after Voltaire's Dr. Pangloss." Because he was "weary from writing six books largely concerned with values," he looked forward to turning out a shorter and more jocular one. In the late 1970s, he discussed with Little, Brown a multimillion-dollar series of about forty books that, using the publisher's access to the resources of its parent company, would combine books, photographs, and television programs. Little, Brown pursued neither of these proposals.[66]

In *People Shapers* (1977), Packard explored the full range of efforts to use human engineering and behavior modification to control humankind. Others had focused on most of the topics that he covered, but no one else had provided such a comprehensive treatment. The core of the book revealed the wide-ranging and "eye-opening, often scary" efforts of scientists and businesspeople to reshape human development, tendencies that disturbed a person, like Packard, who believed in the producer value of harmony between the human and the natural. Irked by the secrecy and hubris involved, Packard singled out several examples for attack. He sharply criticized behavioral psychologists for setting out to tamper with human nature. He disliked new technologies, such as in vitro fertilization, that threatened to undermine what he saw as normal families. He opposed government efforts, especially those used during the Nixon administration, to control dissidence through new methods of surveillance and espionage.[67]

Packard offered his usual combination of horrifying examples, liberal politics, and conservative values. He sought social control of new technologies in the name of enhanced individualism and family integrity. Although he recommended policies that would curtail efforts to shape people's lives, ultimately his solution was more personal. He turned his attention from community responsibility, which he had emphasized in his last two books, to individual rights, albeit making it clear that he was in favor of self-development without narcissism. Man, he wrote after he both acknowledged and adopted the sexism of the language involved, "has the potential for self-mastery and social direction, and he is at his best when he is achieving them."[68]

Named one of the year's notable books by the American Library Association, *People Shapers* received reviews as favorable as those for any of Packard's efforts. The dominant note was that whatever reservations most critics had, what the book revealed deserved serious attention. Especially gratifying was the response of Warren Bennis, a humanistic psychologist on whom Packard had drawn, who placed Packard among the chroniclers of "the most concentrated form of social hell" such as George Orwell, Aldous Huxley, Arthur Koestler, Franz Kafka, Aleksandr Solzhenitsyn. This compliment that "lumps my book with classics," Packard wrote, was one of the "developments that never occurred to me as an author until I came to Little, Brown."[69]

Yet attacks continued. A review in the *New York Times* by Christopher Lehmann-Haupt used a problematic literary device to highlight the weaknesses of the book. "I dropped into Vance Packard's world the other day," he wrote, although he had not actually visited him, "to see what he is viewing with alarm this year." Lehmann-Haupt reported that he had "found this famous trend-spotter with . . . scissors and paste in hand," appearing not "all that alarmed." When asked if he was writing a book, the fictional author responded "everything was people-shaping!" and, pointing to the "conflicting opinions littering the floor," asked, "What did I expect, cohesiveness?" Packard, unhappy that a review "held me up to ridicule" and that it circulated to several hundred newspapers, asked Harriet Pilpel to negotiate a remedy that forced Lehmann-Haupt to acknowledge in print that, not having visited Packard, "the interview was meant to be pure fantasy in the line of comment on Mr. Packard's book." The *New York Times* reviewer, Packard told his editor, "has had a can tied to his tail."[70]

Packard earned about $180,000 from the book, including a remarkable advance of $105,000 from his German publisher. In the late 1950s, Packard had established an effective working relationship with his German publisher, who now pulled out all the stops. He secured from Prime Minister Helmut Schmidt a letter commenting favorably on the book and sent a copy to every member of the West German parliament.[71] The total income from the book, equivalent to about $450,000 in 1994 dollars, rewarded five years of work and exceeded Little, Brown's guarantee, even when adjusted for inflation. Yet once again there were signs of the waning of Packard's appeal, especially in America, where the book did not make it to the best-seller list. Still, *People Shapers* was sufficiently successful to give Packard the leverage to revise his 1975 contract. Already committed to one more book, in 1978 he signed an agreement that provided for the publication of an additional one on "a subject to be mutually agreed upon" and with a guarantee of $80,000 to be adjusted for inflation.[72]

Whatever success *People Shapers* had in the marketplace, it was in some ways disappointing. Packard's proposals to write a different kind of book underscored his feelings about turning out yet another exhaustively researched and highly serious one. What he had written lacked the sense of engagement and vividness that on-the-scene investigation had brought to *Status Seekers* and *Nation of Strangers*. Also missing was a sustained grappling with issues such as how to draw the line between acceptable and reprehensible people shaping. Packard showed his usual fascinated ambivalence, using favorable adjectives to describe the culprits whose efforts he denounced.[73]

He was also tempering his argument. With *Sexual Wilderness* he had raised the possibility of writing with less of an "emphasis upon combative criticism." In 1974 he had told Pilpel that he expected "to be more reflective than combative in handling the material" for *People Shapers*. When a reviewer called him a muckraker and his book an exposé, he balked. These words, he wrote his editor, "imply exposure of conspiratorial shenanigans" and it has been more than a decade "since I have written anything smacking of muckraking."[74] As Packard worked on *Our Endangered Children*, he commented to his editor that "you said your marketing people thought I have been best at exposes showing manipulation." Packard acknowledged that some of what he wrote was in that vein, but he asserted that he also produced what he called "commentary books," a phrase that he used to distance himself from his role as a social critic. Packard knew that the publisher was correct "that some people think of me as an exposer, a Johnny 1-note type," but he insisted that he was "thinking of books— expose or not—that *need* to be written or that I would greatly enjoy writing."[75]

If his books of the late 1950s and early 1960s had demonstrated how powerful people were secretly doing things that were adversely affecting American life, with *Sexual Wilderness* he had begun to turn away from that approach. Though *Nation of Strangers* and *People Shapers* contained plenty of evidence that governments and corporations were manipulating people, Packard did not choose to develop that theme in a concerted way. His struggle with corporate pressures at *American Magazine* now farther behind him, growing more comfortable, further removed from the problems he was descrying, he produced work that was less adversarial. The frightening examples in this book overwhelmed the argument, limiting the book's critical thrust.

Some Children Threatened

By the late 1970s, Packard was at work on his next book, *Our Endangered Children*. The book appeared at a time when there was plenty of evidence to justify such a title. The 1980 census revealed that during the previous decade the number of families headed by an unmarried person, mostly female, increased by more than 50 percent; that almost one child in four was not living with both parents; that more than half of the new households were composed of nonrelated people sharing living quarters.[76] Thirteen million children lived in poverty, with African American children twice as likely to have no employed parent, three times as likely to live in a female-headed household, and four times as likely to be murdered before their first birthday.[77]

With *Our Endangered Children*, authorial independence had a special urgency. When he moved from McKay, Packard established an effective working relationship with his new editor, Larned G. Bradford, but Bradford died before Packard completed the book. Genevieve Young took over, and it was with her that Packard had discussed whether the book was an exposé or a commentary. He had worked closely with women professionals before, but this situation was different. Though he had had heavy editorial supervision at *American Magazine*, by now he was both accustomed to and contractually entitled to independence. So he bristled at what he viewed as his new editor's forcefulness. She was, a colleague reported, "an old-fashioned line editor" who would "rewrite Henry James."[78] Young was playing by a version of standard rules without recognizing the unique situation that Packard had grown used to. Moreover, Eleanor Rawson had not pressed Packard to temper his position on women's issues in *Sexual Wilderness*. With *Our Endangered Children*, Young prodded Packard. "I had a sort of knee-jerk reaction of annoyance to the assumption in the first outline," she wrote, "that it is the mother who is responsible for child raising." She warned Packard about the response of his audience. "I don't know how many feminists you will have as readers, but you're almost sure to get one as a reviewer."[79]

At his first lunch with Young, "she plunged," he later wrote, into a discussion of major changes that she wanted. When Packard showed Young his contract, he reported, "she expressed astonishment. In fact she seemed flabbergasted, and professed never to have seen such" provisions. He reminded her that, having fulfilled his side of the bargain, he was free to walk away.[80] Even as they learned how to work together, Young persisted in pushing Packard to make changes. "Usually," he wrote, "she framed" them "as suggestions," but in several instances she "lapsed into directives." In the end, he agreed to much of what she wanted, a process that improved the book but stalled publication for the better part of a year.[81] Packard was dissatisfied. Meeting his editor's requests, he felt, "aggravated me more than a little though overall a better book emerged."[82] This situation revealed the sharp contrast between the special treatment he had received at McKay and what was happening now. The publisher's production schedule, he wrote when Little, Brown asked that he return galleys almost as quickly as he received them, "leaves me stunned. After a half year of dwaddling [*sic*] everything suddenly becomes split second." The catalog, he noted, had "announced my book in the most routine way" and "repeatedly referred to it as a 'survey.' "[83]

In fact, *Our Endangered Children* was not a survey. Rather, it viewed with alarm what Packard saw as "a deep malaise" that had "rather swiftly come over child-raising" in the United States and other modern societies. Packard pointed to "an anti-child culture that confronts children with a cool, hard world outside their home." Though he acknowledged that millions of children grew up under favorable conditions, he emphasized the "pain, anxiety, and discouraging problems" that threatened "to create a permanent warping of a large segment of our coming generation." He chronicled the hostile conditions that many children faced in hospitals dominated by impersonality and technology, apartment buildings that excluded children, schools overcome by disorder, and television programs that assaulted youthful minds. The entrance of mothers into the work force and the rising rate of divorce were among the factors he felt were most responsible for undermining the health of the family. He expressed concern about the impact on children of absent mothers and inferior day care facilities. He asserted the importance of parental responsibility and of the family as a social institution.[84]

Though hardly romanticizing the treatment of children for much of human history, at key moments Packard made it clear that he took his bearings from a better past. He hailed the way public schools had once stood as "community monuments" that shaped "not only the minds but the character and morals" of young people. He steadfastly held on to traditional notions of motherhood, women, gender roles, and the family. He decried American society's disdain for the life of the woman who stayed home to take care of the children.[85] He paid a good deal of attention to problems in blended families or households headed by single parents, but he did not recognize fully the difficulties faced by children who lived with both natural parents but suffered the consequences of abuse, alcoholism, poverty, or a patched-together marriage.

As the future would prove, Packard correctly understood many of the threatening conditions that children faced and the social consequences that resulted. He seemed torn between his traditional morality and a liberalism that recognized the real conditions that contemporary families were up against. Turning once again from individual rights to responsibility, he blamed the anti-children environment on the "strong emphasis on a quest for sensations, wanderlust, doing your own thing" that had emerged from the counterculture of the 1960s. He attacked what he saw as rejection by feminists of children and motherhood because they were obstacles to career, self-fulfillment, and happy marriage. Though on occasion acknowledging the household responsibilities of the father, Packard persistently saw the care of children as a woman's problem.[86]

Especially troublesome was his selectivity. The book would focus, he remarked, on "typical children coming from increasingly typical families" and not on "those who are delinquents, severely deprived, disturbed or battered." The issue of typicality was, of course, tricky, especially when it came to defining which children were endangered. At a time when others recognized the devastating impact on children of severe cuts in federal programs, Packard focused principally on white, middle-class families. He paid virtually no attention to the special situations of African American and Hispanic children, or even those of white working-class children. He saw affluence—in the form of television, junk food, excessive mobility—more than poverty as the root cause of the difficulties that children faced.[87] For someone who made his mark in the late 1950s by uncovering the means by which corporations, governments, and experts abused their power, here he was relatively mute on the larger institutional situations that shaped people's lives. As recently as with *Nation of Strangers*, he had presented evidence for such a case but did not make it. Now he backed off more, tempering even his analysis in the name of a commitment to family.

More than any of his other books, *Our Endangered Children* had disappointing sales. The earnings, which amounted to around $35,000, contrasted with almost $140,000 that Little, Brown paid him when the cost-of-living provision came into play. The reviews, smaller in number than with the previous books, were generally favorable. There were, of course, exceptions that raised doubts along familiar lines. But compared with the responses to earlier books, there were now remarkably few slashing attacks. Yet Genevieve Young was right: Feminists responded negatively to Packard's concerns about the impact of women's careers on their children.[88] Characteristically, though his book received a review on page 12 of the *New York Times Book Review*, the front-page review in the same issue covered Roger Rosenblatt's *Children of War* (1983), a moving personal story of his travels to talk with children living in war-torn places.[89] Though Packard ascribed his book's poor reception to the situation he had faced at Little, Brown, the showing in the marketplace obviously stemmed from additional factors.[90]

With this book, however, Packard received what was perhaps the most favorable review of his career from a leading academic intellectual—albeit one who was not a sociologist. Christopher Lasch, author of *Haven in a Heartless World* (1977) and *The Culture of Narcissism* (1979), credited Packard with having made it possible to talk about how desirable it was for children to have mothers and two parents "without inviting accusations of antifeminism and reactionary 'nostalgia.'" Taking issue with Packard's policy recommendations, he nonetheless congratulated him for "honest reporting of facts that undercut the complacent assumption that modern society, having freed itself from the provincial moralities of the past, is entering a new age of enlightenment."[91] As evidence of the difficulty of achieving a utopia, Lasch pointed to the problem of combining careers and family, achieving open marriage, and raising liberated children. Lasch's compliments underscored what these two authors shared. Like Packard, the influential historian and cultural critic respected the authority of fathers and criticized those, like feminists and heirs of the counterculture, who he believed were naive about the costs of the quest for progress, liberation, and self-realization.[92] As would become even more obvious when Lasch published *The True and Only Heaven* in 1991, he shared with Packard a moral passion, concern over the demise of meaningful work, worry about the search for false pleasures in consumption, and an emphasis on virtue and independence.

The problems of Packard's book become clear when it is compared with what others were writing. If he had previously offered path-breaking discussions, *Our Endangered Children* entered a crowded field of works on family life and did so without breaking new ground or having appreciable influence on policy.[93] Now he was in an arena filled with ideological land mines. By the late 1970s, feminists had developed a critique of the patriarchal family as oppressive and were working to foster egalitarian households. They saw the entrance of women into the work force not as a trend to be lamented, as Packard did, but as one to be celebrated. Moreover, fighting to make the definition of the family more inclusive, they challenged notions that any one kind of family arrangement was natural.[94] From the Left, advocates for children focused on families devastated by poverty and called for government policies that would guarantee equal opportunity by ensuring that all children benefited from adequate income, health care, education, and legal protection.[95]

In contrast, from conservatives came warnings that feminism, divorce, the welfare system, the heritage of the counterculture of the 1960s, television, individualistic values, and the attacks on motherhood threatened the family. They wanted a much more restricted definition that would put heterosexuality, marriage, and children at the center. Many conservatives in the 1970s and 1980s saw government programs as the cause and not the solution to the problems that poor families faced.[96] Some neoconservatives offered a more secular and restrained version of this approach. Eschewing relativistic values and configurations, they favored the traditional nuclear family that fostered middle-class aspirations and taught self-control.[97]

Packard showed little awareness of the ideological dimensions of the battles raging in America over the family.[98] Though he made clear his willingness to accept a national family policy, he seemed oblivious to the ground that he shared with the Right. To be sure, he did not adopt conservative positions on abortion and school prayer.[99] Yet like the people he would hardly consider his allies, his first instinct was not government programs but action by parents and private institutions. Making it clear how much he had distanced himself from the conflictual view of marriage that Willard Waller presented in the 1930s, Packard offered a list of skills that parents could develop to "help create the melodious kind of environment in which growing children will thrive." At a time when federal programs for children were being cut, Packard, rather than developing an extended critique of policies of the Reagan administration or presenting a full agenda for government action, concentrated much of his attention on practical ways to foster "wise parenting and good community situations."[100]

Similarly, he blamed the neglect of children not on the economic or social system but on working women, divorce, television, and the selfishness inspired by the counterculture. He stressed the importance of hard work and neighborhoods, attacked sexual promiscuity, and offered an antiurban vision. He focused on the middle class, holding up as an ideal the bourgeois family headed by a male breadwinner and a female who assumed the primary responsibility for children. When he read a book that asserted that families "may be composed of groups of friends who rely on one another for help with child-rearing, for advice, and for emotional and perhaps financial support," he found himself "bristling more than admiring, because . . . I am a pretty old-fashioned guy." He wrote to Carolyn Anthony, a woman who combined marriage, career, and child-rearing, that "the problem is that I still think of families as the kinds that you and I have and those I will fight for."[101]

The Impact of Changes in the Media

The fading of Packard's influence also stemmed from other changes. By the late 1960s new developments had begun to challenge his approach. The genre he had perfected had once been in tune with audience expectations. As time went on, the number of readers whose ideas were shaped by mass-circulation magazines diminished. Packard's irony and ambivalence may have dovetailed well with his audience's outlook in the late 1950s and early 1960s, but his stance did not work at a time when readers wanted books that demonstrated more commitment. One particular moment encapsulated these changes. Four 1972 books, he remembered, bumped *Nation of Strangers* off the nonfiction best-sellers list.[102] Carlos Castaneda's *Journey to Ixtlan* provided a guide to spiritual exploration that was much more appealing to audiences than Packard's mixture of moralizing and self-realization. Kenneth P. O'Donnell and David F. Powers's *"Johnny, We Hardly Knew Ye"* benefited not only from the interest in celebrities but also from fascination with the slain president at a time when politics seemed less heroic and more sordid. *Dr. Atkins' Diet Revolution*, published by McKay, was one of many best-sellers that fed the obsession with weight loss. And Alex Comfort's *Joy of Sex*, for which Packard had written a jacket blurb, broke new ground as it guided readers through a sexual paradise that four years earlier Packard had characterized as a wilderness.

Moreover, even if Packard's health had not limited his place in the limelight as a speaker, he would have encountered difficulty in meeting the increasingly demanding requirements for celebrity status. One incident illustrated this change. When his heart attack prevented him from giving a speech at Skidmore during his daughter's last semester there, Abbie Hoffman replaced him. Although it was an illness that prevented Packard's appearance, the situation had considerable symbolic significance. In the spring of 1970, with the war in Southeast Asia raging and feminism flourishing, an audience composed largely of college-age women was probably more interested in hearing from someone as colorful as Hoffman than from the father of one of their classmates who had recently published a book urging them to avoid premarital sex and not be overly assertive in pressing their demands.[103]

But more was at issue than a generational and ideological shift. As a reporter noted after Packard made a disappointing appearance on a television show in 1959, "Packard is no personality boy. The interview was a flop."[104] A colleague remarked that as a lecturer Packard was hesitant and indirect.[105] As a journalist wrote in 1964, though Packard was focused when he was at the typewriter, in performance he could "be a little disconcerting." He talked "slowly, loses the thread of what he is saying, regains it, acts on the whole like a professor at a small college [who is] a little unsure of tenure and [has] an important lecture coming up with the president in attendance."[106]

In the 1950s, 1960s, and even into the early 1970s, Packard had appeared on most of the major television shows. Even had he continued to publish immensely popular and controversial books, his authenticity would have made it difficult for him to be packaged and promoted. Not charismatic, unusually articulate, or telegenic, Packard lacked the ability to project that enabled others to sell books with television appearances and command unusually high fees on the lecture circuit. By the mid-1970s, the best-seller list, the star system of the book world, increasingly relied on television appearances as part of a comprehensive promotional strategy. Among those who wrote attention-getting nonfiction books were Erma Bombeck, Leo Buscaglia, Bill Cosby, Alex Haley, Lee Iacocca, Shirley MacLaine, Miss Piggy, Andy Rooney, Carl Sagan, Richard Simmons, and Chuck Yaeger. More and more, book sales depended on personalities who could perform in public, and Packard was unable to fulfill that requirement by the standards that television demanded.[107]

In addition, by the early 1960s, television documentaries made it possible for people to watch programs that explored the themes that Packard also focused upon: the impact of new technologies, changes in American mores, crises in institutions, the intersection of policy and social change. Like Packard's books, television programs offered social commentaries that used muckraking, relied on interviews with ordinary people and experts, and explored solutions that were both personal and political. The difference was that television coverage was not only more visual and immediate than a Packard book, but it was also less expensive and time consuming for the viewer.[108]

The New Journalism that developed beginning in the mid-1960s compelled the attention of a large reading public that was eluding Packard. Responding to events such as the assassination of President John F. Kennedy and the war in Vietnam, writers now explored the absurdity and disorder of reality. Books by Joan Didion, Norman Mailer, Gay Talese, Studs Terkel, Hunter Thompson, and Tom Wolfe were markedly different from the journalism as social criticism that Packard practiced. Whereas Packard emphasized objectivity achieved mainly by exhaustive research with printed material, the New Journalists blurred fact and fiction as they injected themselves into their narratives, conveyed a sense of crisis, emphasized the consciousness of public events, and used imagination to involve themselves and their readers in the dramas of public life. If Packard was at his best as an observer, some of those who succeeded him hungered to be participants. Some of the most significant books published after the mid-1960s were testimonial and confessional ones.[109] As public figures, members of the new generation of writers were colorful, passionate, involved, and often heroic—qualities that made them compelling stars on the speakers' platform and the television screen. Given the importance of these qualities to the sale of books, publishers may have been increasingly reluctant to place Packard before the television cameras.[110] "The book world is getting beyond me," he wrote to Carolyn Anthony in 1980, as he marveled at how difficult it was to predict what works would rise to bestseller status.[111]

Adjusting to a Different Life

Once the less-than-expected sales of *Our Endangered Children* were clear, Packard took on the task of adjusting to a new relationship with his publisher. He had no illusions about his situation; as he later recalled, he was "obviously over the hill as a big-time author."[112] He was unhappy that Little, Brown had lost so much money on *Our Endangered Children*, in good measure because of the inflation escalator. Moreover, he wanted a new editor, a change of some moment for a publisher to grant. At the time, the contract that governed his next book guaranteed him $80,000, to be adjusted for inflation. There were probably clauses that Little, Brown could have invoked to void the contract—but Thornhill had no desire to take such an unusual step.[113] Packard made clear his desire for a new editor and told Pilpel that he was willing to accept a situation "with my labor being free if desired, until royalty time." He asked only for expenses, a figure set at $50,000 to be charged against future earnings. Fortunately, Packard renegotiated his contract when his success in real estate and publishing had resolved the tension between being free and being a good provider. "At my present stage of life, 68 and reasonably affluent," he wrote Pilpel early in 1983, "I want independence most of all even at the cost of cash."[114] In the fall of 1983, Packard and Thornhill, approaching the situation as two gentlemen, agreed to a new contract that was signed in January 1984.[115]

In March 1984, not long after Packard signed the revised contract, Virginia suffered a major stroke. Although she eventually made a moderately successful recovery, the impact on Vance was considerable. It was painful to watch his beloved wife of forty-five years suffer and struggle. He was able to handle the situation graciously, but their life together would never be the same.[116] Family became even more important to him now than it had been in the past, and his grandchildren were increasingly a source of satisfaction. Moreover, now it was he who had to make all the arrangements for his and Virginia's lives and take the lead in social situations.[117]

The stroke had financial consequences as well. If the reception of *Our Endangered Children* placed in doubt his ability to command substantial royalty income, the stroke threatened Virginia's career as a successful artist. There were also additional expenses: emergency travel from Mexico, bills from doctors and hospitals, and costs of rehabilitation. They had some social security income, no pension, and several hundred thousand dollars in liquid assets. The Packards were used to a situation in which most of their net worth was tied up in real estate. As Vance noted in 1980, "our family economy is based as much on real estate as upon book writing."[118] When they were "feeling affluent and benevolent," they had placed some of the Chappaquiddick land in a conservation trust and given some acreage to the children. Now, new circumstances made it necessary to turn some of what Packard half-jokingly called the "real estate empire" into liquid assets. In the summer of 1984, he sold the Tower House and the Studio House, as well as some of the acreage on Chappaquiddick, sales that grossed about $670,000 but netted much less after taxes and expenses were deducted. Two years later, Vance and Virginia conveyed the Main House to their children.[119]

In 1985, Packard's own heart problems resurfaced, and he underwent bypass surgery in early May. After his surgery he paid increasingly close attention to his health, beginning each day with a walk, playing golf whenever conditions permitted, driving his weight and cholesterol down to much lower levels. By 1988 he was able to write that he was "back to normal, except for some frayed nerves."[120] Despite these setbacks, Packard remained ready to tackle his next writing project.

Barbarians at the Gate, 1984–1989

The Ultra Rich

With *Ultra Rich: How Much Is Too Much* (1989), Vance Packard brought together the major strands of more than half a century of his career. His treatment of the lives of the wealthy reiterated themes he had first developed in his columns at the Boston newspaper, at the same time that it marked a departure from the focus of his books on the middle class. Continuing to blunt his social criticism, Packard once again offered a journalist's fascination with the preposterous. He fell short of developing a critique of the 1980s for which the producer ethic could have provided the basis. During that decade he was free to write as he pleased, not so much on account of the income he earned as a writer as because the appreciation of his family's real estate holdings confirmed his ability as a provider. With this book he continued to prove that he could sustain himself as a writer at the same time that he made clear that financial success greatly beyond the level he had achieved was not worth hankering after.

The core of the book took the reader into the lives of thirty Americans whose net worth averaged $330 million in 1985. Packard blended quotations from interviews with descriptions of how these people built their fortunes and lived their lives.[1] An air of fascination dominated his largely affectionate portraits. He offered human interest and inside dope on the eccentric people he selected. Showing how his subjects contradicted the commonly held image of the wealthy, he emphasized how few of them had extensive formal education and how accident more than skill had built their fortunes. He revealed that many who walked through the pages of the book lived in ordinary circumstances—inhabiting what he saw as modest homes in unexceptional neighborhoods and eating simple food. Although some of his subjects lived lavishly, Packard argued that they, unlike the wealthy of an earlier age, enjoyed fewer opportunities to live differently from millions of other Americans. Commercial services had made large staffs "superfluous." Diets undermined the appeal of rich foods. The anonymity of cities decreased the opportunity for "conspicuous display." VCRs meant that movies were as easily available to the plumber as to the centimillionaire. The IRS, terrorists, and fundraisers also made it prudent for people to live inconspicuously. Consequently, Packard asserted, even as the number of great fortunes was increasing, money was becoming decreasingly important.[2]

At the end of *Ultra Rich*, Packard turned to the question of what society should do about great wealth. He knew the only way he could prevent the book from being "an entertainment" was if he "seriously sought to prove no one should own" more assets than were necessary to live comfortably but not extravagantly.[3] Even though he found many of his subjects "vivid, extraordinary, and admirable personalities," he recommended a progressive tax on wealth that would limit to $25 million the amount of money any one person could hold or transfer. This would allow people like his subjects to live on $1 million a year and end the "increasingly grotesque accumulations of family wealth." He believed that his cap on wealth was "not a revolutionary proposal" and would not undermine free enterprise, which he judged "the most successful method of stimulating economic growth." Limits on assets would "win for these mostly unknown people of great wealth a good deal of public admiration while not affecting their life-styles in any significant way," since most of them lived on $1 million a year anyway. His plan would inspire what he saw as more productive uses of money—venturesome investments, increased revenues for the federal government, strengthened "underpinnings of our democracy," and greater philanthropy. Seemingly unaware that public monies or charitable contributions might be used for conservative ends, Packard optimistically held out the hope that a cap on fortunes would free up funds to deal with AIDS, homelessness, pollution, illiteracy, and educational opportunity.[4]

Packard's analysis and solution rested on assumptions rooted in the producer ethic. He believed that wealth was essential to capitalism but that it was "most efficient, economically and socially," if it was widely dispersed. He distinguished between the productive and the unproductive impact of great wealth, between investments and expenditures that fostered economic well-being and those that were static, such as collecting antiques and buying jewelry. He stood against the ostentation and corruption of what he called "a moneyed aristocracy." There was, he emphasized, "an element of indecency in having so much of the national wealth tied up in a few hands when the nation has so many urgent economic problems." When asked what values he would put in place of striving after money and power, he spoke of honor, service, and creativity.[5]

At times Packard's fascination with his subjects overpowered his capacity to make critical judgments. His approach was that of a tour leader who tried to convey to his audience what he found fascinating about his subjects. When he set out to write the book, he thought about using the interviews to compose in what he called "the Studs Terkel manner," employing "an emphasis on listening to them talk."[6] Though the book did offer extensive quotations, Packard failed to follow Terkel, whose interviews conveyed the vitality and immediacy of the people whose words he recorded. He also missed one of Terkel's central points: that oral histories offered both dramatic social contrasts and the wisdom of ordinary people. Had Packard followed the approach that Terkel used in *The Great Divide* (1988), for example, he could have juxtaposed the stories he collected with interviews from the whole range of Americans affected by the 1980s.

As it was, Packard passed over blemishes in the portraits of the wealthy, mentioning without much judgment the sexism of one person, the joblessness another caused when he moved his business, and the controversy surrounding the pornography that Robert Guccione published in *Penthouse*.[7] Instead, as reviewers noted, what carried the book along was the "delicious" quality of "the life style details."[8] A friend who had known him well since the early 1950s later remarked that Vance was "terribly impressed with people who had lots of money."[9] One observer called his style "chummy" and his portraits "surprisingly sympathetic, given his conclusions." "If he is truly appalled by their obscene affluence," noted the reviewer in the *New York Times*, "he seems not to have let on while in their company."[10] There was a tension between what another observer called "the incisive thinking" of his solution and the rest of the book, which resembled "something you might expect to see serialized in *People* magazine."[11] At key moments, *Ultra Rich* seemed more like an episode in the television series *Dallas* or *Dynasty* than social criticism.

The way Packard selected his subjects also undercut the book's seriousness. At the outset, he decided to concentrate on what he called "the most colorful, preposterous" examples.[12] He was well aware of other books that focused on those whose speculation and greed was so emblematic of the 1980s.[13] When he was writing the book, people asked him if he was including Donald Trump. His response was that he had not, in part because the publicity-hungry real estate speculator was "far less colorful" than others that he did include. This statement overlooked the symbolic power of Trump, Michael Milken, and Ivan Boesky. Similarly, in the book Packard made it clear that he opposed corporate raiders and leveraged-buyout specialists.[14] Yet when he presented one person whose fortune stemmed from such practices, he focused not on how the man made his money but on his idiosyncratic way of spending it. Packard also decided not to include a representative of the idle rich, because he "was more interested in heirs attempting something challenging on their own."[15] When he sought someone who had inherited money from a great turn-of-the-century fortune, he chose not one of the DuPonts or Mellons, who supported conservative causes, but a Chappaquiddick neighbor, a Rockefeller "Cousin," who "said there was no way she could justify all the wealth she has."[16] Inclusion of a new robber baron, a representative of the idle rich, or a person who used inherited wealth for conservative causes would have provided a stronger basis for his recommendation to cap fortunes.

Packard's minimization of the influence of great wealth was also problematic. Although most of the people he interviewed told him they did not see their money in terms of power, their statements were hardly the only evidence available on that point. Great fortunes exercised tremendous cultural force in the 1980s, to say nothing of their political and economic impact. With its emphasis on the symbolic uses of money rather than on the real exercise of power, *Ultra Rich* owed more to Thorstein Veblen's *Theory of the Leisure Class* than to C. Wright Mills's *Power Elite*.[17] In *Ultra Rich*, Packard took a position strikingly different from the distinguished tradition of investigation that, including Mills and G. William Domhoff, explored the connection between wealth and power. In fact, two years before the appearance of *Ultra Rich*, Michael P. Allen's *Founding Fortunes* explored not only how the very rich lived but also how they exercised power.[18]

Packard was well aware of the arguments of these authors. While he acknowledged that many wealthy people "have played rough with their money," that was certainly not the picture that emerged from his stories.[19]

He argued that though a great fortune made power possible, it did "not automatically make a wealth-possessor a power wielder." Rather, he focused on the psychological uses of wealth—as a proof of potency, an extension of the self, or a way to keep score.[20] Packard's subjects, remarked sociologist E. Digby Baltzell, had no sense of belonging to a class or power elite. They had, he said, "no common culture, no common ideals and surely no common sense of duty or *noblesse oblige.*"[21]

As in Packard's other works, in *Ultra Rich* the politics were ambiguous. Packard looked back to an earlier breed who had a sense of stewardship, lamenting the decline of mythic entrepreneurs who achieved great power.[22] He told a reporter from *USA Today* that his book "was totally pro-capitalist."[23] Yet a favorable reviewer noted that "for someone who lives on the right side of the tracks in say, New Canaan, Conn., some of Packard's suggestions are downright treasonable."[24] The central contradiction of the book remained: Between Packard's affectionate approach to the very rich and his proposal to tax their wealth. Packard's statement that millions of Americans did not live very differently from the way his subjects did provided false reassurance for those who did not have hundreds of millions of dollars to cushion them from adversity. Though he voted Democratic during these years and made clear to friends and family his objections to the course of American politics, in the book Packard missed the chance to critique the Reagan administration in a sustained way.[25]

Ultra Rich was much more successful than *Our Endangered Children*, yielding, in addition to $48,000 in expenses, more than $70,000 in income.[26] Foreign sales, especially in Japan and Germany, continued the process, first begun with *People Shapers*, of exceeding the returns from lagging American royalties.[27] If during the 1980s, Packard's royalty income fell, his wealth soared, based as it was on real estate values greatly enhanced by the growing number of multimillionaires to whom New Canaan and Chappaquiddick were desirable locations. The book provided reassurance that fortunes of the ultra rich did not underwrite a style of life vastly different from his own and that they were not happier than he. Proposing to cap their wealth reaffirmed the value of the liberal causes he supported and promised to preserve the opportunity he cherished.

The books on wealth that did reach the best-seller list or command critical attention during the 1980s and early 1990s reveal the distinctiveness of Packard's approach, as well as his distance from the pulse of the American reading public. What casts doubt on his remark about "a decline in cautionary books about the rich" and a shift to ones that were "primarily informational" were the influential ones that took on issues that Packard avoided or slighted.[28] The success of *Iacocca* (1984) and *Trump* (1987) may have spurred him on to write the kind of book that he did. Yet among many best-sellers of the period that showed how hungry Americans were for books on money and power quite different in approach from *Ultra Rich* were *Den of Thieves* (1991), by James B. Stewart; *Barbarians at the Gate: The Fall of RJR Nabisco* (1990), by Bryan Burrough and John Helyar; *America: What Went Wrong?* (1992), by Donald L. Barlett and James B. Steele; and *The Bonfire of the Vanities* (1987), by Tom Wolfe.[29]

Ultra Rich helps make it possible to understand the nature of Packard's political journey. His distinctiveness becomes clear through a comparison of his outlook with that of Middle Americans and neoconservatives whose commitments to the Democratic party, unlike Packard's, became tenuous in the 1970s and 1980s. These were two groups from which Packard kept his distance and yet with whom he shared a grounding in the New Deal and rejection of much of what the late 1960s represented.

Like the lower-middle-class or working-class ethnics who broke with the Democrats after the late 1960s, to a considerable extent Packard based his vision on producer values.[30] He dissented from them or remained silent on issues that were central to them: such as the meaning of the Vietnam War and affirmative action. He spoke from New Canaan and Chappaquiddick, not from the Canarsie section of Brooklyn. Yet unlike limousine liberals, he espoused many traditional social values. Though he remained personally prone to individual self-expression, he opposed self-indulgence. Though he was not conservative on social issues such as abortion and school prayer, he was committed to old definitions of family values. If he remained a defender of reproductive rights, he was against much in contemporary feminism. If his social position made it possible for him to evidence minimal concern over busing, he opposed the black radicalism that had emerged in the late 1960s. Not worried that his children would not make it into the middle class, he had no personal reason to oppose affirmative action.

Sharing common ground but differing on policies also characterizes Packard's relationship to those New York Jewish intellectuals such as Norman Podhoretz, Nathan Glazer, and Irving Kristol, who after the mid-1960s emerged as neoconservatives.[31] Though having in common key generational experiences, the Cold War, anticommunism, and foreign policy were of relatively minor importance to Packard. Reacting strongly against the counterculture of the late 1960s, he differed from these peers when he opposed the war in Vietnam. While Packard rejected black radicalism and post-1968 feminism, he did not follow neoconservatives in developing a generalized sense of the dangers of egalitarianism and entitlement. He may have found the very wealthy fascinating and free enterprise admirable, but unlike Kristol he held back from offering *Two Cheers for Capitalism* (1978). Though he articulated traditional values, evoked a sense of moral decline, and even spoke of threats to Western civilization, Packard remained driven more by optimism than by a sense of doom. Distant from universities, not upset by attacks on Culture, not particularly involved with a commitment to Israel, he remained unaffected by many of the issues that roiled neoconservatives.

Early on, Packard had developed a sense of himself as an outsider, and he had connected that perception with being a nonconformist, a liberal, and a Democrat. In some ways the 1960s had moved him to the right, but he did not explore the tension between his traditional values and his liberal political commitments.[32] Throughout his adult life, Packard, like most of his close personal friends in Fairfield County, kept his liberal faith and remained a FDR Democrat.[33] Success never went to his head, his optimism tempered his outrage, and his social isolation insulated him from the forces that shook Reagan Democrats. Though what it meant to be a liberal changed dramatically between the mid-1960s and the late 1980s, he remained committed to anticommercialism, population control, and protection of the natural environment. By basing his politics on traditional values, he remained true to the life experiences that had shaped him.

In important ways, in *Ultra Rich* he demonstrated his connectedness with his past. Beginning in the late 1930s, he had expressed fascination with wealthy people who lived plainly. Throughout his career, he had argued that riches did not make people happy, at the same time that he had celebrated the American dream of entrepreneurial success. Like others grounded in a producer ethic, what bothered him about the very wealthy was that this new aristocracy might corrupt democracy. As was true in his trilogy, in his 1989 book he placed minimal blame for social ills on individuals. This book, like his others, combined fascination, social criticism, and practical advice.[34] As he had done in the 1950s, he had a tendency to psychologize social problems. He continued to combine bold proposals with fascinating stories—and evidenced no interest in using anything but his pen to bring his recommendations about.

Although *Ultra Rich* underscored the continuities in Packard's outlook, in important ways it marked a break with his past. Packard offered no sermon on how powerful people and institutions were manipulating the lives of ordinary Americans. Despite abundant opportunity to do so, he did little muckraking. He focused not on the middle class but on the very wealthy—a dramatic shift for an author who in 1938 had written that he did particularly not like "the ultra ultra ultra people with dough."[35] These changes involved the closing of the gap, so apparent to observers in the 1950s and 1960s, between angry writer and amiable man. When a reporter in 1968 wrote that Packard, "as pleasantly low-key as they come," struck him as "objective, candid, very much the reporter, not the polemicist," Packard wrote in the margin of his copy of the article "finally, an accurate description!"[36] Though some called him "a stinging social critic," another reporter noted in the 1980s that his looks and demeanor make him "seem more the teacher, the perfect professor."[37] From the mid-1960s until the late 1980s, Packard shifted his self-definition, incompletely and unevenly, from "social critic" to terms that were milder, referring to himself as a "social commentator" or "observer." Eventually he came full circle, writing in 1983, "Basically I've always been a reporter."[38]

"I can't claim too much for my work," Packard said retrospectively, pointing to the increasing amount of money Americans spent on advertising.[39] Such an assessment missed the very important but often intangible ways in which his writings affected America. With his usual modesty, he could also deflate his achievement as an author. Looking back, he remarked that he made more money in his life from appreciation of real estate than from writing.[40] In his years as book author, he commented in 1990 in a way that did not take inflation into account and that invoked a familiar comparison, his average income as a writer was $33,000 "or less than a U.S. plumber's income."[41] Calling himself a "poor author" in front of a lecture audience in 1989, he continued not to think of himself as a wealthy person by standards most Americans would use.[42]

Yet he was proud of the fact that his books covered many of the most important topics of the postwar period.[43] Few free-lance authors do so well over decades—financially or psychologically. Not many authors are able both to enjoy the freedom to write as they please and also to succeed in being good providers. Packard was able to achieve an integrated way of life consistent with his commitments to producer values—pursuing an honest calling, achieving civic virtue, connecting with the natural world, and sustaining his opposition to excessive commercialism.[44]

"I'd have to say it's been a good life," Packard told a reporter in 1986. "For the most part, I've been a very happy man."[45] Yet he had long lived with uncertainty. "I guess you know I'm dying of heart disease, have been for 20 years," he wrote a friend in 1988. Heart disease had felled both his parents in the early 1960s and his siblings in the early 1980s. "I figure I have led a full life and everything else is undeserved bonus." As his seventy-fourth birthday neared, he wrote that if he lived to celebrate his

More than a quarter of a century after the publication of Hidden Persuaders,
*a British periodical features Packard on its cover, asking if he is "still
persuasive after all these years?" (From* Marketing Week,
7 June 1985; used by permission.)

Packard's friend and New Yorker *cartoonist Whitney Darrow, Jr., created this drawing for a 1986 issue of the Sunday supplement of the* Hartford Courant. *Darrow captures essential elements of Packard's life: book after book emerging from his word processor; one hat placed on another; and his dog Thumper at his feet. Waiting at the ready are reminders of his avocations: bowling paraphernalia; golf equipment with tags from courses on Martha's Vineyard, San Miguel de Allende, and Fairfield County, Connecticut; and a sea gull from Chappaquiddick.*
(Used by permission of Whitney Darrow, Jr.)

eightieth in 1994, he would "announce a bounty for anyone who shoots me. Until then the game seems to be to try to proceed with as much dignity and enjoyment of life as circumstances permit." He predicted that to the end, he would remain a writer. He remarked in 1983 that he could not "imagine not being in the middle of a book when I pop off."[46]

Notes

ABBREVIATIONS

ABJ	*Akron Beacon Journal*
AHR	*American Historical Review*
AJS	*American Journal of Sociology*
AM	*American Magazine*
AQ	*American Quarterly*
ASR	*American Sociological Review*
BDR	*Boston Daily Record*
CDT	*Centre Daily Times*
CP	Cindy Packard
CPR	Cindy Packard Richmond
CSJA	Archives, Graduate School of Journalism, Columbia University, New York, New York
CTA	Carolyn T. Anthony
EK	Edward Kuhn, Jr.
ER	Eleanor Rawson
GY	Genevieve Young
HP	*Hidden Persuaders*
HP	Harriet Pilpel
JAH	*Journal of American History*
KR	Kennett Rawson
LGB	Larned G. Bradford
MH	*Methodist History*
NCHS	New Canaan Historical Society
NOS	*Nation of Strangers*
NS	*Naked Society*
NYT	*New York Times*
OEC	*Our Endangered Children*
OMB	*Old Main Bell*
PC	*Pyramid Climbers*
PPLB	Vance Packard file, Little, Brown, Boston, Massachusetts
PPNC	Vance Packard Papers, Packard residence, New Canaan, Connecticut
PPPS	Vance Packard Papers, Rare Books and Special Collections, Pennsylvania State University Libraries, University Park, Pennsylvania
PS	*People Shapers*
PSA	Pennsylvania State University Archives, Pennsylvania State University Libraries, University Park, Pennsylvania
PSC	*Penn State Collegian*
RC	Robert Crandall (pseudonym for VP)

RP   Randall Packard
RR   Ray Roberts
SC   *Summer Collegian*
SS   *Status Seekers*
SW   *Sexual Wilderness*
UR   *Ultra Rich*
VG   *Vineyard Gazette*
VGA   Vineyard Gazette Archives, Edgartown, Massachusetts
VM   Virginia Mathews
VMP   Virginia Mathews Packard
VP   Vance Packard
VPP   Vance Philip Packard
WM   *Waste Makers*
WSJ   *Wall Street Journal*
WW   Willard Waller

NOTE ON SOURCES

In discussions of Packard's career, I have used copies of reviews, features, and other articles from his papers; unless the location is otherwise identified, the material cited is in PPPS. If publication data and citations are incomplete, it is because the publication in the collection does not have all the pertinent information on the source of the article. Usually I have not included these items in the bibliography. Nor does the bibliography contain articles by Packard or, in most instances, by his contemporaries.

PREFACE

1. VP to author, 10 June 1992, author's possession.
2. Buckley, Review.
3. VP to author, 5 November 1990, author's possession.

INTRODUCTION

1. VP, interview with author, New Canaan, Conn., 9 April 1986.

2. Throughout the book, statements about the placement of Packard's works on the best-seller list rely on weekly newspaper clippings, PPPS; only SS reached the annual *Publishers' Weekly* list, ending up in 1959 at the number four position. For those lists, see Hackett and Burke, *80 Years*, and, after 1975, *Bowker Annual.*

3. RP, interview with author, Winchester, Mass., 1 July 1992; VP to author, 9 December 1988, author's possession.

4. Here I am relying on Tompkins, *Sensational Designs*.

5. Radway, "Book-of-the-Month Club," p. 260.

6. See, for example, Jacoby, *Last Intellectuals*.

7. See, for example, Blake, *Beloved Community*, and Westbrook, *John Dewey*.

8. J. S. Rubin, "Between Culture and Consumption," p. 189.

9. In my remarks on the producer ethic, I draw on Blocker, *Retreat from Reform*, pp. 10, 12, 14–16, 27, and 240–41; Clark, *Deliver Us from Evil*, pp. 3, 10, 12–13, 92, 135, 152, 171–72, and 178–79; Gans, *Middle American Individualism*, pp. ix–xi; Lasch, *True and Only Heaven*, pp. 15–17, 66, 193–95, 205–7, 217, 223–24, 274, 303, 394, 431, 477, 495, 505–7, and 530–32; Livingston, *Federal Reserve System*, pp. 45–46; Thelen, *Paths of Resistance*, pp. 3, 11–16, 21, 205, 207, 219, and 225–27.

CHAPTER ONE

1. VP, "Behavioral Changes in Americans since 1950," unpublished essay, March 1993, p. 11, PPNC.

2. Ibid., p. 1. For information on Packard's years in Granville Summit, I have relied on this document and on VP, interview with author, New Canaan, Conn., 23 April 1987; VP, interview with author, New Canaan, Conn., 3 June 1987; VP, notations on map of the area, June 1987, author's possession; VP, "Excerpts from Recollections of My Sister Pauline," around 1977, PPNC; VP, notes from talk with LaRue Packard, around 1977, PPNC; VP, "Boyhood Memories," *Canton Area Historical Society Newsletter* 4 (November 1984): 23–24; VP, notes for a memoir, around 1984, PPNC. His given name was Vance Oakley Packard; his parents named him Vance after Vance C. McCormick (1872–1946), the gubernatorial nominee of the Democratic party in Pennsylvania whom former president Teddy Roosevelt supported.

3. Wood et al., "Soil Survey of Bradford County," pp. 239, 243, and 249; VP, interview with author, New Canaan, Conn., 1 December 1990; VP to author, 3 June 1991, author's possession.

4. "The Packard Family," typescript, PPNC; VP, notes for memoir; Osterud, *Bonds of Community*, p. 142.

5. Obituary for Philip J. Packard, newspaper clipping dated 26 December 1963, PSA; "Citizen of the Week," clipping on Philip J. Packard from Martinsburg newspaper, ca. 1960, PPNC; VP, "Excerpts"; Mabel Packard, sworn statement dated 27 July 1926, PPNC; VP, notes for memoir; VP, notations on document sent to author, 7 April 1988, author's possession; VP to author, 23 July 1989, author's possession.

6. VP, "Behavioral Changes," p. 1; VP, notes for memoir. In this and some other instances, I have made minor modifications in documents in order to make them clearer and avoid distracting the reader.

7. VP, notes for memoir; VP interview, 1 December 1990; VP, "Behavioral Changes," p. 3.

8. VP to author, 23 July 1989; VP, "Excerpts"; VP to author, 14 September 1989, author's possession; VP, "Behavioral Changes," pp. 8 and 14–15.

9. Osterud, *Bonds of Community*, pp. 2, 11, 55–56, 61, 187, 198, 200–201, 244, and 279.

10. VP, "Excerpts"; VP interview, 3 June 1987; VP interview, 1 December 1990.

11. VP to author, 23 July 1989.

12. VP interview, 1 December 1990.

13. Osterud, *Bonds of Community*, pp. 2, 89, 150, 156, 231, 233, 251, and 261; VP interview, 1 December 1990.

14. VP, *NOS*, pp. vii–viii; VP, "Have You Made Any New Friends Lately?" *Reader's Digest* 76 (February 1960): 55; VP, *OEC*, p. 30.

15. Osterud, *Bonds of Community*, pp. 12, 89, 139, 147, 150, 166, 217, 231, 247, and 280.

16. VP, "Behavioral Changes," p. 4; VP, notes from talk with LaRue; VP, "Excerpts"; VP interview, 3 June 1987.

17. VP interview, 1 December 1990; VP, notes from talk with LaRue; VP, "Behavioral Changes," p. 7.

18. The following discussion of the situation that dairy farmers faced relies on Barron, "Bringing Forth Strife"; Eastman, *These Changing Times*, pp. 68–76; Eastman, *Trouble Maker*, pp. 18, 20, 22, 26, and 105. For the involvement of Packard's family in these issues, I am relying on my interview with VP, 3 June 1987, and VP, notes from talk with LaRue.

19. VP interview, 1 December 1990; VP to author, 23 July 1989; VP, notes from talk with LaRue.

20. VP, conversation with Helen L. Horowitz, New Canaan, Conn., 23 February 1991. The condition that Packard had is now called atopic dermatitis. Dermatologists remain unsure about its causes, although it is possible that it stems from a combination of genetic predisposition and stressful conditions. For assistance in helping me to understand eczema, I am grateful to Dr. John R. Crossen, Bruce Goldstein, M.D., Jon M. Hanifin, M.D., and Dr. James E. Lindemann.

21. Shoemaker, *Practical Treatise on Diseases*, pp. 421–22; the timing of the onset and duration of the illness appears in VP interview, 3 June 1987, and VP, "Behavioral Changes," p. 4.

22. Lindemann and Lindemann, *Growing Up Proud*, p. 15.

23. Updike, *Self-Consciousness*, pp. 42 and 48.

24. VP, "Boyhood Memories," p. 23; VP, notes for memoir; VP interview, 3 June 1987; VP to author, 23–24 April 1987, author's possession; VP to author, 14 September 1989; VP to VM, around Christmas 1935, PPNC; VP to author, 25 March 1992, author's possession; VP, "Behavioral Changes," p. 18.

25. VP, notes for memoir; VP, "Behavioral Changes," p. 14.

26. Niebuhr, *Social Sources*, p. 67. This discussion of the heritage of Prohibition draws on Blocker, *Retreat from Reform*, pp. 10, 12, 14–16, 27, and 240–41; Clark,

Deliver Us from Evil, pp. 3, 10, 12–13, 92, 135, 152, 171–72, and 178–79. On American Methodism, see Brunger, "Ladies Aid Societies"; Bucke, ed., *History of American Methodism*, esp. volume 2, chapter 24, and volume 3, chapters 30 and 31; Craig, "Underside of History"; Gorrell, *Age of Social Responsibility*; Gorrell, "Social Creed"; Magalis, *Conduct Becoming to a Woman*; Schmidt, "Present State"; H. E. Thomas and Keller, *Women in New Worlds*; Whiteley, "Ladies' Aids."

27. For information on the years in State College, I have drawn on VP interview, 23 April 1987; VP, telephone conversation with author, 4 May 1987; VP, "Boyhood Memories," p. 24; VP, notes for memoir; and "Not So Long Ago," newspaper clipping, PPNC.

28. VP to author, 14 September 1989; VP, "Boyhood Memories," p. 24; VP, *NOS*, pp. viii–ix; VP, "Excerpts"; VP, "Collegian Days for T & G," unpublished retrospective notes made around 1980, PPNC; VP, notations on 1927 letter to his father, 7 April 1988, author's possession.

29. VP, application to Columbia University Graduate School of Journalism, 1936, p. [11], CSJA; VP, "Influential People in My Pre-Career Days," April 1988, author's possession; VP, quoted in Folkenroth, "Men in the Making," p. 22; VP to author, 5 September 1990, author's possession; VP to author, 9 December 1992, author's possession; VP, draft of application to Nieman Program, spring 1938, p. 1, PPNC.

30. VP, "Boyhood Memories," p. 24; VP interview, 1 December 1990; VP to author, 23 July 1989; the well-known writer Fred L. Pattee (1863–1950) occasionally visited the house (VP, notes for memoir).

31. VP, "Behavioral Changes," p. 18.

32. Gordon Duncan, interview with author, State College, Pa., 8 July 1987.

33. VP, "How the Line Advanced," typescript of speech given 27 June 1932, PPNC; program of "22nd Annual Convention Encampment of the Pennsylvania Young People's Branch Federation of the Women's Christian Temperance Union . . . June 27 to July 2, 1932," PPNC; VP, notations of 17 June 1989, author's possession. For an example of a prank as a Boy Scout, see VP, "Influential People."

34. VP, notes for memoir.

35. Duncan interview, 8 July 1987.

36. VP, notations on copy of high school yearbook, 7 April 1988, author's possession; VP, "Behavioral Changes," p. 20.

37. VP, "Collegian Days"; VP, Nieman application, spring 1938, p. 1; VP, Columbia application, pp. [9 and 11]; "The High School Huddle," newspaper clipping from 1934 *CDT*, PPNC; VP, "Behavioral Changes," p. 20.

38. Little to indicate to Packard's contemporaries that he would gain the level of achievement that he did: Duncan interview, 8 July 1987; exceptional determination: Charles A. Myers, telephone conversation with author, 2 October 1987.

39. Jack H. Light, telephone conversation with author, 25 September 1987.

40. C. J. Noll, quoted in Folkenroth, "Finish First," p. 58.

41. Epigram in *Maroon and Gray* (State College, [1932]), p. 25.

CHAPTER TWO

1. For these categories, see H. L. Horowitz, *Campus Life*, p. 16.

2. VP, interview with author, New Canaan, Conn., 9 April 1986.

3. "An Open Letter to Democrats of Center Co.," *CDT*, 2 November 1936, p. 1. For election statistics, see *CDT*, 9 November 1932, pp. 1 and 4; 4 November 1936, p. 1.

4. Bezilla, *Penn State*, p. 150; Jerome Weinstein, telephone conversation with author, 27 September 1987.

5. VP, notations to author, 7 April 1988, author's possession. In discussing conditions at the university, I have relied on Bezilla, *Penn State*, pp. 150–75; VP to author, 15 September 1989, author's possession.

6. VP, "Behavioral Changes in Americans since 1950," unpublished essay, March 1993, PPNC, p. 21; *PSC*, 23 September 1932, p. 1, and 4 October 1932, p. 1; Bezilla, *Penn State*, p. 158.

7. This discussion of the student peace movement nationwide relies on Eagan, *Class, Culture, and the Classroom*; Draper, "Student Movement of the Thirties," pp. 151–89; Wechsler, *Revolt on the Campus*.

8. *PSC*, 3 May 1934, p. 1; *PSC*, 11 April 1935, p. 1; *PSC*, 16 April 1935, p. 1; Bezilla, *Penn State*, pp. 184–85; VP interview with author, New Canaan, Conn., 23 April 1987; Wittner, *Rebels against War*, p. 7.

9. *PSC*, 8 November 1932, p. 4; Bezilla, *Penn State*, pp. 184–85.

10. Minerva L. Brown, interview with author, New York, N.Y., 17 August 1989. Less than one half of one percent of college students participated in Popular Front activities in the mid-1930s; Perry, *Intellectual Life in America*, pp. 405–6.

11. VP interview, New Canaan, Conn., 1 December 1990.

12. Eleanor Goldsmith, "Legal Chiseling," *OMB* 11 (February 1935): 35.

13. See the following editorials in *PSC*: "Fascism Swaggers On," 8 March 1935, p. 2; "High School Heroes," 22 March 1935, p. 2; "To the American Legion," 26 April 1935, p. 2; "May Day," 30 April 1935, p. 2; "Fascism," 7 May 1935, p. 2; "The War Protest," 11 May 1935, p. 2; no title, 14 May 1935, p. 2; "Poor Mr. Hearst," 21 May 1935, p. 2.

14. VP, application to Columbia University Graduate School of Journalism, 1936, CSJA, pp. [11–12].

15. Harry Henderson, telephone conversation with author, 7 November 1987; Harry Henderson to author, 15 September 1991, author's possession.

16. John A. Brutzman, telephone conversation with author, 15 December 1987.

17. For information on his college years, I have relied on VP interview, 23 April 1987, and VP, interview with author, New Canaan, Conn., 3 June 1987; VP, notes for a memoir, around 1984, PPNC; VP, "Collegian Days for T & G," unpublished retrospective notes made around 1980, PPNC.

18. VP to VM, early 1936, PPNC.

19. VP, "Institution: Slaughter," *OMB* 11 (September 1934): 10 and 23.

20. VP to VM, Tuesday, January 1936, PPNC.

21. VP, "Collegian Days."

22. Ibid.; VP, Columbia application, p. [12]; VP, "Propaganda at Penn State," paper written for Sociology 3, 15 January 1936, PPNC, p. 18; "Total Vote," PPNC, probably spring 1935; VP, notations on "Total Vote," 7 April 1988, author's possession; VP to author, 25 July 1991, author's possession; anonymous letter titled "To the Members of the Collegian Board," PPNC.

23. VP interview, 23 April 1987.

24. For a favorable discussion, probably written by John K. Barnes, Jr., of Social Security legislation and an attack on "left-wingers" who were "continually denouncing the New Deal as the same old potatoes rehashed for present-day swallowers" that appeared in the *Summer Collegian* when Packard was coeditor, see "Notes on the News," *SC*, 1 July 1935, p. 2; on the authorship of this piece, see VP to author, 17 September 1991, author's possession. For information on the Second Hundred Days, I have relied on Leuchtenburg, *Franklin D. Roosevelt*, pp. 130–33 and 150–66.

25. On the long-term weakness of radical commitments by college students of the 1930s, see I. Howe, "New York Intellectuals," pp. 218–19.

26. VP to author, 21 May 1989, author's possession; VP interview, 1 December 1990.

27. VP, "Huey's Hooey," *PSC*, 12 March 1935, p. 2.

28. VP to author, 14 September 1989, author's possession; VP to author, 23 October 1989, author's possession.

29. For this as a general experience, see Pells, *Radical Visions*, p. 169.

30. For parallels, see Cooney, *New York Intellectuals*, pp. 43–46 and 59–60.

31. VP interviews, 9 April 1986, 23 April 1987, and 3 June 1987.

32. VP and John K. Barnes, Jr., "Oil for Chinese Lamps," *SC*, 19 July 1935, p. 2; "Premium on Babies," *SC*, 26 July 1935, p. 2; VP to VM, Sunday afternoon, fall 1935, PPNC. In addition to all the pieces he signed, as well as a few items that, although unsigned, he clipped and saved, I have included as Packard's all of the editorials in the *Summer Collegian* of 1935, because he recollects that he wrote almost all of them (VP interviews, 23 April 1987 and 3 June 1987).

33. Conquest, *Great Terror*, pp. 78–79.

34. VP to VM, early 1936; VP interview, 1 December 1990.

35. Duranty, *I Write As I Please*, pp. 163, 302, 310–13, 338–40. For Duranty's position during these years, see S. J. Taylor, *Stalin's Apologist*; Crowl, *Angels in Stalin's Paradise*, especially pp. 2–4, 146, 150–51, 159, 162–69, and 190; Warren, *Liberals and Communism*, pp. 69, 72–73, 79–80, 84–85, and 171.

36. VP to author, 21 May 1989; VP to author, 14 September 1989; VP to author, 23 October 1989.

37. Duranty, *I Write As I Please*, pp. 102, 122, 163–65, 258, 309.

38. VP to author, 23–24 April 1987, author's possession; VP interviews, 23 April 1987 and 3 June 1987.

39. VP interviews, 23 April 1987 and 3 June 1987; VP, "Medicine Men: One College Man Reports on His Washington Trip," *OMB* 11 (September 1934): 11–13 and 24; [VP], "On Eating Asparagus," *SC*, 7 July 1935, p. 2.

40. VP to VM, early 1936; Packard does not recall being an active member or attending additional meetings (VP to author, 14 September 1989).

41. VP, "Propaganda," pp. 40–41.

42. James Dugan, quoted in VP, "Propaganda," p. 11; VP to VM, Thursday noon, probably September 1935, PPNC.

43. VP interview, 3 June 1987; VP, "Propaganda," pp. 41–43.

44. Brutzman, telephone conversation, 15 December 1987; Robert Goldsmith, telephone conversation with author, 23 March 1988.

45. Gordon Duncan, interview with author, State College, Pa., 8 July 1987; see also VP interviews, 9 April 1986 and 23 April 1987.

46. For the influence of his work in the stacks, see VP, "No Hidden Persua [rest of title illegible]," n.d., PPPS; VP, "From Shelver to Author," n.d., probably early 1970s, PPPS. For a list of books he had read, see [VP], "Essays . . . History," probably early 1936, PPNC, and VP, notations, 7 April 1988 on this document, author's possession.

47. VP, "Behavioral Changes," p. 25. Packard earned an average of 1.64 on a 3.00 scale. The comparative figures were 1.40 for the college, 1.25 for fraternity members, and 1.31 for Phi Delta Theta (*La Vie: The Annual Publication of the Senior Class of Pennsylvania State College* 49 [State College, 1936]: 106); *PSC*, 2 October 1934, p. 2, and 20 September 1935, p. 1; Penn State transcript for VP, 1936, PPNC.

48. VP interview, 23 April 1987.

49. See Packard's two lists: [VP], "Essays . . . History," and VP, Columbia application, pp. [6–8].

50. The following discussion relies on books cited in the bibliography.

51. VP interview, 1 December 1990.

52. For his recognition of a parallel between the two faiths, see VP to VM, Sunday afternoon, fall 1935, PPNC.

53. [VP], "More Outside Reading," *SC*, 19 July 1935, p. 2.

54. VP, "Freshmen Like Customs: A Freshman Explodes a Theory," *OMB* 9 (November 1932): 23–24; VP, "The Freshman—A College Man??," p. 3, unpublished manuscript, dated 1933, PPNC; VP, "Credulous Campuseers," unpublished manuscript, pp. 4–5, PPNC. Internal evidence indicates that Packard wrote this piece not long after "The Freshman."

55. VP, "Credulous Campuseers," pp. 6–9.

56. VP, "1400 Guinea Pigs," *OMB* 12 (September 1935): 14 and 19–20.

57. VP to VM, Sunday afternoon, fall 1935, PPNC; VP interview, 1 December 1990.

58. VP to VM, Friday afternoon, fall 1935, PPNC.

59. VP interview, 1 December 1990.

60. VP, notes for memoir.

61. The information on Virginia M. Packard comes from VP, "Biographical

Material: Virginia Packard," mid-1980s, author's possession; VP, "Biographical Material: Artist Virginia Packard," May 1989, author's possession. See also VP interviews, 23 April 1987 and 3 June 1987; VP, notations "Re Crisis with Virginia," 7 April 1988, PPNC.

62. VMP, interview with author, New Canaan, Conn., 11 April 1992.

63. VP, "The Girls That I Cherish," magazine article, probably *Seventeen*, in mid-1960s, PPNC; VP, notations on copy of article, 7 April 1988, author's possession.

64. [VP], "Large Crowd Will Attend Tonight's Dance—We Hope," tear sheet of *SC* article, summer 1935, PPNC; VP, "Propaganda," p. 25.

65. This discussion draws from VP interview, 23 April 1987, and on the following editorials from the 1935 *SC*: "On Eating Asparagus"; "Oil for Chinese Lamps"; "Premium on Babies"; "We Did, We Didn't," 2 August, p. 2.

66. C. O. Williams to VP and John K. Barnes, Jr., 5 August 1935, PPNC; [A. R.] Warnock, "The Daily Half Colyum," clipping from *CDT*, 1935, PPNC.

67. [VP], "More Outside Reading," *SC*, 19 July 1935, p. 2.

68. Henderson, telephone conversation, 7 November 1987. For evidence of Waller's importance to Packard, see: VP interviews, 9 April 1986 and 23 April 1987; VP to VM, Tuesday, January 1936; VP to author, 23–24 April 1987; VP, draft of application to Nieman Program, spring 1938, PPNC, p. 2; VP, "Outside Reading," about 1936, PPNC; VP, "'An Amiable Skeptic,'" in "Notables Tell about Their Favorite Teachers," Associated Press News Features, 1969, PPNC.

69. VP to Donald J. Willower, 6 February 1987, reprinted in Willower and Boyd, eds., *Waller*, p. [169]; WW, "The Professor Looks at Students," *OMB* 9 (May 1933): 9; VP, *SW*, pp. 245–46; VP, "'Amiable Skeptic.'" For information on Waller's life, see William J. Goode, Frank Furstenberg, Jr., and Larry R. Mitchell, "Willard W. Waller: A Portrait," in Goode, Furstenberg, and Mitchell, eds., *Waller*, pp. 1–110.

70. The following discussion of sociology relies on books cited in the bibliography.

71. Hofstadter, *Age of Reform*, pp. 203–12; Crunden, *Ministers of Reform*, p. 165.

72. Brown interview, 17 August 1989.

73. WW, "Professor," p. 34; Cowley and Waller, "Study of Student Life," pp. 135–36. For a perceptive treatment of Waller's writings on the family, see Lasch, *Haven*, pp. 44–45 and 50–61.

74. Tyack, "Life in the 'Museum of Virtue,'" p. 118.

75. WW, "The Rating and Dating Complex," in Goode, Furstenberg, and Mitchell, eds., "Waller," pp. 171 and 174; WW, *Family*, pp. 13 and 601; WW, *Old Love*, p. 312.

76. Goode, Furstenberg, and Mitchell, "Waller," p. 95.

77. Henderson, telephone conversation, 7 November 1987.

78. WW, "Social Problems," pp. 928–29.

79. Tyack, "Life in the 'Museum of Virtue,'" p. 117.

80. WW, "Professor," pp. 9–10.

81. Pennsylvania State College, *Bulletin, General Catalogue Issue, 1935–1936*, p. 354; VP, class notes, Sociology 3, 1935–36, PPNC; transcript.

82. VP, "Propaganda," pp. 10, 11, 12, 14–17, and 19–21.

83. Brutzman, telephone conversation, 15 December 1987, confirmed the leftward tilt of the new editorial board.

84. VP, "Propaganda," title page; transcript. Although his biography in *Contemporary Authors* lists his degree as a B.S., his college transcript records a B.A.; "Packard," *Contemporary Authors*, pp. 372–77.

85. Conversation reported in VP to VM, Wednesday, December 1935, PPNC.

86. VP, draft of application to Nieman Program, spring 1941, PPNC.

87. W. K. Ulerich, telephone conversation with author, 7 November 1987; W. K. Ulerich, telephone conversation with author, 3 September 1991; W. K. Ulerich, quoted in Folkenroth, "Finish First," p. 56; VP to author, 25 March 1992, author's possession; VP, "Author Paid 'through the Nose' for 1st Newspaper Experience," *CDT*, 1 April 1984, PPNC.

88. John K. Barnes, Jr., to VP, summer 1936, PPNC.

89. VP, "Collegian Days."

CHAPTER THREE

1. Carl W. Ackerman to VP, 6 December 1934, CSJA; VP, application to Columbia University Graduate School of Journalism, pp. [13–14], CSJA.

2. VP, Columbia application, pp. [11–12].

3. Ibid., p. [15].

4. Penn State transcript for VP, PPNC; letters of recommendation for VP, CSJA; handwritten notes of Herbert Brucker and Ackerman, CSJA; VP to Ackerman, 9 July 1936, CSJA.

5. "Texts of Presentation and Citation to Vance Packard, Columbia Journalism Alumni Award, May 8, 1958," PPPS; "Packard," *Contemporary Authors*, p. 372; VP, interview with author, New Canaan, Conn., 9 April 1986; VP, interview with author, New Canaan, Conn., 3 June 1987; VP to author, 14 September 1989, author's possession; Columbia University, "Awards of Pulitzer Prizes," PPNC; VP, notations on Dorsey, "Packard," p. 13, author's possession.

6. Physically bumbling and able to think faster than he could act: John Tebbel, interview with author, Southbury, Conn., 20 July 1987.

7. "Journalism Record Card," CSJA; Columbia University transcript for VP, PPNC; *Growing Pains*, tenth anniversary issue, pp. 22–23, CSJA.

8. VP, interview with author, New Canaan, Conn., 23 April 1987; VP, draft of application to Nieman Program, spring 1938, p. 3, PPNC; VP, "Influential People in My Pre-Career Days," April 1988, author's possession.

9. Pitkin, *Life Begins*, pp. 55 and 107. Although Pitkin's book under other circumstances might have prodded Packard toward a redefinition of success from character to personality, when he first read it Packard was still at Penn State and little interested in the author's message (VP to author, 14 September 1989). Hearn discusses Pitkin's role in promoting new definitions of success (*American Dream*, pp. 139 and 148–51).

10. Florinsky, *Fascism and National Socialism*, pp. v, 261, and 276; Florinsky, *Toward an Understanding*, p. 172. Packard doubts that Florinsky's course significantly affected his view of the USSR (VP to author, 14 September 1989).

11. Packard wrote pieces on corruption in the granting of public transportation franchises in New York City and on discrimination against Jews by Bermuda hotels (VP, paper on Queens franchise, CSJA; VP, "Race Ban in Bermuda Hotels Revealed Here by a Survey," tear sheet of article written in early 1937 for graduate student publication titled *The Pulitzer Press*, PPNC). He also wrote on vote fraud in St. Louis, a story that took its inspiration from a 1902 study by Lincoln Steffens and reflected Packard's interest in carrying on the tradition of Progressive muckrakers (VP, "Ghost-Hunting in St. Louis," manuscript of graduate school paper, PPNC; VP interview, 23 April 1987).

12. "Nazi Berkshire Interests Control Hosiery Empire," *Socialist Call*, 20 March 1937, PPNC; VP, interview with author, New Canaan, Conn., 1 December 1990; VP, "Story behind the Stockings," manuscript article, spring 1936, pp. 2, 3, 7, and 11, CSJA.

13. VP, "Projection of 1937," paper written in late 1936 or early 1937, pp. 1–5, PPNC; VP to author, 14 September 1989. For information on Lewis, I have relied on Dubofsky and Van Tine, *Lewis*, pp. 181–216 and 238.

14. VP, "Projection," pp. 6–9; VP, "Hitler's Newspapers," graduate school paper, PPNC; VP, "German Economic Policy since 1933," graduate school paper, 1937, p. 19, PPNC; VP, "Roll Call on Treaties," manuscript, 1937, p. 1, PPNC. The published version did not contain the quotation cited (VP, comp., "Roll-Call on Treaties," *Current History* 46 [June 1937]: 72–73).

15. Before he began the job in Boston, he was hired by the Hearst-owned *New York American* and then read in the newspaper that it was ceasing publication (Folkenroth, "Finish First," pp. 60 and 62).

16. VP, draft of application to Nieman Program, spring 1941, PPNC; VP, Nieman application, spring 1938, p. 1.

17. VP to Douglas S. Freeman, 10 May 1937, PPNC.

18. VP to Ackerman, 21 November 1937, PPNC, provides the fullest summary of Packard's early work on the paper.

19. The quotation is from Dorsey, "Packard," p. 13. See also *Boston American*, 1 July 1937, p. 1; VP, "My First Week Out or, Cubs Can Have Scoops, Too," undated, probably 1940, PPNC; Robert L. Turner, "The Makings of a Writer," *Boston Globe*, 20 October 1972; VP interview, 1 December 1990; VP to author, 5 September 1990, author's possession.

20. VP to Brucker, 2 October 1937.

21. For a sampling of these themes, see the following articles by Vance Packard in *BDR*: "Judge Dillon," 5 October 1937, p. 20; "Edwin H. Land," 16 October 1937, p. 22; "Sybil Holmes," 20 October 1937, p. 24; "Ruth Gordon," 2 December 1937, p. 24; "Judge Eisenstadt," 8 January 1938, p. 21.

22. This relies on the following articles by VP in *BDR*: "Prof. Sorokin," 6 October 1937, p. 20, and 7 October 1937, p. 22; "J. H. Hammond, Jr.," 27 October 1937, p. 24;

"Henry Cabot Lodge, Jr.," 30 November 1937, p. 20; "G. W. Mitton," 4 November 1937, p. 22; "H. H. Davenport," 13 December 1937, p. 28; "Carl M. Spencer," 4 December 1937, p. 28.

23. VP to Brucker, 2 October 1937.

24. VP to Ackerman, 21 November 1937; VP, "Memo to Mr. Holland," probably fall 1937, pp. 2–6, PPNC; and the following portraits by VP in *BDR* of 1938: "Skywriting," 28 March, p. 22; "Hot-Rivet Catcher," 10 March, p. 24; "Pickpocket Sleuths," 12 March, p. 24. In understanding Packard's journalism, I have drawn on Pells, *Radical Visions*, pp. 195–201, and Boylan, "Publicity for the Great Depression," pp. 159–75.

25. Compare Packard's work with what William Stott described in *Documentary Expression*, especially pp. 12–26.

26. For evidence of this transition in the Depression, see Hearn, *American Dream*, pp. 193–96. Historians have argued that during the first three decades of the twentieth century Americans shifted from producer to consumer values—from character, hard work, self-denial, and religion to personality, relaxation, self-fulfillment, and the psychological: Lears, *No Place of Grace*, pp. xiv–xvii; Lears, "From Salvation to Self-Realization," pp. 3–4; Susman, "'Personality' and the Making of Twentieth-Century Culture," pp. 212–26; Weiss, *American Myth of Success*, pp. 230–34. Packard appears to have made this shift over a very long period of time and in a manner that is more halting and complicated than usually described.

27. VP, "Behavioral Changes in Americans since 1950," draft essay, March 1993, p. 28, PPNC; VP, "How to Enjoy Talking to People," *Practical Psychology*, March 1938, PPNC; VP to Brucker, 2 October 1937; VP to Ackerman, 21 November 1937; VP, Nieman application, spring 1941.

28. VP, "Behavioral Changes," p. 28.

29. VP to Brucker, 2 October 1937; VP to Ackerman, 21 November 1937; VP, Nieman application, spring 1938, p. 5.

30. C. W. Mills, *White Collar*, pp. xii and xvii; Jacoby, *Last Intellectuals*, pp. 94–95, discusses the autobiographical nature of Mills's critique.

31. Mann, *Coming Victory of Democracy*, pp. 9, 17, 26, 32, 50, and 59–61; Mann, "Europe Beware," p. 74; Mann, "'Mass und Wert,'" pp. 89 and 99; Mann, "Mankind, Take Care!"

32. VP to VM, probably summer or fall 1937, PPNC. The quoted passages appeared in a translation by Agnes E. Meyer as "Standards and Values," in *Washington Post* (sec. 3, p. 1), *NYT* (sec. 2, p. 1), and elsewhere on 15 August 1937; and in a different translation in Mann, "'Mass und Wert,'" reprinted in *Order of the Day*, pp. 88–104.

33. VP, Nieman application, spring 1938, pp. 1, 4, and 5.

34. Ackerman to Tyler, 14 March 1938, CSJA; Tyler to Ackerman, 26 March 1938, CSJA; VP to Ackerman, 29 March 1938, CSJA.

35. VP to author, 18 June 1988, author's possession; VP to VM, Thursday, early

May 1938, PPNC; draft of letter from VP to VM, Tuesday night, probably April 1938, PPNC.

36. Draft of letter from VP to VM, Tuesday night, probably April 1938; proving he was a good provider to Virginia's mother, CPR, interview with author, Chappaquiddick, Mass., 16 August 1991.

37. C. Edward Holland to W. T. McCleery, 12 May 1938, PPNC; James P. Murphy to VP, 6 May 1938, PPNC.

38. VP, draft of letter to McCleery, spring 1938, PPNC. Some of his stylistic recommendations relied on *Changing American Newspaper*, a book his Columbia professor Herbert Brucker had recently published.

39. VP to VM, Thursday, early May 1938; VP to Ackerman, 18 May 1938, CSJA; VP to Ackerman, 30 May 1938, CSJA; VP interview, 23 April 1987. For the figures on earnings, see VP, Nieman application, spring 1941.

40. VP interview, 23 April 1987; Edmond Martin to VP, 28 August 1938, PPNC; VP, notations on Martin letter, 7 April 1988, author's possession.

41. VP to VM, summer or early fall 1938, PPNC.

42. VP, "Have You Made Any New Friends Lately?" *Reader's Digest* 76 (February 1960): 57.

43. VP to author, 21 May 1989, author's possession; VP interview, 1 December 1990.

44. Memo from M. J. Wing, 15 March 1940, PPNC.

45. VP, "Truckin' Uncle Sam's Silver," tear sheet dated 30 October 1938, PPNC; VP, "Silent Letters Speak Volumes to Woman Handwriting Expert," tear sheet dated 22 November 1939, PPNC; VP, "A Candid Talk with a Scientist," tear sheet dated 8 November 1939, PPNC; VP, "If an Amishman Wears No Buttons He's One of the Rare White-Tops," undated tear sheet, PPNC; the article on sleep research appeared in *San Diego Evening Tribune*, 22 December 1938; an undated copy of "Industry Meets the Morale Problem" is in PPNC.

46. VP interview, 23 April 1987; VP, notations in response to author's questions, April 1987, author's possession; VP interview, 1 December 1990; "Two Billion Pawns," *New Republic* 100 (30 August 1939): 85; "Stalin's Munich," *New Republic* 100 (30 August 1939): 88–89; John Radnor [pseudonym for VP], "Who Double-crossed Who?" unpublished article written after the signing of the Nazi-Soviet Pact, PPNC.

47. [VP], "Double-crossed"; "Moscow: Berlin: America," *New Republic* 100 (6 September 1939): 114.

48. The following relies on an examination of the weekly section from late March 1940 until mid-June 1942. In order to date Packard's work on this feature, see VP, Nieman application, spring 1941; *World This Week* folder, PPNC; VP, notebook on *World This Week*, probably 1942, PPNC; VP, "Behavioral Changes," p. 32.

49. VP interview, 23 April 1987; VP, notations, April 1987, author's possession.

50. VP, notations, April 1987; VP interviews, 23 April 1987 and 3 June 1987. For Packard's view of events surrounding American entry into World War II, I am

relying on a reading of his articles during the period, including "How War Came to America," tear sheet, sometime after Pearl Harbor, PPNC; VP, "The War's 8 Unanswered Questions," tear sheet, 21 February 1940, PPNC; and more than a score of stories from *ABJ*.

51. VP interview, 23 April 1987.

52. See the following, all from *ABJ*: "The ABC of Russia's Position," 12 January 1941, p. 10D; "Soviet Realizes Hitler Drive May Include Rich Oil Areas," 20 April 1941, p. 12D; "Headliner: Red Army Chief," 22 June 1941, p. 12D; "Will Russia Burn Grain, Blast Oil Wells to Foil Hitler," 29 June 1941, p. 10D; "Russia's Surprise," 24 May 1942, p. 10D.

53. RC, "America First," draft of unpublished article, written between June and December 1941, PPNC.

54. VP, "Behavioral Changes," p. 28.

55. VP interview, 3 June 1987; VP to author, 14 September 1989.

56. This summary relies on VP interview, 1 December 1990, and a series of stories in *ABJ*, including: "Strikes Brings Headache to Defense Work," 30 March 1941, p. 12D; "U.S. Cracks Down As Strikes Threaten Armament Drive," 15 June 1941, p. 12D; "F. R. Wins Showdown With Lewis In Strike," 2 November 1941, p. 12D; "Coal Mine Strike Sends Congress Tempers Up," 23 November 1941, p. 12D; "Labor's Scare," 29 March 1942, p. 10D. On Lewis in this period, see Dubofsky and Van Tine, *Lewis*, pp. 218, 247–60, and 282–304; Isserman, *Which Side Were You On?*, pp. 60–62, 74–75, 77–78, 87, 99, 113, 135, and 164–65.

57. Podhoretz, *Breaking Ranks*, p. 10.

58. VP interview, 1 December 1990.

59. VP, notations, April 1987; VP interview, 1 December 1990; VP, "Behavioral Changes," p. 32; VP to Ackerman, 15 July 1942, CSJA; VP, notations, 7 April 1988. The salary figure comes from VP to author, 3 August 1989, author's possession; VP to author, 14 September 1989.

CHAPTER FOUR

1. VP to author, 21 May 1989, author's possession.

2. Dennis, *Auntie Mame*, pp. 3–4.

3. Ibid., p. 3. Professor Ronald Macdonald of Smith College, who grew up in Darien, says that the local residents assumed at the time that Dennis was writing about their community.

4. VP to author, 21 May 1989.

5. VP, diary, 6 May, 13 May, and 6 June 1947; 8 December 1947 or 1949, PPNC.

6. VP, diary, 16 August 1947; Krutch, *Modern Temper*, pp. 233–34, 240, and 243–44.

7. VP to author, 21 May 1989.

8. VP, interview with author, New Canaan, Conn., 9 April 1986; VP, notations,

7 April 1987, author's possession; Sumner Blossom to VP, 25 May 1947, PPNC; VP, interview with author, New Canaan, Conn., 1 December 1990.

9. King, *New Canaan*, pp. 279–81, 293–94, and 317–21.

10. VP, "The Loyal Order of Sawdust Makers," *AM* 153 (March 1952): 37; VP, *NOS*, p. ix. As a member of the town's planning commission from 1954 to 1956, Packard worked on a master plan that strictly controlled development (VP, interview with author, New Canaan, Conn., 3 June 1987).

11. S. Wilson, *What Shall We Wear*, pp. 23 and 181–82. For another perceptive picture of life in Fairfield County, see Spectorsky, *Exurbanites*.

12. S. Wilson, *What Shall We Wear*, pp. 181–83.

13. Ibid., p. 19.

14. VP interview, 3 June 1987; VP to Betty Hitesman, 16 July 1986, PPNC; VP to Walter W. Hitesman, Jr., 7 March 1944, PPNC; VP, "Behavioral Changes in Americans since 1950," unpublished essay, March 1993, p. 23, PPNC.

15. VP to author, 21 May 1989; "He Lives by His Philosophy," *New Haven Register*, 22 January 1961, p. 11; VP, interview with author, New Canaan, Conn., 20 December 1990; VP, "Biographical Material: Artist Virginia Packard," May 1989, author's possession; VP to author, 25 March 1992, author's possession; VMP, interview with author, New Canaan, Conn., 11 April 1992.

16. VP, "Chappy Has Its Problems Too, but How Near Heaven Dare You Go?" *VG*, 21 June 1974, VGA; VP interview, 9 April 1986; VP, interview with author, New Canaan, Conn., 23 April 1987; VP interview, 3 June 1987; VP, notes for a memoir, around 1984, PPNC; VP to author, 23–24 April 1987, pp. 1–2, author's possession; VP to author, 7 April 1992, author's possession.

17. On the 1906 house, I am using Clarence A. Barnes III, telephone conversation with author, 30 March 1992; VP to author, mid-July 1992, author's possession. For a description of the Stanford White house, I am relying on Travis Beal Jacobs to author, 12 June 1992, author's possession.

18. CP, *Hell's Bells*, pp. v, 5, 6, and 8. In the 3 June 1987 interview, Packard discussed the accuracy and exaggerations of the novel. There are several notable ways in which the novel was different from reality; for example, in the book the maternal grandmother was from a wealthy family and there were four children in the household.

19. Ibid., pp. 17, 18, and 20.

20. Ibid., pp. 5, 7, 8, and 9.

21. Out of bounds, parents did not know how to control: CPR, interview with author, Annandale, Va., 31 October 1991.

22. VPP, interview with author, Goldsboro, Pa., 25 August 1991.

23. More involved: CPR interview, 31 October 1991.

24. CPR, interview with author, Chappaquiddick, Mass., 16 August 1991.

25. Middy Darrow, interview with author, Wilton, Conn., 7 January 1993; Middy Darrow and Whitney Darrow, Jr., to author, 29 April 1993, author's possession.

26. The fullest characterization of Virginia Packard along these lines comes from CPR interview, 16 August 1991.

27. Dominant presence: CPR interview, 16 August 1991; dash and competence: CPR interview, 31 October 1991; strong-minded and outgoing: CTA, interview with author, New York, N.Y., 13 February 1993.

28. Jack Long, telephone conversation with author, 8 June 1992.

29. Whitney Darrow, Jr., interview with author, Wilton, Conn., 7 January 1993.

30. John Tebbel, interview with author, Southbury, Conn., 20 July 1987.

31. John Tebbel, interview with author, Southbury, Conn., 7 January 1993.

32. John Tebbel, interview with author, 20 July 1987.

33. Jack Long, telephone conversation, 8 June 1992.

34. For the story about the hospital, see VPP interview, 25 August 1991.

35. Often telling self-deprecating stories: VPP interview, 25 August 1991.

36. Unassuming and reluctant to put himself forward: Darrow and Darrow to author, 29 April 1993.

37. John Tebbel interview, 20 July 1987.

38. Quite shy and combination of modesty and bravado: CPR interview, 16 August 1991.

39. Gerald Green, telephone conversation with author, 21 December 1992.

40. VP, interview with author, New Canaan, Conn., 9 May 1992.

41. The quotes are from Kacy Tebbel, interview with author, Southbury, Conn., 7 January 1993.

42. Tagalong, background, follower: CPR interview, 16 August 1991; CPR interview, 31 October 1991.

43. VPP interview, 25 August 1991.

44. CPR interview, 16 August 1991.

45. VPP interview, 25 August 1991.

46. Ibid.

47. For information on the children's sense of comparative wealth, see ibid.

48. Mixture of privilege and uncertainty: CPR interview, 31 October 1991.

49. On their parents' relationship, see VPP interview, 25 August 1991; CPR interview, 31 October 1991.

50. Middy Darrow interview, 7 January 1993; Darrow and Darrow to author, 29 April 1993.

51. VPP interview, 25 August 1991; RP, interview with author, Chappaquiddick, Mass., 16 August 1991; CPR interview, 16 August 1991.

52. RP interview, 16 August 1991.

53. CPR to author, 8 April 1993, author's possession.

54. CPR interview, 31 October 1991.

55. VP, *SW*, pp. 246–47.

56. Content in his sphere, removal from world, let Virginia handle problems: CPR interview, 16 August 1991.

57. Darrow and Darrow to author, 29 April 1993.

58. On VP's virtual disappearance, see CPR interview, 31 October 1991.

59. ER, interview with author, New York, N.Y., 16 January 1991.

60. "Sen. Benton to Be Heard Here on Saturday," clipping from *New Canaan Advertiser*, 23 October 1952, PPNC.

61. VP interview, 20 December 1990.

62. VP to author, 21 May 1989.

63. VP, "Why Is a Democrat?" article in a local publication, probably 1956, PPNC.

64. Ibid.

65. VP, interview with author, New Canaan, Conn., 7 June 1987. He also taught classes on magazine writing, from 1941 to 1944 at Columbia's School of Journalism and from 1945 to 1957 at New York University.

66. Clifford Adams to VP, 25 February 1946, PPNC; VP interview, 3 June 1987; VP, 18 June 1988 notations on VP to William Birnie, around 1952, PPNC; VP and Adams, *How to Pick a Mate*, pp. 20, 125, 165, and 205; on poor sales, John Tebbel interview, 20 July 1987.

67. VP interview, 3 June 1987; agreement between publisher and author, 7 February 1949, PPNC; "Human Side of Animals Revealed," *New Canaan Advertiser*, 23 February 1950, PPNC; Joseph Wood Krutch, review of *Animal I.Q.*, *Nation* 170 (25 February 1950): 189.

68. Otis L. Wiese, "Live the Life of McCall's," *McCall's* 81 (May 1954): 27.

69. Meyerowitz, "Beyond the Feminine Mystique," provides a useful corrective to Friedan's picture. The best book on family life in the 1950s, on which this summary draws, is E. T. May, *Homeward Bound*, especially pp. 9–14, 20–33, and 162–81. See also, Friedan, *Feminine Mystique*.

70. For discussion of social and ideological tensions in the 1950s, see L. May, *Recasting America*, especially the essays by Lary May, Warren Susman, and Jackson Lears; Breines, *Young, White and Miserable*, pp. 1–24.

71. This summary draws on Hodgson, *America in Our Time*, pp. 69–83.

72. Pells, *Liberal Mind*, p. 121.

73. This discussion relies heavily on Pells, *Liberal Mind*, especially pp. 185–88.

74. Alfred Politz Research, *Audiences*, though it did not include *AM*, makes clear the diverse audience of similar periodicals.

75. C. P. Wilson, "Rhetoric of Consumption," pp. 43–44.

76. In thinking about these magazines, I have drawn on Ohmann, "Where Did Mass Culture Come From?" pp. 85–101; Murphy, "Tabloids as an Urban Response," pp. 55–69; and Hughes, *News and the Human Interest Story*, pp. 105, 122, and 125.

77. Jack Long, telephone conversation, 8 June 1992.

78. Hughes, *News and the Human Interest Story*, pp. xiv, xviii, 2, 10, 21, 70, 80, 83–84, 86, 101, 105, 122, and 212–13; Cohn, *Creating America*, pp. 6–8.

79. VP, memorandum to Sumner Blossom, PPNC. VP, diary, 8 July 1947, places this memo in mid-June 1947.

80. VP to Sumner Blossom, 12 February 1946, PPNC.

81. Ibid.

82. VP, diary, 8 July 1947; Jerome Beatty, "Parasites of the United Nations," *AM* 146 (September 1948): 37.

83. VP, diary, 8 July 1947.

CHAPTER FIVE

1. "Interesting People," *AM* 107 (July 1943): 107–10, 112, and 114–16. The personal sketches Packard did for the Boston newspaper, the AP, and *American Magazine* bear comparison with what Leo Lowenthal found in his classic study "Biographies in Popular Magazines." At the newspaper, Packard focused on idols of production more than was true of Lowenthal's sample; with Interesting People, Packard's features closely resemble what Lowenthal found.

2. VP to Carl W. Ackerman, 22 September 1943, CSJA.

3. PPNC has a list of the articles he wrote, including more than eighty that appeared under other people's names between February 1944 and January 1953. It is possible that he ghostwrote articles after that date. In discussing authorship, I have drawn on VP, memorandum on magazine authorship, 14 July 1986, author's possession.

4. VP, notations in response to author's questions, April 1987, author's possession; Styles Bridges, "Where to Swing the Ax," *AM* 146 (December 1948): 30–31, 137–38, and 140–41; Homer Ferguson, "Why Not Labor Courts?" *AM* 143 (February 1947): 21 and 98–100.

5. Merlyn S. Pitzele, "Labor's Featherbeds—What They Cost You," *AM* 141 (March 1946): 48–49 and 149–51; John A. Hartford, "Can We Afford to Kill Big Business?" *AM* 150 (October 1950): 24–25 and 92–96; Kenneth S. Wherry, "We Can't Thrive on Security," *AM* 147 (June 1949): 24–25 and 125–28; Hugh Butler, "Government Grads Get Juicy Jobs," *AM* 149 (April 1950): 24–25 and 130–32.

6. Foy D. Kohler, "Our Voice Makes Stalin Jumpy," *AM* 150 (July 1950): 26.

7. VP to author, 21 May 1989, author's possession.

8. On this division, see Podhoretz, *Making It*, p. 290.

9. Guy Irving Burch, "The World Has Too Many People," *AM* 141 (May 1946): 104; see also Nila Magidoff, "Americans and Russians Are So Alike," *AM* 138 (December 1944): 17 and 118–20; Elbert D. Thomas, "American Dollars Fight for Peace," *AM* 142 (November 1946): 26–27, 137, and 139–40; Paul-Henri Spaak, "What You Can Do for Peace," *AM* 143 (March 1947): 23 and 110–12.

10. Mike Monroney, "Can You Afford a White-Collar Job?" *AM* (June 1947): 26–27, 116, and 118; Guy Greer, "Is Your Town Fit to Live In?" *AM* 146 (July 1948): 50–51 and 140–42; Nathan Straus, "Why You Can't Get That New Home," *AM* 144 (December 1947): 21, 130, and 132–34.

11. Ellsworth Huntington, "Where Our Leaders Come From," *AM* 141 (June 1946): 38–39 and 157–59; Carleton S. Coon, "What Type American Are You?" *AM* 141 (June 1946): 52–53 and 128–30; Harvey Zorbaugh, "Your Body Gives You Away," *AM* 143 (June 1947) 52–53; Harriet Bruce Moore, "Are You What You

Eat?" *AM* 151 (May 1951): 46–47. Packard described the process of working with professors in VP, interview with author, New Canaan, Conn., 9 April 1986. When asked at the same time to name books that influenced him in the 1940s, Packard mentioned Huntington's *Mainsprings of Civilization* (1945) and Ralph Linton's *The Study of Man: An Introduction* (1936), two works that explored comprehensive patterns of human lives.

12. William J. Reilly, "How to Avoid Work," *AM* 143 (February 1947): 103.

13. Albert A. Light, "It's No Fun to Be a Millionaire," *AM* 143 (May 1947): 44–45 and 100–2.

14. Peter J. Steincrohn, "Stop Getting Excited!" *AM* 145 (January 1948): 138.

15. Charles C. Spaulding, "What America Means to Me," *AM* 146 (December 1948): 21 and 131. For a similar story on a Native American, see Louis R. Bruce, Jr., "What America Means to Me," *AM* 148 (September 1949): 19 and 121–24.

16. For example, Wernher von Braun, "Why I Chose America," *AM* 154 (July 1952): 115; Mario Pieroni, "Riches at Your Fingertips," *AM* 151 (January 1951): 15.

17. Harold G. Moulton, "Americans Can Be Eight Times Richer," *AM* 149 (February 1950): 46 and 80.

18. See, for example, VP, "The Fabulous Jacksons of Denver," *AM* 152 (September 1951): 21–25, 106–9, and 111–12.

19. Macdonald, " 'Fortune' Magazine," p. 528.

20. WW, "Why Veterans Are Bitter," p. 147; WW, *War in the Twentieth Century*, pp. 3–35 and 478–532; WW, *War and the Family*; WW, "What You Can Do to Help," pp. 26–27, 92, and 94–98; WW, *Veteran Comes Back*, pp. 187–88 and 298–301. In contrast, see VP, "Yanks at Yale," *AM* 139 (April 1945): 46–47 and 89; VP, "GI Wail Call," *AM* 140 (October 1945): 46–47, 122, and 124; Robert Crandall, "Veterans Panic the Politicians," *AM* 142 (August 1946): 24 and 104. Robert Crandall (RC) was a pseudonym that Packard used when he had more than one article in an issue: VP, memorandum on magazine authorship.

21. VP, "Down East Adventure," *AM* 157 (May 1954): 38–39.

22. VP, "Youngsters Wanted for Unlimited Jobs," *AM* 155 (June 1953): 27, 112, and 113.

23. VP, *Animal I.Q.*, p. 192.

24. VP, "They Gambled on Greatness," *AM* 153 (May 1952): 42–45 and 115–18.

25. VP, "He Hit the Jackpot in His Own Hometown," *AM* 158 (November 1954): 22–23 and 92–94.

26. VP, "How to Make a Fortune 'New Style,'" *Ladies' Home Journal* 76 (January 1959): 42–43 and 86.

27. RC, "Hotbeds of Communism," *AM* 143 (June 1947): 22–23.

28. VP, "Russia Seeks the Open Seas," *AM* 140 (September 1945): 34–36; VP, "What's Going On Inside Russia," *AM* 147 (April 1949): 30 and 127–30; VP, notations on copy of article, 7 April 1988, author's possession.

29. VP, "Moving In with the Eisenhowers," *AM* 155 (January 1953): 24–25 and 93–97.

30. VP, "Potatoes and Gravy," *AM* 148 (November 1949): 30–31 and 126–29. For

an earlier, less outraged, and more jocular treatment of government corruption, see VP, "Why Congressmen Never Go Hungry," *AM* 146 (July 1948): 26–27 and 138–40.

31. VP, "The Loyal Order of Sawdust Makers," *AM* 153 (March 1952): 37, 125, and 128; VP, "We're in the Movies Now!" *AM* 154 (October 1952): 39; VP, "I Had My Wife Made Over," *Reader's Digest* 63 (November 1953): 105–8; VP, interview with author, New Canaan, Conn., 3 June 1987.

32. VP, "Why Women Dress That Way," *AM* 144 (September 1947): 46–47; VP, "How to Be Terrific for $9.75," *AM* 145 (June 1948): 46–47 and 100–2; VP, "Potatoes and Gravy," p. 30; VP, "Why Your Auto Insurance Costs So Much," *AM* 155 (May 1953): 28–29 and 108–13; VP, "Learn to Live on Your Income," *AM* 161 (January 1956): 30–31 and 85–88; VP, "It's Fun to Be a Daly," *AM* 153 (February 1952): 42–45 and 86–91.

33. VP, "How Does Your Income Compare with Others?" *Collier's* 138 (23 November 1956): 54–56 and 58–59.

34. VP, "Who Detests You? The Story of Connecticut's Bold Experiment in Democracy," unpublished manuscript, 1945 or 1946, pp. 1, 2, 4, and 10, PPNC.

35. Ibid., p. 4; VP and Adams, *How to Pick a Mate*, p. 139; for a study of ideas about ethnicity in these years, see J. E. Smith, "Creating 'Everyman' after World War II."

36. On the ways that social scientists of the 1950s discussed gender relationships and the family, see Breines, *Young, White, and Miserable*, pp. 25–46.

37. VP and Adams, *How to Pick a Mate*, p. 20. For ghosted articles that endorsed careers for women and spoke of sexuality in an open and relatively democratic manner, see Evelyn M. Duvall, "The Trouble with Most Bridegrooms," *AM* 147 (April 1949): 42–43 and 94–97; Mary F. Langmuir, "Wife Trouble? Get Her a Job!" *AM* 149 (February 1950): 36–37 and 90–93; Elizabeth Force, "What Teen-Agers Want to Know about Sex and Marriage," *AM* 155 (January 1953): 34 and 103–6.

38. VP and Adams, *How to Pick a Mate*, p. 20.

39. VP, "Married Life in a Goldfish Bowl," *AM* 145 (February 1948): 98.

40. VP, "I Sent My Wife to Vassar," *AM* 151 (February 1951): 117.

41. Ibid., pp. 47 and 117–21; VP, "Now You Can Both Rehearse for Parenthood," *AM* 153 (June 1952): 24–27 and 110; VP, "Learn to Live on Your Income," pp. 30–31 and 85–88.

42. RC, "Calling All Women," *AM* 159 (May 1955): 34–35.

43. VP, "Fabulous Jacksons," pp. 21–25 and 106–12.

44. VP, "Marriage for Two: Adventure for Six," *AM* 153 (January 1952): 42–44.

45. See, for example, VP, "Goldfish Bowl," pp. 42–43 and 97–99.

46. Hughes, *News and the Human Interest Story*, p. 155.

47. VP, "Wife Made Over," pp. 105–8; VP, "Go, Man, Go!," draft of talk to 1954 Eastern Conference of American Association of Advertising Agencies, p. 6, PPNC.

48. VP interview, 3 June 1987.

49. John Tebbel, interview with author, Southbury, Conn., 20 July 1987.

50. VP, "Land of Canoes," *AM* 158 (August 1954): 32–33.

51. Ehrenreich, *Hearts of Men*, pp. 29–51.

52. E. T. May, *Homeward Bound*, pp. 16–36.

53. Friedan, *Feminine Mystique*, chap. 2.

54. Compare Packard's articles with the pictures drawn by Meyerowitz in "Beyond the Feminine Mystique."

55. See, for example, the pictures for VP, "Now You Can Both Rehearse for Parenthood," *AM* 153 (June 1952): 24–27.

56. I am grateful to Tom Leonard for information on how mass-circulation magazines covered race in the mid-1950s.

57. VP to author, 23–24 April 1987, author's possession.

58. VP, notations in response to author's interview questions, April 1987; VP, interview with author, New Canaan, Conn., 23 April 1987.

59. VP, notations in response to author's interview questions, April 1987; VP interview, 23 April 1987; James Stewart-Gordon, interview with author, New York, N.Y., 9 June 1987.

60. S. Wilson, *Man in the Gray Flannel Suit*.

61. Compare Packard's articles with those described in Jezer, *Dark Ages*, p. 103.

62. VP interview, 9 April 1986.

63. The quote is from Stewart-Gordon interview, 9 June 1987. For additional information on Blossom, see VP, notes for a memoir, around 1984, PPNC; VP interview, 3 June 1987; Mott, *History of American Magazines: 1865–1885*, 3: 516.

64. William Hart, telephone conversation with author, 15 May 1992.

65. Peter Maas, telephone conversation with author, 5 January 1993.

66. VP, notations in response to author's interview questions, April 1987; VP interviews, 23 April 1987 and 3 June 1987; VP, interview with author, New Canaan, Conn., 1 December 1990; Jack Long, telephone conversation with author, 8 June 1992, confirmed the lack of discussion of political issues or involvement in office politics.

67. Kazin, *Starting Out in the Thirties*, p. 111.

68. Podhoretz, *Making It*, pp. 213–17.

69. Macdonald, "'Fortune' Magazine," p. 530.

70. VP to author, 23 June 1986, author's possession; VP, notes for memoir; VP interview, 3 June 1987; Long confirmed the increasing pressure to link articles and advertisements but did not himself experience pressure from editors to toe a line from which he dissented (telephone conversation, 8 June 1992).

71. VP to author, 23–24 April 1987.

72. Here and throughout the book, figures on real income rely on McCusker, "How Much Is That in Real Money?" pp. 329–32.

73. VP interview, 3 June 1987; VP, notations in response to author's interview questions, April 1987; VP to DeWitt Wallace, 12 November 1951, PPNC; VP to Kenneth McCardle, 19 September 1956, PPNC; Sumner Blossom to VP, 25 May 1947, PPNC; VP interview, 1 December 1990; VP to author, mid-July 1992, author's possession. For data on his success as a writer, see *American Magazine*, Reader

Analysis Bureau, Report no. 18 (June 1944 issue) and Report no. 49 (January 1947 issue), PPNC; "Average Readership Rating of Nine *American* Writers, for the Year Starting August, 1944 and Ending July, 1945," PPNC; VP, "Number of Articles by Each *American Magazine* Writer That Have Been Singled Out for Special Promotion in Newspaper Advertisements Since the Beginning of 1946," memo, probably 1948, PPNC; VP to author, 7 April 1992, author's possession.

74. VP to author, 23 June 1986.

75. VP to William Birnie, around 1952, PPNC; VP to author, 1 December 1990, author's possession; VP interview, 3 June 1987; VP to Wallace, 12 November 1951; VP, draft of letter to DeWitt Wallace, 13 April 1950, PPNC; VP, notations on letter to Wallace, 7 April 1988, author's possession; VP, interview with author, New Canaan, Conn., 20 December 1990; VP to author, 7 April 1992. For information on the relationship between *Reader's Digest* and free-lance authors, see Schreiner, *Condensed World*, pp. 140–43 and 150–51.

76. VP interview, 3 June 1987; Albert R. Perkins to VP, 30 September 1954, PPNC; Sumner Blossom to staff members, 15 February 1954, PPNC.

77. P. C. Smith, *Personal File*, pp. 425, 428, 435, and 439.

78. VP, quoted in Nelson, "Wrong with Sociology," p. 44.

79. T. H. White, *In Search of History*, pp. 415, 416, 438, 447, and 452. For a fictional re-creation of the situation at *Collier's*, see T. H. White, *View from the Fortieth Floor*, especially chap. 4.

80. T. H. White, *In Search of History*, pp. 415, 439, and 426.

81. Jacoby, *Last Intellectuals*, p. 14.

82. VP, "Go, Man, Go!," pp. 2, 6, and 8.

83. VP interview, 23 April 1987; VP, notations in response to author's interview questions, April 1987.

84. Darnton, "Writing News," p. 187.

85. For a perceptive discussion of such a process, see ibid., pp. 175–94.

86. Hughes made these observations about authors of human interest stories in an earlier part of the century (*News and the Human Interest Story*, pp. xviii and 83).

87. VP interview, 23 April 1987.

88. VP to author, 14 July 1986, author's possession; VP, notations, 7 April 1988.

CHAPTER SIX

1. Panicked and pretty desperate: James Stewart-Gordon, interview with author, New York, N.Y., 9 June 1987; in a state of shock: Jane Eager, interview with author, Southport, Conn., 5 June 1986; panicked: John Tebbel, interview with author, Southbury, Conn., 20 July 1987; very hungry: CTA, interview with author, Brooklyn, N.Y., 9 June 1987; quite desperate: VPP, interview with author, Goldsboro, Penn., 25 August 1991.

2. Jack Long, telephone conversation with author, 8 June 1992.

3. VP, notations, 7 April 1988, author's possession; VP to author, 23–24 April 1987, pp. 6 and 9, author's possession; Jim Doyle, "Author of 'Status Seekers' Is Seeking Some for Himself," typescript of feature article for North American Newspaper Alliance, 23 May 1959, PPPS; VP, interview with author, New Canaan, Conn., 4 June 1987; contract between David McKay Company and VP, 6 March 1956, PPNC; VP, interview with author, New Canaan, Conn., 20 December 1990.

4. VP, *HP*, p. 229.

5. D. T. Miller and Nowak, *Fifties*, pp. 106–23 summarizes these themes.

6. Dan O'Keefe, telephone conversation with author, 21 December 1992; Robert Graham, "Adman's Nightmare: Is the Prune a Watch?" *Reporter* 9 (13 October 1953): 27–31.

7. VP to Albert R. Perkins, 23 November 1954, PPNC.

8. VP interview, 20 December 1990.

9. Ibid.

10. VP to author, 23–24 April 1987, p. 7; CTA interview, 9 June 1987.

11. VP to Sumner Blossom, 22 March 1956, PPNC.

12. Mitchel Levitas, "He Used to Be a Status Seeker Himself," *New York Post*, 31 May 1959, p. M2.

13. Brooks, *Great Leap*, pp. 86–92; Lerner, *America As a Civilization*, pp. 307–9; D. T. Miller and Nowak, *Fifties*, pp. 118–20; S. Fox, *Mirror Makers*, pp. 172–217 and 183; Perrett, *Dream of Greatness*, p. 510.

14. Lerner, *America As a Civilization*, p. 309. For critiques of advertising, see [E. B. White], "Notes and Comment," *New Yorker*, 19 January 1946, p. 13, 22 March 1947, p. 23, 22 July 1950, p. 17; C. B. Larrabee, "Thunder on the Right: A Special Report on the Growing Criticism of Advertising," *Printers' Ink*, 7 March 1952, pp. 39–42, 54, 57, 61–63, 66, 68, 73, 79, 80, 83–84, 86–88. For earlier periods, see Cloete, *Third Way*, pp. 119–32; Leff, "Politics of Sacrifice"; F. W. Fox, *Madison Avenue Goes to War*. Mayer, *Madison Avenue*, which appeared in 1958, was less sensational than *Hidden Persuaders*.

15. Frederic Wakeman, *Hucksters* (1946), quoted in S. Fox, *Mirror Makers*, p. 201.

16. An advertising executive quoted in Stephen Birmingham, "The Minstrels of Madison Avenue," *Holiday* 22 (December 1957): 164.

17. Lerner, *America As a Civilization*, p. 307.

18. Ernest Dichter, "How to Perpetuate Prosperity," *Motivations* 1 (April 1956): 8.

19. Robert Sarnoff, quoted in D. T. Miller and Nowak, *Fifties*, p. 118.

20. VP, *HP*, pp. 3, 19, 21, 25, 171, and 227.

21. Ibid., pp. 87–88.

22. Ibid., pp. 4, 184–85, 201–2, 212–13, and 217.

23. Riesman, *Lonely Crowd*, pp. 295 and 305.

24. VP, *HP*, pp. 5, 201, 232, and 236.

25. Ibid., pp. 57, 176, 228, 230, 257, 262, and 263.

26. Ibid., pp. 84–85 and 258.

27. Schudson, "Criticizing," p. 6.

28. Ibid., pp. 3–6; S. Fox, *Mirror Makers*, pp. 185–87; Bauer, "Limits of Persuasion," pp. 107 and 110; Perrett, *Dream of Greatness*, p. 512; Randall Rothenberg (telephone conversation with author, 7 April 1992) and William M. Weilbacher (telephone conversation with author, 8 May 1992) discussed how market researchers and advertising agencies used Packard's material to their own advantage.

29. VP interview, 20 December 1990.

30. VP, *HP*, pp. 208–9.

31. Ibid., pp. 8–9.

32. Tear sheet of advertisement for *HP, Publishers' Weekly*, 1 April 1957, PPPS.

33. VP to KR, probably early to mid-1957, PPPS.

34. VP to KR, 20 February 1957, PPPS.

35. VP to KR, 11 May 1957, PPPS.

36. CTA to VP, 16 May [1957], PPPS.

37. William B. Hart to VP, 9 July [1957], PPPS.

38. VP to KR, 25 January 1957, PPPS.

39. VP interview, 20 December 1990.

40. Contract between VP and David McKay Company, 8 October 1957, PPNC.

41. VP interview, 20 December 1990; VP to KR, Friday night, probably early 1959, PPPS; ER to VP, 18 July 1991, PPNC; ER, interview with author, New York, N.Y., 16 January 1991; VP to author, 23–24 April 1987.

42. VP to author, 23–24 April 1987.

43. "Back Seat of Car Doubles As Office for Vance Packard," clipping from NYU newspaper, June 1959, CSJA.

44. VP to author, 16 June 1993, author's possession.

45. Marchand, "Visions of Classlessness," p. 169.

46. VP, "A Commentary," *Trans-Action* 2 (January–February, 1965): 17–19.

47. Editors of *Fortune, Changing American Market*, pp. 14, 21, 57, 67, 79, 80, and 250.

48. J. E. Smith, "Creating 'Everyman' after World War II," p. 3.

49. F. L. Allen, *Big Change*, p. 291.

50. Lerner reflects and summarizes these arguments (*America as Civilization*, pp. 465–540).

51. Kluckhohn, "Mid-Century Manners and Morals," p. 304.

52. The following summary relies on Perrett, *Dream of Greatness*, pp. 289–92 and 502; Oakley, *God's Country*, pp. 246–47; Marchand, "Visions of Classlessness," pp. 168–69.

53. Perrett, *Dream of Greatness*, p. 290.

54. VP, *SS*, p. 3.

55. Ibid., pp. 8, 10, 308, and 317.

56. Ibid., pp. 7, 99, 132, and 246–50.

57. Ibid., pp. 61–74.

58. Ibid., pp. 74–76 and 92.

59. Ibid., pp. 9–10, 27–28, 34, 114, 116, 122–23, 294–95, and 299–300.

60. Ibid., pp. 7, 257, and 306.

61. Pells, *Liberal Mind*, pp. 191 and 194.

62. VP, *SS*, pp. 9–10 and 307–8.

63. Potter, *People of Plenty*, p. 110. I am grateful to Howard R. Lamar for providing background information on Potter.

64. VP, *SS*, pp. 328–29.

65. Ibid., pp. 8–10, 26, 35, 98, 102, 116, 124–25, and 276.

66. Ibid., pp. 17–21, 90, 118, 195, and 304–5.

67. Ibid., pp. 9, 21, 27, 57, 116, 127, 304, and 358; VP, "How to Make a Fortune 'New Style,'" *Ladies' Home Journal* 76 (January 1959): 42 and 86.

68. VP, *SS*, pp. 340, 346–47, and 351–52.

69. Ibid., pp. 7, 328, and 358–59.

70. Ibid., pp. 35, 85, 87, 94, 122, and 261.

71. Ibid., pp. 22, 24, 41–42, 102, and 179.

72. S. I. Hayakawa, quoted in Ibid., p. 335.

73. VP, *SS*, pp. 41 and 331–34.

74. VP, "Have You Made Any New Friends Lately?," *Reader's Digest* 76 (February 1960): 55–58.

75. Robert Lekachman, review of *SS*, *Commentary*, September 1959.

76. See, for example, Robert Lee, letter to editor, *Christian Century*, 9 December 1959, p. 1443.

77. "America—The Beautiful," *Life*, 3 June 1957. For additional comparisons between Packard and other writers, not all of them favorable to Packard, see, for *HP*: *Houston Post*, 5 May 1957; for *SS*: Orville Prescott, *NYT*, 29 April 1959; Gladys Kessler, *Cornell Daily Sun*; George Christopoulos, *Management Review*, June 1959, p. 85; Donald Cook, *New Republic*, 15 June 1959, p. 19; Levitas, "Status Seeker Himself"; for *WM*, Nate White, *Christian Science Monitor*, 6 October 1960; Gerald Ashford, *San Antonio Express and News*, 2 October 1960; Spencer Klaw, *New York Herald Tribune*, 16 October 1960.

78. This comparison draws on Pells, *Liberal Mind*, pp. 232–48.

79. Bottomore, *Critics of Society*, p. 84.

80. The above summary relies on C. W. Mills, *Power Elite*; C. W. Mills, *White Collar*, especially pp. 239–58 and 274–75; Pells, *Liberal Mind*, pp. 249–61; I. L. Horowitz, *Mills*, especially pp. 236–40.

81. For reviews of *HP*, see William Millis, *San Francisco News*, 25 May 1957; Gerald Carson, *New York Herald Tribune*, 30 June 1957; A. C. Spectorsky, *NYT*, 28 April 1957; Carroll J. Swan, "Are Motivationists Machiavellis?" *Printers' Ink*, 3 May 1957, p. 57. On *SS*, see Reinhold Niebuhr, "Irresistible Joneses" in Berkshire, Mass., newspaper; Prescott, *NYT*; Fred L. Strodtbeck, *Contemporary Psychology*, August 1960, p. 265; Michael M. Mooney, *National Review*, 20 June 1959, p. 150; W. G. Rogers, *Grand Rapids Herald*, 17 May 1959; James W. Arnold, *Best Sellers*, 15 May 1959; *New Yorker*, 16 May 1959. On *WM*, see William Hogan, "Vance Packard's Role as a Social Critic," *San Francisco Chronicle*, 21 September 1960; Marjorie Ragan, *Raleigh Observer*, 2 October 1960; "What 'Waste Makers'

Doesn't Tell," *Salesweek*, 3 October 1960, p. 11; Harry Hansen, *Chicago Tribune Magazine of Books*; *Newsweek*, 3 October 1960, p. 68; Orville Prescott, *NYT*, 30 September 1960.

82. VP to KR, May (Friday) [1959], PPPS.

83. Levitas, "Status Seeker Himself."

84. VP, "A Commentary," p. 19; VP to Jacqueline Thompson, 25 June 1980, PPNC.

85. VP, interview with author, 20 December 1990.

86. Ibid.

87. Contract between VP and David McKay Company, 23 December 1959, PPNC; see also VP to author, 23–24 April 1987, p. 6.

88. VP, interview with author, New Canaan, Conn., 9 May 1992; VP, "Regarding Foreign Publishers Who in the Past Have Published Books by Vance Packard," PPNC.

89. *Time Magazine* 75 (4 January 1960): 34.

90. VP to KR, 29 March 1960, PPPS.

91. VP to KR, Friday, probably mid-1960, PPPS.

92. VP to EK, 27 October 1959, PPPS.

93. VP interview, 20 December 1990.

94. Ibid.; William Zabel, telephone conversation with author, 16 May 1992.

95. VP to KR, 29 March 1960.

96. Editors of *Fortune, Changing American Market*, p. 250.

97. Oakley, *God's Country*, pp. 240–41.

98. B. Earl Puckett of Allied Stores, quoted in D. T. Miller and Nowak, *Fifties*, p. 120.

99. For information on Chase, see Chase, *Tragedy of Waste*, and Westbrook, "Tribune of the Technostructure," especially pp. 396–99.

100. VP, *WM*, pp. v, 6, 7, 10, 16, 20–21, 153, 233, and 245.

101. Ibid., pp. 7, 8, 17, and 25.

102. Ibid., pp. 4–5, 160–67, and 233.

103. Ibid., pp. 186–87 and 189.

104. Ibid., pp. 159–60, 212, 215–31, and 236.

105. Ibid., pp. 159–60, 296, and 299.

106. Ibid., pp. 244–45, 252–53, 264, and 274.

107. Ibid., pp. 200, 273, 284, 286, 287, 290, and 292.

108. Ibid., pp. 16, 294, 296, and 309–11.

109. Ibid., pp. 314, 318, 323, 325, and 326.

110. Ibid., pp. 326–27.

111. Ibid., pp. 184 and 307.

112. D. Horowitz, *Morality of Spending*, pp. xviii–xix.

113. VP, *WM*, pp. 299 and 301.

114. Ibid., pp. 183–84.

115. Ibid., pp. 183–84, 234, 244, 311, and 313.

116. Lewis Nichols, quoted in VP, "Some Thoughts on Possible Questions and Answers for TBR," *NYT*, PPPS.

CHAPTER SEVEN

1. Hackett and Burke, *80 Years*, pp. 14 and 37; "Vance Packard. The Status Seekers," *Book News from David McKay*, ca. 1959, PPPS; clippings from best-seller lists, PPPS.

2. Review of *SS*, *Time*, 8 June 1959, p. 102; clippings from best-seller lists, PPPS. With a few exceptions, the following discussion focuses on reviews published in the United States. PPPS contains foreign reviews, especially those from Great Britain and the Federal Republic of Germany. The collection also contains thousands of Packard's reviews from the United States. For each of the three books, PPPS also has hundreds of items that demonstrate their use in cartoons, editorials, and sermons.

3. Clippings from best-seller lists, PPPS. For a study of the impact of *Hidden Persuaders*, see McInnis, *Books That Influenced the Modern World*.

4. VP to Judith F. Burbank, 3 November 1964, PPNC.

5. "Packard," *Contemporary Authors*, p. 372; "Texts of Presentation and Citation to Vance Packard, Columbia Journalism Alumni Award, May 8, 1958," PPPS.

6. VP, note to author, Thanksgiving 1988, author's possession.

7. Folkenroth, "Finish First," p. 57.

8. VP to author, 24 February 1992, author's possession.

9. Jhan Robbins, interview with author, Northampton, Mass., 22 November 1989.

10. Sarah Stage to author, 25 May 1988, author's possession.

11. Wolff, *This Boy's Life*, p. 207.

12. VP to author, 7 April 1992, author's possession. The income figures for these books, as well as for later ones, include earnings from sales of books in the United States, foreign editions, serial rights in magazines, book clubs—but not lectures.

13. VP to author, 7 April 1992; VP to HP, 1 October 1964, PPNC; VP to HP, 28 November 1968, PPNC; contract between VP and David McKay Company, 30 December 1968, PPNC; Grace C. Fraser, "Reconciliation at 6/30/72," PPNC.

14. Clunker cars and dress unpretentiously: CPR, interview with author, Chappaquiddick, Mass., 16 August 1991.

15. S. Wilson, *What Shall We Wear*, p. 241.

16. CPR, interview with author, Annandale, Va., 31 October 1991.

17. VP, "The Girls That I Cherish," probably *Seventeen*, mid-1960s, PPNC.

18. VMP, interview with author, New Canaan, Conn., 11 April 1992.

19. Whitney Darrow, Jr., interview with author, Wilton, Conn., 7 January 1993.

20. S. Wilson, *What Shall We Wear*, p. 216.

21. For the dating of this shift, see VP, "Biographical Material: Artist Virginia Packard," May 1989; CPR interview, 16 August 1991; VP to author, 25 March 1992, author's possession.

22. VPP, interview with author, Goldsboro, Pa., 25 August 1991.

23. CPR interview, 31 October 1991.

24. VP, *HP*, p. 54.

25. VP, quoted in Mitchel Levitas, "He Used to Be a Status Seeker Himself," *New York Post*, 31 May 1959.

26. VP, interview with author, New Canaan, Conn., 3 June 1987.

27. W. Colston Leigh, Inc., "Statement of Account," for the period between 12 January and 19 October 1961, PPNC; William E. Burrows, "Celebrities, Authors Augment Their Incomes by Delivering Lectures," *WSJ*, 1 April 1969, p. 1.

28. ER, interview with author, New York, N.Y., 16 January 1991.

29. Ibid.

30. VP, interview with author, New Canaan, Conn., 9 May 1992.

31. VP, quoted in Phyllis Meras, "Social Critic Vance Packard—An Amiable Man Who Listens to the Wind and Fishes for Blues," *VG*, 10 October 1969, VGA.

32. "Packard," *Contemporary Authors*, p. 375.

33. VP, *SS*, p. 10.

34. VP, interview with author, New Canaan, Conn., 9 April 1986.

35. William Hart, telephone conversation with author, 15 May 1992.

36. Packard discussed the ways he used campus visits to carry out research and build a network in his 9 April 1986 interview. See Nelson, "Wrong with Sociology," pp. 45–46, on his method in general.

37. VP, memorandum to Sumner Blossom, mid-June 1947, PPNC.

38. C. P. Wilson, "Rhetoric of Consumption," pp. 55 and 64.

39. Nelson, "Wrong with Sociology," p. 46.

40. In writing of the nation's mood at the end of the 1950s, I have benefited from Burner, *Kennedy*, pp. 35–44; Diggins, *Proud Decades*, pp. 348–50; Gitlin, *Sixties*, pp. 11–77; Hodgson, *America in Our Time*, pp. 69–83 and 505–6; Matusow, *Unraveling of America*, pp. 7–12; D. T. Miller and Nowak, *Fifties*, pp. 16–18; Oakley, *God's Country*, pp. 412–15; Pells, *Liberal Mind*, pp. 346–99; Schlesinger, "Challenge of Abundance"; Wilkinson, *Pursuit*, p. 105

41. This discussion relies on Pells, *Liberal Mind*, p. 346; *Prospects for America*; U.S., President's Commission on National Goals, *Goals for Americans*.

42. "Secret Voices: Messages That Manipulate," *Time*, September 1979, p. 71.

43. "The Vanishing Individual," *Newsday*, ca. 1957; several columns by Max Lerner, "Assault on the Mind," *New York Post*, 26 June 1957.

44. Louis Harris and Associates survey, quoted in "Are Thought-Leaders a Threat?" *Printers' Ink*, 26 April 1963, p. 54.

45. Leonard Sloane, "Consumers Spur Industry Response," *NYT*, sec. 3, part 2, 7 January 1973, p. 49.

46. Folkenroth, "Finish First," p. 70; Esther Peterson, telephone conversation with author, 26 July 1993.

47. "'Source of Life Itself,'" *Wilmington, Delaware Journal Every Evening*, 12 November 1957; Jack Patterson, "Invisible Salesman," *Commonweal*, 18 April 1958; "Consumer at a Discount," *Barron's*, 2 October 1961, p. 1. For Packard's testimony before the U.S. Senate on a bill to curb one aspect of excessive advertising, see *NYT*, 13 March 1958. For evidence that the president of the Federal Republic of Germany was interested in *Waste Makers*, see Wehrenalp to VP, 1961,

PPPS. For Packard's discussion of the impact on his writings on policy deliberations, see "Packard," *Contemporary Authors*, p. 375.

48. VP, *WM*, pp. 251–53 and 260–62.

49. There is no mention of Packard in Hays, *Beauty, Health, and Permanence*. However, there is evidence of Packard's impact on those concerned with the environment and population growth: Charles N. Conconi, "An Interview with Vance Packard," *EQM*, March 1973, pp. 19–21 and 23; Chesler, *Woman of Valor*, p. 456; VP, list of the impact of his books, 1970s, PPNC.

50. Though he does not mention Packard, the following discussion of the shift from conservation to environmentalism relies on Hays, "From Conservation to Environment," and Hays, *Beauty, Health, and Permanence*, pp. 3–5.

51. Packard mentioned the pollution of the water supply, but this was a minor note; see VP, *WM*, p. 193. See also VP, "America the Beautiful—and Its Desecraters," *Atlantic* 208 (August 1961): 51.

52. Carson's *Silent Spring* opened with a picture of an earlier America (pp. 1–3).

53. On the importance of a sense of place and nature to him, see CPR interview, 16 August 1991.

54. VP, "America the Beautiful," pp. 52–55.

55. VP, *WM*, p. 307, mentioned the issues of preserving public lands, but this was a minor note in the book.

56. For the argument that writers of the 1950s served as progenitors of the 1960s, see Pells, *Liberal Mind*, pp. 188 and 401–9.

57. Gitlin, *Sixties*, p. 19, highlights the difference between books with and without popular audiences.

58. Arthur M. Schlesinger, Jr., to author, 29 October 1991 and 1 April 1993, author's possession.

59. Eric F. Goldman, "Social and Economic Scene Mirrored," *New York Herald Tribune Book Review*, 15 January 1961, p. 18.

60. Henry, *Culture against Man*, p. 36.

61. Thomas Hayden, "Why This Erupting Generation?" *Michigan Daily*, 22 September 1960.

62. The Port Huron Statement, reprinted in J. Miller, *'Democracy Is in the Streets,'* pp. 334, 338, and 339.

63. Gitlin, *Sixties*, p. 19.

64. Charles W. McCurdy to author, 15 November 1991, author's possession.

65. Willis, "Consumerism and Women," p. 76; Schudson, "Criticizing the Critics," p. 3.

66. Nelson, "Wrong With Sociology," pp. 44–45, discusses Packard's prescience.

67. John Lofflin, "Help from the 'Hidden Persuaders,'" *NYT*, 20 March 1988.

68. Winston Fletcher, quoted in "Are the Persuaders Still Hiding in Wait?" *Marketing Week*, 7 June 1985, p. 45. For other references, see Albert Schofield, "Key Words: Albert Schofield on Vance Packard's Book *The Hidden Persuaders*," *Times Higher Education Supplement*, 3 May 1985, p. 17; "Beyond the Hidden Persuaders," *Forbes*, 23 March 1987, pp. 134, 135, and 138; Randall Rothenberg,

"Capitalist Eye on the Soviet Consumer," *NYT*, 15 February 1989; Bernice Kanner, "Mind Games," *New York*, 8 May 1989, p. 35; Annetta Miller and Dody Tsiantar, "Psyching Out Consumers," *Newsweek*, 27 February 1989, p. 46; "Consumers Are Getting Mad, Mad, Mad, Mad at Mad Ave," *Business Week*, 30 April 1990, PPNC; Hugh Aldersey-Williams, "New Toys for Hidden Persuaders," *New Scientist* 132 (21–28 December 1991): 52; William Glaberson, "Where You Are What You Wear," *NYT*, 9 April 1992, p. B1; Steve Lohr, "Bond Sales from 'The Far Side,'" *NYT*, 22 November 1992; "Che Persuasori," *Panorama*, 6 December 1992, p. 87.

69. Randall Rothenberg, telephone conversation with author, 7 April 1992.

70. Suzanne White to author, 15 October 1991, author's possession.

71. Benjamin Horowitz, interview with author, Northampton, Mass., 19 February 1993.

72. Frank Trippett, "Hard Times for the Status-Minded," *Time*, 21 December 1981, p. 90; "The New Status Seekers," *Los Angeles Times Magazine*, 27 December 1987–3 January 1988, front page.

73. Vivian B. Martin to VP, 29 July 1991, PPNC.

74. "Advertising Everywhere!" *Consumer Reports*, December 1992, p. 752.

75. Kathleen M. Doherty to VP, 10 May 1988, PPNC; "The Fall and Rise of U.S. Frugality," *Time*, 3 March 1980, PPNC.

76. These generalizations rely on examinations of data provided by Dialog, Social Science Citation Index, and BRS Information Technologies.

77. Roell, review of *All Consuming Images*, pp. 1335–36.

78. Clecak, *America's Quest*, p. 16; Dickstein, *Gates of Eden*, p. 69; Diggins, *Proud Decades*, p. 325; Gilbert, *Another Chance*, pp. 118–19; D. A. Horowitz, Carroll, and Lee, *On the Edge*, p. 56; Marchand, "Visions of Classlessness," p. 175; D. T. Miller and Nowak, *Fifties*, pp. 20, 187, and 214; Siegel, *Troubled Journey*, p. 180; Gleason, "Identifying Identity," p. 923; Breines, "Domineering Mothers," p. 602; Oakley, *God's Country*, pp. 231 and 310; Rich, "Best Years," p. 39; Solberg, *Riding High*, p. 262; Wilkinson, *Pursuit*, pp. 26 and 51–53; Higham, "Changing Paradigms," p. 463.

79. This is true, for example, of Pells, *Liberal Mind*.

80. On this tendency, see Jacoby, *Last Intellectuals*, pp. 101–2; Bender, in *Intellect and Public Life*, explores the relationship between academic and civic cultures.

81. Among the relevant books that make no reference in the text to Packard are Chafe, *Unfinished Journey*; Hodgson, *America in Our Time*; Jezer, *Dark Ages*; Matusow, *Unraveling of America*; W. L. O'Neill, *American High*; Pells, *Liberal Mind*; N. L. Rosenberg and E. S. Rosenberg, *In Our Times*; Whitfield, *Culture of the Cold War*; Winkler, *Modern America*; Zinn, *Postwar America*.

82. D'Innocenzo, "A Literature of Warning."

83. Murray, *Losing Ground*, p. 28.

84. Betty Friedan, interview with author, Santa Monica, Calif., 18 March 1987.

85. For Wallace, see *NYT*, 30 June 1990, p. 29; see also Kurt Vonnegut, quoted in interview with D. C. Denison, *Boston Globe Magazine*, 2 September 1990, p. 9.

86. Walzer, *Company of Critics*, p. 22.

CHAPTER EIGHT

1. What follows relies on all of the letters in the Packard Papers at Penn State in the files for these three books, from people who did not know him previously. These letters include a substantial majority, if not all, of those he received; VP, interview with author, New Canaan, Conn., 20 December 1990.

2. The following discussion relies on Radway, *Reading the Romance*, esp. pp. 4–12, 86, and 186–222; Ohmann, "Shaping of a Canon," p. 201, discusses the characteristics of people who buy best-selling books.

3. At a few points in the body of the third book, Packard did draw on his own experiences: VP, *WM*, pp. 47, 75, and 264.

4. VP, *SS*, pp. 10–13; VP, *WM*, pp. vii–viii.

5. VP, *WM*, pp. 3 and 9; see also VP, *SS*, pp. 3 and 11–13; VP, *HP*, pp. 3, 10, and 11.

6. Dust jacket for *HP*, PPPS; unsigned press release, 27 March 1957, PPPS; advertisements, PPPS.

7. Dust jacket for eighth printing of *SS*, author's possession; advertisements, PPPS.

8. Advertisements, PPPS; CTA, press release, 2 September 1960, PPPS.

9. Robert Lekachman, review of *SS*, *Commentary*, September 1959, noted these contrasting responses.

10. K.C., review of *HP*, *Shreveport Times*, 28 April 1957; for *SS*, see GSB, *Albuquerque Tribune*, 16 May 1959; with *WM*, see Spencer Klaw, *New York Herald Tribune*, 16 October 1960.

11. See, for example, Walter Spearman, review of *HP*, *Winston-Salem Journal and Sentinel*, 16 June 1957; review of *SS*, *Albuquerque Tribune*, 16 May 1959.

12. G.R., review of *HP*, *Durham Herald*, 19 May 1957.

13. Fred L. Strodtbeck, review of *SS*, *Contemporary Psychology*, August 1960, p. 265; Ernest R. May, review of *SS*, *Frontier*, September 1959, p. 21; review of *SS*, *Sports Illustrated*, 18 May 1959, p. 13.

14. Klaw, review of *WM*.

15. AM, review of *SS*, *Lewiston Daily Sun*, 2 May 1959, p. 4.

16. Charles Winick, review of *HP*, *Christian Science Monitor*, 30 April 1957, p. 9.

17. For *HP*, see *Huntington, Indiana, Our Sunday Visitor*, 5 May 1957; *Bangor News*, 9 June 1957; *Durham Herald*, 19 May 1957; on *SS*, see Donald Cook, review of *SS*, *New Republic*, 15 June 1959, p. 20; for *WM*, see *High Point Enterprise*, 25 September 1960; Dorothie Erwin, *Shreveport Times*, 16 October 1960.

18. Of the 126 letters, 71 were from help seekers. To fall into this category, the request had to involve something more than an answer to a simple or rhetorical question. Because the categories sometimes do overlap, at times I have referred to a letter in the discussion of one category even though the letter ended up in another. When a letter had more than one purpose, I have categorized it according to its primary thrust.

19. HVA to VP, 24 June 1958, and RLH to VP, 12 March 1958. In order to preserve anonymity, I have used only the initials of the letter writer and the date of the letter.

20. ET to VP, 6 November 1958; DAF to VP, 26 September 1957; RHB to VP, 10 October 1963.

21. Frank Owen, phone conversation with author, 13 November 1990.

22. Ed O'Meara, "Book Marks: Reasons," *Oregon Journal*, 8 December 1957, p. 6C, PPPS; CTA, "A Question Oft Debated, Rarely Resolved," press release, 5 November 1957, PPPS.

23. Bevode McCall to VP, 9 June 1958.

24. SAM to VP, 8 October 1957; VP to SAM, 5 December 1957.

25. Ernest Dichter to VP, 6 January 1958.

26. Louis Cheskin to VP, 7 June 1957; Louis Cheskin to VP, 14 May 1959, PPNC. For evidence that Packard got people in touch with motivational researchers, see Packard's notations on IB to VP, 14 September 1958, and on SZ to VP, 5 February 1958.

27. To end up in the true believer category, a letter had to focus preponderantly on a statement of the letter writer's ideology. Though sparked by something Packard wrote, the letters of true believers tended to be about subjects of more importance to the letter writer than to Packard; they often promoted an ideology so vigorously that it did not seem to matter whether or not Packard was listening. The letters of the converted implicitly or explicitly made it clear that they agreed with the book. Although they often went on to extend or play upon Packard's arguments, they did so in ways that did not fundamentally challenge his position. Unlike the true believers, the challengers were sensitive to the nature of Packard's arguments; unlike the converted, they disagreed with the author's analysis on a major issue. When the disagreement was very friendly or on minor issues, I have placed the letter in the converted category.

28. JFE to VP, 24 March 1958 and 11 April 1958; VP's handwritten note on letter of 24 March 1958.

29. HEM to VP, 28 May 1958.

30. RTM to VP, 13 November 1960. In the longer quote, the capital letters represented words of the letter writer, while the words in lowercase letters were from the original book jacket.

31. See, for example, BGL to VP, 20 February 1958, and TAK to VP, no date.

32. CRG to VP, 19 July 1958.

33. MRM to VP, 20 August 1957.

34. GS to VP, 27 September 1958.

35. FPR and MTR to VP, 31 January 1960.

36. WGL to VP, 18 July 1958.

37. MCM to VP, 1 December 1957.

38. Mrs. Gerald F. Smith to the editor, *NYT Magazine*, 1 June 1958.

39. FD to VP, 22 July 1961; JM to VP, probably fall of 1957; VP to JM, 4 December 1957.

40. JM to VP, probably October 1957. For a similar critique, see Margot Mallary, letter to editor, *NYT Magazine*, 1 June 1958.

41. BH to VP, no date.

42. HCB to VP, 2 February 1958.

43. HLW to VP, 4 August 1960.

44. CA to VP, 11 February 1963.

45. VV-R to VP, 20 May 1958.

46. MRM to VP, 20 August 1957.

47. HLW to VP, 4 August 1960.

48. With this book, 154 letters survive, categorized as follows: from help seekers, 69; true believers, 2; converted, 81; and challengers, 2.

49. FER to VP, 30 March 1960, PPNC.

50. HN to VP, 19 August 1959.

51. AE to VP, 11 June 1960.

52. RSH to VP, 22 September 1960.

53. JD to VP, 5 February 1960.

54. DR to VP, 10 January 1964; JZ to VP, 18 October 1959.

55. MF to VP, 5 December 1960.

56. SHS to VP, 15 July 1959.

57. JLS to VP, 28 August 1960; GF to VP, 24 August 1959; WS to VP, 13 May 1959.

58. HK to VP, August 1960 and 29 September 1965.

59. GR to VP, 2 February 1960.

60. MG to VP, 26 January 1960.

61. VH to VP, 22 August 1959.

62. RB to VP, 3 August 1959.

63. JK to VP, 16 October 1960.

64. EDS to VP, 2 December 1958.

65. DBS to VP, 24 August 1960.

66. For example, see LAF to VP, 29 August 1961, PPNC.

67. MEH to VP, 25 February 1960.

68. JLD to VP, no date.

69. DRH to VP, 21 July 1959.

70. Upton Sinclair to VP, 3 September 1959, PPNC.

71. Mr. and Mrs. SBB to VP, 26 June 1960.

72. JW to VP, 12 January, no year.

73. See, for examples, KSD to VP, 1 August 1963; CME to VP, 2 March 1960; JRL to VP, 14 January 1961.

74. With *WM*, 118 letters survive: from help seekers, 30; converted, 84; true believers, 2; challengers, 2.

75. EDL to VP, 23 September 1961.

76. RG to VP, 3 December 1963.

77. WW to VP, 10 October 1960, PPNC.

78. EM to VP, 25 August 1961.

79. ES to VP, 14 April 1963.

80. LE to VP, 8 May 1964.

81. VK to VP, no date.

82. EM to VP, 25 August 1961.

83. MKC to VP, 12 November 1960.

84. MAB to VP, 16 April 1961.

85. HR to VP, 26 December 1962.

86. CBM to VP, 29 September 1960.

87. DMS to VP, 7 September 1960.

88. JKD to VP, 9 December 1963.

89. ES to VP, 14 April 1963; JD to VP, 30 December 1960.

90. MT to VP, 5 February 1964.

91. HD to VP, 25 November 1960.

92. JKD to VP, 9 December 1963.

93. RC to VP, 29 May 1964.

94. RT to VP, 23 January 1961; EWH to VP, 16 January 1961.

95. GLA to VP, 18 December 1963.

96. GD to VP, 20 June 1960.

97. LE to VP, 8 May 1964.

98. Ibid.

99. RCW to VP, 4 January 1964.

100. Darnton, *Great Cat Massacre*, pp. 249–52, discusses the distinction between intensive and extensive reading.

101. Compare the response to Packard's writings with what happened in the case of Jean-Jacques Rosseau's *La Nouvelle Héloïse*: Darnton, *Great Cat Massacre*, pp. 215–56.

102. Fish, *Is There a Text in This Class?*, pp. 167–73 and 322–37.

103. Radway, *Reading the Romance*, pp. 188, 191–92, 194, and 197.

104. Ibid., pp. 86 and 215.

105. In making these comments, I have benefited from a reading of J. S. Rubin, "Self, Culture, and Self-Culture," esp. pp. 790, 791, and 795.

CHAPTER NINE

1. See Stephen Birmingham, "The Minstrels of Madison Avenue," *Holiday* 22 (December 1957): 81.

2. "In 'Debate' with Packard, Weir Hits Book As 'Malicious,'" *Advertising Age*, 28 October 1957, pp. 82–83; "Weir: 'A Malicious Book,'" *Printers' Ink*, 25 October 1957, pp. 97–98.

3. VP to Edward L. Crow, 2 November 1957, PPPS.

4. For favorable or mixed reviews in industry journals, see "Packard Book Is Searching Probe of Motivationists," *Advertising Age*, 29 April 1957, pp. 2 and 24; James D. Woolf, "'The Hidden Persuaders' Is a Disservice to Advertising," *Advertising Age*, 1 July 1957. On Packard's reaction, see VP, interview with author, New Canaan, Conn., 20 December 1990.

5. VP, "Some Thoughts on Possible Questions and Answers for TBR," probably late 1960, PPPS; see also, VP, letter to editor, *Atlantic*, ca. June 1958; VP interview,

20 December 1990. For a thoughtful essay on the reaction of the business press by Packard's friend and a journalism professor, see John Tebbel, "How to Review a Best-Seller," *Saturday Review of Literature*, 14 January 1961, pp. 39–40.

6. Bauer and Greyser, *Advertising in America*, pp. 13, 14, 23, and 69; Weir, *Truth in Advertising*, pp. 31–34 and 157–66.

7. Ogilvy, *Confessions*.

8. "Is 'The Waste Makers' a Hoax?," *Printers' Ink*, 30 September 1960, pp. 20–22, 24–25, and 28–29; "Packard Hoodwinks Most Reviewers," *Printers' Ink*, 21 October 1960, pp. 58–60; "Has Packard Flipped?" *Printers' Ink*, 10 March 1961, p. 67.

9. "Is 'The Waste Makers' a Hoax?," p. 20.

10. Even before publication, the public relations department of General Foods sent book review editors across the nation copies of a speech by the chairman of the board titled "Consumer Persuasion—Black Art or Key to Economic Progress?"; see Tebbel, "How to Review," p. 39. For major editorial attacks on Packard's book, see "'Planned Waste'—Or a Better Mousetrap," *Fortune*, October 1960, pp. 131–32; "Haste Makes Waste: Vance Packard's New Book Illustrates the Point," *Barron's*, 10 October 1960, p. 1; "Consumer at a Discount: His Critics Underestimate His Wisdom and His Power," *Barron's*, 2 October 1961, p. 1; "On Making Waste," *WSJ*, 7 October 1960, p. 16; "The Taste-Makers" and "The Waste Fallacy," *WSJ*, 19 October 1960; "How to Explain Advertising's Value to Your Workers," *Advertising Age*, 5 June 1961, pp. 10–15.

11. Charles Mortimer, "Persuasion Is Key to Progress," *Salesweek*, 3 October 1960, p. 14; Donald S. Frost, "Packard Harbors Three Fallacies," *Salesweek*, 3 October 1960, p. 12.

12. Ernest Dichter, letter to the editor, *NYT Book Review*, 9 October 1960, p. 53.

13. Ernest Dichter, "Persuasion: To What End?" *Motivations* 2 (June 1957): 16.

14. Joseph C. Ingraham, "Auto Men Restyle Motive of Change," *NYT*. See also Fairfax M. Cone, review of *HP*, clipping dated 12 May 1957.

15. "Major Omission by a Critic," *Detroit Free Press*, 21 April 1961.

16. Edwin Cox, "How Little He Knows of Consumers," *Salesweek*, 3 October 1960, p. 12; "On Making Waste," p. 16.

17. J. Wilfred Corr, letter to the editor, *Atlantic*, ca. June 1958, p. 16.

18. Mortimer, "Persuasion," p. 14.

19. VP interview, 20 December 1990.

20. *Original Texan*, 2 December 1960.

21. Tebbel, "How to Review," p. 40.

22. For evidence of approval of Packard's efforts by sociologists, see Alfred M. Lee to VP, 31 May 1960, PPNC; Lee to VP, 2 February 1965, PPPS; Raymond W. Mack and Bevode C. McCall, quoted on dust jacket, *SS*; review of *SS*, *American Catholic Sociological Review*, Fall 1959, p. 248.

23. A perusal of *Sociological Abstracts* from 1953 until 1984 reveals relatively few references to Packard's work; the most prominent among them was the hostile article "Is Vance Packard Necessary?" *Trans-Action* 2 (January–February 1965): 13–17.

24. ER, interview with author, New York, N.Y., 16 January 1991.

25. Robert J. Havighurst, review of *SS*, *Personnel and Guidance Journal*, February 1960, p. 512; see also Robert Lee, letter to editor, *Christian Century*, 9 December 1959, p. 1443.

26. Morroe Berger, quoted in transcript of "The Open Mind," NBC television, 22 May 1960, p. 4, PPPS.

27. E. Digby Baltzell, quoted in transcript of "Open Mind," p. 4.

28. Joseph Mayer, review of *SS*, *Annals of the American Academy of Political and Social Science* 327 (January 1960): 150–51.

29. William Petersen, review of *SS*, *ASR* 25 (February 1960): 124–26.

30. William Petersen, "Reply to Mr. Packard," *ASR* 25 (June 1960): 408–9.

31. Lewis Coser, "Kitsch Sociology," *Partisan Review*, Summer 1959, pp. 480–83.

32. Seymour M. Lipset, "Vance Packard Discovers America," *Reporter* 21 (9 July 1959): 31–33.

33. Seymour M. Lipset, "The Conservatism of Vance Packard," *Commentary*, pp. 80–83.

34. Seymour M. Lipset, review of *WM*, *Progressive*, January 1961.

35. Lipset, review of *WM*, *Progressive*.

36. Lipset, "Conservatism," pp. 80–83.

37. Lipset, review of *WM*, *Progressive*.

38. "Is Vance Packard Necessary?" pp. 13–17.

39. VP to Quent[in A. Bossi], probably summer 1959, PPPS.

40. VP, letter to the editor, *ASR* 25 (June 1960): 408.

41. VP, "Packard on Vance Packard," *Trans-Action* 7 (June 1970): 10.

42. VP, letter to editor, *ASR*; VP to Judith F. Burbank, 3 November 1964, PPPS.

43. VP, "A Commentary," *Trans-Action* 2 (January–February 1965): 17–19.

44. VP, letter to editor, *Trans-Action* 2 (March–April 1965): 2.

45. Review of *SS*, *Times Literary Supplement*, 15 January 1960, p. 27; review of *SS*, *New Yorker*, 16 May 1959; review of *SS*, *Atlantic* 203 (May 1959): 91–92; review of *WM*, *Newsweek*, 3 October 1960, p. 68; Elmo Roper, "How Powerful Are the Persuaders?" *Saturday Review of Literature*, 5 October 1957.

46. LMG to VP, 2 February 1963, PPPS.

47. In 1991, a prominent sociologist bristled at the description of Packard as a sociologist: Herbert Gans, letter to the editor, *Columbia Journalism Review* 30 (July–August 1991): 6.

48. Donald Cook, review of *SS*, *New Republic*, 15 June 1959, p. 19; H. Reid Strieby, letter to editor, *Trans-Action* 2 (March–April 1965); VP, quoted in "A Talk with Vance Packard," *Bulletin of the Marlboro Book Club*, vol. 6, no. 73, probably late 1960, PPPS.

49. Robert Lekachman, review of *SS*, *Commentary*, 1 September 1959, p. 270.

50. For a classic statement along these lines, see Parsons, "Some Problems."

51. Friedrichs, *Sociology of Sociology*, pp. 57–75 and 93–134, drew the contrast between the prophetic and the priestly. He identified Packard as someone who offered a "narrowly conceived" version of the prophetic (p. 66). For some contem-

porary recognition of the comparability of Mills and Packard, see Petersen, review; Joseph Fletcher, review of *SS*, source unknown, pp. 148–49; Robert Lekachman, review. For discussions of the relationships between sociologists and their audiences, see the essays in Terence C. Halliday and Morris Janowitz, eds., *Sociology and Its Publics: The Forms and Fates of Disciplinary Organization* (Chicago: University of Chicago Press, 1992).

52. On this issue, and on the relationship of academic sociology to its audiences, see Sica, "Rhetoric."

53. Collins, review of *Idea of Social Structure*, pp. 150–54. For a critique from a Parsonian perspective of those, including Packard, who lamented the decrease of individualism and the increase of conformity, see W. White, *Beyond Conformity*.

54. Petersen, "Is America Still the Land of Opportunity?" pp. 477, 480, 484, 485, and 486.

55. Wald, *New York Intellectuals*, pp. 7 and 323–24; for information on Petersen, I am relying on Seymour Martin Lipset to author, 31 March 1992, author's possession, and Neil J. Smelser to author, 4 March 1992, author's possession; Michael P. Rogin, interview with author, Northampton, Mass., 3 October 1990.

56. C.[oser], "American Notebook," pp. 210–13; Coser and I. Howe, "Images of Socialism"; Coser, "What Shall We Do?," p. 163; Coser, "Sociological Theory," p. 154; Coser, "New Political Atmosphere," p. 11; Coser, *Functions of Social Conflict*; Lipset and Smelser, "Setting of Sociology," n. 15, p. 5. For a discussion of Coser's views, see Pells, *Liberal Mind*, pp. 188, 362–63, 366, 381–83, 387–88, and 395–96.

57. Lipset and Smelser, "Setting of Sociology," p. 7.

58. Lipset and Rogoff, "Class and Opportunity," p. 568.

59. Lipset, *Political Man*, pp. x, xix–xx, xxi–xxii, xxv, 1, 442, 445, 446, 454, and 456; Brick, *Daniel Bell*, p. 5. For a discussion of Lipset on which I have drawn, see Pells, *Liberal Mind*, pp. 130–33, 140–45, 178, 181, and 333.

60. Coser, "What Shall We Do?," p. 162; C.[oser], "American Notebook," p. 211.

61. Pells, *Liberal Mind*, p. 121, effectively captures the ambivalence of people such as Lipset.

62. Lipset and Smelser, "Setting of Sociology," pp. 4–5.

63. Ibid., p. 8.

64. Lipset and Smelser, "Change and Controversy," n. 12, pp. 50–51. I. L. Horowitz, *Mills*, n. 30, p. 110, says that Lipset wrote the passage in question. An exhaustive search has failed to turn up a copy of the article by Mills, in a publication called *Paperback Review*, that listed the texts he recommended; therefore it is impossible to determine if he included any of Packard's books. Not surprisingly, though Mills found Packard's work too apolitical, he admired his ability to make sociology accessible to a wide audience (Irving Louis Horowitz to author, 29 January 1992, author's possession).

65. Gitlin, *Sixties*, p. 19, highlights this contrast.

66. Nelson, "Wrong with Sociology," pp. 43–49. See also Edwin B. Burgum, "American Sociology in Transition," *Science and Society* 23 (Fall 1979): 325.

67. Ehrenreich, *Fear of Falling*, p. 18.

68. Gary T. Marx, telephone conversations with author, 12 March 1992 and 15 March 1993.

69. Marx, "Introduction," in *Muckraking Sociology*, pp. 1–3, 5, 12, and 14. For a 1975 critique of the tendency of some sociologists to emphasize "precise measurement over substantive issues" and to address specialized audiences, see Coser, "Presidential Address," pp. 692 and 695.

70. Tyack, "Life in the 'Museum of Virtue,'" p. 118.

71. Goode, Furstenberg, and Mitchell, "Waller," in *Waller*, pp. 74–75.

72. For a discussion of Packard's place in a tradition of popular social science writings, see Thody, "Grammar and Stereotypes."

73. Ohmann, "Shaping of a Canon," p. 205.

74. Macdonald, "Masscult and Midcult," pp. 37, 39, and 53–54; for a thoughtful critique of the debate over mass culture, see Lears, "Matter of Taste."

75. Mary McCarthy, letter to the editor, *Time* 76 (8 August 1960): 2; for an example of McCarthy's celebration of American life, see Mary McCarthy, "America the Beautiful," *Commentary* 4 (September 1947): 201–7.

76. H. Rosenberg, *Tradition of the New*, pp. 271, 274–75, 276, 277, 278, and 283–84.

77. Ibid., pp. 275, 280, 281, 283, and 285.

78. Podhoretz, *Making It*, p. 118.

79. For discussion of these issues, see Gilbert, *Cycle of Outrage*, chap. 7 and esp. pp. 119–21; Macdonald, "Theory of Mass Culture." For a discussion of Packard as someone who, along with others, developed the concept of mass culture, see Pronovost, "Culture."

80. VP, testimony, *Hearings before the Subcommittee on Communications of the Committee on Interstate and Foreign Commerce*, U.S. Senate, 85th Cong., 2d sess., on S. 2834 (Washington: Government Printing Office, 1958), p. 109.

81. W. L. O'Neill, *American High*, pp. 24–27, and Wald, *New York Intellectuals*, p. 230, discuss these questions.

82. For a somewhat similar view in a different context, see Radway, "The Book-of-the-Month Club," pp. 260–62.

83. A. Ross, *No Respect*, pp. 5 and 42–43.

84. Podhoretz, *Making It*, p. xii.

85. Pells, *Liberal Mind*, p. 121.

86. I. Howe, "This Age of Conformity," p. 12.

87. In this discussion, I have drawn on Pells, *Liberal Mind*, pp. 130–261 and 346–402.

88. For this distinction, see Alexander Bloom, *Prodigal Sons*, p. 235.

89. I have found A. Ross, *No Respect*, pp. 12, 49, 50, and 57, useful in understanding these issues.

90. I. Howe, "New York Intellectuals," pp. 241–42.

91. Podhoretz, *Making It*, p. 117.

92. Ibid., pp. 12, 15, and 86.

93. Jacoby, *Last Intellectuals*, p. 90.

94. Kazin, *Walker in the City*, pp. 60 and 169.

95. Podhoretz, *Making It*, p. 117.

96. Norman Houk, review of *HP*, *Minneapolis Tribune*, 2 June 1957; review of *SS*, *Atlantic*, p. 91; Robert C. Moore, review of *WM*, *Boston Globe*, 2 October 1960.

97. Naomi Bliven, review of *WM*, *New Yorker*, 12 November 1960, p. 234; Nate White, review of *WM*, *Christian Science Monitor*, 6 October 1960; Nicholas Samstag, review of *WM*, *Saturday Review of Literature* 43 (5 November 1960). See also Boorstin, *The Image*, p. 290.

98. Saville R. Davis, review of *SS*, *Christian Science Monitor*, 30 April 1959, p. 11.

99. Review of *SS*, *Time*, 8 June 1959, p. 102; John Chamberlain, review of *SS*, *WSJ*, 29 April 1959.

100. Ernest Van Den Haag, "Madison Avenue Witchcraft," *Commonweal*, 29 November 1957, p. 231.

101. Richard C. Kostelanetz, review of *SS*, *Brown Daily Herald*, 3 November 1959.

102. Richard Hoggart, review of *WM*, *Observer*.

103. Loren Baritz, "Of Time and the Ostrich," *Nation*, January 1961, p. 83.

104. See, for example, William Hogan, review of *HP*, *San Francisco Chronicle*, 21 May 1957, p. 23; Cook, review of *SS*, p. 20; review of *WM*, *Newsweek*, p. 69; Philip S. Haring, review of *SS*, *Landscape*, Autumn 1959, p. 38.

105. Irving Kristol, "'I Dreamed I Stopped Traffic . . . ,'" *Encounter*, December 1957, pp. 72–74.

106. Huxley, *Brave New World and Brave New World Revisited*, p. 39.

107. Michael M. Mooney, review of *SS*, *National Review*, 20 June 1959, pp. 150–51; John Chamberlain, review of *WM*, *WSJ*, 7 October 1960, p. 16; Reinhold Niebuhr, "The Irresistible Joneses," in Berkshire, Mass., newspaper.

108. Baritz, *Servants of Power* and *City on a Hill*.

109. Baritz, "Of Time and the Ostrich," pp. 82–83.

110. Marcuse, *One-Dimensional Man*, p. xvii.

111. Al Morgan, review of *HP*, *New York Post*, 5 May 1957.

112. VP to James Wechsler, 4 May 1957, PPNC. For information on Wechsler during these years, see Gitlin, *Sixties*, pp. 54–58.

CHAPTER TEN

1. In VP, interview with author, New Canaan, Conn., 20 December 1990, Packard responded to the major issues that critics raised about his work.

2. The quotation is from a Pittsburgh minister, found in VP interview, 20 December 1990. For a useful discussion of jeremiads, see Bercovitch, *American Jeremiad*, p. xi; E. Long, *American Dream*, p. 189, examines 1950s social criticism as a jeremiad.

3. Crunden, *Ministers of Reform*, pp. x, 3, 15, 165, and 182, provides characteriza-

tions that very much parallel Packard's outlook. John Lyndenberg, review of *SS*, *New Leader*, 21 September 1959, perceptively linked Packard to American traditions; a letter from Sinclair connected *Status Seekers* to Veblen and to the literature of exposé (Upton Sinclair to VP, 3 September 1959, PPNC); for a discussion of Packard as a muckraker, see Stein, "American Muckraking."

4. Hall, "Culture, the Media, and the 'Ideological Effect,'" p. 332, discusses the notion of residual, oppositional cultures.

5. Hofstadter, *Age of Reform*, pp. 186–214, has shaped this comparison.

6. The files in PPPS contain ample evidence of Packard's involvement with Consumers Union.

7. F. C. Howe, *Confessions of a Reformer*, p. 17.

8. The Truman story is from Jhan Robbins, interview with author, Northampton, Mass., 22 November 1989; see also VP, untitled promotional copy, 28 September 1960, PPPS. Wilkinson, *Pursuit*, pp. 51–53, perceptively locates Packard's works within a tradition of cultural analysis. For a sympathetic discussion of the importance of a moral vision in social criticism, one that emphasizes the opposition between corruption and virtue, see Walzer, *Company of Critics*, pp. 9–10.

9. VP to author, 8 April 1993, author's possession.

10. John Keats to VP, 8 October 1960, PPNC.

11. For biographical information, see Keats, *New Romans*.

12. Donaldson, *Suburban Myth*, pp. viii–ix, notes how the myth of the yeoman farmer undergirded critiques of American suburbs in the 1950s; E. Long, *American Dream*, pp. 148–64 and 182–89, provides a cogent analysis of the limitations posed by the backward-looking quality of 1950s social criticism.

13. For a discussion of ways in which reliance on the past has served as an oppositional force, see Hall, "Culture, the Media and the 'Ideological Effect,'" p. 322; Walzer, *Company of Critics*, p. 235; J. L. Thomas, *Alternative America*, pp. 332–33; Newman, *Falling from Grace*, p. 176.

14. Crunden, *Ministers of Reform*, p. x; see also Cohen, "Loss as a Theme," pp. 553–71.

15. Joseph Mayer, review of *SS*, *Annals of the American Academy of Political and Social Science* 327 (January 1960): 150; William Petersen, review of *SS*, *ASR* 25 (February 1960): 125; for the somewhat similar ambivalence of Bruce Barton, see Lears, "From Salvation to Self-Realization," pp. 5 and 29.

16. VP, *HP*, pp. 9, 208–9, 211, 233, and 256; VP, *SS*, p. 3; VP, *WM*, pp. 184, 286–90, and 307; VP, "Resurvey of 'Hidden Persuaders,'" *NYT Magazine*, 11 May 1958, p. 20.

17. Hofstadter, *Age of Reform*, p. 196.

18. RP, interview with author, Chappaquiddick, Mass., 16 August 1991.

19. WW, "Social Problems," pp. 928–29.

20. VP, "Are the Persuaders Still Hiding in Wait?" *Marketing Week*, 7 June 1985, p. 42.

21. See, for example, the favorable reviews of *HP* and *WM*, in the conservative *Shreveport Times* (by KC, 28 April 1957, and by Dorothie Erwin, 16 October 1960).

See also John Tebbel, "How to Review a Best-Seller," *Saturday Review of Literature*, 14 January 1961, pp. 39–40; Eric F. Goldman, in transcript of "The Open Mind," NBC television, 22 May 1960, PPPS; review of *HP*, *Dayton, Ohio, Journal Herald*, 11 May 1957.

22. Nate White, review of *WM*, *Christian Science Monitor*, 6 October 1960.

23. See the following reviews of *HP*: *Hartford Courant*, 5 May 1957; *Washington Post and Times Herald*, 26 April 1957; *Portland* (Oreg.) *Journal*, 16 June 1957; A. C. Spectorsky, review of *HP*, *NYT*, 28 April 1957; also Harry Elmer Barnes, review of *WM*, typescript in PPPS, p. 3.

24. Phyllis Meras, "Social Critic Vance Packard—An Amiable Man Who Listens to the Wind and Fishes for Blues," *VG*, 10 October 1969, VGA.

25. VP, "Comment on a Commentary," in Saxon, *'Oh, Happy, Happy, Happy!'* pp. 3, 4, and 6; VP, typescript of article for Sunday Book Section, *San Francisco Chronicle*, 1959, PPNC; VP, "Some Thoughts on Possible Questions and Answers for TBR," probably 1960, PPPS.

26. VP to CTA, 2 August 1960, PPPS.

27. CTA to VP, 8 August 1960, PPPS.

28. Helen M. Ferrigan to VP, quoting or paraphrasing other people, 23 August 1960, PPPS.

29. VP, interview with author, New Canaan, Conn., 23 February 1991.

30. M. A. Jones to C. D. DeLoach, 26 February 1964; Helen W. Gandy to CTA, 26 February 1964; R. W. Smith to W. C. Sullivan, 3 March 1964. All in FBI file no. 94-59608. I am grateful to Vance Packard for obtaining his files and then passing a copy on to me.

31. VP to author, 17 November 1989, author's possession.

32. Faye Henle, "How the Economy's Critics Really Live," newspaper unknown, 20 January 1961.

33. Transcript of Charles Collingwood television show, ca. 1959, p. E, PPPS.

34. "He Lives by His Philosophy," *New Haven Register*, 22 January 1961.

35. Joan Cook, "Author Reaps Honors, But Not in Own Home," *NYT*, 3 October 1960, p. 27.

36. VP, "Some Thoughts."

37. VP to HP, 1 October 1964, PPNC.

38. Mitchel Levitas, "He Used to Be a Status Seeker Himself," *New York Post*, 31 May 1959.

39. On how Packard talked and thought, see Kacy Tebbel and John Tebbel, interview with author, Southbury, Conn., 20 July 1987.

40. Ehrenreich, *Fear of Falling*, p. 37.

41. VMP, quoted in Martha Emmett, "Hoisted on His Own Status Symbols," *Fairfield County Fair*, 29 November 1959, p. 7.

42. Whitney Darrow, Jr., interview with author, Wilton, Conn., 7 January 1993.

43. Kacy Tebbel, interview with author, Southbury, Conn., 20 July 1987.

44. Jim Doyle, "Author of 'Status Seekers' Seeks Some Status for Himself," newspaper unknown, 24 May 1959.

45. Emmett, "Hoisted."

46. VP, *WM*, pp. 29 and 31.

47. VP, interview with author, New Canaan, Conn., 9 April 1986.

48. VP to KR, 27 September 1957, PPPS; VP to KR, 26 February 1957, PPPS; VP to KR, Tuesday, late 1956 or early 1957, PPPS.

49. VP to KR, probably early to mid-1957, PPPS.

50. VP to KR, 11 May 1957, PPPS; VP to Willis Wing, 16 April 1958, Curtis Brown Ltd. Records, Rare Book and Manuscript Library, Columbia University.

51. Advertisement for *HP*, *NYT Book Review*, 8 September 1957, p. 17; back of dust jacket for *HP*, PPPS; press release for *HP*, 27 March 1957, PPPS.

52. VP to KR, 27 December 1957, PPPS; see also VP to KR, 13 December 1956, PPPS.

53. VP to KR, Saturday, probably early 1957, PPPS.

54. VP to KR, Tuesday, late 1956 or early 1957.

55. VP to KR, 20 February 1957, PPPS.

56. VP to KR, Tuesday, late 1956 or early 1957.

57. VP to KR, 8 January 1958, PPPS; VP to KR, 9 December 1958, PPPS.

58. VP to KR, Friday night, probably early 1959, PPPS.

59. VP to KR, 30 June 1959, PPPS.

60. VP to KR, May (Friday), probably 1959, PPPS; VP to KR, Friday night, probably early 1959.

61. VP, "Prospectus for Class Book," PPPS; dust jacket of *SS*, author's possession.

62. CTA, press release for *SS*, 3 April 1959, PPPS; dust jacket of *SS*.

63. *Boston Globe* and *Chicago Tribune*, quoted in advertisements for *SS*, PPPS.

64. See, for example, the press release: CTA, "Enthusiastic Advance Comments to Vance Packard's 'The Waste Makers,'" 2 September 1960, PPPS.

65. VP to KR, 29 March 1960.

66. Sylvia Porter, quoted in advertisement for *WM*, PPPS.

67. This analysis draws on J. S. Rubin, "Self, Culture, and Self-Culture," p. 794, and J. S. Rubin, "Henry F. May's *The End of American Innocence*," pp. 146–47.

68. E. Long, *American Dream*, pp. 82ff., explores the dimensions of this basic shift, which, she argues, took place in the mid-1950s.

69. Ehrenreich, *Hearts of Men*.

70. Review of *HP*, *Playboy*.

71. In a pamphlet, *Do Your Dreams Match Your Talents?* (Chicago: Science Research Associates, 1960), Packard told his audience of high school students that with purposefulness, ideals, and individualism they could realize their dreams, which he couched in nonmaterialistic terms.

72. E. Long, *American Dream*, pp. 1, 8–9, 82, 86–87, 91–92, and 98.

73. VP, "Abundance: Problems and Potentials," *Social Action* 18 (November 1961), p. 10.

74. VP, in transcript of "The Open Mind," p. 13; VP, in transcript of NBC radio program, "Conversation," 6 May 1957, p. 13, PPPS.

75. VP, "Abundance," p. 5.

76. Ehrenreich, *Fear of Falling*, p. 30.

77. Lears, "Sherwood Anderson," p. 17.

CHAPTER ELEVEN

1. VP, interview with author, New Canaan, Conn., 3 June 1991.

2. VP to EK, 13 June 1960, PPPS; VP to EK, 26 November 1960, PPPS; VP to James Street, 1 November 1962, PPPS; VP, "A Word about Title Possibilities," probably 1962, PPPS.

3. On the concern with positioning the book in relation to Whyte's, see VP to EK, 6 November 1960, PPPS; for another competing book, see Elliott, *Men at the Top*.

4. VP, *PC*, pp. 4, 9, 14, 15, 102, 183, and 267.

5. Ibid., pp. 9, 30–40, 56–65, and 253–54.

6. Packard italicized this phrase; see ibid., p. 308.

7. Ibid., pp. 286–313.

8. For example, see Hugh Stevens, review of VP, *SW*, *Greensboro Record*, 31 August 1968.

9. VP to Street; advertisements for *PC*, PPPS; Bob Wing, review of *PC*, *Shreveport Times*, 28 October 1962; Philip C. Freshwater, review of *PC*, *Sacramento Bee*, 25 November 1962. The letters from readers in PPPS reflected the particularistic focus of the book. Letters exist for all of the books written after 1960, but beginning in the late 1960s they are often scattered throughout the collection at PPNC.

10. VP to EK, 9 May 1964, PPPS.

11. VP to author, 7 April 1992, author's possession.

12. Review of *PC*, *Christian Century*, 31 October 1962; Orville Prescott, review of *PC*, *NYT*, 29 October 1962.

13. Kenneth C. Crabbe, review of *PC*, *Augusta* (Ga.) *Chronicle Herald*, 7 October 1962; review of *PC*, *New York Mirror*, 11 November 1962, sec. 1, pp. 1–2; D. W. Brogan, review of *PC*, *Saturday Review of Literature*, 15 December 1962, pp. 19–20.

14. VP, *PC*, pp. 4 and 275.

15. VP, *NS*, pp. 240–44, tells of some of his activities but uses the appropriate pseudonym "Mr. Diggs."

16. *NYT*, 7 April 1963, p. 77; VP to Paul Hoffman, 9 April 1963, PPNC.

17. VP, interview with author, New Canaan, Conn., 23 February 1991. For impact of this incident, see also CPR, interview with author, Annandale, Va., 31 October 1991.

18. VP, interview with author, New Canaan, Conn., 9 May 1992.

19. VP to William M. Chiariello, 9 February 1964, PPNC.

20. VP to CTA, January 20-odd [1964], PPPS.

21. Kirkus review of *NS*, 16 March [1964], PPPS.

22. Talisman: CPR interview, 31 October 1991.

23. Alex Comfort, review of *SW*, *New Statesman*, 8 November 1968, p. 634. For a discussion of the process of selecting a title, see VP to LGB, 17 September and 1 October 1976, PPLB.

24. VP, *NS*, pp. 4, 13, 207, and 236.

25. Ibid., pp. 299–327.

26. Nan Robertson, "Data Center Held Peril to Privacy," *NYT*, 27 July 1966, p. 41; Nan Robertson, "Data Bank: Peril or Aid?" *NYT*, 7 January 1968, pp. 1 and 52; VP, list of the impact of his books, 1970s, PPNC.

27. VP, *NS*, p. 341.

28. Harold H. Martin, "The Communist Party, U.S.A.," *Saturday Evening Post*, 19 May 1962, p. 20; Robert Gibbon to HP, 13 July 1962, PPNC.

29. John Brooks, review of *NS*, *NYT Book Review*, 15 March 1964, p. 1; VP to KR, Friday 31 [1964], PPPS.

30. VP to Beatrice R. Grant, 26 August 1964, PPNC.

31. BED to VP, 9 April 1964, PPPS.

32. *Brain Watchers* (1962), by Martin L. Gross, had focused on some of the topics that Packard treated.

33. This summary of the field relies on Brenton, *Privacy Invaders*; Dash, Schwartz, and Knowlton, *Eavesdroppers*; M. L. Gross, *Brain Watchers*; Laudon, *Dossier Society*; E. V. Long, *Intruders*; Marx, "Privacy and Technology"; Marx, "Prepared Statement"; Marx, "Communications"; Marx, *Undercover*; A. R. Miller, *Assault on Privacy*; J. M. Rosenberg, *Death of Privacy*; Rule, *Private Lives*; Westin, *Privacy and Freedom*, pp. 3, 195, 248–49, 257, 294, and 378; Westin and Baker, *Databanks*, pp. xiii–xvii and 4; Westin, *Information Technology*; Wheeler, *On Record*.

34. With *Naked Society*, the letters from readers in PPPS were more particularistic in origin and narrower in focus than was true with the trilogy. They contained little passionate protest, evidence of people converted by the book, or challenges on broad issues.

35. VP to author, 7 April 1992.

36. Herbert M. Alexander to KR, 16 April 1964, PPNC.

37. Daniel Aaron, review of *NS*, *New Statesman*, 16 October 1964, p. 584; VP, notations on the review, PPPS; VP, "Seven Steps to Greater Personal Freedom," *Reader's Digest* 88 (April 1966): 123–27.

38. Unsigned memo to VP, probably 1963, PPPS.

39. Michael Shanks, review of *NS*, *Punch*, 7 October 1964.

40. VP, *SW*, pp. 3–5.

41. VP to Baron E. B. von Wehrenalp, 14 January 1967, PPNC.

42. Eleanore B. Luckey and Gilbert D. Nass, "A Comparison of Sexual Attitudes and Behavior in an International Sample," *Journal of Marriage and the Family* 31 (May 1969): 364 ff.; VP, notations on p. 364 of reprint, PPPS.

43. Unnamed academic, quoted in VP to Robert Stein, 3 May 1966, PPPS.

44. VP to Robert Stein, 3 May 1966.

45. VP to CTA, 17 August 1968, PPPS.

46. VP, *SW*, pp. 13, 18, 36, 60, 82, 277, 360–61, 381, 383, 385, 428, and 472; VP, "Working Notes," PPPS; VP, "Working Outline," late 1965 or early 1966, PPPS.

47. VP, *SW*, pp. 13–18 and 428.

48. Ibid., pp. 28–29.

49. Ibid., pp. 36, 60, and 472. Allan Bloom, *Closing of the American Mind*, p. 86.

50. Irvine, *Disorders of Desire*, pp. 11 and 37, discusses these tendencies among sexologists.

51. VP, *SW*, pp. 231, 296, 308, 437, 443, 466–67, and 490. For his reaction to homosexuals, see pp. 80, 128–31, and 390–91.

52. VP to KR, 6 March 1968, PPPS; VP to KR, Memorial Day, [1968], PPPS.

53. CTA to VP, 1 July 1968, PPPS; see also VP to KR, 14 January 1968, PPPS; VP to CTA, Wednesday, [August 1968], PPPS.

54. VP to KR, 23 February 1968, PPNC.

55. *Publishers' Weekly*, PPPS, n.d. p. 48.

56. Kirkus, review of *SW*, PPPS.

57. Jessie Bernard, quote on dust jacket, PPPS.

58. VP to John Keats, 30 September 1968, PPPS; Vidal, *Myra Breckinridge*.

59. VP to author, 7 April 1992.

60. VP to HP, 28 November 1968, PPNC.

61. John O'Hara to Bennett Cerf, 25 February 1961, in Bruccoli, *Selected Letters*, p. 359.

62. Agreement between David McKay Company and VP, dated 30 December 1968, PPNC.

63. Anthony Storr, review of VP, *SW*, *The Sunday Times* (London), 3 November 1960, PPPS.

64. Review of VP, *SW*, *Playboy*, November 1968.

65. Eliot Fremont-Smith, review of *SW*, *NYT*, 16 August 1968.

66. Mintz and Kellogg, *Domestic Revolutions*, pp. 208–9.

67. For a perceptive analysis of the late 1960s as a major turning point in the study of sex, see Irvine, *Disorders of Desire*, esp. pp. 76 and 97.

68. Ira L. Reiss, "How and Why America's Sex Standards Are Changing," in Gagnon and Simon, *Sexual Scene*, p. 49.

69. Gagnon and Simon, *Sexual Conduct*, p. 24; see also Gagnon and Simon, *Sexual Deviance*; Gagnon and Simon, *Sexual Scene*.

70. Advertisement for *SW*, 25 August 1968, source unknown, PPPS.

71. VP, *SW*, p. 281.

72. Hite, *Hite Report*, p. 11; Irvine, *Disorders of Desire*, p. 155.

73. N. O'Neill and G. O'Neill, *Open Marriage*.

74. See William Simon, review of *SW*, *ASR*, pp. 605–6.

75. VP, interview with author, New Canaan, Conn., 20 December 1990, discusses this problem.

76. Simon, review of *SW*.

77. John H. Gagnon, review of *SW*, *Trans-Action* 7 (January 1970): 69–70.

78. VP to Marvin E. Olsen, 19 October 1969, PPPS.

79. VP, letter to editor, *Trans-Action*, PPPS.

80. Kenneth Bridges, review of *SW*, *El Paso Herald-Post*, 14 September 1968, PPPS; VP, marginal marking on review.

81. VP to Raymond Mack, 4 February 1970, PPPS; Raymond Mack to VP, 10 February 1970, PPPS.

82. For an earlier response to commercial music that prefigured Packard's late 1960s attack on youth culture, see VP, testimony, *Hearings before the Subcommittee on Communications of the Committee on Interstate and Foreign Commerce*, U.S. Senate, 85th Cong., 2d sess., on S. 2834 (Washington: GPO, 1958), pp. 109 and 136; for an analysis of his position, see Hill, "Enemy Within," pp. 59–61.

83. Melvin Maddocks, review of *SW*, *Life*, 13 September 1968; see also Geoffrey Gorer, review of *SW*, *Observer*, PPPS.

84. Alex Comfort, review of *SW*, *New Statesman*, 8 November 1968, pp. 634–35.

85. VP interview, 23 February 1991; see also VP interview, 20 December 1990.

86. VP, quoted in tear sheet of article for *Publishers' Weekly*, 5 August 1968, PPPS.

87. VP, *SW*, p. 29.

88. On Packard's attitude toward sexuality, see Tom Maley, telephone conversation with author, 18 February 1992; CPR, interview with author, Chappaquiddick, Mass., 16 August 1991; VPP, interview with author, Goldsboro, Penn., 25 August 1991.

89. Kacy Tebbel and John Tebbel, interview with author, Southbury, Conn., 20 July 1987.

90. VP interview, 20 December 1990.

91. VP interview, 23 February 1991.

92. Ibid.; Connie Sprong, telephone conversation with author, 19 January 1993; Kacy Tebbel and John Tebbel, interview with author, Southbury, Conn., 7 January 1993.

93. VP, "The Reshaping of Man," unpublished manuscript, ca. 1974, PPNC.

94. VP, quoted in Philip H. Dougherty column, *NYT*, 14 November 1972, p. 78.

95. CPR interview, 16 August 1991.

96. VPP interview, 25 August 1991.

97. VP, quoted in Carolyn Anspacher, "Packard Views Negro Revolt," *San Francisco Chronicle*, 19 April 1964, PPPS; VP interview, 23 February 1991.

98. RMT to VP, 21 January 1965, PPPS.

99. Nolan Kerschner to VP, 19 September 1961, PPNC. Packard also headed the National Right to Privacy Committee but resigned when he realized its right-wing bent; VP to author, mid-July 1992, author's possession.

100. Alan Reitman to VP, 9 April 1964, PPNC.

101. Lawrence Bloomgarden to VP, 7 December 1964, PPNC.

102. "Packard," *Contemporary Authors*, p. 372.

103. VP interview, 23 February 1991; VP to Mr. Hollowood, PPPS; VP, "The Kennedy Deal," *Punch*, 1 May 1963, p. 618; Dick Bothwell, "Hedonism Growing in U.S.," clipping from *St. Petersburg Times*, ca. 1963, PPNC.

104. On his feelings toward Nixon, see CPR interview, 16 August 1991.

105. VPP interview, 25 August 1991; RP, interview with author, Chappaquiddick, Mass., 16 August 1991.

106. VP interview, 20 December 1990.

107. VP, "This Is the New Japan," *Saturday Evening Post*, 236 (20 April 1963): 36.

108. VP interview, 23 February 1991.

109. VP to author, 21 May 1989, author's possession; for an announcement of his decision to give speeches, see *Worcester Gazette*, 13 March 1968.

CHAPTER TWELVE

1. VP to author, 15 May 1989, author's possession; VP, "This Strange Era, These Strange Times," unpublished speech, early 1970s, PPNC; VP, *NOS*, pp. x, 321–33, and 334–35.

2. VP to author, 7 April 1992, author's possession. For some of the favorable ones, see Ira Baker, review of *NOS*, *Raleigh News and Observer*, 1 October 1972; James Reston, "'A Nation of Strangers,'" *NYT*, 6 August 1972. In 1975 Monmouth College awarded him an honorary degree; "Packard," *Contemporary Authors*, p. 372.

3. VP quoted in "The Publisher: Good Guy or Bad Guy? Vance Packard and Donald Westlake Differ," *Publishers' Weekly* 203 (30 April 1973): 44.

4. Morris Janowitz, review of *NOS*, *Chicago Sun-Times*, 17 September 1972, sec. 5, p. 18. For the position Janowitz took, see his 1972 article "Professionalization." For an explication of his views that unintentionally helps explain why he would be sympathetic to Packard, see Halliday, "Sociology's Fragile Professionalism."

5. See the following reviews of *NOS* in *AJS*, 79 (July 1973): Amos H. Hawley, p. 165; Claude S. Fischer, pp. 172–73; Brian J. L. Berry, pp. 173–75. The quote is from Fischer.

6. VP, interview with author, New Canaan, Conn., 3 June 1991.

7. Gans, *Levittowners*, pp. v, vi, 417–19, and 432.

8. Herbert J. Gans, "Vance Packard Misperceives the Way Most American Movers Live," *Psychology Today* 6 (September 1972): 20–23, 26, and 28.

9. VP, letter to editor, *Psychology Today* 6 (December 1972): 4.

10. Gans, *More Equality*, pp. xi–xii; Gans, *Levittowners*, p. 432; for his fullest defense of popular culture, see Gans, *Popular Culture and High Culture*, esp. p. vii.

11. VP to GY, 17 June [1979?], PPPS; on the book's lasting impact, see Carin Rubenstein, "The Neighbors Aren't Strangers after All," *NYT*, 7 January 1993, sec. C, p. 1.

12. Pierson, *Moving American*, pp. 38 and 250; Bennis and Slater, *Temporary Society*, pp. 4 and 6; Gordon, *Lonely in America*.

13. VP interview, 3 June 1991; VP, *NOS*, p. 114.

14. Before publication, a historian warned Packard against assuming that mobil-

ity was greater in the 1970s than in the nineteenth century; Peter R. Knights to VP, 6 August 1972, PPNC.

15. For a satire of Packard's approach, see Calvin Trillin, "By and Large: That's America," *Life* 73 (8 September 1972): 20.

16. VP, *NOS*, p. 1.

17. Ibid., pp. 211–27.

18. Peter Michelson, review of *NOS*, *New Republic*, 7 October 1972, pp. 25–27.

19. Lewis, *La Vida*, p. xx.

20. VP, *NOS*, p. 285; David Gelman, review of *NOS*, *Newsday*.

21. VP, *NOS*, p. 2.

22. Michelson, review, p. 26.

23. Gelman, review.

24. VP, "Color and Harmony: What Works and What Does Not Work," [spring or summer of 1973], PPNC, pp. 1–3, 7, 11, and 17.

25. VP to ER, 3 March 1968, PPNC.

26. VP, *NOS*, pp. 283–84.

27. VP, "Color and Harmony," p. 1.

28. In the 1970s he served on a committee to celebrate the fiftieth anniversary of the ACLU and ran unsuccessfully for a position on its national board; Arthur J. Goldberg to VP, 24 February 1970, PPNC; VP to Aryeh Neier, 14 April 1974, PPNC.

29. VP, interview with author, New Canaan, Conn., 1 December 1990.

30. VP, "An Introduction for the Eighties," *HP* (revised edition; N.Y.: Pocket Books, 1980), pp. ix–xi; VP, "We Waste Billions While World Starves," *Connecticut Sunday Herald*, 25 May 1969, NCHS; Martin J. Funke, "Bursting 'American Dream' Fuels Our Gas-Guzzling Nation," *Providence Journal*, 11 October 1979, p. B-7; VP, "The Reshaping of Man or 15 Reasons Why Our Times Will Go Down in Man's History," unpublished talk, about 1974, PPNC; VP, "Need and Strategy for Energy Education," unpublished talk, [1979], PPNC.

31. VP, interview with author, New Canaan, Conn., 23 February 1991.

32. VP to Miss Bailey and Mrs. Wilkin, 28 or 29 September 1962, PPNC.

33. Peter J. Steincrohn, "Stop Getting Excited!," *AM* 145 (January 1948): 138; VP to EK, 10 July [1962 or 1963], PPPS.

34. VP to Helen [at lecture agency], [fall 1964], PPNC.

35. VP, interview with author, New Canaan, Conn., 9 December 1990.

36. Middy Darrow, interview with author, Wilton, Conn., 7 January 1993; Middy Darrow and Whitney Darrow, Jr., to author, 29 April 1993, author's possession.

37. VP to CTA, 15 July 1972, PPPS.

38. VP, interview with author, New Canaan, Conn., 3 June 1987; VP interview, 3 June 1991; Folkenroth, "Finish First," p. 68; VP, marginal note on copy of Folkenroth, "Finish First," author's possession; VP, "Author's Questionnaire," 7 January 1977, PPLB; VP, note to author, undated, author's possession.

39. Sigh of relief: CPR, interview with author, Chappaquiddick, Mass., 16 August 1991; VPP, interview with author, Goldsboro, Penn., 25 August 1991.

40. VP to author, mid-July 1992, author's possession; VP, *NOS*, p. ix. For other discussions of his separation from life in New Canaan, see CTA, "Vance Packard's 'A Nation of Strangers'"; VP, "A Proposal to Simplify Life by Reducing the Moves We Make," around 1979, PPNC; VP interview, 1 December 1990; VP interview, 3 June 1991.

41. VP interview, 1 December 1990; VP interview, 3 June 1991.

42. Nancy Holmes, "At Home: San Miguel Allende," *Town and Country*, February 1983, p. 155.

43. CPR, interview with author, Annandale, Va., 31 October 1991, discussed the financial arrangements of the stays in Mexico.

44. VP to author, mid-July 1992; VP, interview with author, Chappaquiddick, Mass., 14 August 1991; VP interview, 3 June 1991; VP to Thomas Scott and Robert Somerlott, 23 October 1975, PPNC; VP, "Chappy Has Its Problems Too, but How Near Heaven Dare You Go?" *VG*, 21 June 1974, VGA. From 1977 to 1978 he served as head of the Chappaquiddick Island Association; VP to author, Thanksgiving 1988, author's possession.

45. VP to GY, 26 January 1980, PPNC; VP to author, mid-July 1992; VP interview, 3 June 1991; VP interview, 1 December 1990; VP, "A Proposal to Simplify Life"; VP, *NOS*, p. ix.

46. VP, "Go, Man, Go!," draft of talk to 1954 Eastern Conference of American Association of Advertising Agencies, PPNC, pp. 1–2.

47. West, *American Authors*, pp. 144–45.

48. Contract between VP and David McKay Company, 1 January 1973, PPNC; Eric Pace, "M'Kay to Be Sold to British Firm," *NYT*, 11 December 1973; Alden Whitman, "Three Top Editorial Executives at McKay Resign in Policy Rift," *NYT*, 21 December 1974; VP interview, 3 June 1991; VP to June [Robbins], 21 December 1974, PPNC.

49. VP to Alan Latman, probably late December 1974, PPNC.

50. John Tebbel, interview with author, Southbury Conn., 7 January 1993.

51. VP to Scott and Somerlott.

52. Arthur Thornhill, Jr., telephone conversation with author, 8 January 1992; *One Hundred and Fifty Years of Publishing*, pp. 107–8, 110, 119, 177, and 179–80; VP to author, 30 August 1991, author's possession; contract between VP and Little, Brown and Company, 30 July 1975, PPNC.

53. For information on Packard's attitude toward religion, see VPP interview, 25 August 1991.

54. ER, interview with author, New York, N.Y., 16 January 1991; Helen Maley, telephone conversation with author, 19 February 1992.

55. Folkenroth, "Finish First," p. 57.

56. Tom Maley, telephone conversation with author, 18 February 1992.

57. Darrow and Darrow, 29 April 1993; for description of his friends, see VP to author, 23 February 1993, author's possession; VP to author, 14 March 1993, author's possession.

58. Charles Saxon, interview with author, New Canaan, Conn., 7 June 1987.

59. John Fuller, quoted in Folkenroth, "Finish First," p. 72.

60. Linda Matchan, "Vance Packard," *Boston Globe*, 7 September 1983, including quotes from RP and CPR.

61. Charles Saxon, quoted in Dorsey, "Packard," p. 10.

62. Helen Maley, telephone conversation; Matchan, "Vance Packard."

63. Tom Maley, telephone conversation; Middy Darrow, interview, 7 January 1993.

64. Folkenroth, "Finish First," p. 57.

65. VP, "Biographical Material: Virginia Packard," mid-1980s, author's possession; "Portraiture Done with Likeness, Individuality, and Paint Quality," *New Canaan Advertiser*, 7 October 1965, NCHS; flier from Alan-Mayhew, Ltd. (gallery) on Martha's Vineyard, PPNC.

66. VP, "The Super Society," unpublished book proposal, probably 1972, PPPS; VP to author, 5 June 1991, author's possession; VP to LGB, 1 August 1977, PPLB; agreement between VP and Little, Brown, 28 March 1978, PPNC.

67. VP, "Regarding Subject Matter for Packard Book #7 for David McKay Company," [Summer 1973], PPNC; VP, *PS*, pp. 20–25, 72–92, 125–27, and 187.

68. VP, *PS*, pp. 4 and 360. The words in this quotation were italicized in the book.

69. "Packard," *Contemporary Authors*, p. 372; Donald Gould, review of *PS*, *New Scientist*, 16 February 1978, p. 447; Ed Domaingue, review of *PS*, *New Haven Register*, 6 November 1977; Bess White Cochran, review of *PS*, *Tennessean*, 15 January 1978; Warren Bennis, review of PS, *Journal of Applied Behavioral Science* 14 (1978): 236–47; VP to LGB, 15 May 1978, PPLB.

70. Christopher Lehmann-Haupt, review of *PS*, *NYT*, 13 October 1977, sec. C, p. 20; VP to LGB, 22 October 1977, PPLB; Christopher Lehmann-Haupt, "Note," *NYT*, 8 November 1977, p. 31; VP interview, 3 June 1991.

71. VP to LGB, 15 May 1978; VP to author, mid-May 1992, author's possession; VP to author, 30 August 1991; VP, interview with author, New Canaan, Conn., 9 May 1992; VP to author, 7 April 1992; Folkenroth, "Finish First," p. 70. *Naked Society* and *People Shapers* were among the many factors that shaped German public opinion on the issue they covered; *Hidden Persuaders* had some influence on legislation in the European Community on the permissible range of advertising techniques; Wilhelm Steinmüller to author, 15 January 1993, author's possession.

72. Miss Hawkes to LGB et al., 8 August 1977, PPLB; for general income, VP to author, 7 April 1992; agreement between VP and Little, Brown, 28 March 1978.

73. Thomas L. Benson, review of *PS*, *Christian Century*, 23 November 1977, p. 1096.

74. VP to KR, 3 September 1964, PPPS; VP to HP, 26 December 1974, PPNC; VP to LGB, 17 December 1976, PPPS.

75. VP to GY, 17 June [1979?].

76. Hacker, "Farewell to the Family?" p. 37.

77. Edelman, *Families in Peril*, pp. ix–x and 2–3.

78. VP interview, 3 June 1991; Ray Roberts, telephone conversation with author, 12 June 1992.

79. GY to VP, 22 June 1979, PPPS.

80. VP to HP, 23 February 1982, PPNC; to date this meeting, see GY to VP, 22 June 1979.

81. VP to HP, 23 February 1982.

82. [VP to HP], "Re contract with Little Brown" [early 1983], PPNC.

83. VP to GY, 31 March 1983, PPPS.

84. VP, *OEC*, pp. xix–xx, 26–33, and 322–23.

85. Ibid., pp. xvi–xviii, 24–25, 30, 33, 63, and 78.

86. Ibid., pp. 25–32 and 107.

87. Ibid., pp. x and 7–8.

88. VP to author, 7 April 1992; VP to HP, probably January 1984, PPNC; Don Feder, review of *OEC*, *Boston Herald*, 13 November 1983; review of *OEC*, *Kirkus Reviews*, 15 July 1983; Elaine Kendall, review of *OEC*, *Los Angeles Times*, 23 August 1983.

89. Robert Jay Lifton, review of Rosenblatt, *Children of War*, *NYT Book Review*, 28 August 1983, p. 1; Ellen Chesler, review of *OEC*, p. 12.

90. VP interview, 3 June 1991.

91. Christopher Lasch, review of *OEC*, *New Republic*, 8 August 1983, pp. 32–34.

92. See Lasch, *Haven*, esp. pp. 134–41.

93. In understanding the discussions about the family in the period, I have benefited from books cited in the bibliography, including Skolnick, *Embattled Paradise*; Mintz and Kellogg, *Domestic Revolutions*; and Coontz, *The Way We Never Were*.

94. See Pogrebin, *Family Politics*; Bird, *Two-Paycheck Marriage*; Thorne, "Feminist Rethinking"; American Homes Economics Association statement, ca. 1979, quoted in Pines, *Back to Basics*, p. 145.

95. See Kenniston, *All Our Children*, and Edelman, *Families in Peril*.

96. On the Right's position on family issues, see LaHaye, *Battle for the Family*; Murray, *Losing Ground*; and Pines, *Back to Basics*.

97. Kramer, *In Defense of the Family*, pp. 5–6, 25–26, 109–110, and 198.

98. *Our Endangered Children* resembled Berger and Berger, *War over the Family* (1983) in important ways, but the Bergers were acutely aware of the context in which they were writing as they searched for "a middle ground"; Berger and Berger, *War over the Family*, pp. vii and 203.

99. VP, *OEC*, pp. xv–xviii; Theriot, *Nostalgia on the Right*, demonstrates how the new social history should have undermined the conservative depiction of the past.

100. VP, *OEC*, pp. 9, 326, 328, and 343.

101. Roman and Raley, *Indelible Family*, p. 4; VP to CTA, 24 June 1980, PPNC.

102. VP, interview with author, New Canaan, Conn., 20 December 1990.

103. VP interview, 3 June 1991.

104. Jim Doyle, "Author of 'Status Seekers' Seeks Some Status for Himself," 24 May 1959, newspaper unknown.

105. Gerald Green, telephone conversation with author, 21 December 1992.

106. Lewis Nichols, "Talk with Vance Packard," *NYT Book Review*, 15 March 1964, p. 44.

107. On the celebrity status of best-sellers, see Boorstin, *Image*, pp. 163 and 168.

108. Roberts, telephone conversation, first alerted me to the impact of television documentaries; for treatment of their history, see Hammond, *Image Decade*, pp. 12, 54, 80, 151, and 189–90; Barnouw, *Tube of Plenty*, pp. 145, 247, and 284.

109. On the distinction between experience and observation, see ER interview, 16 January 1991.

110. On the New Journalism, see Hellmann, *Fables of Fact*; Hollowell, *Fact and Fiction*, pp. ix, 5, 10–14, 22–26, 32, 38–40, and 48–58; N. Mills, "Introduction"; Wolfe, "New Journalism," pp. 3–52.

111. VP to CTA, 24 June 1980.

112. VP to author, 28 October 1992, author's possession.

113. Most of this summary relies on VP to author, 30 September 1992, author's possession.

114. [VP to HP], "Re contract with Little Brown"; VP to HP, 30 September 1983, PPNC; agreement with Little, Brown, 23 January 1984, PPNC; VP to HP, 10 November 1983, PPNC.

115. VP to author, 28 October 1992.

116. Helen Maley, telephone conversation.

117. On the increased importance of his grandchildren and family, see CPR interview, 16 August 1991; Helen Maley, telephone conversation discussed the role reversal after Virginia's stroke; on Vance's life in these years, see Matchan, "Packard."

118. VP to GY, 26 January 1980.

119. VP to HP, 31 May 1984, PPNC; VP interview, 3 June 1991.

120. VP interview, 20 December 1990; Jo Chesworth, "Who's Minding the Kids?" *Penn Stater*, November–December, 1983, p. 7; VP to RR, 9 July 1988, PPLB; VP to RR, 1 May 1985, PPLB.

CHAPTER THIRTEEN

1. VP, *UR*, pp. vi and 309.

2. Ibid., pp. 310–12.

3. VP to HP, 12 September 1983, PPNC.

4. VP, *UR*, pp. 306, 320, 326–27, 332, 333, and 336.

5. Ibid., pp. 313–14, 317–19, and 321; VP, lecture, City Club Forum of Cleveland, 15 March 1989, tape recording, author's possession. In the original, "an element . . . problems" was italicized.

6. VP to RR, 1 May 1985, PPLB.

7. VP, *UR*, pp. 53 and 63.

8. Maria Gallagher, review of *UR*, *NYT Book Review*, 19 February 1989, sec. 7, p. 21.

9. Whitney Darrow, Jr., interview with author, Wilton, Conn., 7 January 1993.

10. Gallagher, review of *UR*.

11. Ken Roberts, review of *UR*, *Miami Herald*, 19 March 1989.

12. VP to RR, 8 December 1984, PPLB.

13. VP to Mr. Bakel, 29 March 1990, PPNC.

14. VP, *UR*, pp. 316–17.

15. VP, "Packard revised outline, August '86," PPLB.

16. VP, *UR*, p. 4.

17. VP, "THE ULTRA RICH: How Much Is Too Much?" book proposal, [fall 1983], PPLB; VP, "Packard revised outline."

18. M. P. Allen, *Founding Fortunes*, esp. pp. 246–306.

19. VP, *UR*, pp. 208–212. For key works on the relation between wealth and power, see C. W. Mills, *Power Elite*; Lundberg, *Rich and Super-Rich*; and the books by Domhoff listed in the bibliography.

20. VP, *UR*, pp. vii and 308–9.

21. E. Digby Baltzell, review of *UR*, *USA Today*, 10 February 1989.

22. VP, "THE ULTRA RICH: How Much Is Too Much?"; VP, *UR*, p. 21.

23. VP, quoted in interview, *USA Today*, 2 February 1989.

24. John H. Rice, review of *UR*, *Berkshire Eagle*, 12 February 1989.

25. VP, *UR*, pp. 286 and 321. For reviews that saw the book as a landmark in the attack on Reagan, see Robert Reno, review of *UR*, *Newsday*, 14 February 1989; Jonathan Yardley, review of *UR*, *Washington Post*, 18 January 1989.

26. VP to author, 28 October 1992, author's possession.

27. VP to author, 24 February 1992, author's possession; VP to author, 7 April 1992, author's possession; VP, notes on author's letter of 13 May 1992, author's possession.

28. VP, *UR*, p. 11.

29. The bibliography contains a fuller listing of the period's books on money and wealth.

30. On the ideology of Middle Americans in this period, see Lasch, *True and Only Heaven*, pp. 477–532.

31. The following discussion relies on Steinfels, *Neoconservatives*.

32. For his preference for the term "conserving" rather than "conservative" to describe himself, see VP, notations on author's copy of Dorsey, "Packard," p. 21.

33. On the politics of Packard and his friends, I am relying on John Tebbel, interview with author, Southbury, Conn., 7 January 1993; Middy Darrow and Whitney Darrow, Jr., interview with author, Wilton Conn., 7 January 1993; Gerald Green, telephone conversation with author, 21 December 1992.

34. VP, *UR*, pp. 47 and 169.

35. VP to VM, summer or early fall, 1938, PPNC.

36. Tear sheet of article on VP in *Publishers' Weekly*, 5 August 1968, PPPS; VP, notes on proof copy of same, PPPS; see also, Donovan Bess, "Social Critic without a Sting," *San Francisco Chronicle*, 14 September 1963.

37. Andrew J. Shanley, "Vance Packard Turns His Pen to Concern for Plight of Children," *VG*, 8 July 1983.

38. VP, quoted in ibid.

39. VP, quoted in Roy Martin, "Packard and the People Shapers," *Reading* (England) *Evening Post*, 28 February 1978, PPPS.

40. VP, interview with author, New Canaan, Conn., 20 December 1990.

41. VP to Bakel.

42. VP, lecture, City Club Forum.

43. VP to author, 10 April 1992, author's possession.

44. Lasch, *True and Only Heaven*, p. 274, discussed many of these components of the definition of a good life.

45. VP, quoted in Dorsey, "Packard," pp. 8–15 and 20–22.

46. VP, quoted in Linda Matchan, "Vance Packard," *Boston Globe*, 7 September 1983; VP to Jane [Eager?], 4 May 1988, PPNC; VP interview, 20 December 1990; Jo Chesworth, "Who's Minding the Kids?" *Penn Stater*, November–December 1983, p. 7; VP, interview with author, New Canaan, Conn., 9 May 1992.

Bibliography

BOOKS BY VANCE PACKARD

How to Pick a Mate: The Guide to a Happy Marriage. With Clifford R. Adams. New York: E. P. Dutton, 1946.

Animal I.Q.: The Human Side of Animals. New York: Dial Press, 1950.

The Hidden Persuaders. New York: David McKay, 1957.

The Status Seekers. New York: David McKay, 1959.

The Waste Makers. New York: David McKay, 1960.

The Pyramid Climbers. New York: McGraw-Hill, 1962.

The Naked Society. New York: David McKay, 1964.

The Sexual Wilderness: The Contemporary Upheaval in Male-Female Relationships. New York: David McKay, 1968.

A Nation of Strangers. New York: David McKay, 1972.

The People Shapers. Boston: Little, Brown, 1977.

Our Endangered Children: Growing Up in a Changing World. Boston: Little, Brown, 1983.

The Ultra Rich: How Much Is Too Much? Boston: Little, Brown, 1989.

OTHER SOURCES

The following list contains most of the sources on which I have relied. It does not, however, include such items as articles by Vance Packard, reviews of Packard's books, or feature stories on him.

Aldrich, Nelson W., Jr. *Old Money: The Mythology of America's Upper Class.* New York: Alfred A. Knopf, 1988.

Alfred Politz Research, Inc. *The Audiences of Nine Magazines: Their Size and Characteristics.* [New York]: Cowles Magazines, 1955.

Allen, Frederick Lewis. *The Big Change: America Transforms Itself, 1900–1950.* New York: Harper and Brothers, 1952.

Allen, Michael P. *The Founding Fortunes: A New Anatomy of the Super-Rich Families in America.* New York: E. P. Dutton, 1987.

Argyris, Chris. *Interpersonal Competence and Organizational Effectiveness.* Homewood, Ill.: Richard D. Irwin, 1962.

——. *Personality and Organization: The Conflict between System and the Individual.* New York: Harper and Brothers, 1957.

Atkeson, Mary M. *The Woman on the Farm.* New York: Century, 1924.

Auletta, Ken. *Greed and Glory on Wall Street: The Fall of the House of Lehman.* New York: Random House, 1986.

Baldwin, Faith. *Station Wagon Set.* New York: P. F. Collier and Son, 1938.

Bane, Mary Jo. *Here to Stay: American Families in the Twentieth Century.* New York: Basic Books, 1976.

Bannister, Robert C. *Sociology and Scientism: The American Quest for Objectivity, 1880–1940.* Chapel Hill: University of North Carolina Press, 1987.

Baritz, Loren. *City on a Hill: A History of Ideas and Myths in America.* New York: John Wiley and Sons, 1964.

——. *The Servants of Power: A History of the Use of Social Science in American Industry.* Middletown, Conn.: Wesleyan University Press, 1960.

Barlett, Donald L., and James B. Steele. *America: What Went Wrong?* Kansas City, Mo.: Andrews and McMeel, 1992.

Barnouw, Erik. *Tube of Plenty: The Evolution of American Television.* New York: Oxford University Press, 1975.

Barron, Hal S. "Bringing Forth Strife: The Ironies of Dairy Organization in the New York Milkshed, 1880–1930." Paper presented at the annual meeting of the Organization of American Historians, Louisville, Kentucky, April 1991.

Batra, Ravi. *The Great Depression of 1990.* New York: Simon and Schuster, 1987.

Bauer, Raymond A. "Limits of Persuasion." *Harvard Business Review* 36 (September–October 1958): 105–10.

Bauer, Raymond A., and Stephen A. Greyser. *Advertising in America: The Consumer View.* Boston: Harvard Graduate School of Business Administration, 1968.

Baughman, James L. *The Republic of Mass Culture: Journalism, Filmmaking, and Broadcasting in America since 1941.* Baltimore: Johns Hopkins University Press, 1992.

Baym, Nina. *Novels, Readers, and Reviewers: Responses to Fiction in Antebellum America.* Ithaca: Cornell University Press, 1984.

Bell, Daniel. *The Cultural Contradictions of Capitalism.* New York: Basic Books, 1976.

——. *The End of Ideology: On the Exhaustion of Political Ideas in the Fifties.* Glencoe, Ill.: Free Press, 1960.

——. "The 'Intelligentsia' in American Society." In *The Winding Passage: Essays and Sociological Journeys, 1960–1980,* pp. 119–37. [1976] Cambridge, Mass.: ABT Books, 1980.

Bellah, Robert N., Richard Madsen, William H. Sullivan, Ann Swidler, Steven M. Tipton. *Habits of the Heart: Individualism and Commitment in American Life.* Berkeley: University of California Press, 1985.

Bender, Thomas. "The Erosion of Public Culture: Cities, Discourses, and Professional Disciplines." In *The Authority of Experts: Studies in History and Theory,* edited by Thomas L. Haskell, pp. 84–106. Bloomington: Indiana University Press, 1984.

——. *Intellect and Public Life: Essays on the Social History of Academic Intellectuals in the United States.* Baltimore: Johns Hopkins University Press, 1993.

——. *New York Intellect: A History of Intellectual Life in New York City, from 1750 to the Beginnings of Our Time.* New York: Alfred A. Knopf, 1987.

Bennis, Warren G., and Philip E. Slater. *The Temporary Society*. New York: Harper and Row, 1968.

Bercovitch, Sacvan. *The American Jeremiad*. Madison: University of Wisconsin Press, 1978.

Berger, Brigitte, and Peter L. Berger. *The War over the Family: Capturing the Middle Ground*. Garden City, N.Y.: Doubleday, 1983.

Bezilla, Michael. *Penn State: An Illustrated History*. University Park, Pa.: Pennsylvania State University Press, 1985.

Bird, Caroline. *The Two-Paycheck Marriage: How Women at Work Are Changing Life in America*. New York: Rawson, Wade Publishers, 1979.

Bird, Caroline (with Sara Welles Briller). *Born Female: The High Cost of Keeping Women Down*. New York: David McKay, 1968.

Blake, Casey N. *Beloved Community: The Cultural Criticism of Randolph Bourne, Van Wyck Brooks, Waldo Frank, and Lewis Mumford*. Chapel Hill: University of North Carolina Press, 1990.

Blocker, Jack S., Jr. *Retreat from Reform: The Prohibition Movement in the United States, 1890–1913*. Westport, Conn.: Greenwood Press, 1976.

Bloom, Alexander. *Prodigal Sons: The New York Intellectuals and Their World*. New York: Oxford University Press, 1986.

Bloom, Allan. *The Closing of the American Mind: How Higher Education Has Failed Democracy and Impoverished the Souls of Today's Students*. New York: Simon and Schuster, 1987.

Boller, Paul F., Jr., and Ronald Story. "Urban Anguish." In *A More Perfect Union: Documents in U.S. History*, vol. 2, edited by Paul F. Boller, Jr., and Ronald Story, pp. 286–87. 3d ed. Boston: Houghton Mifflin, 1992.

Bombeck, Erma. *Family: Ties That Bind . . . and Gag!* New York: McGraw-Hill, 1987.

——. *Motherhood: The Second Oldest Profession*. New York: McGraw-Hill, 1983.

Boorstin, Daniel J. *The Image, or What Happened to the American Dream*. New York: Atheneum, 1962.

Boston Women's Health Course Collective. *Our Bodies, Our Selves: A Course by and for Women*. Boston: New England Free Press, 1971.

Bottomore, T. B. *Critics of Society: Radical Thought in North America*. London: George Allen and Unwin, 1967.

Bowker Annual of Library and Book Trade Information. New York: R. R. Bowker, 1975–93.

Boylan, James. "Publicity for the Great Depression: Newspaper Default and Literary Reportage." In *Mass Media between the Wars: Perceptions of Cultural Tension, 1914–1941*, edited by Catherine L. Covert and John D. Stevens, pp. 159–75. Syracuse: Syracuse University Press, 1984.

Brecher, Edward M. *The Sex Researchers*. Boston: Little, Brown, 1969.

Breines, Wini. "Domineering Mothers in the 1950s: Image and Reality." *Women's Studies International Forum* 8 (1985): 601–8.

——. *Young, White, and Miserable: Growing Up Female in the Fifties*. Boston: Beacon Press, 1992.

Brenton, Myron. *The Privacy Invaders*. New York: Coward-McCann, 1964.

Brick, Howard. *Daniel Bell and the Decline of Intellectual Radicalism: Social Theory and Political Reconciliation in the 1940s*. Madison: University of Wisconsin Press, 1986.

Brooks, John. *The Great Leap: The Past Twenty-five Years in America*. New York: Harper and Row, 1966.

Bruccoli, Matthew J., ed. *Selected Letters of John O'Hara*. New York: Random House, 1978.

Brucker, Herbert. *The Changing American Newspaper*. New York: Columbia University Press, 1937.

Brunger, Ronald A. "The Ladies Aid Societies in Michigan Methodism." *MH* 5 (1967): 31–48.

Bucke, Emory Stevens, ed. *The History of American Methodism*. 3 vols. New York: Abingdon Press, 1964.

Buckley, Christopher. Review of *In All His Glory: The Life of William S. Paley; The Legendary Tycoon and his Brilliant Circle*, by Sally Bedell Smith. *NYT*, 4 November 1990, sec. 7, pp. 1, 40.

Bulmer, Martin. *The Chicago School of Sociology: Institutionalization, Diversity, and the Rise of Sociological Research*. Chicago: University of Chicago Press, 1984.

Burner, David. *John F. Kennedy and a New Generation*. Glenview, Ill.: Scott, Foresman, 1988.

Burrough, Bryan, and John Helyar. *Barbarians at the Gate: The Fall of RJR Nabisco*. New York: Harper and Row, 1990.

Buxton, William, and Stephen T. Turner. "From Education to Expertise: Sociology as a 'Profession.'" In *Sociology and Its Publics: The Forms and Fates of Disciplinary Organization*, edited by Terence C. Halliday and Morris Janowitz, pp. 373–407. Chicago: University of Chicago Press, 1992.

Carson, Rachel. *Silent Spring*. Boston: Houghton Mifflin, 1962.

Casey, Douglas R. *Crisis Investing: Opportunities and Profits in the Coming Great Depression*. N.p.: Stratford Press, 1980; distributed by Harper and Row.

Caute, David. *The Fellow-Travellers: Intellectual Friends of Communism*. Rev. ed. New Haven: Yale University Press, 1988.

Cayton, Mary K. "The Making of an American Prophet: Emerson, His Audiences, and the Rise of the Culture Industry in Nineteenth-Century America." *AHR* 92 (June 1987): 597–620.

Chafe, William H. *The Unfinished Journey: America since World War II*. 2d ed. New York: Oxford University Press, 1991.

Chase, Stuart. *The Tragedy of Waste*. New York: Macmillan, 1925.

Chase, Stuart, and F. J. Schlink. *Your Money's Worth: A Study in the Waste of the Consumer's Dollar*. New York: Macmillan, 1927.

Chesler, Ellen. *Woman of Valor: Margaret Sanger and the Birth Control Movement in America.* New York: Simon and Schuster, 1992.

Clark, Norman H. *Deliver Us from Evil: An Interpretation of American Prohibition.* New York: W. W. Norton, 1976.

Clecak, Peter. *America's Quest for the Ideal Self: Dissent and Fulfillment in the 1960s and 1970s.* New York: Oxford University Press, 1983.

Cloete, Stuart. *The Third Way.* Boston: Houghton Mifflin, 1947.

Cohen, David K. "Loss as a Theme in Social Policy." *Harvard Educational Review* 46 (November 1976): 553–71.

Cohn, Jan. *Creating America: George Horace Lorimer and the "Saturday Evening Post."* Pittsburgh: University of Pittsburgh Press, 1989.

Coles, Robert. *Children of Crisis: A Study of Courage and Fear.* Boston: Little, Brown, 1967.

Collins, Randall. Review of *The Idea of Social Structure: Papers in Honor of Robert K. Merton* (1975), edited by Lewis A. Coser. *Contemporary Sociology* 6 (March 1977): 150–54.

——. *Sociology since Midcentury: Essays in Theory Cumulation.* New York: Academic Press, 1981.

Comfort, Alex. *The Joy of Sex: A Cordon Bleu Guide to Lovemaking.* New York: Simon and Schuster, 1972.

Conquest, Robert. *The Great Terror: A Reassessment.* New York: Oxford University Press, 1990.

Cooney, Terry A. *The Rise of the New York Intellectuals: "Partisan Review" and Its Circle, 1934–1945.* Madison: University of Wisconsin Press, 1986.

Coontz, Stephanie. *The Way We Never Were: American Families and the Nostalgia Trip.* New York: Basic Books, 1992.

Cosby, Bill. *Fatherhood.* Garden City, N.Y.: Doubleday, 1986.

Coser, Lewis A. "American Notebook: Portraits and Problems." *Dissent* 4 (Summer 1957): 210–13.

——. *The Functions of Social Conflict.* New York: Free Press, 1956.

——. "A New Political Atmosphere in America?" *Dissent* 6 (Winter 1959): 10–11.

——. "Presidential Address: Two Methods in Search of a Substance." *ASR* 40 (December 1975): 691–700.

——. "Sociological Theory from the Chicago Dominance to 1965." *Annual Review of Sociology* 2 (1976): 145–60.

——. "What Shall We Do?" *Dissent* 3 (Spring 1956): 156–65.

Coser, Lewis, and Irving Howe. "Images of Socialism." *Dissent* 1 (Spring 1954): 122–38.

Cowley, W. H., and Willard Waller. "A Study of Student Life." *Journal of Higher Education* 6 (March 1935): 132–42.

Craig, Robert H. "The Underside of History: American Methodism, Capitalism, and Popular Struggle." *MH* 24 (January 1989): 73–88.

Cressey, Paul G. *The Taxi-Dance Hall: A Sociological Study in Commercialized Recreation and City Life.* Chicago: University of Chicago Press, 1932.

Crow, Martha F. *The American Country Girl.* New York: Frederick A. Stokes, 1915.

Crowl, James W. *Angels in Stalin's Paradise: Western Reporters in Soviet Russia, 1917–1937, a Case Study of Louis Fischer and Walter Duranty.* Washington, D.C.: University Press of America, 1982.

Crunden, Robert M. *Ministers of Reform: The Progressives' Achievement in American Civilization, 1889–1920.* Urbana: University of Illinois Press, 1982.

Darnton, Robert. *The Great Cat Massacre and Other Episodes in French Cultural History.* New York: Basic Books, 1984.

——. "Writing News and Telling Stories." *Daedalus* 104 (Spring 1975): 175–94.

Dash, Samuel, Richard F. Schwartz, and Robert E. Knowlton. *The Eavesdroppers.* New Brunswick, N.J.: Rutgers University Press, 1959.

Davidson, Cathy N. *Revolution and the Word: The Rise of the Novel in America.* New York: Oxford University Press, 1986.

——. "Towards a History of Books and Readers." *AQ* 40 (March 1988): 7–17.

——, ed. *Reading in America: Literature and Social History.* Baltimore: Johns Hopkins University Press, 1989.

Davis, Kenneth C. *Two-Bit Culture: The Paperbacking of America.* Boston: Houghton Mifflin, 1984.

DeMott, Benjamin. *The Imperial Middle: Why Americans Can't Think Straight about Class.* New York: William Morrow, 1990.

Denning, Michael. " 'The Special American Conditions': Marxism and American Studies." *AQ* 38 (1986): 356–80.

Dennis, Patrick. *Auntie Mame: An Irreverent Escapade.* New York: Vanguard Press, 1955.

Dickstein, Morris. *Gates of Eden: American Culture in the Sixties.* New York: Basic Books, 1977.

Diggins, John P. *The Proud Decades: America in War and Peace, 1941–1960.* New York: W. W. Norton, 1988.

——. *Up from Communism: Conservative Odysseys in American Intellectual History.* New York: Harper and Row, 1985.

D'Innocenzo, Michael. "A Literature of Warning." Essay accompanying the 1992 exhibit "Books That Most Affected Humankind" at the Port Washington, New York, Public Library.

Domhoff, G. William. *The Bohemian Grove and Other Retreats: A Study in Ruling-Class Cohesiveness.* New York: Harper and Row, 1974.

——. *The Higher Circles: The Governing Class in America.* New York: Random House, 1970.

——. *The Power Elite and the State: How Policy Is Made in America.* New York: Aldine de Gruyter, 1990.

——. *The Powers That Be: Processes of Ruling-Class Domination in America.* New York: Random House, 1978.

——. *Who Rules America?* Englewood Cliffs, N.J.: Prentice-Hall, 1967.

——. *Who Rules America Now?: A View for the '80s.* Englewood Cliffs, N.J.: Prentice-Hall, 1983.

Donaldson, Scott. *The Suburban Myth*. New York: Columbia University Press, 1969.

Dorsey, Gary. "The Absurdly Happy Story of Vance Packard." *Hartford Courant, Northeast*, October 5, 1986, pp. 8–15, 20–22.

Draper, Hal. "The Student Movement of the Thirties: A Political History." In *As We Saw the Thirties: Essays on Social and Political Movements of a Decade*, edited by Rita J. Simon, pp. 151–89. Urbana: University of Illinois Press, 1967.

Dubofsky, Melvyn, and Warren Van Tine. *John L. Lewis: A Biography*. Abridged ed. Urbana: University of Illinois Press, 1986.

Dunaway, Wayland F. *History of the Pennsylvania State College*. State College: Pennsylvania State College, 1946.

Duranty, Walter. *I Write As I Please*. New York: Simon and Schuster, 1935.

Eagan, Eileen. *Class, Culture, and the Classroom: The Student Peace Movement of the 1930s*. Philadelphia: Temple University Press, 1981.

Eastman, E. R. *These Changing Times: A Story of Farm Progress during the First Quarter of the Twentieth Century*. New York: Macmillan, 1927.

——. *The Trouble Maker*. New York: Macmillan, 1925.

Edelman, Marian Wright. *Families in Peril: An Agenda for Social Change*. Cambridge: Harvard University Press, 1987.

Editors of *Fortune*. *The Changing American Market*. Garden City, N.Y.: Hanover House, 1955.

Ehrenreich, Barbara. *Fear of Falling: The Inner Life of the Middle Class*. New York: Pantheon Books, 1989.

——. *The Hearts of Men: American Dreams and the Flight from Commitment*. Garden City, N.Y.: Anchor Press, 1983.

Elliott, Osborn. *Men at the Top*. New York: Harper and Brothers, 1959.

Elson, Ruth M. *Myths and Mores in American Best Sellers, 1865–1965*. New York: Garland, 1985.

Falcoff, Mark, and Fredrick B. Pike. *The Spanish Civil War, 1936–39: American Hemispheric Perspectives*. Lincoln: University of Nebraska Press, 1982.

Fish, Stanley. *Is There a Text in This Class? The Authority of Interpretive Communities*. Cambridge: Harvard University Press, 1980.

Fiske, John. *Understanding Popular Culture*. Boston: Unwin Hyman, 1989.

FitzGerald, Frances. *Fire in the Lake: The Vietnamese and the Americans in Vietnam*. Boston: Little, Brown, 1972.

Flaherty, David. *Protecting Privacy in Surveillance Societies: The Federal Republic of Germany, Sweden, France, Canada, and the United States*. Chapel Hill: University of North Carolina Press, 1989.

Florinsky, Michael. *Fascism and National Socialism: A Study of the Economic and Social Policies of the Totalitarian State*. New York: Macmillan, 1936.

——. *Toward an Understanding of the U.S.S.R.: A Study in Government, Politics, and Economic Planning*. New York: Macmillan, 1939.

Folkenroth, Nancy. "He Wanted to Finish First." *T & G: Town and Gown*, October 1988.

——. "Men in the Making." *T & G: Town and Gown*, March 1993.

Fox, Frank W. *Madison Avenue Goes to War: The Strange Military Career of American Advertising, 1941–45*. Provo, Utah: Brigham Young University Press, 1975.

Fox, Stephen. *The Mirror Makers: A History of American Advertising and Its Creators*. New York: William Morrow, 1984.

Friedan, Betty. *The Feminine Mystique*. New York: W. W. Norton, 1963.

Friedrich, Otto. *Decline and Fall*. New York: Harper and Row, 1970.

Friedrichs, Robert W. *A Sociology of Sociology*. New York: Free Press, 1970.

Gaddini, Eugenio. "Notes on the Mind-Body Question." *International Journal of Psycho-Analysis* 68 (1987): 315–29.

Gagnon, John H., and William Simon. *Sexual Conduct: The Social Sources of Human Sexuality*. Chicago: Aldine Publishing, 1973.

——, eds. *Sexual Deviance*. New York: Harper and Row, 1967.

——, eds. *The Sexual Scene*. Chicago: Aldine Publishing, 1970.

Galbraith, John Kenneth. *The Affluent Society*. Boston: Houghton Mifflin, 1958.

Gans, Herbert J. *The Levittowners: Ways of Life and Politics in a New Suburban Community*. New York: Pantheon Books, 1967.

——. *Middle American Individualism: The Future of Liberal Democracy*. New York: Free Press, 1988.

——. *More Equality*. New York: Pantheon Books, 1973.

——. *Popular Culture and High Culture*. New York: Basic Books, 1974.

——. *The Urban Villagers: Group and Class in the Life of Italian-Americans*. New York: Free Press of Glencoe, 1962.

Gil, Karen M., Francis J. Keefe, Hugh A. Sampson, Cynthia C. McCaskill, Judith Rodin, and James E. Crisson. "The Relation of Stress and Family Environment to Atopic Dermatitis Symptoms in Children." *Journal of Psychosomatic Research* 31 (1987): 673–84.

Gilbert, James. *Another Chance: Postwar America, 1945–1985*. 2d ed. Chicago: Dorsey Press, 1986.

——. *A Cycle of Outrage: America's Reaction to the Juvenile Delinquent in the 1950s*. New York: Oxford University Press, 1986.

——. *Writers and Partisans: A History of Literary Radicalism in America*. New York: John Wiley and Sons, 1968.

Gitlin, Todd. *The Sixties: Years of Hope, Days of Rage*. New York: Bantam Books, 1987.

Givens, Charles J. *Financial Self-Defense: How to Win the Fight for Financial Freedom*. New York: Simon and Schuster, 1990.

——. *Wealth without Risk: How to Develop a Personal Fortune without Going Out on a Limb*. New York: Simon and Schuster, 1988.

Glazer, Nathan. "The Rediscovery of the Family." *Commentary* 65 (March 1978): 49–56.

Gleason, Philip. "Identifying Identity: A Semantic History." *JAH* 69 (March 1983): 910–31.

Goode, William J., Frank Furstenberg, Jr., and Larry R. Mitchell, eds. *Willard W. Waller on the Family, Education, and War: Selected Writings*. Chicago: University of Chicago Press, 1970.

Goodman, Paul. *Growing Up Absurd: Problems of Youth in the Organized System*. New York: Random House, 1960.

Gordon, Suzanne. *Lonely in America*. New York: Simon and Schuster, 1976.

Gorrell, Donald K. *The Age of Social Responsibility: The Social Gospel in the Progressive Era, 1900–1920*. Macon, Ga.: Mercer University Press, 1988.

———. "The Social Creed and Methodism through Eighty Years." *MH* 26 (July 1988): 213–28.

Griffith, Robert. "Dwight D. Eisenhower and the Corporate Commonwealth." *AHR* 87 (February 1982): 87–122.

Gross, John. *The Rise and Fall of the Man of Letters: A Study of the Idiosyncratic and the Humane in Modern Literature*. New York: Macmillan, 1969.

Gross, Martin L. *The Brain Watchers*. New York: Random House, 1962.

Guttmann, Allen. *The Wound in the Heart: America and the Spanish Civil War*. New York: Free Press of Glencoe, 1962.

Hacker, Andrew. "Farewell to the Family?" *New York Review of Books* 29 (18 March 1982): 37–45.

Hackett, Alice P., and James H. Burke. *80 Years of Best Sellers, 1895–1975*. New York: R. R. Bowker, 1977.

Halberstam, David. *The Fifties*. New York: Villard Books, 1993.

Hall, Stuart. "Culture, the Media, and the 'Ideological Effect.'" In *Mass Communication and Society*, edited by James Curran, Michael Gurevitch, and Janet Woollacott, pp. 315–48. London: Edward Arnold, 1977.

Halliday, Terence C. "Sociology's Fragile Professionalism." In *Sociology and Its Publics: The Forms and Fates of Disciplinary Organization*, edited by Terence C. Halliday and Morris Janowitz, pp. 3–41. Chicago: University of Chicago Press, 1992.

Hammond, Charles M., Jr. *The Image Decade: Television Documentary: 1965–1975*. New York: Hastings House, 1981.

Hanifin, Jon M. "Pharmacophysiology of Atopic Dermatitis." *Clinical Review of Allergy* 4 (1986): 43–65.

Haskell, Thomas L. *The Emergence of Professional Social Science: The American Social Science Association and the Nineteenth-Century Crisis of Authority*. Urbana: University of Illinois Press, 1977.

Hayek, Friedrich A. von. *The Road to Serfdom*. Chicago: University of Chicago Press, 1944.

Hays, Samuel P. *Beauty, Health, and Permanence: Environmental Politics in the United States, 1955–1985*. Cambridge: Cambridge University Press, 1987.

———. "From Conservation to Environment." *Environmental Review* 6 (Fall 1982): 14–41.

Heald, Morrell. *Transatlantic Vistas: American Journalists in Europe, 1900–1940*. Kent, Ohio: Kent State University Press, 1988.

Hearn, Charles R. *The American Dream in the Great Depression*. Westport, Conn.: Greenwood Press, 1977.

Hellmann, John. *Fables of Fact: The New Journalism as Fiction*. Urbana: University of Illinois Press, 1981.

Henry, Jules. *Culture against Man.* New York: Random House, 1963.

Higham, John. "Changing Paradigms—The Collapse of Consensus History." *JAH* 76 (September 1989): 460–66.

Hill, Trent. "The Enemy Within: Censorship in Rock Music in the 1950s." In *Present Tense: Rock and Roll Culture*, edited by Anthony DeCurtis, pp. 39–71. Durham: Duke University Press, 1992.

Hite, Shere. *The Hite Report: A Nationwide Study of Female Sexuality*. New York: Dell Publishing, 1976.

Hobson, Laura Z. *Gentleman's Agreement: A Novel*. New York: Simon and Schuster, 1947.

Hodgson, Godfrey. *America in Our Time*. New York: Random House, 1976.

Hofstadter, Richard. *The Age of Reform: From Bryan to F.D.R.* New York: Alfred A. Knopf, 1955.

Hollander, Paul. *Political Pilgrims: Travels of Western Intellectuals to the Soviet Union, China, and Cuba, 1928–1978*. New York: Oxford University Press, 1981.

Hollowell, John. *Fact and Fiction: The New Journalism and the Nonfiction Novel*. Chapel Hill: University of North Carolina Press, 1977.

Horowitz, Daniel. *The Morality of Spending: Attitudes toward the Consumer Society in America, 1875–1940*. Baltimore: Johns Hopkins University Press, 1985.

Horowitz, David A., Peter N. Carroll, and David Lee. *On the Edge: A History of America since World War II*. St. Paul: West Publishing, 1989.

Horowitz, Helen Lefkowitz. *Campus Life: Undergraduate Cultures from the End of the Eighteenth Century to the Present*. New York: Alfred A. Knopf, 1987.

Horowitz, Irving L. *C. Wright Mills: An American Utopian*. New York: Free Press, 1983.

Howe, Frederic C. *Confessions of a Reformer*. New York: Charles Scribner's Sons, 1925.

Howe, Irving. "The New York Intellectuals." In *Decline of the New*, pp. 211–65. New York: Harcourt, Brace, and World, 1970.

———. "This Age of Conformity." *Partisan Review* 21 (January–February 1954): 7–31.

Hughes, Helen M. *News and the Human Interest Story*. Chicago: University of Chicago Press, 1940.

Huxley, Aldous. *Brave New World and Brave New World Revisited*. New York: Harper and Row, 1965.

Iacocca, Lee. *Iacocca: An Autobiography*. New York: Bantam Books, 1984.

Inglis, Fred. *The Cruel Peace: Everyday Life in the Cold War*. New York: Basic Books, 1991.

Irvine, Janice. *Disorders of Desire: Sex and Gender in Modern American Sexology*. Philadelphia: Temple University Press, 1990.

Isserman, Maurice. *If I Had a Hammer. . . The Death of the Old Left and the Birth of the New Left.* New York: Basic Books, 1987.

——. *Which Side Were You On? The American Communist Party During the Second World War.* Middletown, Conn.: Wesleyan University Press, 1982.

"J." *The Sensuous Woman: The First How-to Book for the Female Who Yearns to Be All Woman.* New York: Lyle Stuart, 1969.

Jacoby, Russell. *The Last Intellectuals: American Culture in the Age of Academe.* New York: Basic Books, 1987.

Janowitz, Morris. "Professionalization of Sociology." *AJS* 78 (July 1972): 105–35.

Jezer, Marty. *The Dark Ages: Life in the United States, 1945–1960.* Boston: South End Press, 1982.

Johnson, Michael L. *The New Journalism: The Underground Press, the Artists of Nonfiction, and Changes in the Established Media.* Lawrence: University Press of Kansas, 1971.

Johnston, Jill. *Lesbian Nation: The Feminist Solution.* New York: Simon and Schuster, 1973.

Jumonville, Neil. "The New York Intellectuals and Mass Culture Criticism." *Journal of American Culture* 12 (Spring 1989): 87–95.

Kallet, Arthur, and F. J. Schlink. *100,000,000 Guinea Pigs: Dangers in Everyday Foods, Drugs, and Cosmetics.* New York: Vanguard Press, 1933.

Kazin, Alfred. *Starting Out in the Thirties.* Boston: Little, Brown, 1965.

——. *A Walker in the City.* New York: Harcourt, Brace, 1951.

Keats, John. *The Crack in the Picture Window.* Boston: Houghton Mifflin, 1956.

——. *The Insolent Chariots.* Philadelphia: J. B. Lippincott, 1958.

——. *The New Romans: An American Experience.* Philadelphia: J. B. Lippincott, 1967.

Kenniston, Kenneth, and the Carnegie Council on Children. *All Our Children: The American Family under Pressure.* New York: Harcourt Brace Jovanovich, 1977.

King, Mary L. *Portrait of New Canaan: The History of a Connecticut Town.* New Canaan: New Canaan Historical Society, 1981.

Kinsey, Alfred C., Wardell B. Pomeroy, and Clyde E. Martin. *Sexual Behavior in the Human Male.* Philadelphia: W. B. Saunders, 1948.

Kinsey, Alfred C., Wardell B. Pomeroy, Clyde E. Martin, and Paul H. Gebhard. *Sexual Behavior in the Human Female.* Philadelphia: W. B. Saunders, 1953.

Kleinegger, Christine. "Out of the Barns and into the Kitchens: Transformations in Farm Women's Work in the First Half of the Twentieth Century." In *Women, Work, and Technology: Transformations,* edited by Barbara D. Wright, Myra M. Ferree, Gail O. Mellow, Linda H. Lewis, Maria-Luz D. Samper, Robert Asher, and Kathleen Ciaspell, pp. 162–81. Ann Arbor: University of Michigan Press, 1987.

Kluckhohn, Clyde. "Mid-Century Manners and Morals." In *Twentieth Century Unlimited: From the Vantage Point of the First Fifty Years,* edited by Bruce Bliven, pp. 303–15. Philadelphia: J. B. Lippincott, 1950.

Knightley, Phillip. *The First Casualty, from the Crimea to Vietnam: The War Correspondent as Hero, Propagandist, and Myth Maker.* New York: Harcourt Brace Jovanovich, 1975.

Kramer, Rita. *In Defense of the Family: Raising Children in America Today.* New York: Basic Books, 1983.

Kristol, Irving. *Two Cheers for Capitalism.* New York: Basic Books, 1978.

Krupnick, Mark. *Lionel Trilling and the Fate of Cultural Criticism.* Evanston: Northwestern University Press, 1986.

Krutch, Joseph Wood. *The Modern Temper: A Study and a Confession.* New York: Harcourt, Brace, 1929.

LaHaye, Tim. *The Battle for the Family.* Old Tappan, N.J.: Fleming H. Revell, 1982.

Lapham, Lewis H. *Money and Class in America: Notes and Observations on Our Civil Religion.* New York: Weidenfeld and Nicolson, 1988.

Larrabee, Eric. *The Self-Conscious Society.* Garden City, N.Y.: Doubleday, 1960.

Lasch, Christopher. *The Culture of Narcissism: American Life in an Age of Diminishing Expectations.* New York: W. W. Norton, 1979.

——. *Haven in a Heartless World: The Family Besieged.* New York: Basic Books, 1977.

——. *The New Radicalism in America, 1889–1963: The Intellectual as a Social Type.* New York: Alfred A. Knopf, 1965.

——. *The True and Only Heaven: Progress and Its Critics.* New York: W. W. Norton, 1991.

Laudon, Kenneth C. *Dossier Society: Value Choices in the Design of National Information Systems.* New York: Columbia University Press, 1986.

Lears, T. J. Jackson. "From Salvation to Self-Realization: Advertising and the Therapeutic Roots of the Consumer Culture, 1880–1930." In *The Culture of Consumption: Critical Essays in American History, 1880–1980,* edited by Richard W. Fox and T. J. Jackson Lears, pp. 3–38. New York: Pantheon Books, 1983.

——. "A Matter of Taste: Corporate Cultural Hegemony in a Mass-Consumption Society." In *Recasting America: Culture and Politics in the Age of Cold War,* edited by Lary May, pp. 38–57. Chicago: University of Chicago Press, 1989.

——. *No Place of Grace: Antimodernism and the Transformation of American Culture, 1880–1920.* New York: Pantheon Books, 1981.

——. "Sherwood Anderson: Looking for the White Spot." In *The Power of Culture: Critical Essays in American History,* edited by Richard W. Fox and T. J. Jackson Lears, pp. 13–37. Chicago: University of Chicago Press, 1993.

Leff, Mark H. "The Politics of Sacrifice on the American Home Front in World War II." *JAH* 77 (March 1991): 1296–1318.

Lerner, Max. *America As a Civilization: Life and Thought in the United States Today.* New York: Simon and Schuster, 1957.

Leuchtenburg, William E. *Franklin D. Roosevelt and the New Deal: 1932–1940.* New York: Harper and Row, 1963.

Lewis, Oscar. *La Vida: A Puerto Rican Family in the Culture of Poverty—San Juan and New York*. New York: Random House, 1966.

Lhamon, W. T., Jr. *Deliberate Speed: The Origins of a Cultural Style in the American 1950s*. Washington, D.C.: Smithsonian Institution Press, 1990.

Liebowitz, Nathan. *Daniel Bell and the Agony of Modern Liberalism*. Westport, Conn.: Greenwood Press, 1985.

Lindemann, James E., and Sally J. Lindemann. *Growing Up Proud: A Parent's Guide to the Psychological Care of Children with Disabilities*. New York: Warner Books, 1988.

Lindsey, Karen. *Friends As Family*. Boston: Beacon Press, 1981.

Lipset, Seymour Martin. *Political Man: The Social Bases of Politics*. 1960. Garden City, N.Y.: Doubleday, 1963.

Lipset, Seymour M., and Natalie Rogoff. "Class and Opportunity in Europe and the U.S.: Some Myths and What the Statistics Show." *Commentary* 18 (December 1954): 562–68.

Lipset, Seymour M., and Neil J. Smelser. "Change and Controversy in Recent American Sociology." *British Journal of Sociology* 12 (March 1961): 41–51.

——. "The Setting of Sociology in the 1950's." In *Sociology: The Progress of a Decade*, edited by Seymour M. Lipset and Neil J. Smelser, pp. 1–13. Englewood Cliffs, N.J.: Prentice-Hall, 1961.

Lipsitz, George. *Time Passages: Collective Memory and American Popular Culture*. Minneapolis: University of Minnesota Press, 1990.

Livingston, James. *Origins of the Federal Reserve System: Money, Class, and Corporate Capitalism, 1890–1913*. Ithaca: Cornell University Press, 1986.

Long, Edward V. *The Intruders: The Invasion of Privacy by Government and Industry*. New York: Frederick A. Praeger, 1966.

Long, Elizabeth. *The American Dream and the Popular Novel*. Boston: Routledge and Kegan Paul, 1985.

——. "Women, Reading, and Cultural Authority: Some Implications of the Audience Perspective in Cultural Studies." *AQ* 38 (Fall 1986): 591–612.

Lowenthal, Leo. "Biographies in Popular Magazines." In *Radio Research: 1942–1943*, edited by Paul F. Lazarsfeld and Frank Stanton, pp. 507–48, 581–85. New York: Duell, Sloan, and Pearce, 1944.

Lukas, Anthony. *Common Ground: A Turbulent Decade in the Lives of Three American Families*. New York: Alfred A. Knopf, 1985.

Lundberg, Ferdinand. *The Rich and the Super-Rich: A Study in the Power of Money Today*. New York: Lyle Stuart, 1968.

Lynd, Robert S., and Helen M. Lynd. *Middletown: A Study of Contemporary American Culture*. New York: Harcourt, Brace, 1929.

Lynes, Russell. *The Domesticated Americans*. New York: Harper and Row, 1963.

——. *Snobs: A Guidebook to Your Friends, Your Enemies, Your Colleagues, and Yourself*. New York: Harper and Brothers, 1950.

——. *A Surfeit of Honey*. New York: Harper and Brothers, 1957.

——. *The Tastemakers*. New York: Harper and Brothers, 1954.

"M." *The Sensuous Man: The First How-to Book for the Man Who Wants to Be a Great Lover*. New York: Lyle Stuart, 1971.

McCarthy, Mary. "America the Beautiful." *Commentary* 4 (September 1947): 201–7.

McCormack, Mark H. *What They Don't Teach You at Harvard Business School: Notes from a Street-Smart Executive*. New York: Bantam Books, 1984.

McCusker, John J. "How Much Is That in Real Money? A Historical Price Index for Use as a Deflator of Money Values in the Economy of the United States." *Proceedings of the American Antiquarian Society* 101 (October 1991): 297–373.

Macdonald, Dwight. "'Fortune' Magazine." *The Nation* 144 (8 May 1937): 527–30.

——. "Masscult and Midcult." In Dwight Macdonald, *Against the American Grain*, pp. 3–75. [1960]. New York: Random House, 1962.

——. "A Theory of Mass Culture." *Diogenes*, no. 3 (Summer 1953): 1–17.

McInnis, Raymond G. *Books That Influenced the Modern World: A Reader's Guide to Major Nonfiction Writings of the Twentieth Century*. Forthcoming.

McLuhan, Marshall, and Quentin Fiore. *The Medium Is the Message*. New York: Random House, 1967.

McMurry, Sally. *Families and Farmhouses in Nineteenth-Century America: Vernacular Design and Social Change*. New York: Oxford University Press, 1988.

Madison, Charles A. *Book Publishing in America*. New York: McGraw-Hill, 1966.

Magalis, Elaine. *Conduct Becoming to a Woman: Bolted Doors and Burgeoning Missions*. N.p.: Women's Division, Board of Global Ministries, United Methodist Church, [1973].

Mailloux, Steven. *Interpretive Conventions: The Reader in the Study of American Fiction*. Ithaca: Cornell University Press, 1982.

Mann, Thomas. *The Coming Victory of Democracy*. New York: Alfred A. Knopf, 1938.

——. "Europe Beware." In Thomas Mann, *Order of the Day: Political Essays and Speeches of Two Decades*. [1935] New York: Alfred A. Knopf, 1942.

——. "Mankind, Take Care!" *Atlantic Monthly* 162 (August 1938): 178–84.

——. "'Mass und Wert.'" In Thomas Mann, *Order of the Day: Political Essays and Speeches of Two Decades*. [1936] New York: Alfred A. Knopf, 1942.

Marchand, Roland. "Visions of Classlessness, Quests for Dominion: American Popular Culture, 1945–1960." In *Reshaping America: Society and Institutions 1945–1960*, edited by Robert H. Bremner and Gary W. Reichard, pp. 165–90. Columbus: Ohio State University Press, 1982.

Marcuse, Herbert. *One-Dimensional Man: Studies in the Ideology of Advanced Industrial Society*. Boston: Beacon Press, 1964.

Mark, Eduard. "October or Thermidor? Interpretations of Stalinism and the Perception of Soviet Foreign Policy in the United States, 1927–1947." *AHR* 94 (October 1989): 937–62.

Marx, Gary T. "Communications Advances Raise Privacy Concerns." *Christian Science Monitor*, 2 January 1992.

——. "Prepared Statement Concerning Privacy for Consumers and Workers Act before the Subcommittee on Employment and Productivity, Senate Labor and Human Resources Committee, 24 September 1991." Author's possession.

——. "Privacy and Technology." *The World and I*, September 1990, pp. 523–41.

——. *Undercover: Police Surveillance in America*. Berkeley: University of California Press, 1988.

——, ed. *Muckraking Sociology: Research as Social Criticism*. New Brunswick, N.J.: Transactions Books, 1972.

Masters, William H., and Virginia E. Johnson. *Human Sexual Response*. Boston: Little, Brown, 1966.

Matthews, Fred H. *Quest for an American Sociology: Robert E. Park and the Chicago School*. Montreal: McGill-Queen's University Press, 1977.

Matusow, Allen J. *The Unraveling of America: A History of Liberalism in the 1960s*. New York: Harper and Row, 1984.

May, Elaine T. *Homeward Bound: American Families in the Cold War Era*. New York: Basic Books, 1988.

May, Lary. Introduction to *Recasting America: Culture and Politics in the Age of Cold War*. Chicago: University of Chicago Press, 1989.

Mayer, Martin. *Madison Avenue, U.S.A.* New York: Harper and Brothers, 1958.

Meyerowitz, Joanne. "Beyond the Feminine Mystique: A Reassessment of Postwar Mass Culture, 1946–1958." *JAH* 79 (March 1993): 1455–82.

Miller, Arthur R., *Assault on Privacy: Computers, Data Banks, and Dossiers*. Ann Arbor: University of Michigan Press, 1971.

Miller, Douglas T., and Marion Nowak. *The Fifties: The Way We Really Were*. Garden City, N.Y.: Doubleday, 1977.

Miller, James. *'Democracy Is in the Streets': From Port Huron to the Siege of Chicago*. New York: Simon and Schuster, 1987.

Millett, Kate. *Sexual Politics*. Garden City, N.Y.: Doubleday, 1970.

Mills, C. Wright. *The Power Elite*. New York: Oxford University Press, 1956.

——. *The Sociological Imagination*. New York: Oxford University Press, 1959.

——. *White Collar: The American Middle Classes*. New York: Oxford University Press, 1951.

Mills, Nicolaus. "Introduction," *The New Journalism: A Historical Anthology*, pp. xi–xx. New York: McGraw-Hill, 1974.

Mintz, Steven, and Susan Kellogg. *Domestic Revolutions: A Social History of American Family Life*. New York: Free Press, 1988.

Mitchell, Edward B. "The American Farm Woman As She Sees Herself." In U.S. Department of Agriculture, *Yearbook of the United States Department of Agriculture 1914*, pp. 311–18. Washington: Government Printing Office, 1915.

Morgan, Marabel. *The Total Woman*. Old Tappan, N.J.: F. H. Revell, 1973.

Mott, Frank L. *A History of American Magazines: 1865–1885*. Vol. 3. Cambridge: Harvard University Press, 1938.

Murphy, James E. "Tabloids as an Urban Response." In *Mass Media between the Wars: Perceptions of Cultural Tension, 1914–1941*, edited by Catherine L.

Covert and John D. Stevens, pp. 55–69. Syracuse: Syracuse University Press, 1984.

Murray, Charles. *Losing Ground: American Social Policy, 1950–1980*. New York: Basic Books, 1984.

Nader, Ralph. *Unsafe at Any Speed: The Designed-in Dangers of the American Automobile*. New York: Grossman, 1965.

Nelson, Michael. "What's Wrong with Sociology." *Washington Monthly* 10 (June 1978): 43–49.

Newman, Katherine S. *Falling from Grace: The Experience of Downward Mobility in the American Middle Class*. New York: Free Press, 1988.

Niebuhr, H. Richard. *The Social Sources of Denominationalism*. Cleveland: World Publishing, 1929.

Oakley, J. Ronald. *God's Country: America in the Fifties*. New York: Dembner Books, 1986.

Ogilvy, David. *Confessions of an Advertising Man*. New York: Atheneum, 1963.

Ohmann, Richard. "The Shaping of a Canon: U.S. Fiction, 1960–1975." *Critical Inquiry* 10 (September 1983): 199–223.

——. "Where Did Mass Culture Come From? The Case of Magazines." *Berkshire Review* 16 (1981): 85–101.

O'Neill, Nena, and George O'Neill. *Open Marriage: A New Life Style for Couples*. New York: M. Evans, 1972.

O'Neill, William L. *American High: The Years of Confidence, 1945–1960*. New York: Free Press, 1986.

——. *A Better World; The Great Schism: Stalinism and the American Intellectuals*. New York: Simon and Schuster, 1982.

One Hundred and Fifty Years of Publishing: 1837–1987. New York: Little, Brown, 1987.

Osterud, Nancy Grey. *Bonds of Community: The Lives of Farm Women in Nineteenth-Century New York*. Ithaca: Cornell University Press, 1991.

——. "'She Helped Me Hay It as Good as a Man': Relations among Women and Men in an Agricultural Community." In *"To Toil the Livelong Day": America's Women at Work, 1780–1980*, edited by Carol Groneman and Mary Beth Norton, pp. 87–97. Ithaca: Cornell University Press, 1987.

Packard, Cindy. *Hell's Bells*. New York: Atheneum, 1983.

"Packard, Vance (Oakley)." In *Contemporary Authors*, pp. 372–77. New Revision Series. Detroit: Gale Research, 1982.

Parsons, Talcott. "Some Problems Confronting Sociology as a Profession." *ASR* 24 (August 1959): 547–59.

Pells, Richard H. *The Liberal Mind in a Conservative Age: American Intellectuals in the 1940s and 1950s*. New York: Harper and Row, 1985.

——. *Radical Visions and American Dreams: Culture and Social Thought in the Depression Years*. New York: Harper and Row, 1973.

Perrett, Geoffrey. *A Dream of Greatness: The American People, 1945–1963*. New York: Coward, McCann and Geoghegan, 1979.

Perry, Lewis. *Intellectual Life in America: A History*. New York: Franklin Watts, 1984.

Peters, Thomas J., and Robert H. Waterman, Jr. *In Search of Excellence: Lessons from America's Best-Run Companies*. New York: Harper and Row, 1982.

Petersen, William. "Is America Still the Land of Opportunity? What Recent Studies Show about Social Mobility." *Commentary* 16 (November 1953): 477–86.

Phillips, Kevin P. *The Politics of Rich and Poor: Wealth and the American Electorate in the Reagan Aftermath*. New York: Random House, 1990.

Pierson, George W. *The Moving American*. New York: Alfred A. Knopf, 1973.

Pines, Burton Y. *Back to Basics: The Traditionalist Movement That Is Sweeping Grass-Roots America*. New York: William Morrow, 1982.

Pitkin, Walter B. *Life Begins at Forty*. New York: McGraw-Hill, 1932.

Podhoretz, Norman. *Breaking Ranks: A Political Memoir*. New York: Harper and Row, 1979.

———. *Making It*. New York: Random House, 1967.

Pogrebin, Letty Cottin. *Family Politics: Love and Power on an Intimate Frontier*. New York: McGraw-Hill, 1983.

Polenberg, Richard. *One Nation Divisible: Class, Race, and Ethnicity in the United States since 1938*. New York: Viking Press, 1980.

Pope, Daniel. *The Making of Modern Advertising*. New York: Basic Books, 1983.

Potter, David. *People of Plenty: Economic Abundance and the American Character*. Chicago: University of Chicago Press, 1954.

Pronovost, Gilles. "Culture, Conditions of Production, and Cultural Ideologies." *Society and Leisure* 4 (Spring 1981): 11–23.

Prospects for America: The Rockefeller Panel Reports. New York: Doubleday, 1961.

Radway, Janice A. "The Book-of-the-Month Club and the General Reader: The Uses of 'Serious Fiction.'" In *Reading in America: Literature and Social History*, edited by Cathy N. Davidson, pp. 259–84. Baltimore: Johns Hopkins University Press, 1989.

———. "Reading Is Not Eating: Mass-Produced Literature and the Theoretical, Methodological, and Political Consequences of a Metaphor." *Book Research Quarterly* 2 (Fall 1986): 7–29.

———. *Reading the Romance: Women, Patriarchy, and Popular Literature*. Chapel Hill: University of North Carolina Press, 1984.

———. "The Scandal of the Middlebrow: The Book-of-the-Month Club, Class Fracture, and Cultural Authority." *South Atlantic Quarterly* 89 (Fall 1990): 703–36.

Reuben, David R. *Any Woman Can! Love and Sexual Fulfillment for the Single, Widowed, Divorced . . . and Married*. New York: David McKay, 1971.

———. *Everything You Always Wanted to Know about Sex, But Were Afraid to Ask, Explained*. New York: David McKay, 1969.

Rich, Frank. "The Best Years of Our Lives?" *New Republic*, 7 and 14 September 1992, pp. 38–43.

Riesman, David. *The Lonely Crowd: A Study of the Changing American Character*. New Haven: Yale University Press, 1950.

Rischin, Moses. "When the New York Savants Go Marching In." *Reviews in American History* 17 (June 1989): 289–300.

Roberts, Geoffrey. *The Unholy Alliance: Stalin's Pact with Hitler*. Bloomington: Indiana University Press, 1989.

Robinson, Paul. *The Modernization of Sex: Havelock Ellis, Alfred Kinsey, William Masters, and Virginia Johnson*. New York: Harper and Row, 1976.

Roell, Craig H. Review of *All Consuming Images: The Politics of Style in Contemporary Culture*, by Stuart Ewen. *JAH* 76 (March 1990): 1335–36.

Roman, Mel, and Patricia E. Raley. *The Indelible Family*. New York: Rawson, Wade Publishers, 1980.

Rorty, James. *Our Master's Voice: Advertising*. New York: John Day, 1934.

Rosenberg, Harold. *The Tradition of the New*. New York: Horizon Press, 1959.

Rosenberg, Jerry M. *The Death of Privacy*. New York: Random House, 1969.

Rosenberg, Norman L., and Emily S. Rosenberg. *In Our Times: America since World War II*. 3d ed. Englewood Cliffs, N.J.: Prentice-Hall, 1987.

Rosenblatt, Roger. *Children of War*. Garden City, N.Y.: Doubleday, 1983.

Ross, Andrew. *No Respect: Intellectuals and Popular Culture*. New York: Routledge, 1989.

Ross, Dorothy. *The Origins of American Social Science*. Cambridge: Cambridge University Press, 1991.

Rostenberg, Adolph, Jr. "Psychosomatic Concepts in Atopic Dermatitis—a Critique." *Archives of Dermatology* 79 (June 1959): 692–99.

Rubin, Joan Shelley. "Between Culture and Consumption: The Mediations of the Middlebrow." In *The Power of Culture: Critical Essays in American History*, edited by Richard W. Fox and T. J. Jackson Lears, pp. 163–91. Chicago: University of Chicago Press, 1993.

——. "Henry F. May's *The End of American Innocence*." *Reviews in American History* 18 (March 1990): 142–49.

——. *The Making of Middlebrow Culture*. Chapel Hill: University of North Carolina Press, 1992.

——. "Self, Culture, and Self-Culture in Modern America: The Early History of the Book-of-the-Month Club." *JAH* 71 (March 1985): 782–806.

Rubin, Lillian B. *Worlds of Pain: Life in the Working-Class Family*. New York: Basic Books, 1976.

Rule, James B. *Private Lives and Public Surveillance: Social Control in the Computer Age*. New York: Schocken Books, 1973.

Saxon, Charles. *"Oh, Happy, Happy, Happy!"* New York: Golden Press, 1960.

Schiller, Dan. *Objectivity and the News: The Public and the Rise of Commercial Journalism*. Philadelphia: University of Pennsylvania Press, 1981.

Schlesinger, Arthur, Jr. "The Challenge of Abundance." *The Reporter* 14 (3 May 1956): 8–11.

Schmidt, Jean M. "The Present State of United Methodist Historical Study." *MH* 28 (January 1990): 104–16.

Schreiner, Samuel A., Jr. *The Condensed World of the "Reader's Digest."* New York: Stein and Day, 1977.

Schudson, Michael. "Criticizing the Critics of Advertising: Toward a Sociological View of Marketing." *Media, Culture, and Society* 3 (1981): 3–12.

——. *Discovering the News: A Social History of American Newspapers.* New York: Basic Books, 1978.

Shi, David. *The Simple Life: Plain Living and High Thinking in American Culture.* New York: Oxford University Press, 1985.

Shoemaker, John V. *A Practical Treatise on Diseases of the Skin.* 5th ed., rev. and enlarged. Philadelphia: F. A. Davis, 1909.

Shover, John L. *First Majority—Last Minority: The Transformation of Rural Life in America.* De Kalb: Northern Illinois University Press, 1976.

Sica, Alan. "The Rhetoric of Sociology and Its Audience." In *Sociology and Its Publics: The Forms and Fates of Disciplinary Organization,* edited by Terence C. Halliday and Morris Janowitz, pp. 347–407. Chicago: University of Chicago Press, 1992.

Siegel, Frederick F. *Troubled Journey: From Pearl Harbor to Ronald Reagan.* New York: Hill and Wang, 1984.

Skolnick, Arlene. *Embattled Paradise: The American Family in an Age of Uncertainty.* New York: Basic Books, 1991.

Slater, Philip E. *The Pursuit of Loneliness: American Culture at the Breaking Point.* Boston: Beacon Press, 1970.

Smith, Judith E. "Creating 'Everyman' after World War II: Evaporating Ethnic and Class Distinctiveness in Postwar White Cultural Identity." Paper presented at the annual meeting of the American Studies Association, Costa Mesa, California, November 1992.

Smith, Paul C. *Personal File.* New York: Appleton-Century, 1964.

Solberg, Carl. *Riding High: America in the Cold War.* New York: Mason and Lipscomb, 1973.

Spectorsky, A. C. *The Exurbanites.* Philadelphia: J. B. Lippincott, 1955.

Spigel, Lynn. *Make Room for TV: Television and the Family Ideal in Postwar America.* Chicago: University of Chicago Press, 1992.

Steffens, Lincoln. *The Autobiography of Lincoln Steffens.* New York: Harcourt, Brace, 1931.

Stein, Harry H. "American Muckraking of Technology since 1900," *Journalism Quarterly* 67 (Summer 1990): 401–9.

Steinberg, Salme H. *Reformer in the Marketplace: Edward W. Bok and the "Ladies' Home Journal."* Baton Rouge: Louisiana State University Press, 1979.

Steinfels, Peter. *The Neoconservatives: The Men Who Are Changing American Politics.* New York: Simon and Schuster, 1979.

Stewart, James B. *Den of Thieves.* New York: Simon and Schuster, 1991.

Stonequist, Everett V. *The Marginal Man: A Study in Personality and Culture.* New York: C. Scribner's Sons, 1937.

Stott, William. *Documentary Expression and Thirties America.* New York: Oxford University Press, 1973.

Strasser, Susan. *Satisfaction Guaranteed: The Making of the American Mass Market.* New York: Pantheon Books, 1989.

Suleiman, Susan R., and Inge Crosman. *The Reader in the Text: Essays in Audience and Interpretation.* Princeton: Princeton University Press, 1980.

Susman, Warren. "Did Success Spoil the United States: Dual Representations in Postwar America." In *Recasting America: Culture and Politics in the Age of Cold War,* edited by Lary May, pp. 19–37. Chicago: University of Chicago Press, 1989.

——. " 'Personality' and the Making of Twentieth-Century Culture." In *New Directions in American Intellectual History,* edited by John Higham and Paul H. Conkin, pp. 212–26. Baltimore: Johns Hopkins University Press, 1979.

Talese, Gay. *Thy Neighbor's Wife.* Garden City, N.Y.: Doubleday, 1980.

Taylor, Ella. *Prime-Time Families: Television Culture in Postwar America.* Berkeley: University of California Press, 1989.

Taylor, John. *Circus of Ambition: The Culture of Wealth and Power in the Eighties.* New York: Warner Books, 1989.

Taylor, S. J. *Stalin's Apologist: Walter Duranty, the New York Times' Man in Moscow.* New York: Oxford University Press, 1990.

Tebbel, John. *A History of Book Publishing in the United States.* Vol. 4. *The Great Change, 1940–1980.* New York: R. R. Bowker, 1981.

Tebbel, John, and Mary E. Zuckerman. *The Magazine in America, 1741–1990.* New York: Oxford University Press, 1991.

Terkel, Studs. *The Great Divide: Second Thoughts on the American Dream.* New York: Pantheon Books, 1988.

Thelen, David P. *Paths of Resistance: Tradition and Dignity in Industrializing Missouri.* New York: Oxford University Press, 1986.

Theriot, Nancy. *Nostalgia on the Right: Historical Roots of the Idealized Family.* Chicago: Midwest Research, 1983.

Thody, Philip. "Grammar and Stereotypes: Some Problems in Popsology." *International Social Science Journal* 28 (1976): 375–84.

Thomas, Hilah E., and Rosemary S. Keller, eds. *Women in New Worlds: Historical Perspectives on the Wesleyan Tradition.* 2 vols. Nashville: Abingdon, 1981.

Thomas, John L. *Alternative America: Henry George, Edward Bellamy, Henry Demarest Lloyd, and the Adversary Tradition.* Cambridge: Harvard University Press, 1983.

Thorne, Barrie. "Feminist Rethinking of the Family: An Overview." In *Rethinking the Family: Some Feminist Questions,* edited by Barrie Thorne and Marilyn Yalom, pp. 1–24. New York: Longman, 1982.

Toffler, Alvin. *Future Shock.* New York: Random House, 1970.

Tompkins, Jane P. *Sensational Designs: The Cultural Work of American Fiction, 1790–1860.* New York: Oxford University Press, 1985.

——, ed. *Reader-Response Criticism: From Formalism to Post-Structuralism.* Baltimore: Johns Hopkins University Press, 1980.

Trump, Donald J. *Trump: The Art of the Deal.* New York: Random House, 1988.

Tyack, David. "Life in the 'Museum of Virtue': The Bleak Vision of Willard Waller." In *Willard Waller on Education and Schools: A Critical Appraisal,* edited by Donald J. Willower and William L. Boyd, pp. 109–23. Berkeley: McCutchan Publishing, 1989.

Updike, John. *Self-Consciousness: Memoirs.* New York: Alfred A. Knopf, 1989.

U.S., President's Commission on National Goals. *Goals for Americans: The Report of the President's Commission on National Goals.* Englewood Cliffs, N.J.: Prentice-Hall, 1960.

van Zuilen, A. J. *The Life Cycle of Magazines: A Historical Study of the Decline and Fall of the General Interest Mass Audience Magazine in the United States during the Period 1947–1972.* Uithoorn, Netherlands: Graduate Press, 1977.

Vidal, Gore. *Myra Breckinridge.* Boston: Little, Brown, 1968.

Vidich, Arthur J., and Stanford M. Lyman. *American Sociology: Worldly Rejections of Religion and Their Directions.* New Haven: Yale University Press, 1985.

Wald, Alan M. *The New York Intellectuals: The Rise and Decline of the Anti-Stalinist Left from the 1930s to the 1980s.* Chapel Hill: University of North Carolina Press, 1987.

Waller, Willard. *The Family: A Dynamic Interpretation.* New York: Cordon, 1938.

——. *The Old Love and the New: Divorce and Readjustment.* New York: Horace Liveright, 1930.

——. "Social Problems and the Mores." *ASR* 1 (December 1936): 922–33.

——. *The Veteran Comes Back.* New York: Dryden Press, 1944.

——. *War and the Family.* New York: Dryden Press, 1940.

——. *War in the Twentieth Century.* New York: Dryden Press, 1940.

——. "What You Can Do to Help the Returning Veteran." *Ladies' Home Journal,* February 1945.

——. "Why Veterans Are Bitter." *American Mercury,* August 1945.

Walzer, Michael. *The Company of Critics: Social Criticism and Political Commitment in the Twentieth Century.* New York: Basic Books, 1988.

Warren, Frank A., III. *Liberals and Communism: The 'Red Decade' Revisited.* Bloomington: Indiana University Press, 1966.

Wechsler, James. *Revolt on the Campus.* New York: Covici Friede Publishers, 1935.

Weir, Walter. *Truth in Advertising and Other Heresies.* New York: McGraw-Hill, 1963.

Weiss, Richard. *The American Myth of Success: From Horatio Alger to Norman Vincent Peale.* New York: Basic Books, 1969.

Welter, Barbara. "The Cult of True Womanhood: 1820–1860." *AQ* 18 (Summer 1966): 151–74.

West, James L. W., III. *American Authors and the Literary Marketplace since 1900*. Philadelphia: University of Pennsylvania Press, 1988.

Westbrook, Robert B. *John Dewey and American Democracy*. Ithaca: Cornell University Press, 1991.

———. "Tribune of the Technostructure: The Popular Economics of Stuart Chase." *AQ* 32 (Fall 1980): 387–408.

Westin, Alan F. *Privacy and Freedom*. New York: Atheneum, 1967.

———, ed. *Information Technology in a Democracy*. Cambridge: Harvard University Press, 1971.

Westin, Alan F., and Michael A. Baker. *Databanks in a Free Society: Computers, Record-Keeping and Privacy*. New York: Quadrangle Books, 1972.

Wheeler, Stanton, ed. *On Record: Files and Dossiers in American Life*. New York: Russell Sage Foundation, 1969.

White, Theodore H. *In Search of History: A Personal Adventure*. New York: Harper and Row, 1978.

———. *The View from the Fortieth Floor*. New York: W. Sloane Associates, 1960.

White, Winston. *Beyond Conformity*. New York: Free Press of Glencoe, 1961.

Whiteley, Marilyn F. " 'Doing Just about What They Please': Ladies' Aids in Ontario Methodism." *Ontario History* 82 (1990): 289–304.

Whitfield, Stephen J. *The Culture of the Cold War*. Baltimore: Johns Hopkins University Press, 1991.

Whyte, William H., Jr. *The Organization Man*. New York: Simon and Schuster, 1956.

Wilkinson, Rupert. *The Pursuit of American Character*. New York: Harper and Row, 1988.

Williams, James M. *Our Rural Heritage: The Social Psychology of Rural Development*. New York: Alfred A. Knopf, 1925.

Willis, Ellen. "Consumerism and Women." *Socialist Revolution* 1 (May–June 1970): 76–82.

———. "The Family: Love It or Leave It." In *Beginning to See the Light: Pieces of a Decade*, pp. 149–68. [1979] New York: Alfred A. Knopf, 1981.

Willower, Donald J., and William L. Boyd, eds. *Willard Waller on Education and Schools: A Critical Appraisal*. Berkeley: McCutchan Publishing, 1989.

Wilson, Christopher P. *The Labor of Words: Literary Professionalism in the Progressive Era*. Athens: University of Georgia Press, 1985.

———. "The Rhetoric of Consumption: Mass-Market Magazines and the Demise of the Genteel Reader, 1880–1920." In *The Culture of Consumption: Critical Essays in American History, 1880–1980*, edited by Richard W. Fox and T. J. Jackson Lears, pp. 43–55. New York: Pantheon Books, 1983.

Wilson, R. Jackson. *Figures of Speech: American Writers and the Literary Marketplace, from Benjamin Franklin to Emily Dickinson*. New York: Alfred A. Knopf, 1989.

Wilson, Sloan. *The Man in the Gray Flannel Suit*. New York: Simon and Schuster, 1955.

———. *What Shall We Wear to This Party? The Man in the Gray Flannel Suit Twenty Years Before and After*. New York: Arbor House, 1976.

Winkler, Alan M. *Modern America: The United States from World War II to the Present*. New York: Harper and Row, 1986.

Winn, Marie. *Children without Childhood*. New York: Pantheon Books, 1983.

Wittner, Lawrence S. *Rebels against War: The American Peace Movement, 1941–1960*. New York: Columbia University Press, 1969.

Wolfe, Tom. *The Bonfire of the Vanities*. New York: Farrar, Straus, 1987.

———. "The New Journalism." In *The New Journalism*, edited by Tom Wolfe and E. W. Johnson, pp. 3–52. New York: Harper and Row, 1973.

Wolff, Tobias. *This Boy's Life: A Memoir*. New York: Atlantic Monthly Press, 1989.

Wolseley, Roland E. *The Changing Magazine: Trends in Readership and Management*. New York: Hastings House, 1973.

Wood, Percy O., J. M. McKee, L. M. Skemp, W. B. Nissley, and J. B. R. Dickey. "Soil Survey of Bradford County, Pennsylvania." In U.S. Department of Agriculture, Bureau of Soils, *Thirteenth Report: Field Operations of the Bureau of Soils, 1911*, pp. 231–67. Washington, D.C.: Government Printing Office, 1914.

Zinn, Howard. *Postwar America: 1945–1971*. Indianapolis: Bobbs-Merrill, 1973.

Zorbaugh, Harvey W. *Gold Coast and Slum: A Sociological Study of Chicago's Near North Side*. Chicago: University of Chicago Press, 1929.

Zunz, Olivier. *Making America Corporate, 1870–1920*. Chicago: University of Chicago Press, 1990.

Index